ONE STEP AHEAD

ALSO BY DAVID SALLY

The Numbers Game:
Why Everything You Know About Soccer Is Wrong (with Chris Anderson)

ONE STEP AHEAD

ALSO BY DAVID SALLY

The Numbers Game:
Why Everything You Know About Soccer Is Wrong (with Chris Anderson)

ONE

MASTERING THE ART AND

STEP

SCIENCE OF NEGOTIATION

AHEAD

DAVID SALLY

St. Martin's Press
New York

Library of Congress Cataloging-in-Publication Data

Names: Sally, David, author.
Title: One step ahead : mastering the art and science of negotiation /
   David Sally.
Description: First U.S. edition. | New York : St. Martin's Press, [2020] |
   Includes bibliographical references and index.
Identifiers: LCCN 2019054416 | ISBN 9781250166395 (hardcover) |
   ISBN 9781250272171 (international ed., international, sold outside the U.S.,
   subject to rights availability) | ISBN 9781250166401 (ebook)
Subjects: LCSH: Negotiation in business. | Negotiation.
Classification: LCC HD58.6 .S2575 2020 | DDC 658.4/052—dc23
LC record available at https://lccn.loc.gov/2019054416

First U.S. Edition: May 2020
First International Edition: May 2020

1   3   5   7   9   10   8   6   4   2

To Serena, whom I am always one step behind

I prefer moralists who promise me nothing.
I prefer cunning kindness to the over-trustful kind.

—WISŁAWA SZYMBORSKA, "POSSIBILITIES"
(translated by S. Baranczak and C. Cavanagh)

CONTENTS

ONE STEP AHEAD

PREFACE

One Step Ahead of
One Step Ahead

(or, Where does this book come from?)

I have taught negotiation for the last twenty-five years with two simple aims: to demystify the subject for the MBAs and executives in my classroom, and to help them appreciate the intricacies and subtleties of being a great negotiator.

Each student begins with a different baseline, in terms of both their understanding of how negotiation really works and their comfort level. But there's a fundamental insight that separates the sophisticated negotiators from everyone else. They recognize that while there are different approaches to bargaining—aggressive versus conciliatory, demanding versus persuasive—the key to negotiation is realizing that it's a psychological and social process in which being able to recognize certain things about the person with whom you are negotiating, and adapting your approach accordingly, is crucial. Hence your ability to develop a particular set of observational skills, so that you can suss out your counterpart's strategy and anticipate their tactics, and directorial skills, so that you can guide their performance, frame their perceptions, prime their words, and arouse their wants, is essential.

These advanced negotiation skills are *extremely* teachable. But their development takes hard work and time. A week with executives or a couple of months with the MBAs is enough for them to reduce their fears, gain insights into the game, significantly improve their performances, and in the end realize that this one course is not sufficient. Consequently, many of them come to me with a question I used to dread: "What can we read to keep learning?" My answer had always consisted of three parts: (1) *How to Win Friends and Influence People* by Dale Carnegie (1936), (2) *Getting to Yes* by Roger Fisher and William Ury (1981), and (3) "But neither of those books will get you all the way there. That requires becoming an analytical observer of the people around you. Read novels and biographies, go to plays, watch movies and television, take notes on your families and co-workers, and draw out your own lessons about how people really negotiate and interact."

Number three wasn't that helpful, because the students really didn't know what to look for or how to organize their observations. And so I followed my own advice and started to gather data, studies, theories, experiments, ideas, characters, and stories that illuminated with particular clarity the qualities of the most sophisticated negotiators. Drawing on what I've learned in my class about the preconceptions people bring to the subject of negotiation (some of which my own research has shown to be both debilitating and dead wrong) and utilizing the insights of economics, psychology, and sociology, I set out to write a book that reveals the real world in which negotiations take place.

Why is this book called *One Step Ahead*? We'll explore the research and the details in the chapters to come, but for now, I'll tell you that it's based on my simple observation that the best negotiators, the ones who manage to craft creative deals that achieve the ambitious targets they've set for themselves while leaving their counterparts happy and ready to bargain again in the future, dig deeper into every element of a negotiation—the alternatives, the social pressures, the interests, the biases, the drama, the emotions, the words, the numbers—than their counterparts do. Also, because any negotiation is a constantly evolving process, and every person and situation is different, the best negotiators do not completely predetermine their actions or follow a set bargaining recipe. Rather, they read their counterpart and react; they mold the situation to create the necessary pressures; they improvise.

The need for *One Step Ahead* and the newness and comprehensiveness of its approach will become clearer if we examine the strengths and weaknesses of its two illustrious predecessors.

ONE STEP AHEAD OF
HOW TO WIN FRIENDS
AND INFLUENCE PEOPLE

(or, Good advice, but where is the science?)

Though his book *How to Win Friends and Influence People* continues to sell briskly, Dale Carnegie's personal history is largely forgotten. He grew up on farms in Missouri during the years in which the twentieth century sprouted out of the plowed-under nineteenth. As a young man he attended a local teachers college. Hungry for success and female attention, and unable to throw either a curveball or a spiral, he entered scholastic public speaking contests. One acolyte wrote that Carnegie practiced his talks "as he sat in the saddle galloping to college and back" and "as he milked the cows." By his senior year, he was a trophy-winning speaker.

After an initial attempt to make his living selling bacon, soap, and lard, he lit out for New York City in 1911, enrolling in the American Academy of Dramatic Arts. Despite the training, Carnegie remained more ham salesman, alas, than Hamlet and was not offered any steadily paying acting jobs. Not wanting to return to sales or the Midwest, he convinced several YMCAs in the city to allow him to offer classes on public speaking. The attendance at his courses grew steadily, he aggressively marketed the benefits to potential students, and his renown spread.

Over Carnegie's twenty-plus years of training, he shifted his lessons from public speaking to all forms of "the fine art of getting along with people in everyday business and social contacts." He went searching for a book that was "a practical, working handbook on human relations" and, failing to find one, set out to write one himself. He read biographies and magazine profiles of great men and women, studied "the old philosophers and the new psychologists," and "personally interviewed scores of successful people."

From all of these sources Carnegie distilled a set of precepts that he encouraged attendees of his training sessions to apply out in the world and then recount their successes to future classes. Some of Carnegie's principles were fine pieces of wisdom, and you will find echoes of them in the pages that follow. One of his three fundamental principles in handling counterparts was to "arouse in the other person an eager want." To support the rule "Become genuinely interested in other people," which is a necessary counterweight to our natural egoism, he cited a relevant statistic:

> The New York Telephone Company made a detailed study of telephone conversations to find out which word is the most frequently used. You have guessed it: it is the personal pronoun "I." "I." "I." It was used 3,900 times in 500 telephone conversations. "I." "I." "I." "I."

He saw that getting along with other people is a game, one that can be played honestly and with integrity, but in which you sometimes need to "throw down a challenge":

> That is what every successful person loves: the game. The chance for self-expression. The chance to prove his or her worth, to excel, to win. That is what makes foot-races and hog-calling and pie-eating contests.

To persuade people, "begin in a friendly manner" and "dramatize your ideas" in the manner of a shop owner, with a warm greeting and an intriguing facade. When "the manufacturers of a new rat poison gave dealers a window display that included two live rats . . . , sales zoomed to five times their normal rate."

How to Win is a masterpiece of "anecdata"—one vignette after another, rat-a-tat-tat, targeting a precept until it is holey. No doubts, no hesitations, no limiting conditions. Two can play that game:

> Suzanne Gluck of New York City is a literary agent at WME. One day, she received a document in her in-box. She opened the correspondence to find

a proposal for a book on negotiations titled *One Step Ahead*. She said, "I was very skeptical but I decided to try some of the ideas in my next negotiation. And you know what? They worked! I made tens of thousands of extra dollars in the deal! I signed the author the very next day."

For Carnegie, the testimonies of returning students formed a body of scientific evidence and turned his training classes into a laboratory. His book "grew and developed out of that laboratory, out of the experiences of thousands of adults."

His efforts were many things, but they were not scientific. Some of his numbers were plucked from the thinnest of air. He cited with justified approbation Henry Ford: "If there is any one secret of success, it lies in the ability to get the other person's point of view and see things from that person's angle as well as from your own." Carnegie added, "That is so simple, so obvious, that anyone ought to see the truth of it at a glance, yet 90 percent of the people on this earth ignore it 90 percent of the time." Those "90 percent" figures are concocted. As we will see below, the accurate base rate is roughly 60 percent of people, a proportion that shifts with the identity of the counterpart and the elements of the situation. In truth, *How to Win* still has a bit of the lard salesman in its speechifying.

We can and should admire Carnegie's work and wisdom. But we are blessed with resources he didn't have—decades' worth of progress in economics, psychology, and other social sciences—and we should use them. These developments include the rise of game theory, which allowed the strategic interaction between players, negotiators, businesses, or countries to be analyzed and outcomes forecasted, and the birth of behavioral economics, which increased the empirical accuracy of economic models by replacing the assumption that people are purely rational with the decision-making limitations and biases that cognitive and social psychologists discovered in their experiments.

For example, when Chris Anderson and I analyzed the sport of soccer a few years ago to discover what made teams more successful, we applied O-ring theory from economics to the game and arrived at what would come to be known as "the weak link principle." As we wrote in *The Numbers Game: Why Everything You Know About Soccer Is Wrong*, success in a given soccer match or season is determined more by the relative quality of the weakest player on your team than by that of the strongest. This is in opposition to basketball, a strong-link sport wherein success is controlled by the relative quality of your superstar. This discovery has changed the analysis of soccer significantly, and similar insights about negotiation await you in the chapters ahead. Game theory and behavioral economics will provide the framework that will help us understand the skills and abilities of sophisticated negotiators.

THE *GETTING TO YES* TRAP
(or, Where are toughness and ingenuity?)

Another of Carnegie's principles of persuasion was to "Get the other person saying 'yes, yes' immediately" by talking about matters on which you agree rather than those on which you differ. He described the physical effects of "no" and "yes" in behaviorist, animalist terms: the former causes the "entire organism—glandular, nervous, muscular"—to withdraw and be primed for rejection; the latter causes the organism to be "in a forward-moving, accepting, open attitude." You should continually emphasize to your opponent that "you are both striving for the same end and that your only difference is one of method and not of purpose."

Fifty years on, in their classic work, Fisher and Ury expanded upon Carnegie's precept of rolling affirmation without ever formally crediting him. *Getting to Yes* is the central, revered text in an approach to negotiation that has been variously called principled or interest-based bargaining. This movement arose as a reaction to the traditional, competitive, adversarial negotiations found in the courtroom, the union hall, the military tent, and the corporate boardroom. It has had substantial successes: the role of the ombudsman in many organizations; the growth of the system of alternative dispute resolution, both mediation and arbitration; the rise of deliberative democracy; and the content of many negotiation courses.

Whereas Carnegie proposed thirty principles, Fisher and Ury offered four maxims, each of which is reasonable. They are not, however, all-purpose. Research and experience have shown that interest-based bargaining has some serious limitations:

1. *Separate the people from the problem.* Adversarial negotiations tend to get personal, emotional, strained, and tangled up with the underlying relationship between the parties. *Getting to Yes* recommends that you cooperate with your counterpart to explicitly negotiate relationship issues, on the one hand, and to try to jointly problem-solve the remaining "substantial" issues, on the other.

Sometimes, as in a divorce or a custody battle, the people are the problem. Moreover, there are people who, by virtue of the fact that they are either stupid or not entirely sane, not only won't be separated from the problem but will cling to it. Chris Voss, a former negotiator for the FBI, experienced the limitations of principled bargaining with certain perpetrators: "I mean, have you ever tried to devise a mutually beneficial win-win solution with a guy who thinks he's the messiah?"

2. *Focus on interests, not positions.* Fisher and Ury write, "Interests motivate people; they are the silent movers behind the hubbub of positions. Your position is something you have decided upon. Your interests are what caused you to so decide."

This advice relies on the parties being able to distinguish the two (not at all easy, as we will see) and on a fundamental assumption that negotiators have fixed, independent, identifiable interests. Contrast this with Carnegie's "Arouse in the other person an eager want," which is much more active and forceful. One of his vignettes concerned the wealthy industrialist Andrew Carnegie (to whom he was not related) and his reticent nephews who were attending Yale College and refusing to respond to "their mother's frantic letters":

[He] offered to wager a hundred dollars that he could get an answer by return mail, without even asking for it. Someone called his bet; so he wrote his nephews a chatty letter, mentioning casually in a post-script that he was sending each one a five-dollar bill. He neglected, however, to enclose the money. Back came replies by return mail thanking "Dear Uncle Andrew" for his kind note—and you can finish the sentence yourself.

In *Getting to Yes*, interests are unearthed; in *How to Win*, as well as *One Step Ahead*, interests are crafted and molded.

> 3. *Invent options for mutual gain.* Make the situation a win-win with tactics that are also straightforward: brainstorm cooperatively; don't assume there's a fixed pie; try to solve the other side's problem, not just your own; be creative.

There's an "All You Need Is Love" vibe to this principle: hold hands and generate ideas without criticism, productively support all parties, and then work together to refine the best solution. Creativity is really more "Helter Skelter" and "Stray Cat Blues," as the competitive, complex, conflictual partnerships between Lennon and McCartney and between Richards and Jagger exemplify.

> 4. *Insist on using objective criteria.* Instead of haggling or having a tug-of-war over whose position should prevail, apply "standards of fairness, efficiency, or scientific merit," or look "to precedent and community practice."

As with interests, the very existence of such criteria and their fixity are very much in doubt. The naive bargainer believes that numbers are objective and fair; the sophisticated negotiator knows that a counterpart can pull figures such as "90 percent" out of nothing and that numbers are as easily skewed as words.

At least as important, principled bargaining is susceptible to the tactics and maneuverings of sophisticated negotiators who exploit the other side's belief in cooperation, attention to interests, and sensitivity to fairness. Jim Camp is so opposed to the approach that he gave his book the converse title, *Start with No*, and he writes, "Many, many corporate opportunists and shrewd negotiators in every field understand that a gung ho, win-win negotiator on the other side of the table is a sitting duck."

President Barack Obama often fell into this trap. Critics thought the president's "bipartisan musings [were] gauzy blather at best and, at worst, dangerously provocative, since Republicans would exploit them." One comedian even joked that he could tell when talks between Obama and the Republicans were finished, because Obama would be "missing his watch and his lunch money." Republican congresspeople would dangle their support and potential votes, and the president would reliably stretch for them as an astigmatic mallard does for a puffy snowflake. As one White House aide at the time admitted, the Obama administration, from the stimulus to health care to budget negotiations, would make a proposal that was "simply a predesigned legislative compromise."

You do not want to be a chump. Don't allow a blind adherence to win-win lead to lose-win at the hands of a crafty opponent. Sophisticated negotiation tactics are needed not just by those who seek to conquer territory, destroy their enemies, and extend their duchy but also by those who would defend their city full of peaceful, creative, enlightened citizens. You need to stay one step ahead of your counterpart for defensive purposes as much as for offensive reasons. *Good people need to be able to negotiate with toughness; otherwise, bad people always win.*

The win-win creed is also tied to a larger problem within modern organizations, what *Radical Candor* author Kim Scott refers to as "ruinous empathy": the impulse to avoid offending, confronting, or saying no. In the process of the usual indoctrination conducted by business schools, corporations, law firms, and other organizations, people tend to learn, mistakenly, that a good teammate is someone who is easy to deal with. Obviously, it's in everyone's benefit to get along most of the time, but when it becomes the supreme value it can induce a certain passivity.

I used to have to tamp down excessive aggressiveness in my MBA students and executives. Lately I find the opposite: I have to encourage them to be more determined, more persistent, and more ready to deny the other side when necessary. In *One Step Ahead* we will see evidence that such toughness is the *single most important factor* in being a successful negotiator. And we'll see that being tough does not mean you must be macho, belligerent, belittling, or unpleasant. True toughness arises from persistence and patience, from focus on a goal, from the security that you know what you're doing, and from a willingness to say no firmly and creatively.

THE STEPS AHEAD

(or, The difficult questions a sophisticated, one-step-ahead negotiator needs to confront)

Writing this book has made me a more effective negotiator: I have a broader perspective and more confidence, I see the game more clearly, and I set higher goals, make bigger asks, and say no more easily. Fair warning, though—in the chapters that follow, you will encounter stories, ideas, characters, and principles that will sometimes seem quite distant from the bargaining table. Moreover, some of these people and ideas will refute your intuitions and maybe even make you uncomfortable. My promise to you is that if you hang in and suspend your reservations, you will emerge with a deep understanding of the game of negotiation, and you will be able to have genuine confidence that you can negotiate much more effectively in a wider range of circumstances.

You should expect the path to be difficult. If it were easy, everyone would take it. Those who seek a higher level of insight and performance in any domain are always told by their guides—Socrates, Buddha, Helen Keller, Mr. "Wax on, wax off" Miyagi—that you must look away in order to examine what's in front of you, that you must seek out the most challenging questions, and that you must ultimately derive your own answers.

A beginner's book on negotiation takes your hand and tells you, "Simply do x and y." An advanced book must, of necessity, emphasize the conditional ("If . . . then if . . . then if . . ."), the analogous ("This setting is similar to . . ."), the case study ("This person, with all their various strengths and weaknesses, did the following in this situation with all its real complexities"), and the unanticipated query ("Has it even occurred to you . . . ?"). My job is to present you with the wisest research and deepest knowledge about negotiation and strategic interaction, and to ensure that we encounter the most important questions, some that you know are out there waiting for us and others that you won't fully recognize until we meet on the path:

- Why are there four basic types of negotiator, with respect to strategic depth: ZERO, ONE, TWO, THREE+? How do I distinguish them? Why do I need to be able to change the step I'm on in order to be effective with them?
- Should I always negotiate, or are there times when I'm better off avoiding it?
- Which negotiation styles work again and again, and why is my intuition about profitable personality characteristics often dead wrong?
- What can directors and actors teach me about guiding and participating in the drama of negotiation and about overcoming my fears surrounding it?
- What is the best way to prepare to bargain? Why might it make sense to "come from the cauliflower"?
- What is true toughness? Does toughness crowd out fairness? Is it better for me to be a grave dancer, an umpire, or a Chinese coin?
- How can I, as a woman, be seen as tough and lower the risk of negative feedback?
- Are emotions harmful in a negotiation? How controllable are they, and do they leak through my face?
- How do words really work? How can I persuade my counterparts in a negotiation, should I rely on their promises, and how often will they lie to me?
- Can I find safety and security in a quantitative negotiation? How do I avoid being intimidated by complex models or falling prey to false precision?

– 1 –

THE ENVOYS FOR
ONE STEP AHEAD

MACHIAVELLI, REALLY

(or, Why Florence's infamous diplomat and philosopher
might be a good role model)

On the morning after Christmas in 1502, a body was discovered in the main square of the town of Cesena, in the region of central Italy ruled by Cesare Borgia. The murder's intended audiences were the abused people of the town, the warlords of the surrounding cities, and a visiting envoy from the republic of Florence. The envoy was one counterpart in a set of political negotiations that Borgia, the Duke of Valentinois, had meticulously planned. The murder of Ramiro de Lorca, the brutal Paulie Walnuts to Borgia's Tony Soprano, had multiple meanings for the observers.

As in many negotiations, the incident caused a dispute over what actually had happened and over the numbers. Alexandre Dumas, whose counting abilities we might mistrust since his *Three Musketeers* involved four primary swordsmen, advanced two versions: first, that de Lorca's body had been quartered and left in the square; and second, that his torso had been cut into four pieces while his head was placed on a pike. The envoy from Florence, Niccolò Machiavelli (yes, that Machiavelli), related a different quantitative appraisal in a letter to his city fathers: "Messer Ramiro this morning was found in two pieces on the public square, where he still is; and all the people have been able to see him." The motivation for de Lorca's murder was immediately clear to Machiavelli: "Nobody feels sure of the cause of his death, except that it has pleased the prince." Left unstated was that the pleased Borgia felt absolutely no compunction, no guilt, and no remorse about having ordered the murder of his own lieutenant.

Machiavelli, whose most famous work on the machinations of power was based on his close observations of Borgia, had been negotiating with the prince on an almost daily basis since early October 1502. Borgia's grand plan was to unite all of central Italy under his rule, and he was more than happy to hold the threat of invasion over Florence's head to see what treasures he could extract as ransom. Machiavelli's charge from his city's ruling council (*signoria*) was a tricky one: keep the city from being included in Borgia's imperial plans without being forced to support him with men, arms, and florins. All this while Borgia's capos were filling the streets of the other towns in the region with bodies and blood. The envoy was a big underdog in this negotiation—underresourced, undertitled, homesick, lacking security, with nothing but his wits and his tongue saving him from a blade through the neck.

I know it might seem horribly anachronistic to travel back to the temporal, intellectual, and political heart of the Renaissance. For sure, life was nastier, more brutish, and shorter in those days. And yet, and yet: people were still people; princes, princes; sages, sages; and negotiators, negotiators. The talks between Machiavelli and Borgia involved the highest stakes (the envoy's life and the fate of his hometown), with two supremely sophisticated bargainers using all the words and maneuvers at their disposal.

During his four months of following the court and watching the prince, Machiavelli sent home fifty-two letters. Some documented concrete offers from the prince and some related Borgia's threats, typically made late at night in a darkened throne room. One sinister message, replete with implications similar to those of "Nice place you got here, be a shame if something happened," was:

> I am not lacking in friends, amongst whom I should be glad to count your Signori, provided they promptly give me so to understand. And if they do not do so now, I shall leave them aside, and though I had the water up to my throat I should nevermore talk about friendship with them.

Machiavelli also wrote of the intrigue, mystery, and rumors infusing the court, and of the challenge in gauging Borgia's mind. Just a few lines before reporting de Lorca's fate in his letter of December 26, 1502, Machiavelli noted, "The Duke is so secret in all he does that he never communicates his designs to anyone. His first secretaries have repeatedly assured me that he never makes his plans until the moment of his giving orders for their execution."

Machiavelli's job was to pierce that secrecy, anticipate his counterpart's moves, and somehow arouse in the prince, as Dale Carnegie would state it, an eager want to do right by Florence. Seven years after his negotiations with the duke ended, Machiavelli summarized the responsibility of an envoy, and by extension any negotiator, this way:

> The most important duty of the envoy, whether sent by a prince or a republic, is to *conjecture the future* through negotiations and incidents.

The incident of the dismembered body and other moves that Machiavelli witnessed while at court, as well as Borgia's words as he spoke confidentially, flatteringly, imposingly, and, most of all, strategically, were all analyzed by Machiavelli with one solitary aim, the very aim that animates this book: trying to get one step ahead of his fearsome counterpart. Later on, as a retired envoy, he remembered the specifics of this goal but downplayed the complexity.

> When it comes to your negotiations, you ought to have no difficulty making the right conjecture and weighing what the emperor's intentions are, what he really wants, which way his mind is turning, and what might make him move ahead or draw back.

One writer observes that Machiavelli's deep insight was that a negotiator was "expected to bring *the gifts of a psychologist to the task of a prophet.*" Machiavelli was gifted just so, and in the end, in the face of a terrifying, ruthless duke he would later make infamous in his most legendary book, *The Prince*, he was successful in keeping both his body and his hometown intact and unscathed.

You might conjecture then that I am recommending that you be like Machiavelli when you negotiate. You'd be right, and that puts us in a delicate place. To be "Machiavellian" has come to mean to be a sociopath, to be ruthless, to value the ends above the means, and, ironically, to be Cesare Borgia, to be the Prince. And you might worry that I'm asking you to take on these less than salubrious traits. That, however, would be to credit Machiavelli's reputation rather than to see through to his reality, and to misweigh his intentions, his wants, and the turning of his mind.

Two factors sullied our insightful envoy's character. First, the Church banned all of his writings for many centuries after his death, thus placing infallible papal condemnation at the forefront of societal disapproval. Second, both philosophers and playwrights found it useful, as a near rhyme, to identify "Machiavel" with evil. His name became a kind of meme for the Elizabethan era: Christopher Marlowe's play *The Jew of Malta* features a prologue with these lines:

> *To some perhaps my name is odious;*
> *But such as love me, guard me from their tongues,*
> *And let them know that I am Machiavel,*
> *And weigh not men, and therefore not men's words.*

Shakespeare repeated the association when he wrote of a notorious, chameleonic, politic, subtle Machiavel. Modern personality psychology has legitimized the meme by creating and validating the Mach-IV test, which diagnoses how manipulative, devilish, and "Machiavellian" the respondent is supposed to be.

In fact, recent revisionist scholarship suggests that Machiavelli himself was not Machiavellian. Erica Benner, the author of *Be Like the Fox*, makes a compelling case that a shallow reading of Machiavelli's work, conducted over centuries by critics with ulterior motives or simple minds, has led us to identify him with evil, wickedness, and ruthlessness. That some have been confused should not surprise: our envoy was an ironist, a spy, and an enemy to various lords. So he needed to speak obliquely at times to preserve his own neck and his beloved city, and he "learned how to tread carefully, speak in the right register to particular people, to criticize without seeming to do so."

Shortly after Borgia's murders of de Lorca and other a-loyal allies, Machiavelli's letter to the *signoria* describes the cold-blooded man on his seat of power: "There is the Duke with his unheard of good fortune, with a courage and confidence almost superhuman, and believing himself capable of accomplishing whatever he undertakes." Benner comments that the envoy is letting the *signoria* (and us) "judge whether his words swoon with admiration or ooze scepticism." The former reading leads to Machiavel the evil one, and the latter to a clear-eyed negotiator who knew his letter would be intercepted and scrutinized by Borgia's men, with its contents relayed back to the prince, and then sent on its way to a council of politicians who had their envoy's back to varying extents.

So we'll zig from the well-worn path of history and avoid the obstacle that "Machiavellian" represents, without at the same time losing the guidance of a wise, cunning, and sophisticated person, by considering this overarching advice: In your negotiations, strive to be *Machiavelli-esque* and bring the gifts of a psychologist to the task of a prophet. The Machiavelli-esque negotiator weighs what the counterpart's true intentions are, what they really want, which way their mind is turning, and what might make them move ahead or draw back.†

We have one big advantage over Machiavelli in developing these gifts of psychology and prophecy. We moderns are blessed with a well-developed science of psychology and strategic prediction: the economics discipline of behavioral game theory. To be Machiavelli-esque is to be an *applied* behavioral game theorist—someone who can take the concepts from game theory (moves and payoffs, expectations, dominance, equilibrium, and best response) and combine them with a knowledge of social psychology (decision-making biases, misperceptions, social influences) to develop effective and sophisticated negotiating strategies.

Most people are unmindful, simplistic negotiators. Machiavelli was anything but. He was not only perceptive but multifaceted and flexible.

---

† I will use "they" as a generic third-person singular pronoun because, as we'll see, language matters and gender matters, and the construction "he/she" is, as Clay Davis would say, she-he-eeee-eee-ee-ttt.

He embodied and practiced one of his most famous sayings, "One needs to be a fox to recognize snares, and a lion to frighten wolves." The fox must be clever enough to predict the trapper's intentions and ploys and to doubt its own eyes, since many snares are camouflaged; the lion must be full of toughness, courage, and the integrity to do what its roars promise.

So the task we have set for ourselves here is to make you, reader, a mindful, sophisticated negotiator by helping you understand the science, the evidence, and the stories of those bargainers who were clear-eyed, keen psychologists and accurate prophets, who were able to be both fox and lion, who managed to get one step ahead and thus achieve great things.

WATCHING THE WAY PEOPLE SNORE

(or, How Erving Goffman could see the way that people truly are and really interact)

The nun appeared in the professor's doorway one day in 1968 in Berkeley, California, fully costumed in her black habit, black scapular, white wimple, white coif, and black veil. This particular professor would have instantly appreciated the little dramas, given the time and the place, that her walk to his office created. Had she strolled up Telegraph Avenue, she might have shared a visual frame for a few seconds with the blue-jeaned stoners in the Annapurna head shop; she could have crossed the playhouse of People's Park, nodding at the tie-dye-wearing hippies holding peace signs; her black and white would have made a dramatic contrast with the saffron robes of the chanting Hare Krishnas down Channing Way; in Sproul Plaza, she might have been enveloped by the preachings of "Holy Hubert" Lindsey as he tried vainly to counter the counterculture of the students and to "bless their dirty hearts."

The nun's lay name was Ruth Ann Wallace, and she made this trip to negotiate for a seat in the professor's seminar. It is safe to say that there was not another faculty member on campus who would have been less flummoxed by the sudden appearance of a fully swathed nun at office hours than Erving Goffman.

Goffman was arguably the greatest sociologist of his generation.

Thomas Schelling, the game theorist and 2005 Nobel laureate in economics, said that "if there were a Nobel Prize for sociology and/or social psychology he'd deserve to be the first one considered. He was endlessly creative." This creativity, and the chance to see his mind in action as he taught, was why hundreds of students, including Sister Ruth, tried to get into his seminar.

Goffman's lack of bewilderment at the nun's sudden manifestation was due neither to a devout Catholicism nor to a belief in visions. Rather, his nonchalance arose from a genius for seeing all of life at a remove. Goffman's most famous book was titled *The Presentation of the Self in Everyday Life*, and it documented the ways we all "perform" under the stage lighting of the ordinary sun. He himself practiced what he preached, as one colleague noted:

> Goffman presented himself as a detached, hard-boiled intellectual cynic; the sociologist as 1940s private eye. His was a hip, existential, cool, essentially apolitical (at least in terms of the prevailing ideologies) personal style . . . . [H]e was clearly an outsider. His brilliance and marginality meant an acute eye and a powerful imagination. He had a fascination with other people's chutzpah, weirdness and perhaps even degradation.

What made him such an outsider? Well, if Machiavelli grew up within the confines of a city and within hailing distance of its palaces, Goffman was raised in the hinter-est of hinterlands in Dauphin, Manitoba, population 4,000, the bumper block to a two-hundred-mile railroad spur stretching northwest out of Winnipeg. His father, Max Goffman, and his mother, Anne Averbach, were Russian immigrants who married in 1915. The Goffmans were one of about a dozen Jewish families in the town and were rather well-off, as Max ran a successful dry goods store and invested in the stock market in Winnipeg. Both Anne and Erving's older sister, Frances, as we'll see in a later chapter, were show people, heavily involved in community theater. The young Goffman was at best uninterested in his locale: years later, he gave acquaintances the impression that he felt more marginalized by his rurality than by his Jewishness. He once poignantly said, "One is born near a granary and spends the rest of his life suppressing it."

In a family of characters, one of the most notable was his mother's brother, Mickey "Book" Averbach. Mickey Book was, indeed, a bookie and a card sharp, plying his trades "first from behind the restaurant he and his wife operated, then along the length of the Canadian Railway." He was the favorite uncle—charming, delightful, and glamorous—and according to family members, he looked a lot like Erving.

Maybe due to his uncle's career, Goffman would develop a lifelong fascination with con artists. His second academic publication, "On Cooling the Mark Out," became famous as a study of the actual interpersonal maneuverings that the con artist engages in with the victim or mark. Goffman zeroed in on the defined roles within every con (the roper makes the initial social contact with the mark, the insideman is the expert and authority, the cooler is the consoler for the mark after the sting) and predictable plot points (there is an initial serendipitous event, such as finding a stuffed wallet on the floor or a former colleague in the hotel lobby bar; a small profitable victory; a reluctantly permitted major investment by the mark; and then a snafu causing the money to be irretrievably lost). Also, Goffman took the leap and pointed out that various non-con people and organizations have to cool out "marks" all the time—the wooed has to soothe the refused suitor with an offer of friend status, the restaurant has to placate the hangry waiting customer, the doctor must work with the doomed patient, and the private firm has to deal with the owner's adult child who is "promoted" to VP of special projects.

What emerged from this study and Goffman's subsequent research was an essential insight: every social interaction, and therefore every negotiation, involves role-playing and is inherently theatrical. To view a negotiation dramaturgically is to begin to understand how to operate more successfully, whether you're roping a mark or merely trying to get a raise from your boss. And indeed, framing a negotiation as a drama can have numerous benefits for the bargainer, as we will see in a future chapter, among which are a lessening of the threat presented by conflict, since it is directed at the character we're playing and not our person; a facility in switching roles to meet the demands of the drama; a greater ability to anticipate and respond to other actors and the audience; a dedication to memorizing the script and yet delivering it in the moment; and a heightened sensitivity toward production elements—costumes, props, backdrops, blocking—that can affect performances. In the end, a very sophisticated negotiator has the knowledge and the skills to be a Shakespeare—writer of the script, actor in a role, and director of the play, all at once.

On that afternoon in 1968, the negotiation involved a coveted spot in Goffman's seminar, and the opening scene had been the unexpected appearance of Sister Ruth on the threshold of his office. No self-respecting sociologist self-presenting as a 1940s hard-boiled private eye was going to refuse the chance to find out why this particular "dame" had knocked on his door. First, Goffman said that he was "thrilled" to see her in her anomalous costume. She asked whether she could take his class, and he replied, "No, no, the numbers are all out. I can't seat you." When she expressed her deep disappointment, he told her to close the door, and she thought (maybe exactly as he had hoped), "Boy, am I in trouble." Finally, now that his office had been made both private and backstage, he conceded, "Sister, you can sit at the back of the room, but don't tell anybody."

Goffman was a creator of scenes, small interactions that threatened and sometimes violated the norms of social interaction and expression. Had she shown up in lay clothing, Sister Ruth would not have succeeded. It was her costume that sealed the deal. How could he not let her into his class, knowing what puzzled glances and tentative queries her mute, behabited presence in the back of the room would provoke? As his colleague described earlier, Goffman had a fascination with chutzpah, weirdness, degradation, and testing the boundaries of the social order. If there were witnesses in the hallway who could whisper, "Did you just see that nun go into Goffman's office and close the door?" he would have been delighted. He might not have been a Larry David, curbed and enthused social assassin, but he was well within sniping range. Some of the scenes he wrote, directed, and starred in were the following:

- At an academic conference, he ran up to a group of Berkeley sociology department graduates and said, "Don't go away, because if I don't find anyone more prestigious than you, I'll be back to have dinner with you."
- At one point, Goffman said something like, "The whole point of a dinner party is who isn't invited."

- One non-nun teaching scene: Goffman once scheduled the initial meeting of a seminar at his house, left the front door ajar and the living room chairs set up in a circle, and watched from the wings as the students tentatively let themselves in after a few minutes, sat quietly for a while, and then began to randomly exit. His observations of their behaviors, emotions, and interactions formed the core of that year's seminar.
- And another: After an older student raised her hand and pointed out that his just-finished declamation was the exact opposite of a statement he had made a handful of minutes earlier, he said, "Mrs. Frederickson, don't be so nostalgic."

Goffman's games may have entertained him but they had a very serious purpose as well—they allowed him to plumb below the surface of life and investigate the inner workings of society. He wanted to know how people really are and not how they should or could be. In 1968, he was less interested in protesting the Vietnam War than in discovering how those who protested interacted with a nun in the classroom. His disregard for the political and the normative often put him at odds with his colleagues in sociology. As an outsider, though, he was accustomed to ignoring disapproving eyes and muttered critiques. He didn't want to arouse us to a cause; he just wanted a clear view:

> [The one] who would combat false consciousness and awaken people to their true interests has much to do, because the sleep is very deep. And I do not intend here to provide a lullaby but merely to sneak in and watch the way people snore.

Some biological scientists draw their own blood and test new compounds on their own skin and inside their own veins. Goffman was that type of behavioral game theorist. He observed and experimented with social moves and countermoves, interpersonal strategies of concealment and revealment, and violations of norms and polite speech. He was ruthlessly analytical, though he lacked the mathematics and formal models of economics.

He would extend his acute observations on con artists to other marginal people such as the residents of mental asylums and spies, and he would develop a set of observations that linked these "deviants" with the broader world of those who present their selves on the stage of everyday life (namely, every single one of us). He analyzed the ways that targets, agents, moles, and double agents interact in the same intelligence game, variously hiding and revealing their truths and intentions. The players in the spycraft game, like the rest of us in the normal social game, are distributed up and down a staircase of knowingness and craftiness: they can be naive, unwitting, controlling, uncovering, counter-uncovering, counter-counter, and so on. As we will see shortly, rigorous economic research proves that Goffman's insight is both true and significant.

For Goffman, spies and con artists were not unique. Any interaction, such as a negotiation, revealed varying levels of strategic engagement: sometimes people had their backs turned and didn't even notice; sometimes they remained off to the side with a general awareness that some kind of card game was happening; sometimes they peered around the door frame through the gap in the door and saw an empty living room seemingly set up for a seminar; sometimes they sat solidly in the middle of the room and stared at the black-and-white nun in the corner; and sometimes they planted themselves in the wings, outside the room and closer to the granary, got out their notebooks, and didn't miss a foible or a scheme.

Looking at all of us from his own little empirical corner and observing how we really negotiate, dispute, con, spy, cooperate, present our selves, and converse from different levels on the strategic staircase, Goffman identified the ideal spot:

> The game-theory assumption that one's opponent is exactly as smart as oneself is not a wise one in daily affairs. The subject must put a stop to the cycle of moves and countermoves at the point he thinks will be exactly one step ahead of the furthest step that the observer takes, regardless of how much more devious the subject could be, if necessary.

One step ahead. Ideally, you don't want to be behind or even-stephen, nor do you want to be more clever or crafty than is necessary. You have gained an advantage, but you have not lost touch with your counterpart.

You have not overcomplicated matters, as Michael Jordan once did. At the time, he was being guarded by Steve Kerr of the Cleveland Cavaliers, who was a fantastic shooter but a pedestrian defender. Kerr, who would eventually become Jordan's teammate on the Chicago Bulls, recounts the superstar's mistake:

> And he did this head fake, and he faked one way, then he faked the other, and then he went back to the original way, and I was so faked out by the first fake that I was still there and so I actually stayed in front of him because I was too slow to go for the second fake, he kind of faked himself out. I stayed in front, challenged his shot and he missed it and there was a timeout. In the huddle, [my coach] Lenny Wilkens goes, "Guys, you got to stay in front of Jordan like Kerr just did." I didn't have the heart to tell him it was by accident.

In negotiation, don't be like Mike: One step ahead, as we will see in an upcoming chapter, is where the lion can meet the fox and the psychologist can meet the prophet. One step ahead is where the sophisticated, tough, fair, and Machiavelli-esque bargainer can be most successful.

LEARN TO "PLAY THE PIANO"

(or, Expert performance requires the ability to do multiple things at once)

It wasn't only practice, practice, practice that got pianist Yuja Wang to Carnegie Hall on the evening of May 14, 2016, for a recital that would conclude with Beethoven's *Hammerklavier* sonata, a work that has been described as "difficult" and "impenetrable."

Wang was born in Beijing in 1987, the single permitted offspring of a dancer mother and percussionist father. Six years later she began piano lessons, and shortly thereafter she was performing internationally, with recitals in Australia and Germany. Her adolescence was characterized by the combination of prizes, "youngest-ever" accomplishments, and early admission to the finest schools that distinguishes real prodigies. The common wisdom at Microsoft about hiring the best Chinese engineers back in the early 2000s was, "Remember, in China, when you are one in a million, there are 1,300 other people just like you." Of course, if you're a true genius like Wang and are one in a billion, then there are only 0.3 other Chinese performers like you. As she now enters her thirties, Wang is commonly recognized as one of the world's greatest pianists.

———————

The piano has had a syncopated history in China. The first keyboard instrument, a clavichord, was brought to the imperial court in the Forbidden City in 1601 by evangelizing priests. The emperor designated four of his eunuchs to be trained by one of the Westerners, and from this first quartet of students sprang a slow crescendo of pupils and musicians trained in Western music. Orchestras were formed and conservatories founded. In 1959, for the tenth anniversary of its ascension, the Communist Party allowed Beethoven's Ninth Symphony, with its famous "Ode to Joy" lyrics translated into Mandarin, to be played for the people at the celebration. Just a decade later, Mao Zedong and his Cultural Revolution slammed the lid down, and musicians, scores, and instruments were obliterated. Where once the Shanghai Conservatory had had more than five hundred pianos, by the thirtieth anniversary of the revolution not a single usable one remained.

After Mao died and Deng Xiaoping seized the governmental baton, initiating the era of reform and opening up that has transformed China's economy and society, an accompanying piano fever has replaced revolutionary fervor from Hubei to Hebei, from Henan to Yunnan. Indeed, China has been the global economy's largest producer, and also importer, of pianos. One Chinese composer observes, "For the past fifteen or twenty years, classical music has been very à la mode in China . . . . When I visited my old primary school, I found that, out of a class of forty students, thirty-six were studying piano."

One of the idols of those young pianists is Yuja Wang, and one of their dreams is to emulate her career as an elite soloist who gives concerts with the very best orchestras and players around the globe. As they practice their scales and fingerings, there is one critical aptitude they may not realize that they need, but it is one that Wang and other soloists such as the Canadian pianist Jon Kimura Parker know is essential: negotiating skills. Yes, a live musical performance is in fact a negotiation, one that occurs in public, one that has multiple rounds and multiple parties whose number depends on the piece and the setting but may include the soloist, the conductor, the orchestra, the concertmaster, the composer, the score, the critics, and the audience.

There are many specific issues that need to be hammered out, and there are a variety of processes, some of which may be helpful, others not:

> A soloist and conductor may differ about tempo, articulation, mood, and overall concept, but hopefully they will be able to coordinate their views amicably. If they cannot agree, controversial negotiations should take place in private, not in front of the orchestra.

As Gidon Kremer, a famous violinist, points out, the negotiation extends beyond the two most visible participants: "A soloist and the conductor (or indeed, the orchestra) could be in total agreement about the approach to phrasing, but the solution could still be at odds with the intentions of the composer."

That the negotiations can go quite wrong was made obvious one night, also at Carnegie Hall, fifty-four years before Wang appeared. Conductor Leonard Bernstein strode to the podium, and before the eccentric pianist Glenn Gould was introduced from the wings, Bernstein addressed the audience. He stated that usually a conductor and a soloist "manage to get together by persuasion or charm or even threats to achieve a unified performance." Despite his status and formidable ego, he admitted, "I have only once before in my life had to submit to a soloist's wholly new and incompatible concept and that was the last time I accompanied Mr. Gould." With that warning, he brought the pianist to the stage, and once he lowered his baton, he reluctantly and incompletely submitted to Gould's playing. Some critics found the interpretation too slow, and some audience members booed.

Perhaps there is something about learning the piano that makes a person like Gould or Wang a formidable counterpart in negotiations? That onetime friend turned implacable foe of the instrument, Mao Zedong, who never met a metaphor he wouldn't employ if it was useful, articulated this possibility,

Learn to "play the piano." In playing the piano, all 10 fingers are in motion; it will not do to move some fingers only and not others. However, if all 10 fingers press down at once, there is no melody. To produce good music, the 10 fingers should move rhythmically and in co-ordination.

The pianist, to Mao and for us here, embodies balance, simultaneity, co-ordination, multitasking, and metacognition.

These are the characteristics that allowed Yuja Wang to surmount Beethoven's immense *Hammerklavier* at Carnegie Hall. One critic said that the fugue in the fourth, and final, movement of the sonata

> requires the pianist to do two things at once with the same hand, sometimes trilling furiously with two fingers while articulating a melody with the other two. This requires not only preternatural agility but the ability to think of several things simultaneously and execute two of them with the same hand. Ms. Wang accomplished this with gossamer transparency.

Because she is so talented and so practiced, this kind of parallel processing and deep coordination is routine for Wang:

- "She was listening to harmonies and she was playing in a way that was following and sympathetic as well as asserting herself."
- "She was crystalline, sensitive, and musical. She was utterly composed, with hands and mind in balance."
- Awarding her Artist of the Year for 2017, *Musical America* compared her to "Kali, the many-armed Hindu goddess."

Laboratory tests and scanners have revealed that a pianist's brain and cognitive abilities are atypical. The corpus callosum—the bundle of nerve fibers that connects the left and the right halves of the brain—is larger and transmits signals faster in pianists than in non-musicians. An experienced pianist develops mental scripts that allow complex sequences of actions to flow automatically and free cognitive capacity for attention to be given to emotional expression or overall monitoring. Pianists have a better verbal memory and enhanced executive functions including attentional control, cognitive flexibility, and fluid intelligence. As one review states, "To be a musician is to be a consummate multi-tasker."

———————————

In the pages that follow, we are going to apply Mao's advice to negotiation and learn to "play the piano." To master negotiation as Yuja Wang has done with the piano, we must work on multiple levels at the same time, prioritize balance and coordination, and practice, practice, practice. We can see now that our other two envoys to the world of advanced bargaining, Machiavelli and Goffman, also asked us to multitask and learn to "play the piano" as follows:

1. Talk *and* listen.
2. Perform *and* monitor; act *and* direct.
3. Manifest toughness *simultaneously with* fairness.
4. Execute a plan *while* improvising.
5. Follow *and* assert.
6. Bring the gifts of a psychologist *synchronously* to the task of a prophet.
7. Be the lion *and* the fox: have high integrity *along with* cunning.
8. Be inside the game *and* view the game from the outside.
9. Know what step you are on *and* what step the other party is on.
10. Be a virtuous *and* virtuosic negotiator.

ONE STEP AHEAD OF THE GAME: NEGOTIABILITY

(or, Please don't negotiate all the time for everything)

One of the primary ways a negotiator can get one step ahead of their counterparts is to understand the conventional wisdom on bargaining, especially when it leads adherents in a wrong direction. For example, the typical book on negotiation begins with the ridiculous encouragement that all of life is a negotiation, and you can and should negotiate anything. This is bullshit. You cannot negotiate anything and everything; sometimes you cannot even negotiate crockery.

A number of years ago, in pre–Hurricane Katrina times, my wife and I met a friend of ours, an itinerant folk singer named Peter, for breakfast at Café du Monde in New Orleans. This café is famous for its green-striped awnings, chicory coffee, and plates stacked with mini-mountains of fried beignets coated with an avalanche of powdered sugar. The place is frenetic, crowded with locals, tourists, servers with overloaded trays, and bold, crumb-seeking pigeons.

Since the only bling in folk music is the sound an acoustic guitar string makes when it snaps, Peter had driven himself to New Orleans. In state police profiling terms, as he pointed out to us, folk singers and drug runners are identical: out on the highways in the early morning hours driving decrepit, oversized, generously trunked General Motors vehicles with car tops that are less vinyl than duct tape.

We were having a great Café du Monde breakfast, eating too many beignets and aspirating the powdered sugar and watching it scatter all over our clothes, when Peter announced that he wanted nothing more in life than a genuine Café du Monde coffee cup. These cups are formed of the blandest, beigest, thickest, most unadorned stoneware, a material that you would guess would be completely unbreakable except for the fact that the café's pandemonium was regularly shattered by a server dropping a tray of cups and plates and glasses. The coffee cups would not survive their plummet to the ground, and the ceramic shrapnel would momentarily disperse a gaggle of pigeons from a wide circle.

Peter asked our harried server if he could buy one of the cups, and she replied that the gift shop was right across the street. "No, no," Peter said, "I don't want some souvenir with a cheesy design and logo on it. I want to buy the real thing," and he held the unremarkable cup aloft. Our server said that she would have to talk it over with the manager. Twenty minutes passed—surely one, two, three more cups fell to a clattering, unfortunate, uncompensated early demise. Our server returned with the disappointing news that manager had been unsure—*ka-crash*—and so had gone over to the main office to speak to the higher-ups, who decided—*ka-smash*—that the café would not, in fact, be able to sell one of its coffee cups. There was no negotiation to be had: the disappointment was chicory-tinged. Peter left a few extra dollars in the tip and slipped the beige cup into his bag as we left the café.

Cafés, companies, governments, and societies sanction what can and cannot be negotiated. They create rules and norms to limit or expand the domain of bargaining. For the management of the Café du Monde a coffee cup falling and shattering was regrettable yet tolerable, but losing one in a deal was inconceivable. As Machiavelli and Goffman would advise, the sophisticated negotiator knows that these rules around when and where to bargain make many counterparts very predictable—they will adhere to conventional wisdom—and drowsy with respect to other approaches and tactics. As a one-step-ahead negotiator, you are not asleep: you bargain not because you are supposed to but because it is advantageous to you.

The message of this chapter, as we will see, is not only can't you negotiate everything, but you *shouldn't* try to negotiate everything. Bargaining costs time and mental energy, and it often is inefficient and disadvantageous. You shouldn't waste your time negotiating the price of T-shirts, toothpaste, toasters, and fishing rods at Walmart; you shouldn't waste your relationship negotiating every load of laundry, pickup of the kids, and dog walk with your spouse. You, therefore, can get one step ahead by having a clearer idea of *when* to negotiate, and this chapter will present realistic guidelines based on how much bargaining costs you personally, the potential efficiency of simply paying the posted price or running an auction, and the chance that a victory you have at hand will turn into a stalemate.

BUYING IS CHEAPER THAN ASKING

(or, The deep urge to avoid negotiating in the car dealership)

The trend in human history has been toward the elimination and containment of negotiation. Where once the shepherd and the farmer had to barter over the relative exchange rate of lambs for sheaves, no doubt helped by whatever the rate was the last time they traded, the invention of money and prices meant that trades could happen more efficiently and more quickly. The peddler has been replaced by the corporation, the bazaar by the mall, the souk by the supermarket, and the creaky roadside wooden stand by Etsy. Haggling was pushed aside in favor of faster methods— posted prices, pricing handbooks, auctions, price-labeling guns, and bar codes.

The Germans, noted lovers of competency and experts on efficacy, including the wordiness of their aphorisms, have a saying, *Kaufen ist wohlfeiler denn bitten*, or "Buying is cheaper than asking." There are two factors that can make this proverb come true—time and stress—and no place reveals the relative expense of asking/negotiating more clearly than the car dealership.

Everybody, even a laid-back folk singer, complains about how long it takes to negotiate the purchase of a car, whether it is a 1993 Oldsmobile 88 or a 2019 Subaru Outback. On the automobile website Jalopnik, one frustrated guy detailed his experience at the dealer: "[We] sent them an email with a link to the car on their lot that we wanted. We came in and it still took 4 hours to complete the deal and we sat around for almost 3 hours waiting for 10 minutes of paper work . . . . Dealership[s] waste your time in order to wear you down." Buying is cheaper than asking because buying is usually *quicker* than asking.

Maybe it's the uncomfortable chairs; maybe it's the Styrofoam cups, weak coffee, and non-dairy creamer. But whatever it is, some buyers, both prospectively and retrospectively, severely misvalue the time it takes to ask: "I negotiated for my most recent car. I got $2,200 knocked off the car. But I really didn't get a 'deal.' For the pleasure of me actually doing this I wasted 2.5 hours of my life while the rep pretending he was talking to his sales manager told me they needed to look at the trade again, etc." For 99 percent of us, grossing $880 per hour, as this gentleman did, is an excellent return on our time, even if the coffee is bad and the bargaining (and salesperson's cologne) is painful.

So let's agree to be rational and sensible about bargaining. If it's $2,000 for a few hours of your time and it's the only way to save that much, then definitely ask, and ask well. If it's $2 on your basket of odds and ends while the Target cashier calls the supervisor and the line of disgusted customers extends behind you well past the candy bars and lip balm, then just buy. In general, though, let's admit that if it were only the return on your time, the line between buying and asking would be drawn for most of us much closer to $2 than to $2,000.

The insightful car buyer knows that the minutes in the showroom don't only pass by ever so slowly, tick by tick by tick, they also create an investment, and that investment begins to demand some kind of positive return. This is one version of the famous sunk cost fallacy: "I've put so much gosh-darned time into this particular deal, I really better make it happen no matter what price the salesperson offers me." Note that the psychological obligation experienced by the prospective buyer might also include the salesperson's invested time as well. Those in sales rely on this, as voiced by John Steinbeck in his imagined inner monologue of the blokes selling jalopies to Okies fleeing the Dust Bowl in *The Grapes of Wrath*: "Get 'em under obligation. Make 'em take up your time. Don't let 'em forget they're takin' your time. People are nice, mostly. They hate to put you out. Make 'em put you out, an' then sock it to 'em." Dealerships waste your time not only to wear you down, as the first Jalopnik commenter wrote, but also to load a commitment on top of you. Think about the last time you bought a car or another big-ticket item—did you begin to feel some sense of debt to the salesperson? Don't.

Let's turn here in our test drive to the other source of dread as you walk into the showroom: the mental cost. A 2014 survey of American car buyers by Edmunds.com revealed that relative to haggling over the price of a car, one in five would rather embrace a nunnish celibacy for the next month, 29 percent would refrain from touching their iPhone for the weekend, and one in three would rather stand in line at the DMV or squeeze into the middle seat in coach. Without a doubt, bargaining is stressful, and one of the hoped-for benefits of this book is that a deeper understanding of negotiation will lessen that strain and pain. There is a tremendous amount of psychological security in knowing what you're doing and knowing what ploys the other side might be pulling. This knowledge, and the confidence that comes with it, will put you one step ahead.

Misterdestructo, the screen name of another car buyer, explained on Jalopnik why he flees bargaining and embraces CarMax, a U.S. chain of no-haggling used car outlets, to avoid slimy used-car dealers. He knows he's paying more, but admits, "I'm not good at the negotiations and getting involved in that makes me feel like I'm being taken advantage of in some way. I'm paying more for the peace of mind I get from shopping at CarMax, and that's fine with me."

A decade ago, journalist Chandler Phillips went undercover to work for several months as a car salesman and learn the tricks of the trade. The result was a great series titled "Confessions of a Car Salesman," and one of his revelations was, "The system was not set up for educated people who thought for themselves, it wasn't to help customers make informed decisions. The system was designed to catch people off guard, to score a quick sale, to exploit people who were weak or uninformed." The system targets unsophisticated negotiators.

So Misterdestructo is not all wrong, and I have compassion for his plight. Of course, it's always possible to skip the negotiation and just pay the sticker price at any dealership, thereby eliminating all the costs of asking and negotiating. But that won't solve the larger problem, because the tricks used by car salespeople are utilized by many other negotiators in many other settings. If your impulse is to acquiesce, always buy and never ask, you will end up getting ripped off a lot.

As with the time savings, you need to price at rational economic levels the peace of mind you get when you avoid negotiating. Another Jalopnik commenter admitted to Misterdestructo that the reduced stress of buying at CarMax is worth a little more: "BUT, a little more is like $50. Could you honestly spend $2500 for a better 2 hours than you would elsewhere? No, no two-hour buying experience is worth that much." Our journey through these pages is intended to reduce the fear of bargaining tactics and the stress of asking so that you are not paying more than $50 to avoid negotiating.

In fact, experts in car buying suggest that there is a better way for Misterdestructo to get the best deal and avoid negotiation than simply fleeing to CarMax. The best buying process for a new car or a used car that's fairly common is this: (1) Identify what make and model you want. (2) Lay out your specifications, being as detailed and complete as possible (transmission, mileage, accessories, fabrics, and so on) but no more than necessary (e.g., does the color really matter to you?). (3) Focus only on the lease rate or purchase price for the car and disregard financing or trade-in credit. (4) Create an electronic auction by emailing at least three dealers in your region, making sure that their addresses are visible (no BCC's) so they know they are competing. Write out your specifications and tell them that you want their best *total, out-the-door* price, one that includes all fees, licensing, and so on. (5) Print out the most attractive offer and proceed to the dealer to close. Be fully prepared to refuse the dealer's inevitable attempt to put you under obligation and renegotiate. (Don't let Jerry Lundegaard talk ya into that TruCoat there, even if he very, very persuasively argues, "Yeah, but that TruCoat.")†

It might be true that buying is often cheaper than asking, but your goal is to compare *buying well* and *negotiating effectively*, and to choose the method that yields the greatest net value. That comparison swings to bargaining in some predictable ways. Negotiation is more likely the better choice when the stakes are high, when the product or service is complex and has few substitutes, when there are important post-deal consider-

---

† See the polite couple paying $400 for that TruCoat there in the Coen brothers' movie *Fargo* (1996).

ations, and when there are multiple issues beyond price to be decided. Very importantly, the advantage swings to negotiating when you are not fearful, anxious, inexperienced, naive, ignorant, or unaware, when you understand the game inside and outside and are not snoring—so finish the rest of this book! (After all, I put in a lot of work on the previous pages [you don't want to put me out!] and you've invested many minutes getting to this point . . . .)

ADMIRAL JOY'S REGRET

(or, How to not let a winning advantage slip from your grasp)

Being clear-eyed about negotiability—when to bargain and when to avoid it—can be an advantage not only when $50 is at stake but also when thousands of lives may be on the line. Few people have ever felt this as keenly as Admiral C. Turner Joy did, and few people have ever had as many regrets.

Joy was the senior delegate for the United Nations Command (UNC), including the United States and the Republic of Korea (South Korea), in armistice talks with China and the Democratic People's Republic of Korea (North Korea) during the conflict on that peninsula in the early 1950s. He summarized his learnings from those peace talks in a bluntly titled tome published at the height of the Red Scare, *How Communists Negotiate*. One major theme of the book was the Communists' implicit adherence to von Clausewitz's famous saying "War is the continuation of policy with other means," so much so that the inverse was also true for them—"Diplomacy is the continuation of war with other means." Joy credited their seamless approach, battling spirit, and willingness to offend for their success against his "Occidental" side: "The measure of expansion achieved by Communism through negotiations is impossible to disassociate from what they have achieved by force, for the Communists never completely separate the two methods."

If you brush aside Joy's full-on Cold War rhetoric, the casual racism and name-calling, and his stiff, repetitive, military-grade prose, you can perceive the Machiavelli-esque appreciation the admiral had for the effective tactics of the Commies:

- "They carefully set the stage," including giving the Americans much shorter chairs and placing a North Korean flag that was six inches taller than the United Nations flag in the center of the conference table.
- With respect to their negotiating team, "force of intellect is the primary consideration. Reputation, rank, and position are of secondary consideration . . . . Persistence and an unruffled demeanor in the face of logic seemed to be the prime characteristics of their negotiating group." Hmmm, smart, persistent, and calm negotiators—those tricky Reds! And, by implication, woe to the "Occidentals" on Joy's side, who were selected based on the non-performance-related criteria of reputation, rank, and position.
- "They seek an agenda composed of *conclusions* favorable to their basic objectives." In modern parlance, they anchored the discussions by strategically embedding their first offers in the wording of the agenda items. For instance, item one on their agenda was the establishment of the 38th parallel as the military demarcation line between South and North, in contrast to the United Nations' first agenda item, agreement on a demilitarized zone.
- They "delay progress" (I've got to check with my manager/supreme leader) and "hope to exploit to their advantage the characteristic impatience of Western peoples."

Admiral Joy bemoaned the opportunity lost in the spring and fall of 1951, two years before the final armistice agreement was signed and the killing stopped, when the Eighth Army was advancing, supply lines to the North Korean troops had been decimated by the navy and air force, and, in a fire-and-fury manner, "talk of extending United States air action to Manchuria was rampant, complete with ominous overtones of the atomic bomb." All this momentum was halted by the armistice talks, particularly by orders from Washington telling the negotiators to agree to "a provisional truce line with a thirty-day time limit, thereby giving the Communists a respite from United Nations Command military pressure" and "a sorely needed breathing spell in which to dig in and stabilize their battle line." Joy felt that this directive from President Truman and the senior generals in the Pentagon severely reduced his leverage at the bargaining table. He knew it would have been far better to make the establishment of the truce line the last item on the agenda and keep alive the threat that successful fighting would continue to push the line north during the peace talks.

As many a military leader before him had when the guns were finally silenced, the fog cleared, and hindsight was at hand, Joy was certain that victory had been there for the taking, if only, if only: "I am convinced beyond any doubt that had our powerful offensive during the autumn of 1951 been continued, we would have had an armistice in Korea a year earlier than we did." The twelve extra months of military and civilian casualties weighed heavily on his mind, and "shoulda, coulda, woulda" suffuses the pages of *How Communists Negotiate*. As he reflected on this missed opportunity and the successful Communist bargaining tactics while writing in 1955, a year that began with the Pentagon's announcement that it would be developing nuclear-armed ICBMs, Joy had powerful advice for any future American leader who might find herself or himself maybe sixty-two (to pick a random number) years into the future, negotiating with, or engaged in a war of words with, the leadership of North Korea:

> Whatever may be the ultimate judgment of history regarding the significance of the Korean Armistice, those who must deal with the problems of today can learn from it certain sharply pertinent lessons. Taken to heart, this painfully acquired knowledge may save us all from the creeping disaster of unskilled effort in later negotiations between our world of freedom and that of tyranny.

The creeping disaster of unskilled effort in later negotiations, no doubt.

So, was Joy right? Were the Korean armistice talks costly? Can it be true that peace negotiations in general aren't an unalloyed good? Do we misapprehend negotiability not only on the individual level but on more macro levels as well—"we *should* negotiate everything"?

These are the questions that a young political scientist at UCLA, Eric Min, is attempting to answer. Min has scoured the military archives, historical records, and leaders' memoirs to compile a database of the tens of thousands of days with armed conflict and peace talks over the last two centuries. For each of these days, Min has documented how many battles took place, the results of the battles (favorable to the attacker or to the defender), and whether the combatants negotiated.

Some simple numbers show that World War II created a different relationship between war and diplomacy. Before 1945, 11.5 percent of war days had armistice talks; after 1945, 27.5 percent did. Moreover, after the defeat of the Axis powers, negotiations began earlier in subsequent wars than they did previously—with about a tenth of the war completed in the modern era as opposed to a third of the war for the conflicts from 1813 to 1945. The staggering body counts of the two world wars, the advances in killing technology, the dawn of the nuclear age, the creation of the United Nations, the drafting of the Geneva Conventions in 1949, and the spread of instantaneous and visual media have all led to a prevailing norm that negotiations should begin as soon as possible after the shooting starts. This norm provides cover and disguise for any armistice-suing side: Min writes that belligerents are more protected from looking weak and can claim that they're begrudgingly going along with the international community.

The daily battle database allows Min to calculate a measure of momentum by summing up the battle results for the previous sixty days of the war. The first fifteen months of the Korean War were distinguished by huge surges and *Game of Thrones*–like army movements:

- In the opening months of 1950, the North Koreans invaded across the 38th parallel and almost pushed the South Korean and American troops off of the peninsula.
- On September 15, 1950, General Douglas MacArthur led UNC forces on the famous landing at Incheon behind enemy lines, cutting the North Koreans' supply lines, and in the succeeding two months they were pushed to the northern edge of the peninsula at the Yalu River.
- However, on November 25 came another big swing of momentum, as tens of thousands of Chinese soldiers crossed the river and pushed the UNC troops steadily back down to the 38th parallel.

Figure 1 shows Min's calculation of fighting momentum for the entire war, including the initial big swings, first for North Korea, then for the

UNC, then for the combined Communist side. We can see that the data support Admiral Joy's sense of regret as the battlefield momentum created in the spring of 1951 ebbed away over the rest of the year.

We cannot conclude from this chart whether Joy's attribution of the lost advantage to armistice talks is a general phenomenon. It is possible that the Korean War is just an exception to the general rule that peace negotiations have no real impact on combat and quickly bring wars to an end when one side has a big advantage over the other. To test that, Min applies a number of sophisticated statistical methods to his entire dataset of post-1945 war days, battles, and negotiations. These methods allow him to tease out the effect of negotiations while controlling for such factors as whether the combatants were democracies, had nuclear weapons, were neighbors, had highly developed economies, and so on. Some of his results are startling.

First, Min shows that Joy's sense that the talks gave the Communists "a sorely needed breathing spell" is broadly correct. The number of battles on days with negotiations is 19 percent lower than on days without talks. Second, there is a big first-mover advantage in war: the initiator of the war is likely to seize momentum right away and, on average, to maintain an advantage throughout the war. Similarly, the attacker in a given battle

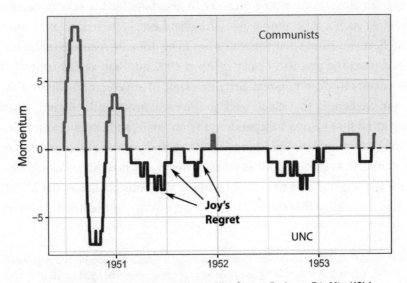

Figure I: Combat Momentum in the Korean War. Source: Professor Eric Min, UCLA.

has a two-thirds chance of winning. So both the target in a war and the defender in a given battle are struggling against the odds. Min's analysis reveals that the target in a war has the most to gain from negotiations, as combat momentum will on average switch to its side if talks occur and then break off. Armistice talks do seem to allow the disadvantaged side to, as Joy feared, "dig in and stabilize their battle line." Third, since they provide this breathing spell and can reverse momentum, peace negotiations extend the war and push armistice further into the future. This extending effect is greater the more lopsided the results on the battlefield are on behalf of the initiator of the war.

There is a perverse effect here. Once a war is started, armistice talks can delay the silencing of the guns and potentially increase the number of casualties.[†] So Admiral Joy was right to feel the weight of unnecessarily lost souls on his conscience and to wish that there had been some way of persuading his superiors in Washington to not press for negotiations. In addition to his sense that the chance for decisive battles had been denied, Joy came to know what Machiavelli understood firsthand: namely, that negotiation can be a refuge for the weak and the failing.

Margaret Thatcher, in her memoir, described the overwhelming din of peace advocates during the Falklands War with Argentina: "I was under an almost intolerable pressure to negotiate for the sake of negotiation. At such a time almost everything and everyone seems to combine to deflect you from what you know has to be done." Argentine forces had sailed from the mainland early in April 1982 and had seized control of the islands to dispute Great Britain's claim of sovereignty, one in a series of challenges that dated back to the early nineteenth century, when Argentina first gained independence from Spain and Spain granted England dominion over the islands. These challenges were often motivated by domestic Argentine politics when various leaders or juntas would perceive the wag-the-dog benefits of making symbolic claims on the Malvinas, as they called the islands. In the spring of 1982, as the British military

---

† The actual trade-off in deaths and injuries would be the reduced casualties on negotiation days, with 19 percent fewer battles, weighed against those generated by the additional days of fighting.

task force steamed south and Thatcher publicly disavowed any interest in peace talks, troop totals quickly outnumbered the residents of the barren, rather forlorn islands, and the conflict became a deadly enactment of Argentine writer Jorge Luis Borges's description: "Two bald men fighting over a comb."

Thatcher, the "Iron Lady," would not be deterred from grabbing the comb. Papers released thirty years after the war reveal that her ideological soul mate, President Ronald Reagan, phoned her on June 1, when British troops had successfully pushed all the Argentine forces into the capital city, Stanley, and were on the verge of victory. His message, according to secret notes of the call, was that "the USA considered it imperative that the UK should show that it was prepared to talk before the Argentinians were forced to withdraw. As the UK now had the upper hand militarily it should strike a deal now." Thatcher refused, comparing the Falklands to Alaska (a rather dubious comparison), and she pushed the fighting for another two weeks, until the commander of the Argentine garrison in Stanley surrendered. Thatcher saw that negotiations likely would only erode Britain's military and political advantage.

Another example of advantageous non-negotiating comes from a much less violent setting but one still involving mortality and morbidity: drug prices in the American health care system. In 2012, Americans spent over $1,000 per capita on pharmaceuticals, 33 percent more than was spent in Canada, and twice the average for all countries in the economically developed world. A handbook written for biotech executives and financial analysts who are trying to model the economics of new drugs under development in corporate laboratories states that the correct rule of thumb is that the future price of a medicine in the United States will be twice that in Europe. So not only were drug prices high in 2012, but industry executives were counting on them staying that way well into the future.

Like a seasonal outbreak, feverish reactions to pharmaceutical prices emerge in the media with some regularity and then usually subside. Once these outbreaks resolve, the underlying price disease persists. A large part of the condition is created by extended patent protection in the United States that suppresses competing medicines. Other developed countries have shorter patent terms that are usually coupled with price controls. In

the United States, the drug companies do their utmost to resist any restrictions on their ability to set prices, such as allowing the government
to negotiate.

The most well known of these efforts occurred in 2003 with the pas-
sage of Medicare Part D, which gave American seniors coverage for their
prescriptions. There was a non-interference clause in the legislation that
explicitly prevented the Secretary of Health and Human Services (HHS)
from interfering with "the negotiations between drug manufacturers and
pharmacies"; from excluding any drug from the formulary, no matter how
expensive or ineffective; and from instituting any kind of "price structure." The secretary of the Department of Veterans Affairs (VA), on the
other hand, *is* allowed to interfere and negotiate, and as a result, the VA
pays substantially less than Medicare for the same medicines—one study
found a savings of 45 percent. The Medicaid program features a number
of controls and caps on prices, and an analysis by the Office of Inspector
General in 2015 found that out of 200 commonly prescribed drugs, net
costs for Medicaid were less than half of the net costs for Medicare for 110
medications, and only five medicines were cheaper for Medicare participants than for those in Medicaid.

We can tell how valuable the ban on negotiation is to the drug manufacturers by how hard their lobbying group, the Pharmaceutical Research
and Manufacturers of America (PhRMA), has fought for it on Capitol Hill.
In a session that bled from the morning of Friday, November 21, 2003,
into Saturday's dawn, after representatives had had only a few hours to
review the thousand-page final version of the Medicare Part D bill, House
Republican leaders pulled out all the stops to get the bill passed. Among
the events that occurred during a night one senior Republican said was
the "ugliest" he had ever experienced were C-SPAN cameras "somehow"
freezing as pharmaceutical lobbyists prowled the floor of the House; the
vote being called at 3:00 a.m.; President George W. Bush being woken up
in the wee hours to make several arm-twisting phone calls; HHS secretary
Tommy Thompson, who would subsequently become a health care lobby-
ist, buttonholing members in the aisles; $100,000 in campaign funds be-
ing offered to assist a retiring congressman's son claiming his father's seat;
and Republican Speaker Dennis Hastert extending the voting window

from its usual fifteen minutes to almost three hours to gather up the last few yeas in what was "the longest electronic vote in congressional history."

Subsequent years have seen the industry and PhRMA continually interfering so as to keep the non-interference clause. Presidential candidate Barack Obama had run on a platform that advocated for removing the restriction on negotiating Medicare drug prices, but early in the complex process of creating and passing the Affordable Care Act (ACA), his administration was given an incentive to retain the non-interference clause by PhRMA's offer of a $150 million media campaign in support of Obamacare (and the implied threat that interference would lead to the same size campaign against the ACA).

Surely President Donald Trump, who promised during the 2016 campaign to void the ban on Medicare negotiation and said that the drug makers were "getting away with murder," has pharmaceutical executives reaching for their bottles of Xanax or other anxiolytics to calm their nerves, right? You might have thought so, especially when he began his January 31, 2017, meeting with PhRMA with the statement "We have to get prices down. We have no choice." Then the cameras stopped rolling and the media were ushered out. By the time the meeting broke up, Trump had swallowed a full dose of PhRMA's reality-bending *kauf* syrup: "I'll oppose anything that makes it harder for smaller, younger companies to take the risk of bringing their product to a vibrantly competitive market. That includes price-fixing by the biggest dog in the market, Medicare, which is what's happening." PhRMA understands—as both Thatcher and Joy did, as a car salesman would confess after a shot of Pentothal, as Misterdestructo should come to realize, and as an itinerant folk singer with enough room for a coffee cup in his satchel learned—that sometimes the greatest success comes from not negotiating and, especially, from not negotiating well.

SUMMARY

- Do *not* negotiate for everything, and especially do not *unthinkingly* negotiate: consider your non-bargaining options and all of the costs and benefits.

- Buying is often cheaper than asking.
- In war, the aggressor or the winning side can lose its advantage during armistice talks. If you're strong and have the upper hand and can get to the close without negotiating, then do so.
- Logically, then, negotiation is sometimes the refuge of the weak (Florence in Machiavelli's time) and the failing.
- Negotiating (or not negotiating) might be the law, but if it's just a norm, even a strong norm like holding peace talks, you should consider violating it. In this way, be more like Thatcher and Joy and less like Truman.

STRATEGIC SOPHISTICATION I: NEGOTIATION HAPPENS IN OUR MINDS

RISK: THE GAME OF WORLD CONQUEST

(or, Placing game theory on our table)

An episode in *Seinfeld*'s sixth season features a subplot in which Kramer, the most wildly unpredictable character on the show, plays the board game Risk with Newman ("Hello, . . . Newman"), the most obviously selfish and blatantly scheming character. Six hours into the famously neverending game (and early in the episode), Kramer backs slowly through Jerry's front door. He is carefully carrying the board, which has tens of blue and red army pieces distributed in territories throughout the global map. Trailed by Newman, Kramer kicks the newspaper off Jerry's table and gently places the board down.

Kramer explains that his opponent has to go to work, and they need "to put the board in a neutral place where no one will tamper with it." When Jerry objects to being their Switzerland, Kramer tells him it's essential, since the two players "are engaged in an epic struggle for world domination. It's winner take all. People cannot be trusted." In particular, Kramer knows that Newman is untrustworthy, and Newman knows that Kramer knows this. Kramer also believes (correctly, as it turns out) that Newman will plan a sneak attack on the neutralized board and that if Newman wins the game and takes over the world, he would make a "horrible leader" who would bring suffering to the "little people."

The story ends with the two wannabe emperors sitting on the subway

carrying the still open board with Kramer's blue troops now clearly
outnumbering Newman's dwindling red ones. Standing and holding a
pole nearby is a grim Slavic-looking fellow with a long dark wool coat, a
red scarf, and a black ushanka on his head, ear flaps tied up top. Newman
is reluctant to make his next move in the game:

KRAMER

```
I've driven you out of Western Europe and
I've left you teetering on the brink of
complete annihilation.
```

NEWMAN

```
I'm not beaten yet. I still have armies in
the Ukraine.
```

KRAMER

```
Ha ha, the Ukraine. Do you know what the
Ukraine is? It's a sitting duck. A road
apple, Newman. The Ukraine is weak. It's
feeble. I think it's time to put the hurt
on the Ukraine.
```

USHANKA

```
I come from Ukraine. You not say Ukraine
weak.
```

KRAMER

```
Yeah, well we're playing a game here, pal.
```

USHANKA

```
Ukraine is game to you?! How 'bout I take
your little board and smash it?!
```

To an economist, however, Ukraine *is* a game; Risk is (obviously) a
game; a pricing war between Uber and Lyft is a game; the Cold War was
a game; two arrestees being interviewed in separate rooms, each offered a

reduced sentence to rat out the other, is a Prisoners' Dilemma game; and, most importantly for us here, a negotiation is a game.

A game is a strategic interaction. It is, as the inventors of game theory, John von Neumann and Oskar Morgenstern, stated, "simply the totality of the rules which describe it." The key rules are those that govern the number of players, their possible moves (the actions and choices they can take), the flow of information (who knows what, who knows what someone else knows, et cetera), the outcomes resulting from terminal combinations of moves (the sidewalk collision when pedestrian 1 chooses to move left at the same time as approaching pedestrian 2 chooses to move right), and the players' payoffs from those possible outcomes (a bruised nose and a dropped cup of coffee).

A strategy is an action plan developed by a player that uses some or all of the information available to them and that prescribes a move at each stage of the game. At its most basic, used-car level, negotiation is the buyer choosing an offer from the set {$0, $1, $2, $3, . . .}, and the owner responding with one of {Yes, No}. One buyer's strategy could be "bid $3,000 no matter what," and one owner's strategy could be "say no to every offer less than $5,488."

Game theory analyzes pared-down, mathematical models of games. It is the science of action planning and implementation: it predicts what strategies players will develop and what choices they are likely to make. It incorporates the notion of *best response*: a player choosing an action that is the best answer to the action they anticipate their opponent will take. A best response is a player getting one step ahead of another.

In theory, best responses could be infinitely reflected—I choose the best response to your response to my response, and so on. In practice, real players are much more limited in their strategizing and mental mirroring—many act without any, or very limited, anticipation. In this chapter, we will discover the relevant game theory: a basic mathematical version of Risk; a group of players for whom the strategizing of social interaction does not come naturally; a number-guessing game that distributes people up and down Goffman's staircase of knowingness and craftiness; and a closer look at people who are zero mental steps into a game. By applying these learnings to negotiation, we can fulfill Machiavelli's instruction and have an easier time "making the right conjecture and weighing what the [wannabe] emperor's intentions are, what he really wants, which way his mind is turning, and what might make him move ahead or draw back."

COLONEL BLOTTO:
THE GAME OF TROOP PLACEMENT
(or, An illustration of the mental interworking of strategy)

Like a number of things in life, game theory is easier to show than to describe abstractly. Let's examine the Colonel Blotto game, an abridged version of Risk that involves placing forces in separate locations. It is a mathematical model of Machiavelli's missions to determine how Borgia had arrayed his forces across central Italy. A version formalized by analysts at the Rand Corporation in 1950 may have helped Admiral Joy distribute the navy's ships across the Korean peninsula's ports and straits.

In the game, you are Colonel Blotto and you have 100 troops at your disposal. Your counterpart, let's call them Ushanka, has the same number of troops. There are five potential battlefields to which you are both allocating troops. If you place more troops than Ushanka does on a given battlefield, you win the battle and a point; the same or fewer troops results in a stalemate or a loss and yields you zero points. Your objective is to win more points than Ushanka so that you win the war. How do you decide to spread your forces across the five locations?

One natural solution is to send twenty soldiers to each spot. If Ushanka does that also, then both sides get zero points because every battle is a draw. But you might figure out that if Ushanka distributes 20-20-20-20-20, then you could allocate 20-21-18-21-20 and win two battles, giving you two points to your opponent's one. Or maybe battlefield #5 is in Ukraine, so you know that Ushanka will decide to keep it strong and pick 0-0-0-0-100, so you can confidently choose 25-25-25-25-0 and win four points to their one. Or maybe Ushanka is pretty smart, thinks Blotto is dumb, and will pick 20-21-18-21-20 also, so you should really weaken field #3 a little further and go 20-22-16-22-20 and retain your advantage . . . . You can see that the mental interweaving, or iterative reasoning, as economists call it, gets pretty complicated pretty quickly.

Variants of Colonel Blotto have been used to generate insight into a variety of competitions and conflicts—guerilla warfare, political party spending in elections, viruses versus the immune system, and phishers against internet users. Some of these variants have been tested with human subjects to see what choices they would actually make as Blotto or Ushanka. One large-scale experiment with hundreds of participants was conducted on Facebook: the easy choice of 20-20-20-20-20 was the second-most-popular strategy, while the most popular was 34-33-33-0-0, which will always defeat the even allocation.[†] The sixth-most-popular choice was the naive Ushanka-protecting-Ukraine strategy 100-0-0-0-0, which, as you will see if you test it, cannot defeat any other allocation. The strategy that was victorious most often was 36-35-24-3-2, a non-obvious clumping to say the least. In addition, there were some mental quirks in people's troop distributions: they treated battlefields #1 and #5 differently than those in the middle, and they changed their strategy if their counterpart was a friend rather than a stranger.

But you, esteemed reader, might respond, "This is all a little abstruse. It's all well and good for strategists at Rand, wargamers, nerds, and even Kramer and Newman to think like this, but how is it going to make me a better negotiator in real life? How can game theory get me to the Machiavelli-esque ideal of bringing 'the gifts of a psychologist to the task of a prophet'?" To see why the degree of mental reasoning and the proper weighing of the intentions of other people are essential not just to negotiations but to most of social life, we must turn to those people who, at least sometimes, have to do without.

LOOKING GLASS:
THE GAME OF MINDSIGHT
(or, Why negotiation is all of life)

Suppose you had trouble supposing. Suppose every interaction you had left the other person with the sense that something was amiss. Suppose you could not hint or snark or keep a conversation on track. Such impairments

---

† 34-33-33-0-0 includes all permutations of these clusters across the five fields—0-0-33-34-33, 33-0-33-0-34, and so on.

in imagination, social functioning, and communication are central to the diagnosis of autistic spectrum disorder (ASD).

Neurotypical people can be befuddled by those with ASD: "One is welcomed and bid goodbye with the same impersonal kindness as if contact were only real as long as it lasted during concrete presence." Naoki Higashida, the young ASD author of the bestseller *The Reason I Jump*, admits, "True, we don't look at people's eyes very much. 'Look whoever you're talking with properly in the eye,' I've been told again and again and again, but I still can't do it. To me, making eye contact with someone I'm talking to feels a bit creepy, so I tend to avoid it." No eye contact means no iterative looking: you can't see them seeing you seeing them seeing you, and so forth.

All along the autism spectrum, images of transparency and metaphors of glass recur. Temple Grandin, animal rights activist and subject of an eponymous HBO movie, says, "People around me were transparent . . . . Even a sudden loud noise didn't startle me from my world." Donna Williams remembers that when she was a little girl, "my bed was also surrounded and totally encased by tiny spots that I called stars, so that it seemed to me I lay in some kind of mystical glass coffin." A mother writes, "Autism is when your two-year-old looks straight through you to the wall behind—through you, her father, her sister, her brother, or anybody else. You are a pane of glass."

For neurotypicals, other people are mirrors, as we are for them, which means it's mirrors all the way down to our genes. Charles Horton Cooley, an influential predecessor of Goffman in the field of sociology, captured this idea in his "looking glass self" theory, which describes how essential the mental pinging back-and-forth is to our lives:

> Society is an interweaving and interworking of mental selves. I imagine your mind, and especially what your mind thinks about my mind, and what your mind thinks about what my mind thinks about your mind. I dress my mind before yours and expect that you will dress yours before mine. Whoever cannot or will not perform these feats is not properly in the game.

As I believe, and as I believe you believe since you read Chapter 2, we cannot say that all of life is a negotiation, but we can say, because of the mental interweaving, that *a negotiation is all of life*. Negotiating is smiling, frowning, hinting, directing, joking, crying, mimicking, angering, delighting, confronting, refusing, shunning, engaging, pleasing, disappointing, sharing, competing, understanding, confusing, learning, arguing, educating, denying. This potentially infinite regress of mirroring and the involvement of all parts of social life are why a successful negotiator requires psychology and prophecy. Game theory can be particularly valuable here because certain games expose exactly how deeply we and our counterparts look into the mirror.

Individuals with ASD may have difficulty not just dressing their minds but dressing, period. Higashida, again: "As an adult, I know that it's not good to wear grubby or inappropriate clothing, and choosing clothes has become a fraught area—I'm simply not in the habit of thinking about my wardrobe and appearance. When I look in a mirror, I never know what it is exactly that I ought to be checking out." How do neurotypicals get dressed so easily, both body-wise and mind-wise? The answer coming from both cognitive science laboratories and neuroscience scanners is a brain network with the somewhat confusing label "theory of mind" (ToM). ToM is the hardwired system through which neurotypicals quickly and automatically understand and predict the emotions, thoughts, and intentions of other people. Basically, ToM allows us to have mindsight—or, as we'll also call it, mentalize.

The capacity of the system typically increases throughout childhood, a fact that is demonstrated by performance on "false belief" tests. One of the most common tests happens like this: The participating child is seated in front of a medium-sized diorama of an apartment. The child sees two puppets come in the front door, one tall and skinny and with wild hair ("Hi, my name is Kramer, giddyup"), and one short and stout and in a postal uniform ("Hello, . . . Newman"). The child sees Kramer place the Risk board on Jerry's table and sees that Newman sees. The two puppets depart. Kramer comes back into the apartment alone (the child sees that there's no Newman) and moves the board into the freezer in Jerry's kitchen. Kramer exits—after snagging a handful of grapes, a peach, and a banana from the refrigerator. Now, the child is asked, where will Newman look for the board when he breaks into the apartment? Four-year-old neurotypical children correctly answer, "The table!" ASD children of the matched mental age incorrectly answer, "The freezer," as do younger neurotypical kids, because their ToM is not developed sufficiently to distinguish what's in their heads (board in the freezer) from what's in Newman's (board on the table).

This mental state is a first-order false belief because Newman has a mistaken impression of objective reality in his mind. A second-order false belief is this: Now puppet Newman crouches to the side of Jerry's couch and watches Kramer move the board to the freezer. Kramer, as oblivious as ever, does not see Newman. The question for the test subject is, "Where does Kramer think Newman thinks the board is?" Neurotypical children have to be around six years old to reliably get the correct answer: "The table!" Older children with ASD struggle with this depth of mental mirroring.

One objection you might have is that the wrong answers just reveal a confused observer, not one lacking mindsight. A second, analogous experiment cleverly refutes this possible interpretation. This time a child is shown the diorama of Jerry's apartment and is given a Polaroid camera with which to photograph the venue. The child looks through the lens and snaps. The Kramer puppet comes in alone again, board, freezer, yada-yada, making the photograph "false," and then the child is asked, "Where will the board be in the photo?" ASD children have no difficulty reading the "mind" of the camera, since they answer correctly that the board will be on the table in the Polaroid. ToM is neurally and evolutionarily homed in on other people.

Many adults with ASD still lack a spontaneous, automatic ToM and are not properly in Cooley's and our social game. As the glass imagery suggests, those with ASD do not reflect other minds to the same extent; they have in a sense passed through the looking glass. We learned long ago from Alice, the heroine of Wonderland, exactly what it's like when you live on the non-reflective side of the mirror: you have difficulty with social interaction and relationships (none of the animated objects seem to be able to see you or hear you), language (poetry is jabberwocky), and emotions (if you don't write your feelings down, as the White King attempts to do in his ever-present notebook, you might never remember them).

The looking-glass self allows those without ASD to handle faces, imaginary play, and pronouns with aplomb. Neurotypicals are transfixed by human faces and store them so accurately that we can instantly tell one person from another as long as the chin is at the bottom and the brow at the top. To many with ASD, another's face is simply one more object in a world with many and is shelved in memory as though it were a household item, "as a yellow plastic bowl with a wide circumference." Kramer and Newman have no problem pretending nearly to the point of belief that they're emperors in a struggle for world conquest, but from the other side of the looking glass, "it was when everyone was playing like cowboys and Indians and cops and robbers and things and I didn't get it because all these people were pretending to be like a cowboy or a robber and I didn't understand why. For obvious reasons, because they weren't, they were just a bunch of school kids running around." Finally, mindsight blinds neurotypical people to how much reflection and mental translation pronouns require: when I say "I," you know I mean me and not you. Experiments show that pronouns are much more confusing for those with a damaged innate ToM.

Nevertheless, individuals with ASD can, with grit and determination, compensate enough to join the social game. In the looking-glass world Alice notes that the White King keeps a memorandum book in which he records his memories, emotions, and other mental content. Similarly, many people with ASD compensate for a malfunctioning ToM by explicitly, studiously learning "the myriad rules of human interaction one by one, by rote . . . because the criterion of 'how would I feel if' is unavailable."

Higashida relates his approach to conversations: "First, I scan my memory to find an experience closest to what's happening now. When I've found a good close match, my next step is to try to recall what I said at that time. If I'm lucky, I hit upon a usable experience and all is well. If I'm not lucky, I get clobbered by the same sinking feeling I had originally, and I'm unable to answer the question I'm being asked." Temple Grandin has a visual version of the White King's book: her experiences "were like a library of videotapes, which she could play in her mind and inspect at any time—'videos' of how people behaved in different circumstances. She would play these over and over again and learn, by degrees, to correlate what she saw, so that she could then predict how people in similar circumstances might act."

The way that Grandin and others with ASD make their way back through the looking glass into the social game should remind us of the way that Goffman, himself an outsider from the granary, could see so deeply into the ways that we interact. Even if mentalizing (what your mind thinks about what my mind thinks about . . .) could be an infinite series of reflections, and false beliefs could run to many orders, neurotypicals often use very simple rules to interact. Although these rules and norms are learned with difficulty by most people with ASD, occasionally that struggle helps them to see rule-bound reality better than we do because we think we're playing cops and robbers, or a game of world conquest, when we're just kids running around. Sometimes we falsely believe that we're awake and deeply sophisticated, and that just allows Goffman and some of those individuals with ASD to sneak in, watch the way we snore, and record it in their memorandum books.

Still, though, the hacked-out social prophecies of those with ASD often have a fair degree of inaccuracy and are occasionally wildly wrong. Cooley would say, and we have seen, that people with ASD are not properly and performatively in the social game. One prevalent theory about autism is that it is "a disorder of prediction" that causes an individual with ASD to inhabit "a seemingly 'magical' world wherein events occur unexpectedly and without cause." So on the neurotypical side of the mirror, mindsight and theory of mind are essential to accurate social prediction and to performing well in a negotiation. We need to understand, then, how much mental pinging back-and-forth there is in real interactions, how much strategic sophistication there is within negotiations when conducted among neurotypicals, and how much snoring there is. To answer these questions, we need to train our looking glasses on a beauty contest.

BEAUTY CONTESTS: THE GAME OF NUMBER PROPHESY

(or, The game that distributes players on the staircase of strategic sophistication)

Miss Helen McMahon was the winner of a contest conducted in the autumn of 1913 by the *New York Times* to select "The Girl of To-Day" ("to-day" clearly being well before Second Wave feminism). Readers were asked to submit a photograph of a contestant who they felt was "most typical of

The Girl of To-day
Picture Section
Part 2

The New York Times

Christmas Number
Sunday.
December 7, 1913

THE GIRL OF TO-DAY   507 West 171st Street, New York
MISS HELEN McMAHON,

Source: Library of Congress

the American girl today," and a judging panel of seven artists would pick the winner. One of the artists framed the challenge as "We are not here to pick the prettiest of the lot," and another added, "But The Girl of To-Day must certainly look up-to-date."

What might be most interesting about this retrograde competition are the comments of the judges and nominating readers as they struggled with the idea of "typical." Some felt she should be from a city, and especially New York City; others thought the Midwest, and especially Indiana; she should be lithe and slender; she should be distinguished by alertness and independence; she should be "a glittering creature, lacking poise, but clean cut and pleasant"; one complained that it didn't really matter because she couldn't possibly hold a candle to The Girl of 1863; some thought she "was drifting toward masculinity, and that she was apt to take a cocktail and a cigarette"; a YWCA secretary felt she should be a "compound of sunshine and steel"; Booth Tarkington, a writer famous for his depiction of Hoosier life in such novels as *The Magnificent Ambersons*, said that she "made him think of tennis rackets, turkey trotting, flat-soled shoes, college pins, and the 'biological' view of life."

John Maynard Keynes, the British economist who helped the world understand the Great Depression, pointed out the degree of mentalizing that contests like The Girl of To-Day might require. He writes:

> It is not a case of choosing those faces which, to the best of one's judgment, are really the prettiest, nor even those which average opinion genuinely thinks the prettiest. We have reached the third degree where we devote our intelligences to anticipating what average opinion expects the average opinion to be. And there are some, I believe, who practice the fourth, fifth, and even higher degrees of this game.

Keynes believed the stock market was essentially akin to the *Times* contest, since investors are trying to identify the stock that average opinion will eventually select as the most attractive. The underlying value of the stock was less important than its potential popularity and comeliness in the eyes of others, and those others' conjectures about yet others' conjectures of value. Following Keynes's lead, economists label games involving the estimation of average opinion "beauty contests."

The winner of the beauty contest among various "beauty contest" games—the one that is clean-cut, pleasant, and flat-soled—was popularized by economist Rosemarie Nagel in 1995. It is a variant of the standard guessing game in which a group of players tries to come closest to a target number between 0 and 100. In Nagel's version, the target number is generated by the players themselves, computed as some fraction of the average of all of their guesses. The person who comes closest in either direction to this cropped average wins. This is an unambiguously ToM, Keynesian game: players need to anticipate where the average, "typical" guess will be and then adjust downward, a process that depends on making assumptions about the other players and their conjectures.

As a numerical example, suppose there are ten players whose guesses are equally spaced between 0 and 90, that is, 0, 10, 20, 30, . . . , 90. Assume also that the target is set at two-thirds of the average of the guesses. We can work the arithmetic: summing the guesses gives a total of 450, and dividing by 10 (for the number of players) yields an average guess of 45. Taking two-thirds of that shows that the target is ㉚, and the winner would be the person who was closest (in this case, the guesser of 30).

So suppose you're about to play this game, with an allowed number range of 0 to 100 and a target of two-thirds of the average guess, for a $100 prize with the nineteen people who are closest in space to you right now as you read this—your family and neighbors, the other patrons of the coffee shop, passengers in the nearby rows on the plane or train, whatever. Make your guess for the target—The Number of To-Day—right now.

> Enter your guess in the box here, either visibly with a pen or a pencil or invisibly with the tip of your finger on the page or screen.

Notice as you do so how your mind is working through it. Do you want to just pick a number without wasting much time? Do you want to try to figure out what the others would do? Do you think they even understand the game? Force yourself to go a little further, to the second order: Are some of them anticipating that you and the others are anticipating? If so, how many of the others are doing this extra thinking? With each and every bit of insight that you credit the others with, do you see how The Number of To-Day is shrinking?

Because of the structure of the game, your guess reveals how sophisticated you are and how clever you believe the other players are. Assume, for the moment, that all the players except for you are not even bothering to think through the game. These are the zero-step players because they refuse to enter into the strategic domain, forgoing any consideration of what might be the best move. In a way, these ZEROs have their eyes closed to the game and they are, to use Goffman's image, really deeply snoring. If you are strategic, you would choose the best response to these naive co-participants, some of whom might choose a large number and some a small number. As we will see, these ZEROs—their unpredictability and Kramer-ness, their density, and their distribution—control a lot of the final look of the game. In the absence of any additional information, the best you can do is to assume the highs and lows balance out and the ZEROs come in around 50.

Acting a single step ahead would make you a ONE here, and you would select 33 (the number closest to two-thirds of a little less than 50, since your guess gets folded into the average).[†] You have a good chance to win the game if your prediction about the ZEROs being randomly scattered between 0 and 100 is true, and if your assumption that no one is as smart as you is also correct. ONEs are one step into the game and understand enough to make moves that will narrowly and blindly fulfill their self-interest. A ONE is equivalent to the person I once knew who was a very poor driver and rejected the idea of defensive driving with this dismissal: "Everyone else just has to watch out for me."

A TWO is a more defensive, semi-alert driver, aware that the game is filled with those who are predictably charging straight ahead and those who are chaotically weaving all over the place. A TWO is using strategic thinking and their theory of mind to try to get one step ahead of opponents who are ONEs and ZEROs. If a TWO conjectures that everyone else is a ONE, they guess 22.[‡] As we will see when we review the results from actual laboratory tests of the beauty contest, in many instances this would often be a good guess for The Number of To-Day.

THREEs would assume that some of the others are TWOs and would choose an even smaller number (maybe around 14), and so on down the number line. Deeper levels comprising experienced players, game masters, Machiavelli and Borgia, economists, rationalist writers such as Jorge Luis Borges and Hilary Mantel, and the financial men that Keynes believed were four and five steps in exist in smaller and diminishing numbers. Let us group these THREEs, FOURs, FIVEs, and so on into the THREE+s—these are the players who are sometimes capable of conjecturing very complex futures if necessary.

Mind-seer, you might be thinking, "wait a second. If he's combining all the deeper levels into one category, then there must not be a whole

---

[†] Because the nineteen ZEROs would be choosing randomly, the expected total of their guesses is 950, since the best conjecture for each of them is that they end up in the middle of the range. The one-step player solves the following equation to determine x, which is their best guess: $2/3 \times (950 + x) / 20 = x$.

[‡] The solution to $2/3 \times ((19 \times 33) + x) / 20 = x$.

lot of difference among them for all intents and purposes." Very clever deduction on your part! And, for all of us, a big relief! It is a rare negotiation in which we won't be 99 percent effective by employing the four classifications of strategic sophistication—ZEROs, ONEs, TWOs, and THREE+s—on ourselves and the other bargainers.

How deep do you have to go to win this game? Fortunately, the beauty contest and the depths of strategic thinking have been one of the most active research topics in behavioral economics, and so an answer can be found in the tens of experiments that have been run around the globe in the last two decades. Let's start with my classroom, where 327 of my negotiation students have played the game: their predictions of The Number of To-Day are arrayed in Figure 2. Moving from left to right along the number line, you can see that 22 students picked zero; 12 picked 1; more than 10 percent picked 13, 14, or 15; there are spikes at 22, 33, 50, and 67; and two students, with a very cracked and cloudy (maybe intentionally and perversely so?) looking glass, forecast 100. Across all the semesters, the average guess of my students was a little less than 27; multiplying that by two-thirds gives a target of just below ⑱.

Rosemarie Nagel's original experiment in 1995 with German college students resulted in an average of about 36 and, hence, a target of ㉔. The same number emerged as the winner from a later, online version played by more than two thousand students from around the globe. Colin Camerer, an economist at Caltech, tested groups such as the university's board of trustees, CEOs, elderly people, and high school kids, and all ended with targets between ㉙ and ㉒.

Also, Nagel had her students play the game three more times, and the target shrank steadily, to ⑯ to ⑪ to ⑥. One of the reasons the target is lower with my negotiation students than Nagel found at first is that some of them had seen the contest in another course.

There have been three versions of this Number of To-Day contest run in actual periodicals, two by Nagel and her colleagues in a Spanish newspaper and a German magazine, and one by Richard Thaler, the eminence grise of behavioral economics and 2017 Nobel Prize winner, in the *Financial Times*. The lovely winners, full of Spanish sunshine, German steel, and pecuniary glitter, respectively, were ⑰, ⑮, and ⑬. The winner for the *Financial Times* was lower not because the readers consisted mainly

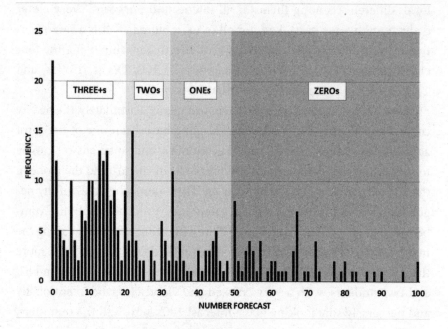

Figure 2: Beauty Contest Guesses by My Negotiation Students

of Keynes's supposed THREE+s but because there were fewer ZEROs who picked numbers above 50. This dearth may not be due to the lack of ZEROs in the readership of that paper (although a variety of financial masters of the universe gathered in a bar on Wall Street might tell you otherwise); rather, it may simply be because Thaler included an example in the instructions in which 20 was the winning number. The anchoring effect of numbers is something we will encounter deeper into the book.

The overall distribution of guesses and the target are interesting to economists and relevant to negotiators for a number of reasons. First, none of these Numbers of To-Day is ⓪, an absence that made some economists' hearts grow fonder and others' flutter. The latter group were orthodox game theorists who knew that John Nash, the 1994 Nobel Prize winner portrayed by Russell Crowe in *A Beautiful Mind*, had proved that every game has a "solution." The solution, called a Nash equilibrium, is a stable set of strategies in which no single player has an interest in independently changing their plans if everybody else holds to their own plans. One condition that can foster a Nash equilibrium is if the players are completely clairvoyant mind-seers whose shared mental looking-glass reflections are endless. We can eavesdrop on the mind-talk in the heads of these infinitely sophisticated players: *Everybody else is at 45, so I'm going to 30; but they are thinking that too, so really they're at 30, so I'm going to 20; again, though, they're already there, so I'm going to 13*; and so on, as The Number of To-Day gets skinnier in the myriad mirrors. Once it collapses down to ⓪, then you have a Nash equilibrium, since no solo THREE+ would want to pick a higher number.[†]

Those with the fluttering hearts are the behavioral economists, members of a field created by Thaler and a pair of psychologists, Daniel Kahneman and Amos Tversky, whose unique complementarity was profiled in Michael Lewis's *The Undoing Project*. The prediction that players in the beauty contest would all pick 0 was yet another example of how orthodox economics made terrible forecasts. The orthodoxy assumed people were hyperrational, deeply mentalizing, objective data processors, or "Econs," as Thaler labels them in *Misbehaving*. "Econs" always choose the Nash equilibrium, maximize their utility, ignore irrelevant options, and so on. Thaler, Kahneman, and Tversky thought they could gain insight and accuracy by modeling all of us as "Humans," creatures who often make merely satisfactory choices, are willfully ignorant and sometimes altruistic, are strategically shallow, pay attention to social cues, and are anything but objective. Behavioral economists know that predicting the world is made up of only "Econs" or THREE+s is as erroneous as supposing it is full of just ZEROs.

Almost all tests of the beauty contest show the same regular heaping of guesses as in Figure 2. There are piles at 0 and 1, at 13 through 15, at 22, at 33, and at 50 and 67. In behavioral economics, this pattern arises from what is called level-k thinking and what we have been calling steps. As shown in the chart, only ZEROs are found at the upper end of the number line; primarily ONEs are found near 33; the TWOs, near 22; the THREEs, near 14; and the other THREE+s down to zero.

The ZEROs and naive THREE+s are not going to win the beauty contest: the former group might not care, and the latter group often can take

---

[†] Depending on the number of players, the fraction that the average is reduced by, and whether decimal answers are allowed, the number 1 can also be a Nash equilibrium.

solace in being smarter than the other players and "solving" the game by choosing the Nash equilibrium. But solving is not winning: zero is actually a terrible prediction when most targets range from (24) to (15). Naive THREE+s are a great example of being too clever by half (or, really, too "devious")—being five or six steps into the contest and well past Goffman's ideal spot of one step ahead of, in this case, the most typical player. As our initial review of the laboratory results shows, in many populations it's the TWOs centered around 22 who are the better prophets and often end up winning.

The skeptical part of your brain (and it's an essential part if you're going to be a sophisticated negotiator) might be asking, "How do we know that these steps are not just a result of differing abilities in arithmetic and logic?" Good point. I can respond with two counters.

Researchers Konrad Burchardi and Stefan Penczynski cleverly added an element of negotiation to the beauty contest by pairing participants and allowing them each to send one text to the other to convince them of the best number to guess together. They found strong evidence that the size of the guesses for The Number of To-Day explicitly matched the depth of subjects' thinking. For instance, a ZERO whose starting guess was 77 sent this message—"i do not have a suggested decision as it is not based on any logic. i cannot predict what the other teams will play and cannot figure out how to work out what would be the best decision to make"—to a TWO whose initial number was 23 and who sent a very different message: "the problem is that we have to be BELOW the assumed average—which is tricky cos how should we know? lets think about what's going on in ppl's minds: they're all facing the same question, so i reckon they'll go for rather small numbers, at least below 50 so let's try being below that as well and do something like 25 or maybe even 20 which would be two thirds of their 30–40." The ZERO is completely baffled, while the TWO is anticipating getting one step in front of a bunch of ONEs.

A dozen years after her original paper was published, Nagel and a neuroscientist, Giorgio Coricelli, ran a beauty contest in which the participants were placed into a brain scanner when they made their guesses. Two tasks for each contestant were simply to pick any number between 0 and 100 and to do some stepwise calculations, such as $\frac{2}{3} \times \frac{2}{3} \times 66$. Then they played a beauty contest either with nine other people or against a computer, which, they were told, would choose nine random numbers. This latter condition is equivalent to being told that you're playing with nine mindless ZEROs, so mentalizing is not necessary. The first outcome of the testing was that the reaction time of participants seemed to follow a pattern of deeper thought: it took the average subject two seconds to choose any random number, seven seconds to guess against the computer, and nine seconds to guess against other people.

Brain scanning could give a clue to the thoughts that were different during the nine seconds. The fMRI machine Coricelli and Nagel used detects when an area of the brain receives a gush of blood flow caused by the particular mental activity the person is engaged in. Compared to random number picking and calculating, the beauty contest activated the areas of the brain involved with ToM and mentalizing, and TWOs had significantly more blood flow in the medial prefrontal cortex than less sophisticated choosers did. The medial prefrontal cortex (mPFC) is an area of the brain behind the upper forehead involved in understanding other people's intentions and social cognition in general.

Lastly, the brains of the ONEs and the ZEROs (the Newmans and the Kramers) in this study were far less active in the regions that support the Yuja Wang–like executive functions "related to performance monitoring and cognitive control." Combined with the lower activity in the mPFC, this dormancy means that the less sophisticated are not able to override their initial impulses and their prepotent guesses for The Number of To-Day; therefore, they are not very strategic. ZEROs and ONEs get an early mental impression and can't or won't move away from it.

MENTAL REAL ESTATE:
THE CENTRAL GAME OF NEGOTIATION

(or, Theory of mind plays a direct role in successful negotiation)

Colin Camerer, the researcher who tested the beauty contest on the Caltech board of trustees and other specialized groups, is one of the founders of neuro-economics, a field that combines brain science with behavioral economics. It is the neuro-economists who keep many of the fMRI machines at universities buzzing and clanging, filled with undergraduate subjects whose brains are scanned as they play different games and make various choices. His research, as we will see in the next two sections, has been essential to discovering the workings of level-k thinking and strategic sophistication. One of his studies can provide the last piece of our puzzle: direct evidence that theory of mind and mentalizing are critical not only to winning beauty contests, solving false-belief tests, and, as Cooley wrote, dressing our minds to be properly in the social game, but also to succeeding in a negotiation.

Camerer and his associates tested a simple buying and selling game for a hypothetical object—say, an illustrated version of Lewis Carroll's *Through the Looking-Glass*. Two players, Bjorn and Sally, are matched; Bjorn is the buyer and Sally is the seller for sixty consecutive transactions. Each round Bjorn, the buyer, is told in secret how much he values the book (a number between 1 and 10). He will open the game by suggesting a possible price to Sally, the seller, who then sets the actual sticker price for the book. If her price is more than Bjorn's secret value, then there's no deal; if it's equal or lower, then there is a deal, with the seller getting her price and the buyer getting the difference between his value and what he paid. A numerical example: Bjorn is told his value for this round's book is 7, he suggests a price of 3, Sally sets a price of 5, and a deal is made with the seller getting 5 and the buyer 2 (= 7−5). If Sally priced it at 8, there would be no deal, since that price would be greater than Bjorn's value of 7.

As always, sellers want to sell high and buyers want to buy low. Buyers will have to shade their suggestions at least a little: if they propose their actual valuation and the seller agrees, then they will net nothing from the deal. However, if they always suggest a low number, then buyers might just ignore the suggestion and set prices on their own. You can see that the buyer's suggestion becomes a single piece of the mental clothing Cooley was highlighting, since it has to both cover and reveal in just the right way.

With two THREE+s and full mentalizing, this is not much of a negotiation: the Nash equilibrium is for Sally to completely ignore Bjorn's suggestion (since he has an incentive to lie), so the buyer just blurts out random jabberwocky and the seller sets her price at 5 or 6. As with other games, however, real players don't act this way. Camerer and his co-authors find that ZERO buyers employ a simple rule: Suggest a fraction of your value every time. On average, they shave 43 percent off their valuations, so a sophisticated seller learns something when a ZERO buyer says 4 rather than 1. ONE buyers believe they are dealing with simplistic ZERO sellers who will accept and trim every suggestion so as to make a little profit, and so they propose consistently low numbers, some even saying 1 over and over again.

We're going to need our own ToMs in order to understand the more sophisticated buyers. ONE sellers think they're dealing with ZERO buyers whose suggestions are informative. Accordingly, they naturally move their final prices in sync with the proposals. TWO buyers know ONE sellers do this, so they misrepresent in a cunning way—their proposed bids are sometimes high when their value is low. TWO buyers capitalize on what is a false belief of the ONE sellers (namely, that their buyer is a ZERO) by, for example, saying 1 and inducing the seller to set the price at 2 when their real value is 10. TWO buyers will even sacrifice small profits and try to build credibility with their sellers by saying 6 when their value is 4.

The results of this experiment demonstrate directly the presence of and importance of mentalizing in negotiation. ZERO buyers earned significantly less than ONE and TWO buyers, and each category of buyer showed different levels of activation in the areas of the brain identified with mentalizing and ToM. Solely based on areas of the prefrontal cortex that activated when the buyer was making their suggestion, Camerer and his colleagues could distinguish which of the first three steps of strategic sophistication the buyer occupied. Cooley's metaphor of dressing the mind is more real than he could ever have fathomed.

Both literally and figuratively, then, negotiation takes place in the mind. This fact yields an interesting variant on the oldest cliché in real estate. In my classroom, students simulate the negotiation over a two-bedroom, one-bathroom, 1,000-square-foot condominium in Cambridge, Massachusetts. Both sides have a great deal of additional information: a map of the city, photos of the condo, and, most importantly, a database of almost five hundred recent sales of condominiums in the city. The best deal for an owner will usually be 20 percent higher than the worst deal, a difference worth tens of thousands of imaginary dollars.

When the students and I debrief the exercise to determine the sources of the big variance in prices, typically we share an aha moment. The catalyzing question is this: *What determines the valuation of the condo?* There are various good answers: the number of bedrooms, the quality of the interior, the square footage, and so on. Some sellers and buyers will point to the prices of specific condos in the database that were very comparable to this one. Some quants will have built a financial model using the entire database, and they will assert that the value is located in the model's underlying regression equation.

At some point, a student with real estate experience will trot out the old saw that it's all about "location, location, location." I will respond enthusiastically, "Yes! But where?" My question almost always receives a quizzical look: Can't I read maps? Don't I see the condo is on the outskirts of Harvard Square? Duh? "No, no," I say, "where, where? *What* location?" Silence, shrugs. At last I point to my own head, tapping my temple. *This* is where the value is located in every negotiation: in your mind and the mind of your counterpart. Those mental valuations are not fact; they are fancies, opinions, perceptions. So you can discern them and shape them, both in your mind and in the other person's, through forecasts, incidents, arguments, tactics, and observations.

SOME CLUE: THE GAME OF ZEROs

(or, How people are distributed on the strategic sophistication staircase)

Two topics in the behavioral game theory literature are whether ZEROs actually exist and whether their choices are completely random. To an orthodox economist, it seems an unfathomable way to live; to a behavioral economist, of course there are ZEROs among the "Humans," and their decisions may be irrational and yet still partially predictable.

A revelatory example: Who?—my brother, Steve; where?—in our aunt and uncle's house outside of Boston; with?—our much younger cousin, Peter. The occasion was a big family gathering and Peter, only a few years

old at the time, was being a bit whiny. Steve came to the rescue and asked our little cousin if he wanted to play a game. After an enthusiastic yes, Peter toddled over to the game cabinet and with some difficulty slid a box out of the pile. It was Clue—perfect. They sat on the rug, and Peter patiently watched as Steve laid out the board: he got the scholarly Professor Plum, Colonel Mustard, the turkey-trotting Miss Scarlet, and associates situated in their proper starting places; distributed the weaponry into every single room, lead pipe in the ballroom, candlestick in the billiard room, and so forth; shuffled the clue cards, slid the mystery cards into the target envelope, dealt some out, and put the rest on the board; found two pencils with a point but not too sharp because Peter could hurt himself; carefully ripped a clue sheet from the pad and handed it to Peter so he could record what he knew and what he learned about this particular pretend homicide; saw that everything was set; and finally said, "You go first." Peter looked up at Steve and innocently pointed out, "I can't read." Hah—our little cousin, due to no fault of his own, was zero wobbly steps into the game.

Peter is not standing alone in the ZERO lineup: he is joined by people from all walks of life, including chess players. More than six thousand chess players took part in an online beauty contest at the website Chess-Base and the target was ㉑, right in the "normal" range, which means there were plenty of guesses above 50. At an international tournament in Paris in 2010, another study found a majority of the chess players were ZEROs when it came to guessing games, even among those with a grandmaster rating. There are two key points here: you can find ZEROs anywhere, and someone who is very sophisticated in one setting is not necessarily so in another.

Nonetheless, it's useful to try to get a sense of how people are distributed in a Blotto-like fashion on the steps of strategic sophistication. No one has done more credible work to figure this out than our friend Colin Camerer. Along with other colleagues, he has tried to build a general model of the cognitive staircase and then has tested it to see how well it predicts the results in a wide variety of experiments on different strategic games. Looking at a decade's worth of beauty contest results, Camerer finds that the average distribution of strategic types looks like Figure 3. Using a more recent set of studies on strategic sophistication, I find an

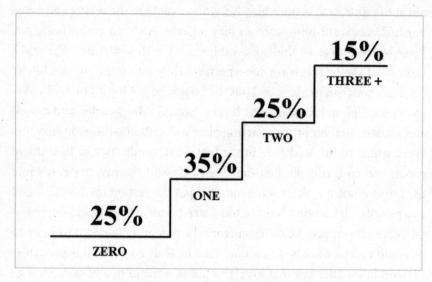

Figure 3: The Staircase of Strategic Sophistication

average allocation to the four steps quite similar to Camerer's. This means that, all else being equal, if you meet another typical adult in a game or a negotiation, there's a one-in-four chance that they're a ZERO.

This base allocation is handy knowledge for making psychologically informed forecasts of your counterpart's behavior. It is also a useful starting point to anticipate factors that will predictably shift the clumpings. You are more likely to meet someone who will choose a naive or unsophisticated strategy when:

- *The game is unfamiliar and fresh.* As we've seen before in the beauty contest, the average guess is highest among those who have never seen the game before and are making their initial guess.
- *The game is complex.* This is why the car salesperson wants to negotiate the new car, financing, the trade-in, and accessory option packages all at the same time.
- *The setting is perceived to be cooperative instead of competitive.* People activate a higher level of strategic sophistication when they are at risk of losing or being defeated by their counterpart, but they are more

likely to be a ZERO or ONE when they are working together, or getting to yes, with the other side.

- *The rules are intricate.* Non-strategic players have a harder time learning the rules and make more mistakes in a subsequent quiz. A THREE+ such as New England Patriots coach Bill Belichick or former Manchester United manager Alex Ferguson will know the rules backward and forward and will have identified where all the holes and constraints are.
- *The players are under time pressure.* In one guessing game experiment, participants were given either thirty seconds or three minutes to come up with their guess. With more time for contemplation, the average fell significantly, from 43 to 36.
- *Your counterpart has a lower cognitive capability.* The general finding is that subjects who score better on a variety of tests of general intelligence and cognitive ability choose lower numbers in the beauty contest and are more likely to win a variety of guessing games.
- *Your counterpart is stressed, sleepy, or cognitively overloaded.*

So yes, ZEROs are real, but are they predictable? Recall that in our original discussion of the beauty contest logic we said that those who were non-strategic would typically pick randomly between 0 and 100 and so would average out at 50. As a large group, then, the ZEROs might be predicted, but as individuals, they are seemingly unforeseeable. Except that's not always true. In Burchardi and Penczynski's experiment, shallow types could be identified by the non-strategic messages ("it is not based on any logic") they sent their partners, so the researchers could then see whether the ZEROs' number guesses were evenly spread across the line. It turns out that only 18 percent of the ZEROs' guesses (instead of half) were below 50, and there were clusters at 50, 66, and 100.

When you're lost in the city, you look desperately for a landmark, something that sticks out of the confusing landscape: the Empire State Building in midtown Manhattan, or Nelson's Column in London's Trafalgar Square. In the blur of a situation "not based on any logic," a salient object or move can provide great relief to the wanderer. It is the one card sticking up out of the fanned hand in Old Maid; it is prioritizing the protection of your homeland in Risk; maybe for the judges in one beauty contest it was the lacy white collar that popped out from the darkened background of Miss Helen McMahon's portrait; and for ZEROs in the beauty contest, it is the nice round numbers 50 and 100 and the simply calculated $\frac{2}{3} \times 100$.

When you're lost in the wilderness, you try not to die and you stay on the beaten trail. The same is true of ZEROs in the strategic forest. Camerer and his co-authors find that unsophisticated people across a wide range of games play by avoiding any action that potentially has the worst outcome. ZEROs might just want to stay alive and avoid any and every chance of a loss. In a hazy strategic situation, doing the "usual" thing, the "right" thing, or the "safe" thing is a very attractive option.

That means you can make ZEROs predictable in a negotiation by giving them an obvious, prominent option, maybe one where there is no possible downside, or by presenting them with strong arguments about how "this is the way we have always done it" or "this is absolutely the right way to handle the situation." Nonetheless, the strategic naïf often remains largely capricious. However, there is one other option if you're negotiating with a ZERO: shove them in a specific direction. And—no offense—I'll point you down the road to Chapter 4 to learn more about this option and other sophisticated negotiating strategies, and when you get there, there are a number of very distinguished people of means and substance I'd be pleased to introduce to you.

SUMMARY

- One foundational aspect of social life is the interworking of mental selves. Autism reveals that a fluid theory of mind and mindsight/ mentalizing are necessary to be *properly* in the game. As a consequence, though all of life is not a negotiation, a negotiation involves all of life—smiling, angering, joking, competing, sharing, confusing, and the rest.
- The value of any issue in a negotiation, not just real estate deals, is determined by location, location, location—namely, where and how that issue sits and is dressed in your mind and the mind of your counterpart.

- People can be distinguished by how deeply they step into a game. The base rate among neurotypicals for strategic sophistication is ZEROs (25 percent), ONEs (35 percent), TWOs (25 percent), and THREE+s (15 percent). This distribution is why the ideal point of staying one step ahead of your counterpart varies. Behaving with maximum sophistication is usually not the best approach.
- There will be more ZEROs and ONEs when the game or negotiation is complex, unfamiliar, competitive, or has intricate rules, and when the players are under time pressure, are stressed, or are low in cognitive capability.
- ZEROs are inherently unpredictable. However, you might be able to make an accurate forecast if you can create an option for them that is salient, appropriate, or safe.

—4—

STRATEGIC SOPHISTICATION II: THE GAME OF CONFIDENCE

ZEROs to ONEs: THE CON GAME

(or, The sometimes futile attempt to educate a mark)

Bill Bain, the founder of the global consulting firm that bears his name, believed devoutly that strategic thinking could be developed. That is why, as we'll see, he called it an "elixir" that could transform the mid-level executive into a "king of that little world." However, as Bain's clients would come to realize, the lessons are often discomfiting and painful. In Chapter 3, we learned a formal kind of strategic thinking from beauty contests. Now we'll turn to a less attractive strategic inter-action in which our primary teachers will be confidence artists. Their livelihood and liberty depend upon being clear-eyed about where their counterpart is on the cognitive staircase and having no false beliefs about how the other assesses them. The two key lessons they have for negotiators are:

1. When your counterpart is a ZERO, the best approach might be to educate them and transform them into a ONE, so as to ensure more predictable behavior.
2. It is easy to get one step ahead of those who misperceive you as a ZERO.

In a justly famous scene from his memoir, Benjamin Franklin described disembarking on a Philadelphia wharf as a seventeen-year-old naïf in 1723. He remembered, "I was in my working dress, my best clothes being to come round by sea. I was dirty from my journey; my pockets were stuff'd out with shirts and stockings, and I knew no soul nor where to look for lodging."

As he wandered near the market house, Franklin met a boy eating bread who directed him to the nearest bakery. There, unsure of the local prices, he told the baker to give him what he could for three pennies. Franklin got more than he bargained for—"three great puffy rolls":

> I was surpris'd at the quantity, but took it, and, having no room in my pockets, walk'd off with a roll under each arm, and eating the other. Thus I went up Market-street as far as Fourth-street, passing by the door of Mr. Read, my future wife's father; when she, standing at the door, saw me, and thought I made, as I certainly did, a most awkward, ridiculous appearance.

A century on, as Karen Halttunen describes in *Confidence Men and Painted Ladies*, an innocent, somewhat befuddled young man wandering in the big city was thought by many citizens of the time to be a prime target of those sinful hypocrites who could "reduce the American republic to social chaos." Franklin encountered neither a confidence man nor a painted lady (at least on this walk), but his countless successors, pulled by the Industrial Revolution, were believed by the clergymen, teachers, and moralists of the time to be in grave peril. In 1850, Reverend John Todd advised,

> The moment the inexperienced youth sets his foot on the sidewalk of the city, he is marked and watched by eyes that he never dreamed of. The boy who cries his penny-paper, and the old woman at her table professedly selling a few apples and a little gingerbread, are not all who watch him. There is the seducer in the shape of the young man who came before him, and who has already lost the last remains of shame. There is the hardened pander to vice who has as little remorse at the ruin of innocence as the alligator has in crushing the bones of the infant that is thrown into his jaws from the banks

of the Ganges; and there is she—who was once the pride and hope of her parents—who now makes war upon virtue and exults in being a successful recruiting-office of hell.

Welcome to the City of Brotherly Love, fine young sir!

What these gloomy advice givers didn't realize was that the naive country youth was not necessarily the best target for confidence men— too empty in both brain and pocket. Yet another century on, in the glory time for the C-gees (con men) during the Roaring Twenties, there was no doubt who was their best target or mark—the property developer:

> A Babbitt who has cleared half a million in a real-estate development easily forgets the part which luck and chicanery have played in his financial rise; he accepts his mantle of respectability without question; he naïvely attributes his success to sound business judgment. And any confidence man will testify that a real-estate man is the fattest and juiciest of the suckers.

Real estate men may be both flush and inured to making secretive deals, but a few, even in the pyrite-plated skyscrapers of New York City, may lack the nous to be the very best chumps.[†] "In fact, highly intelligent marks, even though they may tax the ingenuity of the con men, respond best to the proper type of play. They see through the deal which is presented, analyze it, and strike the lure like a flash." The best marks are ONEs (and TWOs if the C-gee is highly skilled) because they are deep enough in the game to see their potential payoff and have a predictable intent.

Unsophisticated chumps, on the other hand, might need to be educated. Two key actors in the con game, or C, are the roper, who first identifies and steers the mark, and the insideman, who interacts with the mark in the negotiated transaction. The roper and insideman have to possess the patience and tutoring skills to transform "stupid or 'lop-eared' marks" who "are too dull to see their own advantage, and must be worked up to the point again and again before a ray of light filters through their thick

---

† Thanks to David Maurer's extensive research, in addition to "chump," we have these other synonyms for "mark": "apple," "egg," "fink," "John Bates," "savage," and "winchell."

heads. Sometimes they are difficult or impossible to beat." As a character in David Mamet's C movie *House of Games* says, "You can't bluff someone who isn't paying attention."

It is not always simple to get the lop-eared to pay attention. It can be difficult for a diplomatic insideman to convince an unsophisticated mark—in the con parlance, to give them the tale (that is, show them how they can profit)—even in a very legitimate negotiation with minimal downside. Scene: The prime minister of Australia is on the phone with the president of the United States. The two men exchange hellos, pleasantries, and commonalities of their identities—a love of golfer Greg Norman and of commerce, and a loathing for terrorists and for illegal immigrants.

The prime minister, Malcolm Turnbull, turns the conversation to, as he not so innocently phrases it, "some people on Nauru and Manus Island." These "some people" are asylum seekers from various countries in South and Southeast Asia who crossed the ocean in jerry-rigged sloops. Unlike Franklin, these refugees never got the chance to debark on the wharf because of Australia's non-negotiable stance of never accepting refugees who arrive by boat, based on a political rationale of discouraging human smugglers. Instead, two thousand of these "some people" were held in detention centers on the two remote islands.

In a previous negotiation, the Obama administration had pressed the Australian government to change its policy, and had agreed to take some of the asylum seekers in exchange for Australia welcoming some people from Central America who had tried to enter the United States. Heather Higginbottom, the deputy secretary of state who negotiated the deal, explains that America "sought to immediately relieve the suffering of these refugees and agreed to resettle up to 1,200 after they went through the U.S. government's rigorous refugee screening processes. (Refugees are subject to the most thorough vetting of any visitor to the United States.)" Now Turnbull wants Trump to honor his predecessor's agreement.

On the phone call, Trump, hard on the heels of his executive order banning immigrants from seven Muslim-majority countries, asserts, "Somebody told me yesterday that close to 2,000 people are coming who are really probably troublesome. And I am saying, boy that will make us look awfully bad. Here I am calling for a ban where I am not letting anybody in and we take 2,000 people. Really it looks like 2,000 people that

Australia does not want and I do not blame you by the way, but the United States has become like a dumping ground."

Turnbull asks the president to hear him out and let him describe the deal. The PM explains to his counterpart that there's no chance a Middle Eastern terrorist will leave the two islands and land in America: "Every individual is subject to your vetting. You can decide to take them or to not take them after vetting. You can decide to take 1,000 or 100. It is entirely up to you. The obligation is to only go through the process. So that is the first thing. Secondly, the people—none of these people are from the conflict zone. They are basically economic refugees from Iran, Pakistan, and Afghanistan. That is the vast bulk of them. They have been under our supervision for over three years now and we know exactly everything about them."

Trump naturally asks why Australia won't let them in, Turnbull describes the non-negotiable, anti-people-smuggling policy, and Trump replies with apparent admiration, "That is a good idea. We should do that too. You are worse than I am." Working up to the point and hoping that a ray of light filters through, Turnbull lays out the payoff—"This is a big deal to Australia, and we'll be in your debt"—and gives Trump the script that will work: "Yes, we can conform with that deal—we are not obliged to take anybody we do not want, we will go through extreme vetting."

Losing the plot instantly, Trump objects, "Why is this so important? I do not understand. This is going to kill me. I am the world's greatest person that does not want to let people into the country. And now I am agreeing to take 2,000 people and I agree I can vet them, but that puts me in a bad position." Working up to the point for the second time, Turnbull patiently tutors that it's not two thousand refugees and it fits with Trump's policy of extreme vetting. Trump rejects the proposed script. No light yet, just thick darkness: "I hate taking these people. I guarantee you they are bad. That is why they are in prison right now. They are not going to be wonderful people who go on to work for the local milk people."

Laboring up to the point again while ignoring the implications for American regional dairy employment, Turnbull soldiers on, trying to educate Trump on the deal and why it's in his best interest to implement it. Trump responds that it will show him to be a dope, beholden to Obama's incompetence, and it's a stupid, stupid, rotten deal. He concludes with a question: "Suppose I vet them closely and I do not take any?" Turnbull, certainly thinking that here's the ray of light filtering through at last, replies, "That is the point I have been trying to make." Finally, the ZERO is wised up to ONE and is pointed in the right direction, which will be more than satisfying for all concerned.

Not so fast. In a wildly tacking series of objections, Trump re-re-asks, "Who are they?"; brings up boats, World Trade Centers, and Boston bombers; presents the tautology of people being from wherever they are from; says it's foolish; and then anchors with, "Why do you discriminate against boats? No, I know, they come from certain regions. I get it."

Nope, didn't get it. Turnbull begins toiling toward the point yet again. He has no more success this final time as the two negotiators conclude with the following exchange:

> TRUMP
>
> I am going to get killed on this thing.

> TURNBULL
>
> You will not.

> TRUMP
>
> Yes, I will be seen as a weak and inef-
> fective leader in my first week by these
> people. This is a killer.

> TURNBULL
>
> You can certainly say that it was not a
> deal that you would have done, but you are
> going to stick with it.

> TRUMP
>
> I have no choice to say that about it.
> Malcolm, I am going to say that I have no
> choice but to honor my predecessor's deal.
> I think it is a horrible deal, a disgust-
> ing deal that I would have never made. It

```
is an embarrassment to the United States
of America and you can say it just the way
I said it. I will say it just that way.
As far as I am concerned that is enough
Malcolm. I have had it. I have been mak-
ing these calls all day and this is the
most unpleasant call all day. Putin was a
pleasant call. This is ridiculous.
```

As we've seen, when you are negotiating with someone who is a ZERO, you are going to have difficulty predicting their strategy unless one of their options is especially salient, proper, or safe, or unless you can tell the ZERO the negotiating tale, point out the right direction, give them specific instructions to wise them up, and let them walk forward as a ONE. But sometimes the only thing you can do—as Turnbull tries with the forcing move hidden in his final phrase, "you are going to stick with it"—is to try to shove them down the right city street.

MISUNDERESTIMATED:
THE GAME OF HIDE-AND-NOT-MUCH-SEEK

(or, The various ways TWOs can be seen as ZEROs)

Lookee here, pal, I know all this chitchat about confidence games can be a little upsetting. I freely admit I'm acting as both roper and insideman, getting you mixed up with the C. I swear, though, I'm not trying to make you a C-gee, just a fly-gee (an outsider who understands the play), and, more importantly, a fly-gee who is both Joe Hep (wise to what's happening) and humble. Strategic insight into the game and humility distinguished the visitors to Chicago and Miami who avoided being Limehouse Chappie's or Barney the Patch's next victim. I want you, as a negotiator, to be Joe Hep, cautious, and self-effacing.

David Maurer, the non-playing disciple of the grift whose bible *The Big Con* I've been quoting for the last few pages, agrees with Erving Goffman: confidence men "prosper through a superb knowledge of human nature; they are set apart from those who employ the machine gun, the blackjack, or the acetylene torch. Their methods differ more in degree than in kind from those employed by more legitimate forms of business."

Edgar Allan Poe writes that the practitioner of the con game "rightly considered, is a compound, of which the ingredients are minuteness, interest, perseverance, ingenuity, audacity, nonchalance, originality, impertinence, and grin."[†] It's hard to come up with a better list of qualities we would all want as advanced negotiators.

The C is a negotiation with very, very asymmetric information—only one side knows that the wallet stuffed with twenties wasn't "lost" or "found," that the satchel is filled with dollar-sized rectangles of newsprint, or that "the big store" with betting windows crowded with eager customers of means and distinction, boards toting win, place, show, and the odds for each horse in the upcoming race, and a scratchy feed from the track announcer, "Here they come, spinning out of the turn," is a Potemkin parlor. In the end, the mark says yes and hands their money over voluntarily; that's why the con game, as we said, is not robbery. The confidence that is thrown and earned in this setting is continuous with the confidence that lubricates a normal negotiation.

What the C-gees understood quite well is that many people throw their confidence irrationally—they are all too willing to overcredit their own abilities and downgrade the abilities of others. Unwary and unthoughtful negotiators use surface information to discredit their counterparts. There are three classic settings in which this happens: when the other is from the hinterlands (The Hayseed), when the other appears incompetent and disorganized (The Inept), and when the other is crazy and emotional (The Kramer). I'm going to tell you each of these negotiating tales so that you can avoid making the same mistakes and so that you can take advantage when your counterpart miscasts you.

The Hayseed

The first play is well described and probably embellished by Mark Twain from the chapter in his memoir *Life on the Mississippi* titled "The Professor's Yarn." The professor, in his earlier guise as "a humble-minded young

---

† "Grin" means "projective triumph," or the enjoyment of competitive advantage, according to one critical review.

land-surveyor," was the fly-gee on a boat bound for California. There were three professional gamblers among his fellow passengers and one particularly cloying cattleman from interior Ohio, notable for "his countrified simplicity and his beaming good-nature," Mr. John Backus.

Mr. Backus was blessed with an "easy-working jaw" that was never more frictionless than when the subject was cattle: "At the bare name of a bull or a cow, his eye would light and his eloquent tongue would turn itself loose . . . he knew all breeds, he loved all breeds." One day Mr. Backus asked the surveyor to visit his stateroom, where he "unlocked an old hair trunk, tumbled a chaos of shabby clothes aside, and drew a short stout bag into view for a moment, then buried it again and relocked the trunk. Dropping his voice to a cautious low tone, he continued, 'She's all there—a round ten thousand dollars in yellow-boys.'"

When the ship docked in Acapulco and the crew hoisted some beeves in slings onto the deck, Mr. Backus exclaimed loudly enough for all the passengers, including the gamblers, to hear, "What *would* they say to it in *Ohio*. Wouldn't their eyes bug out, to see 'em handled like that?—wouldn't they, though?"

From that point forward, for the rest of the two-week voyage to San Francisco, the gamblers continually attempted to corral the innocent cattleman, who resisted with a resolve Reverend John Todd would have approved of: "Oh, yes! they tag around after me considerable—want me to play a little, just for amusement, they say—but laws-a-me, if my folks have told me once to look out for that sort of live-stock, they've told me a thousand times, I reckon."

No doubt the grifters knew they had a mark to steer, but the cattleman was in no mood to be moved until the moon rose on the final night of the trip and the mook finally grabbed his moola from the bottom of the trunk. The future professor approached the door of the gamblers' stateroom, which was "a-crack," and saw the Ohioan gambling on cards while he drained glass after glass of champagne, proclaiming it delicious "cider," as the gamblers dealt the cards, lifted their glasses to their mouths, and then tossed the bubbly over their shoulders.

At dawn, the boat passed through the Golden Gate strait and the surveyor returned for one last look. It was a grim scene—"Backus's eyes were heavy and bloodshot, his sweaty face was crimson, his speech maudlin and thick, his body sawed drunkenly about with the weaving motion of the ship." A final hand was dealt, five cards to each player. Backus discarded none of his, while the three professionals each took one or three new cards. Two of the grifters dropped out as the bets grew exponentially, from $1 to $10 to $100 to $500 to the "foolish bull-driver's" entire bag of yellow-boys. The remaining gambler called with his own large bag of coins and threw his cards triumphantly on the table—four kings! He reached for the pile of gold, only to be stopped by his suddenly coherent "friend from the rural districts": "Four *aces*, you ass!" thundered Backus, covering his man with a cocked revolver. "*I'm a professional gambler myself, and I've been laying for you duffers all this voyage!*"

A week later in downtown San Francisco, the surveyor stumbled upon Backus, "arrayed in the height of fashion," not a cow patty in sight, who told him, "I don't really know anything about cattle, except what I was able to pick up in a week's apprenticeship over in Jersey just before we sailed. My cattle-culture and cattle-enthusiasm have served their turn—I shan't need them any more."

It can be an extremely powerful position in a negotiation to be underestimated—or as former president George W. Bush, himself an example of the phenomenon, put it, "misunderestimated." Heedless city types mark those who are, or seem to be, from the hinterlands, the granary's shadow, based on a regional accent or an enthusiasm for down-home (and not downtown) culture. These slickers might have heard that their bargaining counterpart was raised in a "two-room home [that] required a 40-foot walk to the outhouse" and overlooked how sophisticated and formidable he really was. Welcome to the true tale of Jon M. Huntsman Sr.

Huntsman built the multibillion-dollar chemical company that bears his name. His career in packaging and chemicals was launched by the plastic egg carton, and its first stage peaked with the clamshell polystyrene container that kept Big Macs and Quarter Pounders with Cheese warm and unsmushed. Huntsman, a devout Mormon, located his company headquarters three hundred yards from the canyon Brigham Young and his party of pilgrims stumbled out of and into the Salt Lake valley.

He had descended from a long line of pioneers who were, by and large, a little more enamored of polygamy, tobacco, and drink than the average Latter-Day Saint. But as he presents himself in his memoir, Huntsman was more of a straitlaced, charitable, and faithful person. He was also civic-minded, taking a three-year sabbatical from his business to serve his country by working for President Richard Nixon, first as an administrator and then as staff secretary in the White House.

He had enough of a leonine backbone to survive the Nixon administration with his integrity intact, but after returning to the container business, he also had enough cunning to counter the direst of threats from a key customer. In a meeting at McDonald's headquarters, senior executives gave Huntsman an ultimatum—hand over "the legal and technical rights to the clamshell and stop selling to competitors." Huntsman describes the vulpine stillness, craftiness, and effectiveness of his response:

> I listened quietly to their demands, then picked up the phone. I remarked that perhaps we ought to speak to the US Attorney General Richard Kleindienst about this and dialed the White House phone number from memory, asking to be put through to Kleindienst. One of the McDonald's guys took the phone from me, gently placed it on the cradle, and assured me I had misunderstood them. Some scrambled from the room while those who remained said all they meant to do was to increase McDonald's orders with Huntsman Container Corporation. I knew what they meant and refused to be bullied. From that day until I sold the business, the relationship was smooth.

Here and elsewhere, Huntsman was smart enough not to needlessly correct mistaken impressions: What fox doesn't want to be misidentified as a bunny or a hen?

Having sold the container business in the late 1970s, he set out to build a chemical company through acquisitions. His first target in 1982 was a polystyrene plant in Ohio that the Shell Oil Company wanted to sell. Huntsman managed to buy the plant for $42 million with no cash down. Shell executives were so impressed by Huntsman's creativity and appetite for risk that they gave him a Twain-inspired statue titled *The Riverboat Gambler* when the deal closed. Huntsman Chemical made many more debt-funded acquisitions through the rest of the 1980s and the 1990s, and *Fortune* magazine reported that thirty-five of the thirty-six companies Huntsman acquired over these fifteen years were highly profitable. The most significant deals were the $1.1 billion purchase of Texaco's specialty chemical operations in 1994 and the $2.8 billion for four businesses of Imperial Chemical Industries in 1999. Each of these agreements doubled the size of Huntsman's business.

Huntsman refers at many points in his memoir to the advantage of being a "friend from the rural districts" during this acquisition spree: "In fact, operating out of Utah sometimes has the effect of disarming competitors. They assume we are hicks from the sticks and often let down their guard. Too late, they realize their miscalculation." Indeed, when the team from Huntsman toured the ICI facilities in England during the negotiations, the local executives seemed to catch a whiff of hayseed and cow chip: "Rumors spread that a bunch of 'morons' from Utah were buying the company."

A disguise can last for a longer time than you think. There was a saying among con men that "you can't knock a good mark." There was a Mr. Hubbell of Kansas whom the police themselves couldn't even knock: he "was tied up with the Christ Kid when the officers arrested the Kid. He was being played for $50,000 and was most indignant at the interruption. Even when he learned that he was being played on the rag [a stock market con], he refused to believe it and insisted on posting bond for both the Christ Kid and his insideman."

One reason for this tenacity is that you can't knock a first impression. Malcolm Gladwell in his book *Blink* calls this the "Warren Harding error," perfectly appropriate for us here since he was president during the zenith of the C-gee. Harding, due to his handsomeness, his Roman bearing, his physical grace and virility, his resonant voice, and his small-town manners, struck many observers of his time exactly as The Man of To-Day. A string of strong and uncorrected first impressions led this particular Ohioan from the interior of the state eventually to the White House. In truth, Harding was an empty suit, unintelligent, with a laboring jaw that uttered "an army of pompous phrases moving over the landscape in search of an idea," an unsophisticate with a wandering eye and a lack of self-control.

Gladwell views Harding's uninterrupted rise through society as a symbol for the fact that many times our initial, thin-slice impressions resist all attempts at correction and all contrary evidence, even that delivered by an authority like the cop arresting Christ Kid. To not fall prey to the error of positively judging Harding or negatively judging Backus or Huntsman requires an effortful, two-level mental process of consciously correcting the automatic initial impression. Doubting oneself is essential for the one-step-ahead negotiator.

Gladwell portrays this process in the person of Bob Golomb, the sales director for a Nissan car dealership in New Jersey. Golomb's mantra is to never prejudge and to assume that everyone has the same chance of buying a car. One of his best customers is a "friend from the rural districts":

> I have a farmer I deal with, who I've sold all kinds of cars over the years. We seal our deal with a handshake, and he hands me a hundred-dollar bill and says, "Bring it out to my farm." We don't even have to write the order up. Now, if you saw this man, with his coveralls and his cow dung, you'd figure he was not a worthy customer. But in fact, as we say in the trade, he's all cashed up.

Not every negotiator is capable of overcoming the Harding error, especially with only a handful of opportunities to do so. Such correction takes a Yuja Wang–like diligence and ability, and this is why misidentification can last. You can hide in a disguise, either intentionally or not, and most people will not seek the real you very diligently.

Still, though, if you show up continually to the same riverboat, steamship, or market, your disguise as a foolish bull-driver, a rural ZERO, a bumpkin, a yokel, will eventually be discovered by even the most lop-eared counterparts. Huntsman had to deal with the reality of revelation by the end of his acquisition spree, as the *Wall Street Journal* reported: super-profitable deals were harder to find "because the company can't sneak up on potential sellers, playing the role of the Utah rube. Says one investment banker, 'Now, companies are saying to themselves, if Huntsman wants to acquire us, maybe we shouldn't sell after all.'" By that time, of course, he had raked in a huge pile of yellow-boys out of the pockets of many overconfident executives and bankers who would have been better served to have recognized who Huntsman really was when they first met him.

The Inept

The second form of misunderestimation relies not on the visible signs—dress, accent, manner—of a person's outsiderness, but rather on the conspicuousness of their fumbles and stumbles. George W. Bush was looked down upon not because he was a Texan but because of his malapropisms, his mishandling of Hurricane Katrina's destruction in New Orleans, and the lack of planning for the wars in Afghanistan and Iraq. Six years into his presidency, the single word most closely associated with him among hundreds of survey respondents was "incompetent."

W. may well have earned that label honestly by being a very bad "decider," but being mistakenly categorized as a bumbler is not necessarily disadvantageous. The great theorist of war and combat Sun Tzu had this advice for China's emperor and his generals: "Even though you are competent, appear to be incompetent." This is a favorite tactic among harassed bureaucrats and sullen teenagers, as any parent who has tried to get their thirteen-year-old to do the dishes ("I thought you said 'Watch the dishes'") or mow the lawn ("I couldn't find the gas can") can attest.

Feigned incompetence was also the calling card of one of the great detectives in popular culture, Columbo. As portrayed by Peter Falk, Columbo was Sherlock if Holmes dressed himself in a dirty, rumpled, beltless tan trench coat; kept a ratty notebook instead of a faultless memory; never jumped to conclusions and therefore never ran out of questions ("just one more thing"); and never let the suspect know his was the superior intellect until the steel bracelets were closed around the suspect's wrists.

I witnessed a Columbo at Bain & Company when I worked there. The company was still small at this time, and when I walked down the main corridor of the Boston headquarters, I would pass by the offices of the firm's four founders. Mythological figures all, they were known as the Count, the Bear, the Fox, and Bill. The last was the aforementioned Bill Bain, the mild yet intimidating, country yet urbane, soft-talking yet fierce, plain yet hypnotic, democratic yet authoritarian leader who had led his team from the Boston Consulting Group (BCG) to strike out on their own.

Bill—you called him that, but you also didn't call him that, if you know what I mean: you kept all hints of familiarity out of your greeting—invented a new form of consulting centered on a version of strategic sophistication applied to corporate competition. The innovation coalesced for him when he was at BCG and was pitching the top team of Union Carbide on a new engagement. Bill told them that to succeed "either you were a lot smarter, or you're a lot better prepared and think more strategically." If you were Machiavelli-esque and thorough and looked at the game as a whole, you could gain an advantage over your adversaries. Bill recommended that "we really try to look at your entire business as an intricate competitive environment where your profits and your security at the end of the day depend on how you wend your way through this three-dimensional bunch of armed robbers out there."

Bill followed that meeting a few days later with a written proposal for Union Carbide to hire him and his team (and BCG) on a continuous basis, with recurring monthly fees of $25,000, to conduct a "classic strategy study," which, since it was the first of its kind, was essentially ghostware and would be "classic" only if the team spoke Latin.

Subsequently, Bill was reportedly irate to find out that another BCG partner had copied his epistle and sent it to one of Union Carbide's competitors. As he told one biographer, he could not indulge this profanation:

> If you read the proposal, you're talking about someone ending up as the master of a three-dimensional competitive world, and part of that means putting into place each of these other competitors by the action you take, which causes them to do certain things without knowing what they're doing or why they're doing it. You want your client to be the king of that little world, and you want everyone else to be his subjects. You don't start sending the same elixir to all his subjects.

It appeared that the leadership of BCG did not value the sanctity of this revelation or the preciousness of the elixir, and this was one reason Bill led his group out into the start-up wilderness.

No one, maybe not even Bill, could have prophesied how successful Bain & Company would become. The firm quickly became a king in its own little consulting world and attracted the best clients and employees. A typical Bainie was almost impossible to misunderestimate, as they—present company excepted (obviously)—were highly credentialed, from the top schools in the world, "articulate, attractive, meticulously well groomed, and exceedingly charming," "cut out of the same cloth."

There was one senior colonel in this uniformed consulting army who was an ongoing misfit: the Fox. Pat Graham, Bill's right-hand man at both BCG and Bain, was tweedy and professorial, self-effacing and mild-mannered. Growing up in the small town of Galesburg, in the interior of Illinois, Graham embodied a certain midwestern plainspokenness. An observer might guess that he would have a hard time making an impact in the CEO's office or the client's boardroom during the high-stakes presentations that were so critical to Bain's success.

Naturally, the four founders took these face-to-face negotiations very seriously. For Bill, preparation was critical, as one reporter wrote: "Like a pole vaulter, Bain devotes most of his time to preparing for the event—say, a meeting with a chief executive. Physical preparation is as important to Bain as mental preparation. He jogs daily and plays a serious game of tennis. When he walks into the client's office, Bain is in top form and in control of the situation." The Bear (Ralph Willard) stated, "You don't walk in with your tie loose and with facial hair and talk sloppily in a situation like that . . . . You have to be a little stiff. You can't be casual." The Count (John Halpern) began a boardroom presentation by declaring imperiously, "This strategy will make everyone in this room rich."

The tale of the Fox is a little different. The setting was the boardroom of the Firestone Tire and Rubber Company. Harvey Firestone created his company at the turn of last century in Akron, and he sold Henry Ford the first tires for the Model T. Following two decades of growth and innovation, Firestone tires might have been Ohio's second-most-popular export after President Harding himself. The company flourished through World War II and the booming car culture of the postwar decades. However, Firestone's fortunes declined through the 1970s due to energy costs, poor investments, and overcapacity. When Graham shambled into the Firestone boardroom, the firm was looking bankruptcy squarely in the eye, since it had a heavy debt load and hundreds of millions of dollars of losses per year.

The story goes that the Fox stood up at the front of the room. As usual, he did not look overly formal, buttoned-up, or meticulous: not as haughty as the Count, not as intimidating as the Bear, and not as mesmeric as Bill. He did not turn on the projector or reach for a slide. Instead, he patted his pockets as if searching for something. The boardroom grew uncomfortably quiet, and Firestone's directors must have wondered whether their extremely expensive consultant was unprepared or inept. At last the Fox seemed to find something: he pulled a scrap of paper from a pocket. Slowly he unfolded it, read it, and nodded to himself. What was it—a dry cleaning slip, a shopping list? What was this ZERO doing? How much was Bain getting paid? Did he have the least idea of how important the Firestone executives were? The Fox took another awkward beat or two to half stuff the paper back in his pocket. Finally he looked up and said quite clearly and matter-of-factly, "Everybody in this room should be fired."

The contrast of message and messenger cut through the board members' arrogance and defensiveness and prepared them to accept the bad news the Fox was about to deliver and to implement the radical actions that were necessary to save Firestone.

This tactic of surface incompetence can come in quite handy during negotiations. There are a number of ways to execute it. Roger Dawson, in his book *Secrets of Power Negotiating*, says that he asks for the definitions of multisyllabic words and for the counterpart to go through the numbers just one more time because he's just not getting it. You can use repetitive or obvious questions whose answers you should already know. You can "forget" that the meeting was today, you can leave your notes at home or bring them in a messy folder that is a chaos of shabby papers, or you can pat your literal or figurative pockets cluelessly for the key fact or message. You can have an Excel model that keeps crashing, fails to update, or spits out gibberish. You can hire an incompetent agent to negotiate on your behalf: Francis Bacon, in his essay "On Negotiating," advised, "In choice of instruments, it is better to choose men of a plainer sort, that are like to do that, that is committed to them, and to report back again faithfully the success, than those that are cunning." If you have a cunning agent, you can force them to bungle by withholding key pieces of information or by issuing confusing instructions.

All this bumbling and fumbling causes the typical counterpart's mind, in line with Cooley's interworking metaphor, to believe that the inept negotiator's mind is dressed in a dirty, rumpled, beltless tan trench coat. That awful coat is sufficient evidence for most counterparts who are looking for reasons to quickly decide that others are maladroit, blundering morons. If you are on the receiving end of this gambit, it takes the mental effort and discipline of Bob Golomb, the New Jersey car dealer, to look past the trench coat and see the Armani-suited mind below.

The Kramer

Lastly, and most obviously, you can be judged a ZERO because you're acting irrationally. No need for interpreting signs of outsiderness or a lack of aptitude; the observer sees you and your crazed Kramer look busting in right through the front door.

Across the Hudson River from New York in Newark, New Jersey, Hess Corporation had twenty-three empty brownfield acres on which it hoped to locate a new 655-megawatt natural-gas-fired electric power plant. In 2011, Hess bargained with General Electric over the purchase of the turbines and supporting equipment and services necessary to get the plant up and running.

Both sides had large negotiating teams. For Hess, there were various executives, a senior lawyer from White & Case, and two ex-GE power plant consultants to help "keep GE honest" about all facets of the contract. The GE side included a sales representative and a young female lawyer. Hess's lawyer was an experienced, sophisticated operator who seemed to have an unerodable advantage over his callow GE counterpart. The latter recognized this as well and pursued the only strategy she could—the Kramer.

One participant summarizes how the talks spooled out:

> She was irrational, emotional, "silly," argumentative, and snipe-y throughout the entire negotiation. Her irrationality gave her a fighting chance—she kept the pace of the negotiation slow (so as not to miss anything); she frustrated others with her thick-headedness. This slow pace also added pressure onto the Hess negotiators as the time to reach agreement was running out. There were many conversations we had outside of the conference room where the lawyers would say "we don't want to push too hard on this issue because she might do x, y, z and throw us off course again."

What the young lawyer figured out is that if the other side decides you're a ZERO because you appear to be a hick or a bumbler or a Kramer, then they will rationally behave as a simple ONE, educating you, conceding to you, making you obvious and very proper proposals, and not even bothering to make offers they think you won't like or understand. Then you can outflank them as a TWO quite easily and without getting very deep or complicated: they'll pick 33 and you can pick 22.

The strategy is a pianistic two-level operation: act like a ZERO and think like a TWO. There is a parallel process a single step up: allow others to judge you as a ONE (narrowly self-interested, blindly altruistic, lucky, or flawed) but plan like a THREE.

In many social settings there are groups that are marginal, either because of small numbers or because of cultural norms. Marginality is typically associated with negative stereotypes that naturally prime misunderestimation—tourists, immigrants, people of color (in America and Britain) or white people (in Nigeria and Japan), women in institutions of power and authority, those with ASD, people with disabilities, children, the elderly, the unattractive, southerners in the rest of the United States, the white shooting guard in basketball and the black goalkeeper in soccer, the server, the assistant, the working stiff, poets in banks, and engineers in nightclubs.

The Kramer (as well as The Hayseed and The Inept), whether you're executing it as someone who is marginal or someone who is central, carries risks for both ego and reputation. It takes a basic humility and willingness to lose face and be judged a ZERO when you're really a TWO or a THREE+. You need to ignore public acclaim and overvalue the admiration of those who naturally see behind the disguise—yourself, your family, and those who know you best.

Fostering misunderestimation can carry large reputational costs. Since they were both at the top of their corporate pyramids, neither Huntsman nor the Fox faced any broader career concerns. The young lawyer on the GE side, however, must be very careful that she is not identified as a ZERO by her company superiors—the ones who evaluate her, pay her, and promote her. If your negotiating counterpart thinks you're incompetent, that's one thing, but if your boss or shareholders or spouse thinks you're inept or crazy, that's quite another.

You may feel uneasy about these strategies. Aren't they manipulative? There are a few answers that you might find satisfactory. First, the choice of being disguised might not be up to you: the surrounding environs or your counterpart might have already placed the mask upon your face. The tourist in a foreign land, the good ol' Alabama boy in New York City, the woman in private equity or tech, the young neophyte printer in pre-revolutionary Philadelphia—all are marked before they put their feet on the wharf. Second, you might want to forswear camouflage, but others might not. The fly-gee is less at risk for becoming a mark if they use their knowledge and insight appropriately. Knowing what we know now, you can productively doubt whether the ZERO who's staring at the blank wall, wrapping the stalk of hay around their index finger, searching through their messy folder for the memo, or looking at you wild-eyed is really that shallow in the game. A little bit of well-informed suspicion can be very helpful to maintaining a strong defense against being exploited or conned.

Finally, the evidence we examined previously about the looking-glass world, from those with ASD and those who have made decisions while lying in a brain scanner, suggests that "manipulating" is far too loaded a term. The fact of manipulation is not sufficient to disqualify these and other similar tactics, because neurotypicals are always manipulating even if we're unaware of it—that's the interweaving and interworking of the social mind, that's the automatic firing of our ToM and mentalizing neural system. A century ago, Mary Parker Follett had the same insight: "I never react to you but to you-plus-me; or to be more accurate, it is I-plus-you reacting to you-plus-me. 'I' can never influence 'you' because you have already influenced me; that is, in the very process of meeting, by the very process of meeting, we both become something different."

I argued in Chapter 1 that for those of us who aspire to be sophisticated and pragmatic negotiators, Machiavelli-esque should replace Machiavellian, so let's restrict the term "manipulating" and use more broadly Cooley's "interworking" or "interweaving." The accusation of manipulation can't just be about the means, because the means are ubiquitous and hardwired; rather, it has to include a judgment about the ends to which the "interworking" is put.

MAGICAL ELIXIR

(or, The improvability of strategic thinking)

This chapter and Chapter 3 have been long and complex. We've met a lot of different characters (a partial list: Kramer, Newman, Ushanka, Blotto, Naoki Higashida, Alice, Miss Helen McMahon, Rosemarie Nagel, Colin Camerer, Ben Franklin, Malcolm Turnbull, Mr. Backus, Jon Huntsman Sr., Warren Harding, and the Fox) and heard a variety of stories about strategic thinking. So let's start this final section with an exercise: go back to the box on page 57 and recall your original guess in the beauty contest game. What number would you write down now? Have the identities of the nineteen people closest to you in virtual or real social space changed? Has your perception of their identities changed? You now know the base rates of strategic sophistication, so you could apply those clumpings and forecast that you're dealing with five ZEROs (rounding up 25 percent of 19), seven ONEs, five TWOs, and two THREE+s. Since I'm dealing with the same base rates for you as a *clearly* well-above-average reader, I would conjecture that there's a 60 percent chance that you want to adjust your guess downward by 10 or more, a 5 percent chance that you need to add 20 to it since you guessed 0, 1, or 2, and a 35 percent chance that you leave your guess as is or tweak it by a few slots on the number line.

In any case, you should feel much more confident in this second round of guessing. And that is one point of these chapters: we've managed to make you Machiavelli-esque, able to bring the gifts of a psychologist to the task of prophesying the beauty contest. And if you can do it there, you can do it in the more complex setting of a typical negotiation.

Research shows that Bill Bain's faith in the augmentation of strategic thinking is not misplaced. Computer scientists and artificial intelligence (AI) researchers are busy trying to endow their machines with theory of mind, mindsight, and the steps of strategic sophistication in order to transform them from ZEROs with the robotic equivalent of ASD into THREE+s. One group in the Netherlands has had success developing a second-order ToM in both machines and humans by training each in the structure of a game layer by layer and by giving each the command to think of what the counterpart thinks they think. This is exactly what we've been trying to do in this chapter and Chapter 3: reveal the complex structure of strategic sophistication step by step and factor by factor, and issue you the command to stop snoring and incorporate this principle into your negotiations.

Now we see that Bill Bain's "elixir" of strategic thinking is not actually that magical. It is not some secret, complex formula. It is merely, as many a C-gee and Bill himself knew, bottled tap water. It is a purified version of the same presentation of your self and interpretation of the other's self— the I-plus-you reacting to you-plus-me—that you're sipping throughout the day. It is a filtered version of our typical theory of mind and mentalizing capabilities and our interweaving social actions.

The key, as Bain understood well, is to have the confidence to enter the game and to expend the effort to identify each layer and every detail, as the computer scientists are doing with their mentalizing machines. We need to do the same. The key for us here is to understand the particular rules, norms, and tendencies of the negotiation game itself. The remainder of the book will explore these critical elements: drama, acting, performance, preconceptions, anticipation, preparation, toughness, fairness, gender, emotions, words, numbers, and so on. A deeper understanding of these elements along with the tap water of strategic sophistication can transform us all into brilliant one-step-ahead negotiators, able to both play the game and see the game.

SUMMARY

- The C-gee and Bill Bain understood, as did Dale Carnegie, Niccolò Machiavelli, Erving Goffman, and Mary Parker Follett, that the negotiation game can be controlled and your counterparts put into place by the actions you take.
- When negotiating with a ZERO, the best option often is to educate them in the deal so they become more predictable ONEs.
- Many people use small visible hints to quickly label other bargainers "rustic," "incompetent," or "crazy" and assume they're ZEROs. Therefore, an effective strategy is to *act like a ZERO but think like a TWO*. This disguise might be forced upon you by the world or your

counterpart, or you might, in certain circumstances, actively culti-
vate this misunderestimation.

- Work hard to avoid judging people (and situations) on first impression (that is, the Harding error): use the strategic sophistication
base rate of 25 percent ZEROs, 35 percent ONEs, 25 percent TWOs,
and 15 percent THREE+s, and look for real clues to make adjustments. This will be true not only for assessments of sophistication
but also for evaluations of all other counterpart characteristics, such
as toughness and fairness.

- Anyone can be a mark, even you, even me, so be skeptical and critical. One of the Fox's pieces of wisdom is "Be suspicious about anything that everyone else believes."

- Foster your ability to go deep into the game of negotiation, but in
any particular setting, aim to be one step ahead of your counterpart.
That is the position of maximum confidence.

ONE STEP AHEAD IN THE GAME: DIRECTING THE DRAMA

(or, Making the metaphor of negotiation as a drama conceivable)

It is incontrovertible that the 1987 movie *The Princess Bride* has one of the great portrayals of strategic thinking in its famous "battle of wits" scene between Vizzini, the sophisticated-and-doesn't-he-know-it Sicilian, and the mysterious Man in Black. The object of their mental swordfight up and down the cognitive staircase is Princess Buttercup, the Man in Black's one true love, whom Vizzini has kidnapped.

Incongruously, as the Man in Black crests a hill in pursuit of his love, he finds Vizzini waiting, having already created a picnic scene with a white handkerchief stretched across a large table-like rock, on top of which are two goblets, a bottle of wine, and some food. The Sicilian sits at the far side of the table-rock with his long knife pointed at the lovely throat of the bound and blindfolded Buttercup.

In conceit, able as he is, the Sicilian's plan is a model of what to do when coming up against long odds: the Man in Black is faster and stronger and a better fighter, so fleeing and dueling are poor options. His best chance lies in the mental and verbal jousting of a negotiation. Vizzini hopes that his hospitality (knife and hostage aside) and staging will befuddle his adversary and yield him an even greater advantage.

Inconsiderately, Vizzini boasts that his counterpart is "no match for my brains," and the bemused Man in Black responds with a mental challenge of his own. He instructs the Sicilian to pour wine into both goblets, then hands him a tube, encouraging him to smell it. Vizzini sniffs the material and passes the tube back, indicating dismissively that he smells nothing. The Man in Black replies that the tube contains iocane, a deadly and un-detectable poison, and then he turns away from the table with the goblets in hand, seemingly to add the poison to one of them. Facing his opponent again, the Man in Black shuffles the glasses back and forth in the air be-fore placing one in front of himself and the other in front of Vizzini, de-claring, "Where is the poison? The battle of wits has begun. It ends when you decide and we both drink and find out who is right and who is dead."

Inter-conceivably, Vizzini exposes the thoughts of the other:

> But it's so simple. All I have to do is divine from what I know of you. Are you the sort of man who would put the poison into his own goblet, or his ene-my's? Now, a clever man would put the poison into his own goblet, because he would know that only a great fool would reach for what he was given. I'm not a great fool, so I can clearly not choose the wine in front of you. But you must have known I was not a great fool; you would have counted on it, so I can clearly not choose the wine in front of me.

Further and further, ONE, TWO, THREE, the cogitator expounds until he creates a distraction that causes the Man in Black to turn his head, where-upon he switches the goblets. Then, laughing to himself, he says, "Let's drink—me from my glass and you from yours." Both drink, and the Man in Black says, "You guessed wrong." Vizzini tells him that he switched the glasses and that his enemy is as foolish and blundering as those who would "get involved in a land war in Asia" or who would "go in against a Sicilian when death is on the line. Hahaha, hahaha"—then he keels over dead, *clunk*, never realizing that both goblets were poisoned and the true game was who had built up a tolerance to iocane. (This should be a re-minder to all one-step-ahead negotiators about the need for humility and the importance of clearly understanding the scope of the game.)

This famous scene never would have existed without another, earlier negotiation. This one was staged not as a picnic on a rock in a beautiful setting but as a climbing pilgrimage by two supplicants to an idol. None of the participants was a hostage; only a script was. The hostage-holder and idol was William Goldman, one of Hollywood's great screenwriters, the author of the screenplays for *Butch Cassidy and the Sundance Kid* and *All the President's Men* and of the 1973 novel *The Princess Bride*. After the novel was published, 20th Century Fox bought the film rights and Goldman wrote the initial screenplay. However, after a dozen years of eager proposals, thorough prenuptial contracts, and left-at-the-altar productions, the book acquired an iocaned reputation: a great piece of work, yes, but those who backed it keeled over and were fired, or their studios folded, or their money dried up. Goldman eventually decided to buy the film rights back from the studio because, he says, "I didn't want some idiot destroying what I had come to realize was the best thing I would ever write."

The pilgrims were Rob Reiner, the former actor and young director, and his producing partner, Andy Scheinman. Reiner had just directed two hit movies (*This Is Spinal Tap* and *The Sure Thing*) when the following negotiating scene occurred:

OPEN ON

The typical office of a Hollywood studio heavyweight, an *atasteful* space with median furnishings and median objets d'art. Rob REINER sits on a low-slung couch and the Paramount EXECUTIVE sits high up in her leather chair.

> EXECUTIVE
>
> We love your films. What do you want to do next?

> REINER
>
> Well, you don't want to do what I want to do.

> EXECUTIVE
>
> No, that's not true. I want to do what you want to do.

> REINER
>
> No, no. You want me to do what you want to do.

```
                        EXECUTIVE
        No, no. I want to do what you want to do.
        What is it?


                        REINER
        The Princess Bride.


                        EXECUTIVE
        Well, anything but that.
```

The executive was happy to attempt interest-based bargaining, but not if it led her to have to drink from that particular poisoned goblet.

Reiner, who'd fallen in love with *The Princess Bride* upon his first reading of an advance copy of the novel years earlier, was undaunted. He also pitched an executive at Columbia Pictures. The executive issued the ultimate backhanded compliment to the famous screenwriter—"You've got to be careful with William Goldman scripts. He tricks you with good writing"—and then poured cold water on Reiner: "You'll never get the rights anyway, as Goldman will never let anyone make it!"

In spite of this welter of stop signs, Reiner and Scheinman approached Goldman. The writer was known in Hollywood for being a curmudgeon and, as he himself writes, a leper—he lacked the sunniness of Southern California, which he forswore for New York City and its inherent "abrasiveness," which was essential for his writing. To the city, then, and an apartment tower at the top of which the screenwriter was ensconced:

We hear the somewhat muted sounds of New York City: a siren, a jackhammer, a car alarm, street chatter.

OPEN ON

Elevator doors as they open and two men, Rob REINER and Andy SCHEINMAN, emerge into the hallway. They walk uncertainly to the front door of William GOLDMAN.

CUT TO

REINER's trembling hand as he nervously pushes the doorbell. In a few seconds,

CUT TO

the door opens and GOLDMAN fills the frame.

                              GOLDMAN
          Princess Bride is my favorite thing I've
          ever written in my life. I want it on my
          tombstone.

GOLDMAN retreats into his apartment, the other two (and camera) follow, and they all
sit. GOLDMAN takes out a notebook and a pencil, and with a glower makes apparent
that he is ready to be pitched.

                              REINER
          Mr. Goldman, I've read these other drafts
          and . . . I . . . what I want to do is go
          right back to what you have in your book.

GOLDMAN is quiet.

                              REINER
          We can't do the prologue, but let's have
          [a grandfather] telling a grandson or a
          father telling a son.

GOLDMAN writes and is quiet.

                              REINER
          Let's interrupt the story just the way the
          book does.

GOLDMAN writes and is quiet.

                              REINER
          Let's protect what we love about this
          book.

Still quiet, GOLDMAN gets up to get a glass of water from the kitchen. REINER turns to
SCHEINMAN.

                              REINER
          Geez, I don't know. I hope this is going
          okay.

GOLDMAN returns and the other two men look up at him uncertainly.

GOLDMAN

Well, I just think this is going great.

The three spent the rest of their meeting sharing notes about turning the book into a memorable movie. Reiner says that as he left Goldman's apartment he was walking on air, and that Goldman's "yes" was the greatest moment of his career.

Think about the drama of the pilgrimage to see a great person. The key to the narrative logic—and, therefore, to the negotiation—is worthiness. It is necessary that the supplicants physically journey (Goldman writes, "In Hollywood, *you* travel to the power"), that they manifest signs of awe and nervousness, and that they know the sage's teachings and scriptures backward and forward. Reiner and Scheinman did all that, and then they delivered the line that was so effective and confirmed their worthiness— "Let's protect what we love about the book." The rhetoric was fitting and powerful: "we" = the two of us *alongside* you; "love the book" = devotion to the word; "protect" = safeguarding the truth and bringing it wholly into the future.

Vizzini's picnic rock and Goldman's high-rise apartment join the other sets we have already examined—the boardroom at Firestone, the faux betting parlor of the big con, the car dealer's showroom, the stage at Carnegie Hall, the professor's office with a nun in the doorway, and the darkened throne room of an Italian medieval castle. All along, we've been using a theatrical framing. What if we were to take that metaphor—negotiation as drama—deadly seriously? What insights could we gain?

Another scriptwriter named William, one who tops the pantheon, wrote these lines a long time ago:

All the world's a stage,
And all the men and women merely players

Making some ado about nothing withal, an insightful and sophisticated player can think about these lines as they declaim them:

- The world is a stage, yes, as long as we realize that it is more than just the flat wooden platform illuminated by the overhead lights and gazed upon by the audience. It is also the sets, the costumes, the curtains, the trapdoors and the mechanical lifts, the wings, the backstage, the special effects, the crew, the audience itself, et cetera. So the world is a stage in the fullest sense; put otherwise, all the world's a theater.
- All the men and women merely players? Surely not. Shakespeare himself was literally player, playwright, and director. Many, maybe most, men and women are merely players: they put the same costumes on day after day, they enter, they hit their marks, they read their lines perfunctorily, and they exit. But some are actors, improvisers, and directors, and they have partial control over the play before it is staged and during its performance.

For now, though, let's shine a spotlight on the metaphor of negotiator as actor in a theatrical production. This lens can be immensely liberating for the reluctant or fearful negotiator.

One of the main pieces of advice I can give to any bargainer is to *stop taking the drama so personally.*

Thinking of yourself as a mere actor in a play achieves this depersonalization. If your counterparts get aggressive or insulting, they are not insulting you, they are skewering your *character*, your *role*. Further, they are simply doing their job: they have to follow the script, and you are obliged to do so as well. You are not allowed to flee the stage or remain mute, and this limitation, ironically, frees you up because you are no longer fully and solely responsible for everything you say and do—the playwright made you do it.

Lynda Obst, a well-respected and successful Hollywood producer who got her big break with the hit *Flashdance*, came to this very insight after her early years of taking every studio no, note, and demand as a personal slight. In her memoir *Hello, He Lied*, Obst writes,

> When I'm fighting with the studio over days or money during production, no matter how mean they get, I keep remembering, *"I'm playing the role assigned to me by God, and they're playing the role assigned to them by God"* [emphasis added]. They have to say the things that they are saying, and I have to say

the things I am saying . . . . Interestingly, I lose if I capitulate, because then I'm not playing the role assigned to me by God . . . . I don't personalize it anymore because I know there's an algorithm to the whole endeavor. I know it, and they know I know it, and they know I know they know it, and it makes them feel better to know I'm not going to collapse.

God, for Obst, is just the Great Screenwriter in the Sky, and Obst's words are merely Her Words, channeled. Notice that being a character means that Obst feels emboldened, refuses to capitulate, and is much tougher and obstinate. She is invulnerable to the mean words and hurtful moves of the studio in a way that her younger self was not. Moreover, she is now sophisticated enough to perceive the mental interweaving between studio and producer that makes it common knowledge that both sides are playing characters they have been assigned. Because of her job and the situation, Obst must slip on the mask of "tough producer," of one-step-ahead negotiator, and simply recite the lines drafted by the Great Screenwriter in the Sky.

KNOW YOUR LINES AND DON'T BUMP INTO THE FURNITURE

(or, An effective negotiator delivers scripts with power and avoids mistakes)

Of course, even being a mere actor can seem daunting. Acting is a craft that people work their whole lives to perfect, that the elite receive golden statues for. But one such statue winner, two-time Best Actor Spencer Tracy, simplified the job in a way that might provide some comfort for the nervous negotiator: "Know your lines and don't bump into the furniture."

KNOW YOUR LINES

Frances Goffman Bay, sister of Erving, was a professional actor, and their mother, Anne Averbach Goffman, a petite, attractive, extroverted woman, had been heavily involved in the local community theater during the young family's years in small-town Canada. Anne was the most assimilated of the Averbach family, including her brother Mickey "Book," but she retained traces of her Eastern European accent. She loved to sing and dance and act. One family friend remembered seeing Anne leave dress rehearsal for a local production of *The Mikado* and run down Main Street in her Japanese-style costume, with full makeup and beehive hair, to cook dinner for her husband and two children. No wonder that three decades later her son was unsurprised by a nun in a full habit manifesting in his Berkeley office doorway.

Frances left school at the age of seventeen to pursue an acting career. A Winnipeg newspaper praised her acting mettle as a twenty-year-old: "Miss Goffman has an abundance of temperament, but she proves in her handling of a scene of hysterics that she is able to keep it under control." During World War II, she took her fine temperament and hysterical control from the stage to the radio waves, hosting a popular Canadian Broadcasting Corporation program for the overseas troops and becoming "the girlfriend of the armed forces," a rousing Toronto Rose. After the war, she married her childhood sweetheart, Chuck Bay, and though her career was on hiatus, she still performed, as her brother would have pointed out, the roles of housewife, mother, and spouse.

It wasn't until after her son's tragic death as a young adult that Frances Bay returned to her profession at the age of sixty. She carved out a niche as a character actor on television and in the movies, specializing in older ladies who were off-kilter, sometimes menacingly so (as in David Lynch's *Blue Velvet*) and sometimes wackily so (as in Adam Sandler's *Happy Gilmore*).

One of Bay's most famous roles was as a patron of a famous Jewish bakery on *Seinfeld*. In the episode titled "The Rye," George Costanza's parents, Frank and Estelle, are driving into the city from Queens to have dinner with the wealthy parents of their son's fiancée, Susan Ross, at their Fifth Avenue townhouse. Frank, conscious of his hinterlandedness, insists on going out of their way to pick up a marble rye from Schnitzer's Bakery because he wants "to show these people something about taste!"

The dinner party is a disaster, and the complaints on the drive back to Queens are copious: "And who doesn't serve cake after a meal?" Sitting in the backseat, George discovers the loaf of bread in the bag. Because the Rosses did not serve it, Frank has taken the marble rye back—after all, as George's mother points out, "people take buses to get that rye." George and Jerry's dubious solution is to purchase another marble rye, get the Rosses out of their house, and then, unseen, relocate the second loaf to the Rosses' kitchen, where everyone might think it had been overlooked. A real theory of mind maneuver. Jerry arrives at Schnitzer's one step and a numbered ticket behind a frail-looking Frances Goffman Bay. A non-negotiation ensues: Frances buys the last marble rye on the shelf and refuses Jerry's offers of $12 and $50 for it. Jerry resorts in the end to grappling unmanfully with the elderly woman on a snowy city sidewalk, telling her, "Shut up, you old bag!" and then sprinting away with the bread under his arm as she shouts, "Stop, thief! Stop him! He's got my marble rye!"

Bay believed that there was no great secret to being a good actor, just "loving it and training," "dedication and tenacity." She agreed both with her brother's view on the omnipresence of acting and with *A Practical Handbook for the Actor*, which advises, "To put it simply, anyone can act if he has the will to do so, and anyone who says he wants to but doesn't have the knack for it suffers from a lack of will, not a lack of talent." Viola Spolin, the inventor of modern improv, writes, "Everyone can act. Everyone can improvise. Anyone who wishes to can play in the theater and learn to become 'stage-worthy.'"

As with strategic sophistication, we are endowed with the capability to act; we just have to put our mind and body to it. We can perform as a marble-rye lady, as a hayseed titan of specialty chemicals, as an admiral frustrated by the Commies, as a poised and dual-processing pianist, as a tough Hollywood producer, and as a pragmatic envoy from Renaissance Florence. Tapping into this natural performing ability is essential to becoming a one-step-ahead negotiator and to embodying the optimal characteristics we will describe in the next set of chapters. For now, though, we want to understand: How do actors (and, therefore, negotiators) really *know* their lines?

First, actors have to prepare and read their pages of their script. The presence of scripts in real-life bargaining is a theme of sociologist Ray Friedman's insightful book on labor negotiations, *Front Stage and Backstage*. Friedman was allowed to be the note-taking observer inside the room for bargaining sessions between many different unions and companies. He was present at International Harvester, the farm equipment company whose roots lay in McCormick's mechanical reaper and whose union negotiations were forever scarred by the Haymarket Riot of 1886, when a labor relations manager described what years of bargaining had wrought:

> The script was written and you could just about predict what was going to be said, what the union's list would look like, what our list would look like, how meetings would go, and how the adjournments would happen.

Generations of negotiators at International Harvester had written virtual labor and management bibles whose verses were supposed to be recited by one side and answered by the other.

Performance suffers either when someone hasn't learned the play or is too verbatim in reading its lines. One company's lawyer was driven crazy by an inexperienced union negotiator who was heedless of the script:

> I found that to be one of the most difficult negotiations because the signals coming across the table did not mean anything; he did not understand the language of negotiation . . . . He would put things aside and not discuss them at all, and you thought they were dead. Normally when that happens they are gone. With this guy, they weren't gone. When you were starting to get close on the other issues, they would reappear.

In another deal, it was the Southwestern Bell Telephone company negotiators who weren't performing because they had simply memorized their lines at a surface level, leaving their union acting partner hanging: "Nothing I said made any impact. It was mechanical. They had speeches, dialogue prepared. We were honest, from the gut."

Sophisticated negotiators do not treat their lines casually. They follow the advice of another famous teacher of acting, Stella Adler: "Your job as actors is to understand the size of what you say, to understand what's beneath the word." ZEROs babble, ONEs are literal and mechanical ("I want that rye, lady!"), TWOs are figurative or indirect ("You don't want to do what I want to do"), and THREE+s seek to discover what ideas, motivations, emotions, and choices are beneath the words ("Let's protect what we love about this book"). Echoing Lynda Obst's imagery and referring to the play *Henry V*, Adler said, "I'm always urging you to find ways to gain size. You must see these lines are full of strength, power and authority. The words come from God, through Shakespeare, to you." We will come back to the power of words in a future chapter.

The last part of really knowing your lines is the understanding that a given line is interwoven into a dialogue with both past and future words. In this sense, as Stella Adler also taught, "Acting is reacting." Meryl Streep, an actor supremely dedicated to her craft, says, "Acting is just listening, so if you're really there with a person, you're picking up what they're about." That brings us face-to-face with a bit of a quandary: How do you truly listen when the other side is following a script?

I posed this puzzle to David Feldshuh, the playwright of *Miss Evers' Boys*, an award-winning dramatization of the Tuskegee syphilis experiment. Feldshuh is also a physician and a professor of theater at Cornell University, and as a young man he studied both mime and Zen—is there anything quieter than a novitiate clapping with one hand while trapped in a nonexistent box?—so he's well positioned to consider paradoxes of talk. There is, of course, no simple answer. However, Feldshuh says that Zen holds part of the answer due to its emphasis on awakening the practitioner to the present reality. The premise, in parallel with Goffman's image of watching regular people snore, is that most everyone moves through life asleep. One koan is "People of these days see this flower as though they were in a dream."

While you could stare at a blank wall for a full day and eat a small bowl of rice grain by grain, as Feldshuh did during his monastic training, there are a couple of easier ways to partially see through the somnolent haze. First, he says, be aware that there's more than one choice for each actor even if the words in the line are the same. In a light singsong voice and combined with a wink, "Shut up, you old bag!" means something quite different than a spittle-flecked, angry "Shut up, you old bag!" The actual performance and execution leave many, many degrees of freedom for the actor—tone, pitch, tempo, volume, emphasis—so even though a script might limit the possible choices, it does not necessarily drive the number down to zero.

Moreover, think of Feldshuh's training as a mime: performance is not just words, it's your body. Facial expressions, eye contact, gestures, movements, and posture are critical. For example, one observer of American diplomat Richard Holbrooke's performance during the negotiations to end the conflict in Bosnia noted, "He gets this dyspeptic look on his face so that they have to ask him, 'What is it?,' and he'll say, 'I'm worried. I don't know if it's going to work.' He uses all these performance acts to achieve his goals."

Second, Feldshuh says, speak and listen with a purpose—your character's purpose. Lynda Obst's goals, ones she shared with Rob Reiner and Andy Scheinman, were to get a green light from the studio and then to overcome all obstacles to get her movie made. This purpose—"I lose if I capitulate"—animated the delivery and authority of the words written for her by the Great Screenwriter in the Sky.

DON'T BUMP INTO THE FURNITURE

The second part of Spencer Tracy's advice on how to be a good actor was to avoid stumbling on set and accidentally moving the sofa. The idea is that mistakes during a play or a negotiation can take on an outsized importance. Erving Goffman notes that these picayune discrepancies can ruin the expressive coherence of a performance, whether it's the loose screws sitting on top of the appliance after the departure of the repair person, a soccer player tripping on their shoelaces as they make their way onto the pitch, or a negotiator mispronouncing the name of their counterpart. Goffman writes, "The impression of reality fostered by a performance is a delicate, fragile thing that can be shattered by very minor mishaps." Think of the sudden, all-encompassing hush that takes over a restaurant (other than places like the chaotic Café du Monde in New Orleans) when a server or a bartender drops a glass.

The asymmetry between the cost of a blooper and the gain from words and actions that fit the script reveals the artistic nature of performing as a negotiator. Goffman again: "We should not analyze performances in terms of mechanical standards, by which a large gain can offset a small loss, or a large weight a smaller one. Artistic imagery would be more accurate, for it prepares us for the fact that a single note off key can disrupt the tone of an entire performance."

One way actors avoid bumping into the furniture is by participating in multiple thorough rehearsals. The actor not only memorizes their lines but runs them through over and over. Practice is just as useful for a negotiator. In one hospital dispute witnessed by sociologist Ray Friedman, the union's lead bargainer asked her team "to rehearse their arguments, then assigned those arguments to particular people: 'You do the "sacrifice of the past" argument, you do the "insurance is your responsibility" argument, and I will do the "flagship" argument. Otherwise, we will caucus. Stay poker faced. Except, if *we* talk, all nod your head.'"

Rehearsals are one thing, but when the seats are filled, the actor's lot becomes much more stressful. Playwright Richard Maxwell cautions the actor in *Theater for Beginners*, "You face an audience and prepare to speak. Fear will be there, if you're alive. There is, of course, no shortage of feeling up there. It is an extreme act, unusual, testing you in unparalleled ways." Stress will make it more likely that the performer or negotiator stumbles and creates small discrepancies. This tendency is ironically heightened by the additional stress caused by following Goffman's and my advice to pay close attention and don't make a mistake.

Stress causes cortisol levels to rise in the negotiator, and that rise might cascade into fear and anxiety, and then into a deep desire to flee the stage and quit the spotlight as quickly as possible. The result for many anxious negotiators is much less effective bargaining. In one study, half of the participants listened to the shower-curtain-clutching theme from the movie *Psycho* while negotiating, and the other set listened to the placid, inoffensive "Air" from Handel's *Water Music*. The shower-curtain-clutchers earned 10 percent less profit from the deals that were completed and were the only participants to flee the negotiation before a deal was done.

Fear not, though, because all is not lost: as for the actor, the combat pilot, and the penalty-taking soccer player, stress can be a benefit to the negotiator. Research gives us three ways to help the anxious bargainer:

- *Knowledge.* The simple fact is that stress is not all bad. Anxiety can make you watchful, can help you be present, and can give you purpose, all qualities that Cornell's Feldshuh says can help an actor speak and listen effectively. In one experiment, simply being given this knowledge (i.e., "people who feel anxious during a negotiation might actually do better") helped subjects whose cortisol levels spiked during a negotiation *actually do better*.
- *Reappraisal.* The psychologist Kathleen O'Connor and her co-authors

demonstrated that those who view the negotiating drama as a "threat" will underperform those who view it as a "challenge." Another researcher, Alison Wood Brooks, shows that you can get to the reappraisal of the situation as a challenge by telling yourself "I'm excited" instead of "I'm nervous" or "I've got to settle down." In other words, effective negotiators don't suffer stress and persist; rather, they get excited and kick ass.

- *Inhalation.* Feldshuh tells his students that every effective performance begins with the actor taking the time to pull in a deliberate full breath. There is solid scientific evidence that diaphragmatic breathing can reduce cortisol and stress. An intentional inhalation can help the negotiator see clearly and avoid bumping into the furniture on the bargaining stage.

COMMAND THE IDIOM

(or, The need to be both inside and outside the script, the play, and your performance)

The wrestler André the Giant, all eighty-eight inches and quarter ton of him, was fearful, hesitant, and brimming with cortisol as rehearsals for the entire cast of *The Princess Bride* got under way at the Dorchester Hotel in London in the summer of 1986. André had been targeted for years by Goldman, a fan of professional wrestling, to play the role of Fezzik, the behemoth who switches sides from Vizzini henchman to Man in Black ally, even as the jinxed script was failing to find a studio home. Nobody could embody Fezzik as well because, as Goldman writes, "André, for me, was like the Pentagon—no matter how big you're told it's going to be, when you get close, it's bigger."

After their successful negotiation with the great screenwriter, Reiner and Scheinman agreed that André was perfect. A global schedule of wrestling appearances made him a hard man to pin down, however. The two producers had almost given up hope of securing him for the role when they received a message that André would meet them in twenty-four hours in Paris. Walking into the hotel bar the next day, Reiner says, they saw "a land mass sitting on a barstool." The three men went to a private room so André could audition, and it was pretty rough: neither producer could understand a word he said. Physically, though, he was perfect, and Reiner and Scheinman offered him the role. André enthusiastically replied, "I do it, boss!"

The strong man was going to need help just learning Fezzik's lines, of which there were many—forever rhyming, said with a chiming, with perfect timing, sometimes while climbing. Scheinman says that he and Reiner came up with a fix: "Rob and I ended up recording all of André's scenes on tape. Rob did André and I did whoever else was in the scene. And André would walk around in headphones, with that tape playing all the time. Listening, figuring it out."

By that cool summer morning in London, André knew his lines, but he did not *know* them yet. During the first table read of the script, he was only capable of reciting his lines in a rote manner, with aching sluggishness. Contra Stella Adler, there was nothing beneath his words, and despite his deep baritone, the size of what he said was minuscule. The actors and Reiner, Scheinman, and Goldman all broke for lunch at an outdoor restaurant, at which André pincered himself in between the arms of a standard metal café chair. After the meal, they all returned to the hotel and resumed rehearsals.

This time André practiced a scene with Mandy Patinkin, who was playing Inigo Montoya, the swordsman who was driven to avenge his father's death. Goldman remembers how the interaction between the actors' characters played out:

> Mandy, as Inigo, tried to get Fezzik to go faster. And Andre gave back one of his slow, rote memory readings. They went back and tried it again and again, Mandy as Inigo asking Andre as Fezzik to go faster—Andre coming back at the same speed as before—
>
> —which was when Mandy went, "Faster, Fezzik"—and slapped him hard in the face.
>
> I can still see Andre's eyes go wide. I don't think he had been slapped outside a ring since he was little. He looked at Mandy and it was all so sudden and there was a brief pause . . .
>
> And Andre started speaking faster. He just rose to the occasion, gave it more pace and energy and you could almost see his mind going, "Oh, this is how you do it outside the ring, let's give it a try."

Notice that it was role-playing that gave Patinkin the license to be aggressive and hit Fezzik, all the while hoping not only that the strong man would not react in kind but also that he would grow in acting size to match his physical size and realize the strength, power, and authority of his lines in the script.

By the time the cameras were rolling, André was capable of delivering one of the best lines of the movie, his yet-still-rhyming retort to Vizzini's plea of "No more rhymes now, I mean it!": "Anybody want a peanut?" His performance is a testament to the power of rehearsal and to his innate dramatic talents. As Reiner says, "His acting instincts, because he had never done it before and because he was a natural actor from being in the wrestling ring, were always pure. He never made false moves; he did things that were totally natural."

As most professional wrestlers are, André was sensitive about the identification of his sport, or "sport," with theater. It was one of the few things this most agreeable, warmhearted colossus would dispute:

OPEN ON

A spare commissary on a movie lot in the countryside of England. REINER, SCHEIN-MAN, PATINKIN, and ANDRÉ THE GIANT sit around a table having lunch.

                        PATINKIN
        So this wrestling thing, it's obviously
        all fake, right?

                    ANDRÉ THE GIANT
        What do you mean?

                        PATINKIN
        It's all planned, right? It's all fake?

                    ANDRÉ THE GIANT
        Nooooo, boss.

Patinkin could have pursued his argument by pointing out that the grappling action in the ring, if not "fake," was at the least thoroughly scripted.

And at this point in the chapter, we all could retort along with André, "And that's different from life how, boss?"

Not surprisingly, Erving Goffman, writing in the late 1950s when television had made big stars of Gorgeous George, Antonino Rocca, and Verne Gagne, found professional wrestling a perfect example of how performances in life were balanced between scripted and improvised:

> When we watch a television wrestler gouge, foul, and snarl at his opponent we are quite ready to see that, in spite of the dust, he is, and knows he is, merely playing at being the "heavy." . . . We seem less ready to see, however, that while such details as the number and character of the falls may be fixed beforehand, the details of the expressions and movements used do not come from a script but from *command of an idiom*, a command that is exercised from moment to moment with little calculation or forethought.

By having command of the idiom, sophisticated negotiators can rehearse thoroughly and know the entire script backward and forward, and yet improvise and be strategically spontaneous when the opening presents itself. This command naturally camouflages their role-playing from the eyes of the counterpart. The less advanced negotiator merely plays the heavy and plods through their lines, much like the maladroit company owner whose union opponent finally had to tell the first's lawyer, "You are better off telling your client not to sit in negotiations or not to speak, because he is sending signals that some of my people are picking up, and I know he does not mean what he is saying."

Yes, this clueless owner was giving a poor performance and was not helping his cause in the least, but the lawyer also was failing in his role by letting his client disrupt the overall play. The ability to improvise or to get a faltering play back onto the script calls on the duality we've used pianist Yuja Wang to symbolize: the actor must be both inside and outside the play, speaking and listening with purpose while monitoring the overall action carefully as well. Goffman refers to this as dramaturgical discipline: "While the performer is ostensibly immersed and given over to the activity he is performing, and is apparently engrossed in his actions in a spontaneous, uncalculating way, he must none the less be affectively disassociated from his presentation in a way that leaves him free to cope with the dramaturgical contingencies as they arise." Command of the idiom is manifest in the ability to improvise without stress and to quietly nudge the furniture back into place when a fellow actor has displaced it.

In general, then, we can map our categories of strategic sophistication to Spencer Tracy's advice on performing and André the Giant's experience in the following way:

ZEROs: do not know their lines; say whatever comes into their head without listening to the other side; make multiple gaffes (André doesn't know his lines and smashes the furniture).

ONEs: know their own lines but tend toward rote recitation; recognize the end of the counterpart's line but only because that's their cue to start talking; in big trouble if the other side goes off script or fails to recite their lines; always make a few errors (André can mimic what Reiner does on the tape and bumps the furniture).

TWOs: know the script; can help their counterparts get back to it when they forget a line or make a misstatement; bring size and weight to their words because they are present and are listening (André has listened to Scheinman on the tape and understands his own line as a reaction to the other character's line, and he moves smoothly among the furniture).

THREE+s: consider the script as more of an outline; lines emerge organically from the action of the drama; many errors are handled without the audience knowing; improvisation is seamless; can say yes and take advantage when the counterpart goes off script; bumped furniture is repositioned (André has command of the idiom of acting).

...BUT WHAT I REALLY WANT TO DO
IS TO DIRECT

(or, Using the techniques of directors to stage negotiations and identify wants)

In the theater, there is one participant who is expected to have complete command of the idiom, the script, the furniture, and the cast—namely, the director. If our purpose in this chapter is to take quite seriously the metaphor of negotiation as a drama, don't we naturally then have to see what skills and insights directors have? We will find that the sophisticated, Machiavelli-esque negotiator is both actor and director.

Again, I turned to Cornell theater professor David Feldshuh as my sensei in this field, and he strongly recommended a short book by William Ball, founder of the American Conservatory Theater (ACT), titled *A Sense of Direction*. The book is distinguished by its practical, specific advice. Some of the topics—dressing room assignments, technical rehearsals, offstage romantic relationships—are less relevant to negotiation, but some are startlingly pertinent.

First, Ball has a special technique to guide the drama and release the creativity of all the participants: "We are looking for some object, picture, statement, photograph, sketch, or fabric that shall not only be like the production, but, in the director's mind, shall be the production itself." Read those last lines carefully: the key is not that the play is *like* something but that it *actually is* that thing. This strictness can bring unity, order, and—through the process of giving the actors some limits to react to—creativity to the production. Some examples of metaphors Ball suggests for certain plays are "a household of robots," "a vanilla-and-strawberry ice-cream sundae," "Rembrandt's painting *The Night Watch*," and "a cockfight."

In hindsight, we can apply this technique to some of the negotiating scenes we have already examined, admittedly in a way the participants themselves might not have thought of at the time. Admiral Joy and the North Koreans: the music and lyrics, "and the rocket's red glare." Reiner, Scheinman, and Goldman: a child's hand-drawn Valentine. The Fox (Pat Graham) at Firestone: the smell of burning rubber. Buying a car: ¯_(ツ)_/¯ . Trump and Turnbull: a toy boat caught in the swirl of draining dirty bathwater.

The guiding metaphor can help the director prevent any false notes from creeping into the physical production. A negotiation is a delicate, fragile drama, and small staging errors can be shattering. The script in the International Harvester talks mentioned earlier might have been firmly established, but from the union's perspective, management mishandled its costumes: "One guy on their side came in wearing an ascot, . . . so after they left, some of the guys were putting napkins on so they could have their little ascots on. It looked like some of these guys came out of the yacht club or something to meet with us." If you're dealing with a relatively sophisticated counterpart, look at your staging and costuming through their eyes. Do you really want to wear a black turtleneck to the pitch meeting at Apple, an ascot to union talks, or a tracksuit to the banking interview?

The director's command of the idiom allows for some parts of the narrative to be communicated efficiently through signs and physical elements. Cy Feuer, the legendary producer of the original production of *Guys and Dolls*, claimed that he saved more than an hour of running time from the first act by using uniforms instead of explication to capture the main characters' histories and natures. Feuer said, "The ingénue, Sarah Brown, was described at great length in the script as a rigid, sexually moralistic spinster," so he and director George S. Kaufman simply gave her "the costume of the Salvation Army."

In a non-fictional example recorded by Ray Friedman, the lead negotiator for one management team "brought a deck of cards with him during the last days of negotiations" and made sure that his union counterpart saw them. Hence he had no need to say out loud that he was happy to string the process all the way out to the deadline. Moreover, his union counterpart knew that he knew that the unwritten script called for both sides to hold out until the last minute before agreeing. The one-step-ahead negotiator can use costumes, props, and composed stagings (e.g., the Communists sitting on higher chairs during talks with Admiral Joy) with strong connotations as a test of the strategic sophistication of the counterpart. Does the counterpart see and interpret the clue correctly? If so, the counterpart is unlikely to be a ZERO.

One of the most perplexing things for negotiators who are following the prescriptions of *Getting to Yes* is how to differentiate an "interest" from a "position." As we saw earlier, Fisher and Ury offer the following guidance: "Your position is something you have decided upon. Your interests are what caused you to so decide." If this strikes you as unclear, you are like many of the students and executives I have taught, and you are joined by the line-reciting union representatives at Southwestern Bell we saw before, whose roteness may have been caused by their training in interest-based bargaining: "I did not understand the process. We did not have a good feeling for what was an interest and what was a position."

In a crucial section of *A Sense of Direction*, we learn how Ball helps every actor portray a character. The actor might be overwhelmed by a myriad of factual aspects of the character—habits, appearance, hopes, weaknesses, hobbies, accent, mannerisms, and so forth. Only one of this large set is the golden key to understanding and portrayal, and "that technique is the systematic and thorough pursuit of the *wants* of the character." We're right in the same neighborhood as *Getting to Yes*: the interests of a negotiator seem identical to the wants of a character.

Importantly, however, Ball gives the actor/negotiator specific tools to get deeper and gain clarity. First, wants should always be captured by verbs, not nouns or adjectives: rather than "I want the _____" or "I am _____," the insightful formulation is "I want to _____." For example, rather than "I want a spouse," the actor-as-character should say, "I want to WIN so-and-so's heart"; rather than "I want more money," "I want to GAIN respect"; rather than "I am frustrated," "I want to DISCOVER a way out"; rather than "I want your script," "I want to PROTECT your words."

Second, in keeping with the cognitive staircase, "a superior, more subtle, and certainly more actable expression of the want will include the person to whom the want is directed and the response sought from that person." So, for example, "I want to AWAKEN *my father's enthusiasm*," and "I want to PERSUADE *Buttercup to kiss me*." Third, a given verb may be actable, but there may be more evocative versions. For instance, "I want to TAKE the marble rye from her" could be upgraded by using SEIZE, or APPROPRIATE, or COMMANDEER.

Finally, there are two "crowbar" questions that, Ball claims, will always get the director and actor out of trouble and pry open any scene:

- What are you trying to GET the character to do?
- What are you trying to MAKE the character do?

If we scroll all the way back to the beginning of the chapter and Lynda Obst's insight, shared by both Goffmans, that being a negotiator is playing a character in a social drama, then the crowbar question becomes "What are you trying to GET your negotiating-person to do?" You yourself, the actor, may feel that you are unworthy of the want or don't wish to force it upon the other actors, but your negotiating-person *requires* the want as a directed verb. Also, for the one-step-ahead bargainer, "What is my counterpart trying to MAKE their negotiating-person do?"

We can map Ball's directorial insight to the levels of strategic sophistication: ZEROs—random (*I don't know what I want*); ONEs—plain verbs and nouns (*I want to succeed*, or *I want my* x); TWOs—interests as directed simple verbs (*I want to tell the old bag to give me the marble rye*); THREE+s—interweavings of wants among the players, and choosing the verbs to enhance performance. Obst wants to CONVINCE the studio to GREENLIGHT her movie; the Fox wants to SHOCK the Firestone board out of its complacency; Machiavelli wants to SAFEGUARD Florence from the whims and power of Borgia; Reiner and Scheinman want to REASSURE Goldman that his book will be safe in their hands.

THE SPACE WHERE MASKS
AND PROPS ARE STORED

(or, Why the backstage might be the most important negotiating venue)

One of the most poignant aspects of André the Giant's life was that he could never be hidden in the wings. When he walked into a bar or restaurant, all eyes would open wide, lift up and up, and gawk at him. Even off the canvas mat, it was as though he carried the bright lights and wrestling ring ropes with him wherever he strode.

The very same evening of the cast's first read-through of *The Princess Bride*, André sat at the bar of the Dorchester Hotel with some of his new colleagues. One of the big man's favorite drinks was a concoction he called "The American"—a beer pitcher that fit into his huge hands as a coffee mug fits in ours, filled with a pour from every bottle of hard liquor on one of the bar's shelves. Cary Elwes, who played the Man in Black, describes what happened late that night:

When it came to last call he got up to leave but never made it to the front door, instead passing out cold in the lobby . . . , an unconscious 500-pound Gulliver spread out on their very ornate carpet. A meeting was held and the wise decision was made to leave him there . . . . For safety purposes, both to protect him and any passersby, they decided to place a small velvet rope barrier around André, who was by now snoring loudly enough to shake the lobby walls.

As Jonathan Swift might agree, a giant is defined by the ropes that tether him in public view.

It was thus that André was denied one region of the human drama that Goffman felt was critical to our health, sanity, and performance—the backstage. The backstage is where "individuals attempt to buffer themselves from the deterministic demands that surround them"; where the boss can be avoided for periods of time, and the audience at all times; where the faux French waiter can remove his accent, drop his silver tray, and fart in the general direction of those co-workers who irritate him; where costumes can be unbuttoned, brows mopped, shits taken, makeup adjusted, audience cursed; and where, in general, the "stage props and items of personal front can be stored in a kind of compact collapsing of whole repertoires of actions and characters."

Left alone, late at night, Machiavelli and Borgia could reach agreements that would not be possible during the day when Borgia's court was present. The drama onstage may be one of conflict and dispute, but the actors playing warring characters may be quite friendly behind the curtain, hanging out in each other's dressing rooms. Friedman, in his study of union-management negotiations, contrasts the irrational demands and performative fist-pounding of the main table with the problem-solving, creativity, and agreement that occurred in private meetings in hotel rooms, union halls, and executive suites. The backstage, unmasked meeting was incredibly effective for one company lawyer: "No [labor] committee members, no management members, let's see if we can settle it. Without all the posturing and such, we settled in a half hour."

The creation of a viable, productive backstage—that is, a second, hidden venue for talks—may be one of the most important moves a sophisticated bargainer/director can make. A country can absolutely refuse to negotiate with terrorists and can demonstrate its adherence to the pledge by leaving the stage unoccupied, the wings empty, and the lobby doors locked. Meanwhile, its diplomats or proxies can enter through the back door, sit in a cramped room among the heaped props and collapsed sets and retired masks, and talk.

In November 1993, in the wake of yet another bombing by the Irish Republican Army, British prime minister John Major replied to a member of Parliament, "If the implication from the honourable gentleman's remarks [is] that we should sit down and talk with [IRA head] Mr. Adams and the Provisional IRA, I can only say to the honourable gentleman, that would turn my stomach over and that of most people in this House, and we will not do it." Within a few weeks, it was revealed that the British government had, in fact, been having back-channel conversations with the IRA for more than two decades.

Fifteen years on, the identity of the back-channel creator was revealed: Brendan Duddy, a mild-mannered proprietor of a fish-and-chips shop in Derry, Northern Ireland. Duddy, who had the girth, the complexion, the scarred forearms, the ready smile, and the patience of a man who loved to immerse battered fish in hot oil, had been raised a staunch Republican. His chippy was a popular hangout for Catholics in town during the 1960s, including a polite and innocent young man who delivered boxes of hamburger patties to the shop and who would linger to chat up the girls: future IRA leader Martin McGuinness. Duddy had lately come to feel that the violence on both sides was futile, and he started to work as a covert peace-seeking intermediary in 1972, the year that began with the slaughter of Bloody Sunday in Derry and continued six months later with tens of IRA bombs exploding in central Belfast on Bloody Friday.

The next year Duddy was approached by Michael Oatley, an agent of the British Secret Intelligence Service (MI6) who had just been posted to Northern Ireland. While neglecting the agent's most magnificent feature, his Mercury-winged eyebrows, Duddy described meeting Oatley for the first time: "six-foot, handsome, perfect language, perfect ability, perfect specimen comes in, grey suit, tie, and the lot." Despite the government's ban on any contact with the IRA, Oatley felt that he "could bend the rules a little bit" and began a relationship with Duddy. Oatley framed the connection with a metaphor that minimized any violation of the government's prohibition: "I was able to report to my superiors in Northern Ireland Administration that I had established what you might think of as a hollow bamboo pipe—if one sort of blew down it gently, the person at the other end might feel the pressure and blow back."

The effectiveness of a back channel relies on its status as mere puffs of air, simple chats, non-negotiations, or pre-bargaining. In another case, that of the secret talks held in the mid-2000s by special envoys from Pakistan and India over the territory that had been disputed since the partition, they "were developing what diplomats refer to as a 'non-paper' on Kashmir, a text without names or signatures which can serve as a deniable but detailed basis for a deal."

Duddy hosted frequent "just-talkings" between government and IRA representatives in the humble back parlor of his home. It was, he says, "a simple room in a simple family house," with a coal-burning fireplace, an overstuffed armchair, two aged sofas, and a surprisingly sought-after stout wooden chair that was everyone's favorite, maybe for its proximity to the fire. The domesticity of this backstage was the key to its magic: Duddy said, "Eventually somebody is dying for a cup of tea and says, 'I'll make a cup of tea,' and you have to ask somebody who you're not very happy about, 'Would you like tea? Do you want sugar in it?' It breaks it down. And then, of course, what happens after that is somebody says, 'When you're there, would you get a bucket of coal?'" These homey discussions laid the groundwork for the announcement of an open-ended cease-fire in early 1975.

The fish-and-chips man gives us a sense of what kind of determination, patience, and listening effort is required, even backstage, when the negotiators are bitter enemies and the talks involve such high stakes: in a typical four-hour dialogue, "there would be half a sentence that mattered and you trained yourself to listen for that half sentence . . . and it was that half sentence which made the difference, either way." The sophisticated bargainer may have to sift through pages and pages of scripted lines to find the single half-sentence that can be used to advance their interests and meet their goal.

The meetings in the back parlor continued, but without much substantive progress. In truth, there were cracks of fatigue in the commitment of some IRA partisans to violence. The British notes on the final secret meeting at Duddy's home in February 1976 characterized one IRA commander as having "an emotional (but not angry) outburst" about the six years of suffering and the destruction of "both the physical and spiritual qualities of life." The British government misperceived these words (and other clues) as representing not merely hairline fractures in IRA resolve but rifts that with more pressure might cause the organization to crumble. One senior British diplomat denied Duddy's plea for the continuation of peace talks, replying, "If the IRA is losing support, why should we aid them by giving them a way out?" As a result, the cease-fire, which had been weakening for months, ended officially in March 1976.

Despite a renewed government emphasis on cutting off all communications with the enemy, Oatley remained in touch with Duddy. The MI6 agent encouraged him to "brief the new IRA leadership, including Martin McGuinness, about the existence of the channel and inform him that it could be reopened whenever they wanted." In late 1980, when IRA inmates began a hunger strike to dispute their judicial status as "criminals" rather than "political prisoners," Oatley "produced a set of proposals as to how the matter might be managed with a formula." (Note Oatley's reliance on a "formula"; we will revisit it in a future chapter.) He flew to Belfast's Aldershot Airport to meet with his contact. Belying the clandestine nature of the meeting, Oatley arrived wearing a red carnation in his lapel, and Duddy teased him that they might as well be meeting in the city center on top of the Christmas tree. Oatley's thirty-four-page proposal was accepted and the strike ended, but it was soon violated by prison authorities, causing a second hunger strike that resulted in the death of Bobby Sands and nine of his IRA comrades in 1981.

For the next decade, there were few puffs of air in either direction through the hollow bamboo pipe. As the elegant Oatley neared retirement in early 1991, Duddy asked him to come to Derry for a final meeting over dinner. Bernadette (Bernie) Mount would cook and host at her house, which had served years earlier as the bed-and-breakfast for the IRA representatives who stayed overnight after the back-parlor fireside chats at the nearby Duddy home.

OPEN ON

A simple small dining room in Derry, Northern Ireland. Seated around the table are the hostess, Bernie MOUNT, DUDDY, Duddy's wife, MARLO, and Agent OATLEY. The small talk is friendly with a hint of guardedness, and all are relaxed but vigilant.

There's a knock at the back door.

MOUNT

Who the fuck is that?

DUDDY

I forgot to tell you, that's Martin.

MOUNT

I don't have enough dinner left, we've eaten it all.

DUDDY

He's not here for dinner.

Martin MCGUINNESS enters the dining room and takes a seat.

Oatley and McGuinness, despite their status as sworn enemies, talked for several hours. Both men could afford to be disarmed because they were backstage. Oatley says of McGuinness, "I thought him very serious and responsible about the situation that he occupied. I didn't see him as somebody who actually enjoyed getting people killed. So, I found him a good interlocutor . . . in some ways, rather like talking to the ranking British army officer of one of the tougher regiments." Oatley, being the sophisticated negotiator that he was, could distinguish the actor from the role, even one so bloody as IRA commander.

For the next couple of years, the back channel conducted gusts that applied pressure to both sides until a set of events and misunderstandings triggered by Prime Minister Major's expression of revulsion brought the talks out into the open. A few weeks after Major's speech, the *Observer* pulled back the curtain and revealed the existence of the back channel to the public. Two days before the revelation, the leadership of the IRA requested that Duddy (code name Mr. Brown) send along his own pneumatic pink slip: "As a result of difficulties, of which you are aware, we wish to replace Mr. Brown. We would welcome your advice on how to proceed with this. We will forward our suggestions in the near future."

Duddy was out, but the peace process he helped sustain culminated in cease-fires, shakily in 1994 and solidly in 1997, and in the negotiation and signing of the Good Friday Agreement in 1998. Among its many elements, the agreement contained a formula (Oatley must have smiled approvingly) for the final disposition of the sovereignty of Northern Ireland—the six counties would remain part of the United Kingdom until such time as there was a majority vote in both Ireland and Northern Ireland supporting reunification.

Martin McGuinness died in March 2017, and Brendan Duddy followed him to the Great Beyond two months later. Duddy's former companions and those of us who have come to learn his story are naturally compelled to ask the courageous, determined, peace-seeking, mediative chippy proprietor, "When you're there, would you get a bucket of coal?"

SUMMARY

- Think of a negotiation as a play in which you are filling a role that has been assigned to you by the Great Screenwriter in the Sky. Remember that it is the *character* you are portraying who is the subject of the drama, not your inner self.
- Know your lines. Recognize the social scripts in the interactions all around you; memorize and learn the lines; deliver them with the strength and size of André the Giant. Remember how many options your counterpart has in speaking their lines, so listen, really listen, for the subtleties and the critical half-sentence Duddy spoke of.
- Don't bump into the furniture. "The impression of reality fostered by a performance is a fragile thing" and is sometimes ruined by picayune discrepancies, minor mishaps, or incorrect details, such as wearing the wrong clothes or forgetting a name. Rehearse, rehearse, rehearse.
- Anxiety and stress are normal and can actually help your performance. That knowledge alone can help the negotiator/actor whose cortisol is spiking. View the negotiation as a "challenge" rather than a "threat," and tell yourself, "I'm excited." Lastly, take a deep, deliberate breath.

- Through study and experience, command the idiom of negotiation: improvise when the moment is right, and help your counterpart get back to the script. Seek to be both actor and director, as the best negotiators are able to perform immersively and yet also monitor the overall drama from above.
- The crowbar questions are:
    - What are you trying to GET your negotiating-person to do?
    - What is your counterpart trying to GET their negotiating-person to do?
- Together, these questions can unlock many negotiations, leading to successful gambits like Rob Reiner's "Let's protect what we love about the book."
- If the drama on the front stage is not delivering on your interests, create a backstage as a venue for honest just-talkings and creative non-deals.

ONE STEP AHEAD OF YOUR PERSONALITY

(or, The traits that we believe make the negotiator)

Imagine that you find yourself backstage at an old theater and among the dramatic bric-a-brac you discover a heap of trunks containing costumes. One trunk has "Negotiator" painted on its top. You open it, and inside there are numerous masks. You notice that they are each labeled— "prepared," "tough," "fair," "creative," "rational," "emotional," "trustworthy," and "communicative." You slip on the emotional mask and find that your feelings start to flow, from happiness to sadness to bittersweetness. Next, you wear the rational mask and notice that your emotions have been replaced by cost-benefit calculations and thoughts of efficiency and optimization. In this manner, you try on all the masks in the trunk.

While these eight masks don't capture every essential trait of the advanced negotiator, they would appear on almost everybody's top-twenty list. These characteristics have been the focus of much research, are cited as keys to success in the memoirs of negotiators, and are promoted by many excellent books on negotiation—*The Mind and Heart of the Negotiator* (Thompson), *Negotiating Rationally* (Bazerman and Neale), *Difficult Conversations* (Stone, Patton, and Heen), and *Bargaining for Advantage* (Shell).

Masks affect actors themselves, but audiences even more so. You might object that we can't wear and remove our personalities quite that easily (though our personal characteristics might not be quite as fixed as we sometimes believe them to be), and you'd be right. But remember this essential fact: we rarely negotiate with someone who has seen the results of our Myers-Briggs, FIRO-B, or Big Five personality test, and so *what matters is their perception of who we are.* We need not alter who we are, only the negotiating-persona that our counterparts observe.

Having tried on the masks of prepared, tough, fair, creative, rational, emotional, trustworthy, and communicative, you might naturally ask the question, which is most essential and which are less important? In the pages ahead, we are going to find out what you think the answer is, what the average businessperson thinks the answer is, and then what the performances of hundreds of negotiators with different personalities suggest is the reality.

Whether we know it or not, all of us have a general mental model of negotiation based on our own experiences of bargaining and our interpretation of the general drama of social life. In particular, we all have a sense of what personal characteristics a great negotiator should have. The survey that follows is designed to reveal your mental model of personality traits and negotiating success, so please give it some thought and answer these questions:

Negotiators form opinions about each other based on prior reputations and behavior within an actual deal. Also, one important measure of negotiating performance is how much value or profit a negotiator captures over a whole set of different deals through time. Based on your experience, what is the general relationship between perceived personal qualities and negotiating performance?

1. When they think you are *prepared,* your captured value
   ☐ Decreases greatly
   ☐ Decreases slightly
   ☐ Does not change
   ☐ Increases slightly
   ☐ Increases greatly

2. When they think you are *tough,* your captured value
   ☐ Decreases greatly
   ☐ Decreases slightly

☐ Does not change

☐ Increases slightly

☐ Increases greatly

3. When they think you are *fair,* your captured value

☐ Decreases greatly

☐ Decreases slightly

☐ Does not change

☐ Increases slightly

☐ Increases greatly

4. When they think you are *creative,* your captured value

☐ Decreases greatly

☐ Decreases slightly

☐ Does not change

☐ Increases slightly

☐ Increases greatly

5. When they think you are *rational,* your captured value

☐ Decreases greatly

☐ Decreases slightly

☐ Does not change

☐ Increases slightly

☐ Increases greatly

6. When they think you are *emotional,* your captured value

☐ Decreases greatly

☐ Decreases slightly

☐ Does not change

☐ Increases slightly

☐ Increases greatly

7. When they think you are *trustworthy,* your captured value

☐ Decreases greatly

☐ Decreases slightly

☐ Does not change

☐ Increases slightly

☐ Increases greatly

8. When they think you are a *good communicator,* your captured value

☐ Decreases greatly

☐ Decreases slightly

☐ Does not change

☐ Increases slightly

☐ Increases greatly

You can compare your survey responses with those I received from three hundred MBAs and one hundred executives of a Fortune 100 company, shown in the pie charts in Figure 4. Most people believe that the more you are perceived as prepared, trustworthy, and a good communicator, the more value you will get out of a deal. Four out of five respondents agree that these characteristics are profitable for the negotiation actor (as shown by the two lightest-shaded wedges, with big or small upward arrows). Fairness and creativity are seen a little less positively, with more people believing the latter trait doesn't have much of an impact, while more believe being seen as fair might lead to the bargainer performing less well. A substantial wedge of businesspeople (more than a third) think that being perceived as rational is a "meh." The two traits that are seen as potentially most damaging are toughness and emotionality. More than a quarter of people think that being seen as tough will decrease the value you capture from your deals (the two darkest wedges with down arrows), while almost three-quarters think that being seen as emotional will leave you crying over spilled profits.

Overall, the average ranking of the eight negotiator masks is:

1. Prepared
2. Communicative
3. Trustworthy
4. Creative

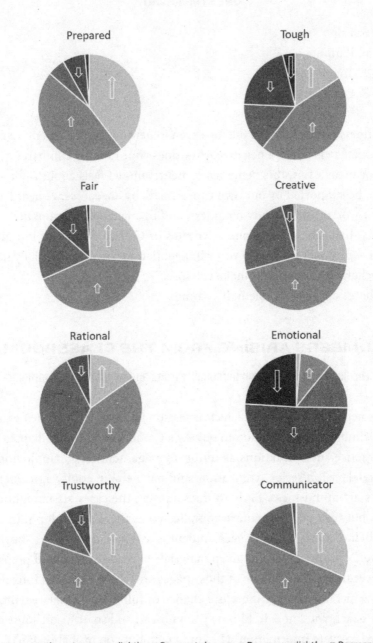

Prepared

Tough

Fair

Creative

Rational

Emotional

Trustworthy

Communicator

■ Increases greatly ■ Increases slightly ■ Does not change ■ Decreases slightly ■ Decreases greatly

Figure 4: Mental Model of Personal Characteristics and Negotiating Success

5. Fair
6. Rational
7. Tough
8. Emotional

Toughness is the closest of the top seven to neutral, and being emotive or passionate nets out as a negative. How does your ranking compare?

For many of us, this benchmark mental model feels about right and would be supported by our own experiences, by anecdotes we hear from our co-workers and family members, and by many of the proponents of interest-based bargaining and advocates of *Getting to Yes*. It's intuitive: positive personal traits help you win negotiations, while potentially negative characteristics might make you lose.

There's only one problem. It's wrong.

NUMBERS ARISING FROM THE CLASSROOM

(or, The source of the data on personality traits and negotiation performance)

In my negotiation course, each class session involves at least one negotiation simulation. In addition to buying a Cambridge condo (Chapter 3), we practice such situations as union-management talks, employment offers, television series syndication, and partnership equity agreements for a start-up business. Early in the semester, the cases are straightforward, but they get much more complicated as the weeks roll on. In the days before a class session, each student is assigned a role (e.g., "buyer," "lawyer," "proprietor") and given materials to read through and prepare however they choose. Some of those pages are labeled "general information," which means that there is a chance of full mental interweaving (I know a fact, you know it, I know you know it, and so on), and some are labeled "private information" (I know a fact, but you probably don't).

During class time, the students negotiate. I emphasize the importance of taking the simulated situation as seriously as possible. I also partially base their final grades on their outcomes in the dozen cases they negotiate. Sell high, buy low, find creative solutions, walk away from bad deals, resolve disputes, and so on, and you are more likely to get an A; sell low, buy high, and needlessly reach an impasse, and you might get a C. As an economist, I appreciate incentives.

After the negotiating period is up but before we reassemble as a class, each negotiator rates their counterpart(s) anonymously on eight essential personal qualities. The raters are asked to assess, on a scale from 1 to 10, if their counterpart was prepared, tough, fair, creative, rational, emotional, trustworthy, and a good communicator, and whether the negotiation strengthened their relationship. At the end of the semester, I gather all these ratings and produce a feedback report for each student. The feedback helps the students understand and recalibrate how they are perceived by others.

Once we're assembled back in the classroom, the first thing I do is to reveal all the outcomes. Students instantly scan the columns to see if their deal was relatively good or bad, high or low. There are groans, laughs, reddened cheeks, joy, anger, shakes of the head. Typically—and this is why negotiation matters and why you're bothering to read this book—the range in outcomes is quite wide. There are big winners and losers, medium outcomes, and a bunch of deals around the average. The remainder of the time in the session is spent in lecture and discussion figuring out why this person captured so much value and another so little, while a third negotiation ended in impasse.

Later, I take all of the students' outcomes and standardize them. The statistical process—calculating z-scores—is straightforward and one you may be familiar with. First, take all the outcomes and figure out the average. Next, calculate the standard deviation, a measure of how spread-out the deal numbers are. For example, if the Cambridge condo sold for $149,000, $149,000, $151,000, and $151,000, then the average is $150,000 and the standard deviation is $1,154, but if the deals were $119,000, $119,000, $181,000, and $181,000, then the average would be unchanged while the standard deviation would be much larger, $35,796. Finally, the z-score is the number of standard deviations an outcome is from the average. For instance, if a negotiator sold their condo for $170,000 when the average was $150,000 and the standard deviation was $15,000, then their z-score would be +1.33.

The point of this statistical standardization is to level the playing field and be able to compare and combine performances in different deals. You can see this most easily on playing fields. Baseball's George Brett had a batting average of .390 in 1980, which was lower than Ted Williams's .406 in 1941, but relative to major league batters in their seasons, Brett had a higher z-score (3.6 vs. 2.8) and so, arguably, was better. Golfer Padraig Harrington won the 2008 British Open with a score of 3 over par, many more strokes than Tiger Woods's winning score of 18 under par in the 2000 Masters, but their performances relative to the tournaments' fields were very close (z-scores of 3.1 and 3.2, respectively).

So at the end of the course, by adding all of a student's z-scores for each negotiation, we can get a measure of their overall performance. The more consistently a negotiator bought low or sold high, or traded off items of less value for those of higher value, or gained concessions without reciprocating, or created profitable solutions to mutually shared problems, or wrote creative contract clauses that constrained the counterpart, or quickly and cheaply satisfied the counterpart's requests, or outwitted and outargued or outwilled the counterpart, the more total value they would have captured. The average student will still be at zero in total. The very best might be at +8 or +10, and those who struggled badly would be at -8 or -10, having been consistently below average, sometimes disastrously so.

By the end of the quarter I also have multiple feedback sheets on each negotiator, and I can calculate an average perception. I check those perceptions—this person is not trustworthy, that person is very creative, and so on—against total performance to determine which personal characteristics are associated with being an above-average or below-average negotiator. We now are in a position to assess your intuition (and the average mental model) about whether it helps you or hurts you as a bargainer to be seen as very rational or unemotional, and to assess the effects of all eight negotiator masks.

CORRELATIONS AND DISAGREEMENTS

(or, How the evidence on personality traits disconfirms our benchmark mental model)

We are going to examine a series of scatter charts with each point representing one out of almost a thousand individual negotiators. The height of a point will be determined by the person's negotiating performance, their total *z*-score from multiple deals. A point's horizontal position will reflect the extent of the perceived character trait, such as "prepared": to the left are negotiators who are perceived as unprepared, while to the right are those who seem to have all the facts absolutely straight and at their fingertips.

The charts will also show a trend line passing through the cloud of points representing the correlation between performance and mask. If "prepared" is really essential to negotiation success, then the line will climb out of the bottom left-hand corner toward the top right of the chart; if the trait doesn't make much difference, the line will just be horizontal across the middle; and if it is harmful, the line will dive toward the bottom right corner.

Our benchmark mental model suggests that the trend lines for prepared, fair, creative, trustworthy, rational, and communicative should be sharply rising, the line for toughness should be much more level, and the one for emotional should decline. What correlation lines did your survey answers predict?

The evidence says that four of the eight traits are a good match to the expected pattern—prepared, communicative, creative, and rational.

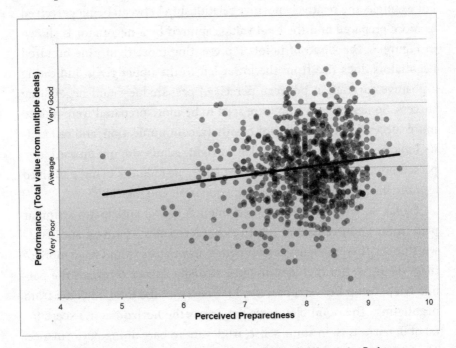

Figure 5: The Relationship Between Perceived Preparedness and Negotiation Performance

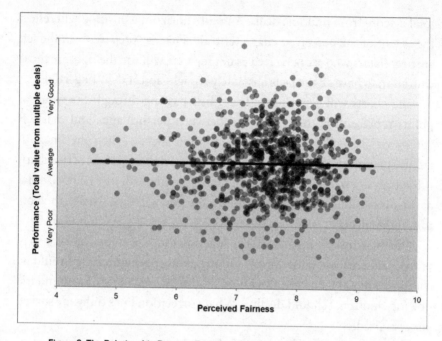

Figure 6: The Relationship Between Perceived Fairness and Negotiation Performance

For example, the relatively positive relationship between being perceived as more prepared and the total value captured by a negotiator is shown in Figure 5. The cloud of points representing more than nine hundred negotiators does rise from the lower left to the upper right, indicating a positive correlation between perceived preparedness and negotiating success. So negotiators who were seen to be more prepared were indeed more successful. The graphs for creativity, communication, and rationality look similar—moving from left to right, gently sloping upward, dispersed point spatters—and represent better negotiators being perceived as more imaginative, mellifluous, unequivocal, and logical.

So far, so good. The benchmark mental model anticipates a similar pattern for another pair of positive characteristics—fairness and trustworthiness. It seems sensible that better negotiators would have more of these qualities, but the data disagree strongly. Figure 6 reveals the flat-line relationship between perceived fairness and the total outcome from negotiating. The point cloud lies flat across the horizon at a z-score total of 0; fairness is, in some sense, irrelevant to bargaining performance. The fairest negotiator (the farthermost right point, at about 9.25) had a middling performance, while the performances of the four least fair negotiators (the leftmost points, at about 5.00) offset each other, with two a little above average, one at zero, and the last a step below average. On trend, the fair and the unfair enjoy the same level of bargaining success, as do the trustworthy and the treacherous. This flatness raises a question that we will answer shortly: Can the one-step-ahead negotiator safely ignore being seen as fair and trustworthy? Maybe just low craftiness without high integrity is enough.

The remaining two traits—toughness and emotion—are surprises and require a severe redesign of the benchmark mental model. The default pattern, projecting that these personal qualities will be of modest help and may even harm performance, is way off here. Toughness, as shown in Figure 7, is the single strongest correlate with bargaining performance. In general, you will get more profitable deals the more that your counterpart perceives you as tough. Sophisticated negotiators know that their priority is to craft their performances—setting the stage, writing the script, wearing the costume and makeup, delivering the lines, and avoiding the furniture—to convince the audience of their toughness and spine.

Toughness is essential to winning the game. Lynda Obst, the Hollywood producer, agrees that when studio executives "understand that I will maintain my position no matter what they say, in a funny way they know the picture is going to be okay—that I'm strong enough to do my job . . . . *They want me to win even though they are fighting me*" (emphasis added). Toughness is a willingness to press your advantage, assert yourself, and use your leverage. Both Machiavelli and Admiral Joy would applaud the way the irreplaceable, cunning Judge Judy negotiates her television contract renewals with CBS: "And we go to the Grill on the Alley with the president of the company. We sit across the table, and I hand him the envelope and I say, 'Don't read it now, let's have a nice dinner. Call me tomorrow. You want it, fine. Otherwise, I'll produce it myself.' That's the negotiation." Brava.

The chart also reveals that perceived toughness by no means guarantees success. The line does not shoot straight to the ceiling; moreover, many points are scattered quite far from the trend. The two toughest negotiators (at 9.5 on the scale) performed relatively poorly: both were below average, and one well below. There is a cluster of bargainers (between

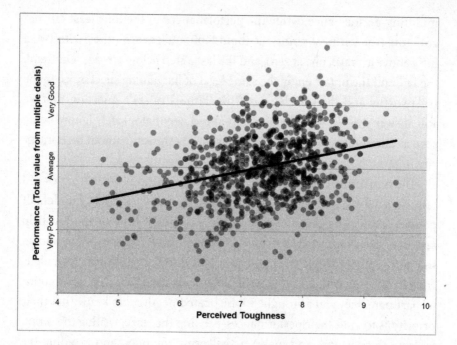

Figure 7: The Relationship Between Perceived Toughness and Negotiation Performance

8.5 and 9) who failed to capture the average amount of value, and a group of four negotiators a little above average in toughness (around 7.6) who were among the poorest performers.

The mismatch between the evidence and the mental model tells us that we don't really understand the personal characteristic of toughness. A sophisticated conception of the perceived trait combined with execution and good acting can lead the negotiator to "smart tough." This is the quality essential to TWOs and THREE+s; ONEs and ZEROs, by contrast, pursue and practice "dumb tough."

Conventional wisdom often suggests that emotions are the stumbling blocks preventing effective bargaining. Our benchmark mental model anticipates that perceived emotionality would cause performance to suffer and that the correlation line would fall from left to right. Against these expectations, the data cloud, as captured in Figure 8, actually moves upward: more emotional negotiators generally capture more value over multiple deals. In fact, the rise and positive correlation are statistically

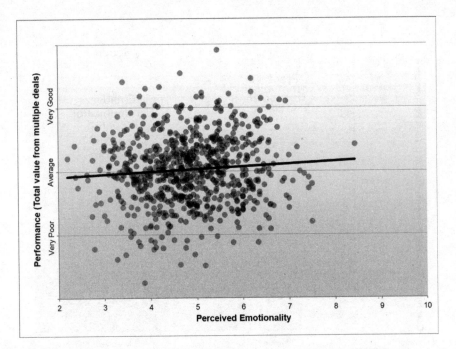

Figure 8: The Relationship Between Perceived Emotionality and Negotiation Performance

indistinguishable from those for being perceived as more prepared, rational, and communicative.

Upon reflection, it shouldn't surprise us that emotions might be helpful to the negotiator; after all, we spent Chapter 5 analyzing bargaining as theater and negotiators as actors. Emotions certainly play an important role in delivering your lines, understanding the size of what you say, identifying the verbs that underlie motivation, and bonding with counterparts backstage. As we will explore in an upcoming chapter, the one-step-ahead negotiator should embrace, backslap, punch the arm of, and tousle the shaggy hair of emotions.

The overall fit between the benchmark mental model and the evidence from the classroom is shown in Figure 9. Again, the most important differences are the underestimation of toughness and emotions and the overestimation of fairness and trustworthiness. The effective, sophisticated negotiator has a mental schema and acts in accordance with the relative ranking and positioning of the character traits in the right-hand column

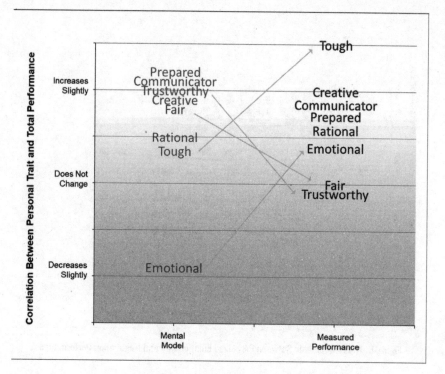

Figure 9: Intuition and Data on Personality and Negotiation

of the chart. Having you learn and act upon this true relative ranking is one of the most important lessons of this book.

A LITTLE BIT OLD SCHOOL

(or, Toughness might not be as costly as you fear it is)

Wait—is this a modern negotiation book that emphasizes, as two of its key themes, *scheme more shrewdly* and *be tougher*? On the one hand, of course not. As our earlier discussion made clear, "scheming more shrewdly" would be a crude synonym for the natural principles of strategic sophistication that require thoughtfulness, insight into human nature, planning, analytical thinking, and psychology, and that help to make you Machiavelli-esque and able to conjecture the future.

For many of us, especially those who were raised in Western traditions, toughness is naturally characterized as masculine, belligerent, belittling, explosive, unpleasant, and self-involved. A more insightful, modern version, as we'll see in a couple of chapters, suggests that true toughness arises from determination, from focus on a goal and a constituency, from integrity, and from a deep knowledge of the negotiation game. The stereotype of toughness is all exterior, but true toughness is all interior. You roll up your sleeves not to fight but to sweat, persist, and work. The best thing about this correct interpretation of toughness is that it is available to both men and women, and to people from all cultures.

On the other hand, yes, the approach and advice here are a bit revisionist and old-school. As we discussed in the preface, there is an endemic softness induced by the ways *Getting to Yes*, team-building, and creativity are often mistaught and misapplied. This is one reason the benchmark mental model is miscalibrated and fails to see that toughness is the number one negotiator mask and emotionality can be productive.

Interest-based bargaining promotes togetherness over individuality: it asks negotiators to stop facing off across a table and to work side by side to solve their mutual problem. One of its presumed benefits is that it "facilitates constructive, positive relationships between previous adversaries." The corollary is also assumed: if you don't follow the prescriptions of *Getting to Yes*, then you're risking that your positive relationships will shatter. You shouldn't be tough, especially old-school tough, with your friends, acquaintances, and social network. However, the modern one-step-ahead negotiator doesn't automatically cave in the face of the objection "But I thought we were friends . . ."

The presumption of an irreparable antagonism between toughness and healthy relationships appears in the responses to my mental model survey. Following the same pattern as with negotiating performance, the survey asks, "A given deal may be the final straw between the partners or may lay the foundation for future business. Based on your experience, what is the general relationship between perceived personal qualities and relationship building?" The numbers reveal the shared intuition: the fairer and more trustworthy the other side thinks you are, the more your relationship is strengthened, while the tougher and more emotional they think you are, the more your relationship is weakened. Not surprisingly, in this setting, toughness and emotion are the only negative traits of the eight we've been examining.

Recall that in the wake of a simulated negotiation that ended in a contract or an impasse and might have involved much argument and some bad feelings, each of my students rated how much the interaction had improved or damaged their relationship with the other person. So we can graph similar correlations as before, this time with how much the negotiation strengthened the relationship on the vertical side of the chart. The pattern of the benchmark mental model is that the trend line should plunge to the bottom right for toughness, since it naturally leads to sundered relationships, and it should sky to the upper right for fairness. The results are shown in Figure 10.

Surprisingly, the trend line for toughness is almost perfectly horizontal: statistically it is indistinguishable from a truly level line. On average, then, the degree of the negotiator's toughness has absolutely no effect on the closeness of the relationship. Of course, you can see from the wide scatter of points that there were certainly some very tough bargainers whose counterparts disliked them intensely after the interaction. However, there are also many soft negotiators who had harmed their connections with their counterparts by the end of the bargaining.

One objection might be that these negotiations were not "real." Fair point, but remember that the stakes were heightened by having students' actual grades on the line. Also, if the concern is that the simulated negotiations involved role-playing and acting, then we should recall the imaginary retort from André the Giant, "And that's different from life how, boss?" Finally, at the very least, the data demonstrate that toughness does not inevitably weaken affiliation: there are social situations and actors for whom toughness leaves their associations intact. We've already seen Lynda Obst strongly assert that Hollywood is just such a situation, and Martin McGuinness and Michael Oatley would have agreed that Brendan Duddy's back parlor is an example as well. And I'm guessing that if you think back over your own personal history, you'll remember a time when you mustered up the courage to be very tough in a conversation or negotiation and in the end you got along better with that counterpart.

In contrast to the wide dispersal of points in the top chart of Figure 10, the bottom chart for fairness features data clinging tightly to the trend

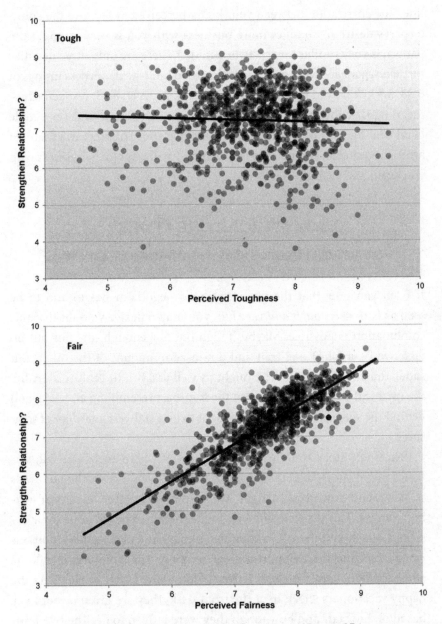

Figure IO: Relationship Quality, Perceived Toughness, and Perceived Fairness

line. The correlation between your being perceived as fair and the counterpart's desire to conduct more business with you is very strong. (The pattern is very similar for trustworthiness.) There are only three negotiators who managed to be well above the trend line—with fairness ratings of 6.33, 5.93, 7.27, and relationship ratings of 8.33, 7.47, 8.73, respectively—meaning that they were seen as at least partially unfair and yet people liked dealing with them. If you can convince your counterparts that you are just, equitable, and reasonable, then they will want to do business with you again and again.

A MYTHICAL CREATURE?

(or, Authentic negotiators who were super-tough and super-fair)

If I tell you now that the one-step-ahead negotiator has to aim to be seen as *both very tough and very fair*, you may reflexively doubt that this combination is possible. Maybe "tough but fair enough" or "fair but no pushover"—a lot of one trait and a non-zero amount of the other. But super-tough and super-fair? I might as well ask you to capture a griffin, the mythical creature that was "in the fore-part resembling an Eagle, and behind the shape of a Lion" and thought to be a stalwart guardian of treasures.

No single story could prove this case, but where anecdotes fail, statistics might succeed. Let's turn again to the evidence from the hundreds of MBAs and executives I taught. We need to do another analytical sorting exercise. This time, imagine we invite them to a beach hotel for a no-strings-attached (other than attending a mandatory presentation on our wonderful time-share opportunities) vacation. This hotel has five floors and each floor has five suites lettered from A to E, left to right. As the happy vacationers check in at the front desk, they are given a room key based on how fair and how tough they were judged to be. The two hundred least fair negotiators will be assigned rooms somewhere on the first floor, while the two hundred fairest will be on the fifth floor. Their suite letters will be determined by how tough they were thought to be. The two hundred least tough bargainers will all be in the A suites, while the two hundred toughest will be in the E suites. So if you receive room key 1A, you were evaluated as being both unfair and a pushover; down the hall in 1E, you'll find all the very unfair toughies. Those bargainers who were about average in both fairness and toughness crowd into the suite in the middle of the hotel, 3C. Upstairs in 5A, all the really fair pushovers are standing in the living room with their luggage trying to figure out the most just and sensitive way to decide which bed everyone gets.

If toughness and fairness are strongly and negatively correlated—that is, if you choose to be perceived as really tough, you've got to be a bastard, and if you're really fair, you're a marshmallow—then the suites on the diagonal from 5A down and across to 1E should be packed. Common sense suggests that some people are just really bad negotiators, so suites 1A, 2A, and 1B will have some occupants, and also that there's some noise in assessing other people's qualities, so the rooms near the main diagonal (3B, 2E, et cetera) will have some residents as well. But importantly, 5E should be vacant because those who are super tough and super fair are mythical creatures. We can draw a simple sketch of the beach hotel as a five-by-five set of squares, and we can represent the number of occupants with a circle. The bigger the circle, the more student negotiators in the suite; no circle at all, empty room; a small dot, one person. If toughness and fairness work in complete opposition, then the chart should show big circles along the diagonal and small dots most everywhere else.

As Figure 11 demonstrates, however, suite 5E is packed with negotiators who were seen as *both the toughest and the fairest*. Moreover, the noise coming from next door and up through the floor lets us know that suites 5D and 4E also have plenty of negotiators in them, people who almost topped out on both qualities.

The evidence seems compelling: certain people can be both very tough and very fair, they can have both high integrity and low cunning, they can be both Machiavelli-esque and just, and they can be griffins and protect the treasure. But do you think *you* can? Or is it just impossible to alter your negotiating personality?

Research has shown that your answer to this question is important. If you think great negotiators are born and their personalities are set in stone, then you will likely not bargain as effectively as those who think personality is more malleable and mutable. Two psychologists at Berkeley

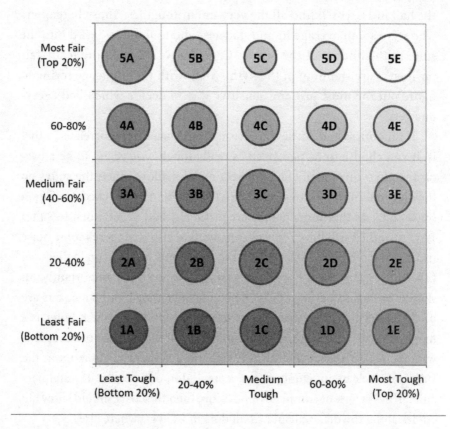

Figure II: Negotiators Arrayed by Toughness and Fairness

had half of the participants in their study read an article titled "Negotiation Ability Is Changeable and Can Be Developed," while the other half read an article titled "Negotiation Ability, Like Plaster, Is Pretty Stable over Time." Even this simple intervention with two fairly boring essays had a huge impact: both sides were convinced by their own essay, but the "malleable" negotiators captured almost twice as much value as the "fixed" negotiators did when they completed a deal with each other.

Of course, the premise of this book, from the analysis of negotiability and strategic sophistication to the exploration of negotiation as theater and the negotiator as actor, has been that negotiation ability is highly changeable and improvable. So this belief is not only correct but valuable:

it benefits you to believe you can develop your negotiating ability and change your bargaining persona as if it were a mask.

In *A Guide to Diplomatic Practice*, one of the classics of the genre, Sir Ernest Mason Satow, a long-serving diplomat of the British Empire in Japan and elsewhere in Asia, offered another list of the chief attributes of the successful negotiator:

> In addition to knowledge of affairs in general and comprehension of the interests of his own country in particular, . . . knowledge of men, which enables one to interpret looks and glances, an elasticity of demeanour which overcomes the weak man by earnestness and the strong man by gentleness, readiness to understand the opponent's point of view and skill in refuting his objections.

You've made it this far into the book, fair reader, so I imagine you too are convinced about the elasticity of demeanor. The experiment above, Satow, and I concur that you should hold fast to it, and in particular to the belief that you too can learn to be very tough and very fair, well prepared, well spoken, highly rational, and properly emotional and creative.

The belief in mutability might not be sufficient on its own. It leaves open the question, change to what? To answer that, in succeeding chapters we will examine, in depth and in turn, what it means for a sophisticated negotiator to be prepared, tough, fair, emotional, communicative, and rational with respect to numbers. Understanding the scientific research and the stories of negotiators who have worn these masks most successfully will you get one step ahead of your counterparts who have only glancing knowledge of these traits.

SUMMARY

- The common intuition (average mental model) on how to be an effective, profitable negotiator ranks key personality factors in this order: prepared, good communicator, trustworthy, creative, fair, rational, tough (positive but closest to neutral), and then, negatively, emotional.

- The data from more than nine hundred students over more than ten thousand negotiations suggests that our benchmark intuition is miscalibrated in some important ways:
  - The mental model is correct about the positive effects of being seen as prepared, a good communicator, creative, and rational.
  - There is zero correlation between being perceived as fair or trustworthy and the performance of these negotiators with respect to value captured.
  - Toughness is clearly the number one positive factor in negotiating success.
  - Rather than being a hindrance to performance, emotionality can be a significant positive factor.
- The mental model on relationships anticipates that toughness will be very damaging, while fairness and trustworthiness will be very binding. The data support our intuition on the last two factors but not on toughness: surprisingly, being seen as a marshmallow does nothing to promote affiliation.
- In sum, toughness makes you more successful in deals and does not necessarily hurt your relationships; fairness does not gain you value but does promote strong relationships.
- The good news is that real negotiators are able to be seen by their counterparts as both very tough and very fair. The two characteristics do not crowd each other out.
- The evidence and received wisdom are that elasticity in demeanor is both achievable and valuable: superior negotiation ability and traits can be learned and developed.

— 7 —

ONE STEP AHEAD
OF PREPARATION

(or, Our initial meeting with the envoy
of superior preparation)

The door United Nations diplomat Giandomenico (Gianni) Picco faced late one August night in 1991 certainly did not open onto a wonderland or "the loveliest garden you ever saw." Rather, it was the front entrance of the Iranian Embassy in Beirut, and the streets outside were some of the harshest and most dangerous in the world. In his desperate quest to free the Western hostages held by Hezbollah and its affiliates in Lebanon, Picco had bravely come to the embassy alone and with only the vaguest assurances.

Picco had hoped to find a Hezbollah representative waiting to negotiate inside the embassy. He was disappointed to meet only the Iranian chargé d'affaires, who had no directions or details for him and said little more than that meetings with the kidnappers would involve "inconveniences." Moreover, the Iranian would not leave the safety of his compound: "Oh no, Mr. Picco, I do not know these people. It is going to be between you and them." The chief took his leave, and a functionary completed the dismissal by waving Picco away: "Finished here. Go! Go! Go! Finished here! Finish! Finish!"

That was how he found himself alone on a pitch-black, rubble-littered street, hemmed in by bullet-pocked walls, without an entourage or security. As he turned south toward a Shiite neighborhood, he saw a shadowy figure in the distance who walked steadily in front, never allowing the diplomat to either approach or to lose contact. After ten minutes, he heard a car approaching from behind at great speed. As the car door opened, Picco turned toward a wall, since he realized that "the most dangerous thing for me to do would be to see these people and be able to recognize them." He was shoved into the backseat and his head was pushed down to the floor.

After a half hour, the car stopped. A hood was placed on his head and he was led from the car up three flights of stairs and seated on a sofa. Once the hood was removed, he dared not swivel his head, but he could see a fairly large room with walls and furniture anonymized by draping white sheets, and a welcoming bowl of fruit on the ghostly coffee table in front of him. He could sense many presences behind him, and he could hear the metallic slotting, bolting, and loading of weapons and a beep from some kind of signal-scrambling machinery. Two men wearing ski masks emerged from his peripheral vision; one sat and one stood in front of him. The incredibly high-stakes bargaining was about to begin.

It had taken years of experience and weeks of preparation by Picco to get to this dangerous place. He had worked within the United Nations for eighteen years, and early in his career he had become a trusted assistant to Peruvian diplomat Javier Pérez de Cuéllar. Picco had demonstrated his creativity and his appreciation for the game and drama of negotiation early on. He had figured out a way to both honor and subvert the young diplomat's typical role as secretary in high-level meetings: since senior officials were overly sensitive about having their words disregarded, he "had developed a system of fake writing, jiggling my pen up and down on the pad so that the result looked like an EKG." Machiavelli would nod his approval to his countryman and fake-scribble on his own parchment.

Not all of his learning took place in well-appointed conference rooms and hotel suites. When posted to Afghanistan as part of the effort to end the Soviet occupation there, he learned the power of indirection and patience in the Kabul rug markets from an Afghani colleague:

Take your time and never reveal your intentions. You shouldn't pause when you first see something you like, but continue your inspection of the merchant's entire stock. Then concentrate on a carpet you have no intention of buying and pronounce it excellent but too expensive. It is permissible to take another look at the carpet you really want, but say nothing and courteously take your leave. A few days later, return to the shop and resume discussions with the merchant, ensuring that the carpet you really want is still there. When the negotiations on the unwanted carpet come to a crunch, refuse the price offered to you and name your lower price for the second best, which is, of course, the carpet you really want.

When Pérez de Cuéllar was elected to the position of UN secretary-general in 1982, he brought Picco along. Together, during Pérez de Cuéllar's decade in charge, the two men expanded the remit of the office from merely reactive peacekeeping to more active peacemaking. The first real test of this new approach was their success in bringing the bloodshed of the Iran-Iraq War to an end in 1988. The contacts Picco established in Tehran and the credibility he built with them during the peace negotiation would prove crucial during the Beirut hostage negotiations.

At the beginning of 1991, there were six Americans, most famously AP journalist Terry Anderson, held hostage, as well as two Germans and three Britons, including Terry Waite, the Archbishop of Canterbury's emissary whose efforts to secure the release of the kidnapped men had resulted in his being taken hostage himself. Waite's personal fate was never far from Picco's mind as he undertook the mission that would eventually bring him to that besheeted room in Shiite Beirut sitting across from two ruthless killers.

THE PROTOCOL OF PREPARATION

(or, The guiding checklist of preparation)

Diplomats from Machiavelli to Picco share a deep understanding of certain key elements in negotiation: the need to speak carefully, the benefits of being clever, the power of the right word or phrase to unlock a barrier, the central role of protocol, and the importance of preparation. One of the quieter but still astounding facts in Picco's memoir, *Man Without a Gun*, is the amount of time he spent planning for his first encounter with the spiritual leader of Hezbollah, Sheikh Fadlallah, in April 1991.

Picco writes in his memoir that he spent a month preparing for the meeting. Thirty days of planning for a three-hour meeting! That's the rational choice this expert negotiator made when his life was on the line. What could Picco have possibly been thinking about for that entire month?

The protocol of preparation begins with a checklist. As with all lists, it is imperative to have a visual representation: the one-step-ahead negotiator knows that their memory is fallible. The planning document I personally use is shown in Figure 12. In a two-party negotiation, I write "Me" as the heading of the middle column and the name of my counterpart as the heading of the last. The version I use with beginning students has fewer rows, and they submit one before each in-class negotiation. A big part of what we are doing in the class (and what you and I are working together toward here) is to learn how to prepare thoroughly and effectively. The plans reveal each negotiator's level of strategic sophistication: early in the semester, the ZEROs and the ONEs (well more than 60 percent of the class at that point) will sketchily fill in the middle column with their own interests and issues but will leave the right-hand column blank, unwittingly assuming that it is superfluous. Once again, we see that the less strategic and inexperienced don't naturally and automatically consider their counterparts.

Part of what filled Picco's preparation the month before meeting with Fadlallah was that he had to think through all the other parties involved in addition to Hezbollah—Iran, the group's funder and sponsor; the American, British, and German governments; the foreign and defense ministries of Syria and Israel; the families of the hostages; the secretary-general and his colleagues at the United Nations; and so on.

There's no doubt that going through the preparation checklist for even a single counterpart can be a challenging task. The frustration can echo that expressed in the email we saw earlier by the confused participant in the beauty contest game: "I do not have a suggested decision as it is not based on any logic. I cannot predict what the other teams will play." That's why the ZEROs and ONEs leave the rightmost column empty in their planning documents. As we've seen, however, there is a logic based on the drama of negotiation and the wants of the counterpart, and each negotiator has the capacity for prediction either through their typical theory of mind or through atypical compensating mechanisms. At least some of the future can be forecast: it just requires determination, practice, and accommodation.

Directing Metaphor _____

Participant:		
Level of Strategic Sophistication		
Other Key Personal Characteristics		
Interests (Wants as Directed Verbs)		
Negotiable Issues (Agenda)		
Alternatives to a Negotiated Agreement		
Best Alternative to a Negotiated Agreement (**BATNA**)		
Reservation Point (or, Walk-Away Point)		
Target (or, Goal)		
Alternatives Within a Negotiated Agreement, and **BAWNA**		
Tactics and Offers (Moves, Countermoves, Countercounters)		
Script (Lines, Questions, Answers, Phrases)		

Figure 12: The One Step Ahead Planning Document

Preparation for a negotiation is fundamentally an exercise in optimistic pragmatism. Recall the negotiations Yuja Wang has as a soloist with the conductor and the orchestra. Yes, she may have to spend time communicating her preferences, and she may need to make some concessions, but ultimately she has some measure of control. The one-step-ahead negotiator retains this sense of agency and realizes that they not only conjecture about the future but conjure it as well. You should be pragmatic (thorough, diligent, insightful, rational, unbiased) in your conjecturing and optimistic (hopeful, ambitious, creative) in your conjuring. That balance begins with the right kind of planning. In the pages that follow, we will work down through the rows of the preparation checklist, with a special focus on alternatives, the reservation point, the target, and offers, so that you, like Picco, are ready to face whatever comes your way in a negotiation.

NOT MIGHTIER, BUT IT'S ALL YOU GOT (METAPHOR)

Gianni Picco was a creative, practical planner. Before venturing out that night in August to the streets of Beirut, he had thought through his costume and props, and maybe, without realizing it, a possible metaphor for his whole series of negotiations over the hostages. He wore a double-breasted blazer, a shirt and tie, and expensive loafers, and he carried with him only his UN identification card, a photo of his son, a folder with a pad of paper, and a pen. His costume signaled his status as both a diplomat and an Italian, and his props were meant to be unthreatening and easily vetted.

The terrorist seated across from Picco began an opening monologue. Deeper into the discussion, he would introduce himself as Abdullah. Both American and Israeli intelligence would later confirm to Picco that, with a high degree of probability, the masked man was really Imad Moughniyeh, one of the world's most wanted men, likely involved in the 1983 Beirut bombings of the U.S. embassy and U.S. Marine barracks that resulted in hundreds of deaths, and in the 1985 hijacking of TWA Flight 847 in which a U.S. Navy diver, Robert Stetham, was tortured and killed. As the man spoke, Picco opened his folder and uncapped his pen.

His writing instrument might have been both his key prop and his directing metaphor. Yes, he was unarmed and a man without a gun, but in his own mind he was a "commando with a pen." The pen represented both the bit of control he had over the situation and how much was resting in his hands. He describes the pianistic demands: "During our meetings, I was a commando force of one playing all the roles at once: note taker, speaker, listener."

Later in the process, in a different whited-out room, after Picco had been to Israel to broker a possible trade of Lebanese prisoners for Israeli and Western hostages, his silver pen was seized and not returned. Hezbollah was obviously worried that the Mossad had bugged it. Picco was furious beyond all reason with this offense, and when he safely reentered the Iranian embassy at one in the morning, he told the Iranian diplomat who opened the door for him that he would no longer negotiate with Hezbollah unless his pen was returned. He had a tactical concern that the group would plant something in his pen, but his overriding concern was one of symbolism. He told the Iranian, "Please let them know I am most upset. It is a matter of principle, and I find it very offensive. I want this settled right now." By 4:00 a.m. Picco received assurances that the pen would be returned that night, which it was along with an apology. He was powerless, unarmed, and vulnerable, but the pen represented his edge, his one advantage.

LOOKING INTO THEIR EYES (STRATEGIC SOPHISTICATION)

After our earlier examination of strategic sophistication, there are a few things we know. First, it is better to overestimate rather than underestimate a counterpart's degree of sophistication as you plan. Second, whatever degree you reckon your opponent really has, you are aiming to behave exactly one step further along. Third, whether through disguise or failing to correct the other's misimpressions, you might choose to perform and manifest the signs of a ZERO or a ONE. With respect to preparation, should you bring multiple thick binders to the talks or just a crumpled, torn piece of paper, as the Fox did at Firestone? (As Picco's costume and manner revealed, he was not playing the game of misunderestimation.)

Fourth, you should be biased in how you update your assessment of the counterpart once the bargaining begins. If you see signs your counterpart is more sophisticated, give them greater weight; if you see signs of naivete, especially on the surface or ones that appear easily manipulated, give them less weight.

Back to Picco's very first meeting with the masked man. After he finished his opening monologue, Moughniyeh "asked me a question unexpected in this environment, one that revealed political sophistication: 'Who sent you? Is it the secretary-general or the Security Council?'" Picco marveled that the masked man understood some of the internal politics of the United Nations and the maverick role that Pérez de Cuéllar had carved out. Picco answered honestly that his mentor, acting alone, had sent him. Abdullah appeared pleased with the answer and said that that was why they would be dealing with him.

Having no idea of the quality of person Hezbollah would send to talk to him, Picco could have made only the vaguest guess in his preparation. Now, though, he quickly and strongly updated his assessment of his masked counterpart to "very astute." Picco was once asked in an interview, "What is it like to negotiate with people who are masked?" (Again, we all should hear the giant voice in our heads saying, "And that's different from life how, boss?") Picco replied, "I tried to overcome the difficulty of negotiating with somebody who I don't know who it is by looking into their eyes. I often do that whether people have a mask or not. And it is important in my view even though in some cultures it may be considered to be unpolite." What he perceived in the gaze of his counterpart was confidence and authority, "a man who knew how to take decisions by himself."

The eye contact and the sophisticated question helped Picco realize that his personal situation was all the more dangerous because his opponent was formidable, and so he needed to craft all of his answers with extreme care. His realization was very accurate: one former CIA agent said that Moughniyeh was "probably the most intelligent, most capable operative we've ever run across, including the KGB or anybody else."

DISOBEDIENCE (INTERESTS)

As a reflection of his personal courage and determination, Picco's chief interests would have been ranked as follows:

1. GET the Hezbollah groups to RELEASE the hostages unharmed.
2. GET Israel to RELEASE the unjustly detained Lebanese prisoners.
3. PROVE to the world the full capability of the secretary-general's office.
4. CONVINCE the groups to NOT KIDNAP him.

As he sat on the white-sheeted sofa and began discussions with Abdullah, Picco was also convinced that he knew Hezbollah's overriding interest:

1. OBEY the directives of our Iranian paymasters.

The Italian envoy had made a number of trips in the prior weeks to Tehran as well as meeting with Iranian diplomats in New York, Geneva, and Damascus, and he had hammered out an agreement that Iran would ensure the release of the hostages. In exchange, the secretary-general would implement Paragraph 6 of UN Resolution 598, the agreement that brought a cease-fire to the Iran-Iraq War. To implement Paragraph 6, Pérez de Cuéllar would appoint a commission to determine responsibility for starting the war, a determination that the leadership of Iran was certain would land in the lap of Saddam Hussein and Iraq.

It was another surprise, then, when Abdullah told Picco that they were here not just to execute Picco's agreement with Tehran but to negotiate themselves: "We are not Iranian, we are Lebanese. So, we want something from you too. We have our own requests." Picco's optimism for a quick and easy solution was thus dashed.

FIXING THE LINES (ISSUES/AGENDA)

Since this first meeting was not simple implementation, it meant that Picco would have to endanger himself repeatedly over the succeeding months. The basic pattern was set: visit the Iranian embassy in Beirut late at night, walk out alone onto the streets, hear the car coming and stare at the wall, lie below the backseat, be hooded and ushered into an unknown apartment, negotiate with Abdullah, and then, after reversing the previous steps, walk safely, *inshallah*, back through the embassy door to debrief his Iranian counterparts before being driven back to the UN compound. There might have been a pattern, but there was no real protocol: he was not only a man without a gun, but a man without an agenda. He had no control over the schedule of meetings or the topics to be discussed.

Picco, and diplomats in general, understand the power of an agenda and a list of issues in structuring and organizing a negotiation. If an issue is listed on the agenda, then it is "legitimate." As with many other elements in a negotiation, there is an anchoring effect, so it is harder for new issues to get on the agenda once it has been set. This means the initial draft is extra critical. If an issue is high on the list, then it is assumed to be more important, and it provides a point of leverage if it remains unresolved when your counterpart wants to discuss an item lower on the list.

We saw earlier that Admiral Joy admired the Communists' ability to compose an agenda with "conclusions favorable to their basic objectives." Joy wrote that if there had been talks between the two sides to arrange a UNC-Reds baseball game, the American agenda would be as simple as a shelled peanut:

1. Place the game is to be played
2. Time the game is to start
3. Selection of umpires

while the Communist agenda would be cracker-jacked:

1. Agreement that game is to be played in Shanghai
2. Agreement that game is to be played at night
3. Agreement that umpires be Chinese officials

The admiral felt that the biggest mistake on the United Nations Command side of the negotiations was to allow the first item on the agenda to be fixing the military demarcation line. Admitting to a lack of strategic sophistication, Joy wrote, "We failed to foresee the use that the Communists would make of the chronological order of the agenda items." Having to fix the truce line early in the process created a "de facto cease-fire," shielding the Communists from all military pressure and allowing them to stall and obfuscate.

Both Picco and Joy were wise enough to know that one limitation of rigorously agenda-based bargaining is that the sequential settling of issues might prevent value-creating trade-offs across items, when one side gets everything it wants on one issue in return for conceding completely on another issue. Splitting the difference item by item can be very inefficient. Another danger (or opportunity) is that an agenda issue can be strictly diversionary, the equivalent of the most expensive rug at the dealer's, and a negotiator might give a concession on that item when none is needed.

UTILIZING THE MULTIVERSE (ALTERNATIVES/BATNA)

Picco's options were just as circumscribed as those of his compatriot five centuries earlier. Pérez de Cuéllar did not compel Picco into the white room as the *signoria* did Machiavelli to the dark ducal apartment. In fact, the secretary-general often did not realize how much risk his assistant was taking on. Because Picco felt both that his mission was just and that he was uniquely positioned to achieve it, he believed that he had no real alternative. He knew that there were other efforts being conducted to free the hostages. The Americans had opened up a Swiss channel, and the Israelis were also making their own attempts. The Italian, however, felt that these efforts were unlikely to succeed because none of the American, Swiss, or Israeli diplomats had his level of credibility, which was based not on his impartiality but rather on his ability to deliver agreements and actions.

The standard advice offered in most negotiation books is to multiply your alternatives, the possible paths you could pursue if a deal with this particular counterpart is not forthcoming. The negotiator is also advised to identify the first-ranked of the possible outside paths, and that becomes your BATNA, the best alternative to a negotiated agreement. The better your BATNA, the more leverage and power you should feel in the negotiation. When your alternatives are sufficiently numerous and identical, you should lever yourself right out of a negotiation and into an auction, as discussed in Chapter 2 for buying a new car.

A strong BATNA allows a negotiator to utter the hoariest line in the bargaining script: "I have another offer." Without a doubt, this line can often extract an increased and desperate bid from a counterpart, especially an inexperienced or unsophisticated one. Picco was neither. Two months on from his initial August encounter with Abdullah, Picco met in Damascus with Iranian ambassador Mohammed Hassan Akhtari. The Italian had been knitting together a deal among the various parties that involved matching releases, including, in the blunt shorthand of the ongoing talks, "nine plus one": the freedom of nine Lebanese prisoners and the return of one body from Israel's "inventory." Akhtari was a stout, bushy-bearded cleric who, as Picco puts it, "came from a culture that taught the greater a man's power and authority, the more softly he should speak. Listeners therefore had to be silent to hear what he had to say." Akhtari told the UN envoy that he had received a much better offer than "nine plus one" via another channel. Picco had a very effective response at the ready: "As always, when confronted with such counteroffers, real or imagined, *I would always recommend accepting the better one*" (emphasis added). This reply can be delivered straight, as Picco did, or with a bit of an edge; the key is to communicate to your counterpart and to yourself that your offer is solid and immune to being raised.

Leverage is determined not just by the best of your alternatives but also by how optimistically they are framed. There are three helpful psychological maneuvers one-step-ahead negotiators can utilize. A recent set of experiments demonstrated that negotiators who unpacked their positive alternatives (that is, listed them completely and in more detail) bargained more effectively and profitably. For Picco, then, the Swiss could save the hostages, the Americans could save the hostages, the Pakistanis could, the Red Cross could, and so on. Though the experiments did not examine this directly, it is logical that doing the opposite—assessing your counterpart's alternatives, and unpacking the negative ones (for Abdullah, this or that hostage could fall ill and die, the Americans could attack, the Israelis could infiltrate, et cetera)—would be beneficial as well.

The second mental move is to describe imaginary or very low-probability alternatives, including wondrous coincidences and seeming miracles. In keeping with the unpacking approach, these imagined alternatives should be positive for you and negative for your opposition. Experiments on what the researchers called the "mental simulation of having an attractive alternative" instructed some sellers of a secondhand CD or a used car to imagine they already had a strong offer in hand and then to mentally savor that illusory offer. These fantasizing sellers had an asking price that was on average 39 percent higher than those without an imaginary alternative. In another setting, job candidates with an imagined positive option negotiated signing bonuses that were 14 percent higher (after an initial ask that was 28 percent higher). It pays to be the Walter Mitty of the multiverse of bargaining alternatives.

Third, if when you are preparing you find that all the options, even the imaginary ones, are bad, there's still one way to boost your performance. The common wisdom is that it is better to have even a bad outside option than no option at all. Three social psychologists, Michael Schaerer, Roderick Swaab, and Adam Galinsky, conducted an online survey in which 92 percent of the respondents preferred negotiating a job offer while holding an unattractive alternative rather than while having no other offer at all. Seems obvious. Here too, though, the common wisdom turns out to be wrong. The psychologists' experiments demonstrated convincingly that although negotiators with no alternative will indeed feel less powerful, they will nevertheless bargain more aggressively. Someone with a bad alternative will anchor on it and will be more likely to meekly accept any deal that's a little better.

One simulated negotiation they tested involved an antiques dealer and an heirloom sugar bowl. The dealer had originally purchased the bowl for a client who was willing to pay €600 but pulled out of the deal because the bowl had a small flaw, despite the fact that similar bowls could sell for up to €1,000. The participants acting as the dealer were split into three groups: the first were told they had no other offers for the bowl and should expect none in the future; the second had one offer for €45; and the third had a sweet alternative, a bid for €450. After bargaining with a potential buyer, the average negotiated prices for the sugar bowl were €619, €430, and €658, respectively. Not having another buyer for the sugar bowl was statistically the same as having a reasonable offer in hand and much better than having an anchoring low-ball alternative.

In this third case, then, the challenge for a preparing negotiator is to explore all your options with as much creativity and out-of-the-box thinking as possible. Upon discovering that all the real and multiversal alternatives are bad, place them in a mental strongbox. Then draw on your newly enhanced acting skills and pretend that you have no alternatives at all.

One other way to achieve this emptying is to make the negotiation itself unique, so it is fundamentally incommensurable with all other paths. For example, you can load notions of duty, responsibility, obligation, or purity onto the negotiation. Transcendent values can seem to banish all other alternatives. When Picco was asked by Moughniyeh in that white room why he was doing what he was doing, his "answer was very simple: I thought it was the right thing to do. I thought that's what a UN official should do." A negotiation that is a "must" eliminates all the other possible paths in the multiverse that are "could." Destiny banishes alternatives from the mind.

Having learned a bit more about Picco's motivations, Abdullah complained that he couldn't control all the kidnapping subgroups that were making various demands and thus couldn't guarantee the release of the hostages. The duty-bound, alternative-lacking Picco was able to aggressively challenge his opponent's authority ("Who was really in charge?") and his strength (if a few people could extort Hezbollah, didn't "that say a great deal about the weakness of the group itself?"). A few minutes later, Moughniyeh asked when their next meeting would be, implying that the Italian would be neither kidnapped nor killed that night, and Picco protested that he "was not prepared to leave as yet" since there was "much to accomplish in the here and now." While Machiavelli quickly took his leave from the black room when dismissed by Borgia, the modern envoy with no alternatives and no BATNA was willing to stay in the white room and risk everything.

THE CONSTRUCT (RESERVATION POINT)

The reservation point is a knife's edge: on one side you have to turn down the offer, and on the other side you make the deal. For it to have meaning, the blade has to be sharp and the negotiator has to respect the clean cut between acceptable and unacceptable.

Suppose when Picco's hood is removed, he sees that he is in a white room, but in this version there is no bowl of fruit on the table, only a sealed envelope. This time he hears no sounds at all; the hairs on his neck stand up because he senses he is absolutely alone. He is so certain of this that he dares to turn his head, and he sees nothing but snowy blankness in every direction, just as Neo does when Morpheus first brings him to the Construct in *The Matrix*. He picks up the envelope and sees that it says "Gianni" on it in Allah's writing. He opens the envelope and pulls out a card inscribed in the same hand. It says: "I'm the All-Aware, the High and Mighty—you get the point. I've pulled you out of time and space for just a moment. No person knows you are reading this and no one will know what you decide. There is an offer concerning the eleven hostages on the other side of this card, and because I am All-Controlling, it is the only offer you will ever receive. After you read it, nod your head to accept or shake it to decline." Picco flips the card over and reads, "See Waite." That is, he would be allowed to visit Terry Waite, just a single hostage, to make sure he's okay, but with no guarantee of his release. Picco thinks, then nods.

For the advanced negotiator, the reservation point (RP) is set with cold, clear economic rationality. You set the RP in the Construct, away from all social influences, with only the knowledge you carry in your head, with as little sanguinity and skew as possible, and by answering the same hypothetical question: If you were given one ultimatum offer, where is the knife's edge between yes and no? The answer should be pinned to the hip of the real BATNA, and any wedge of distance between it and the RP should be justified by a measurable fact and objective evidence.

For example, let's suppose you are the antiques dealer with the lovely sugar bowl and you have another offer of €450 in cash. If a customer approaches with a Visa card and the bowl in hand, then your RP should be €459.20 to allow for the 2 percent credit card processing fee you will be charged. This is one example of a transaction cost that can differ widely among various counterparts. Other instances of legitimate transaction costs to build into the dealer's RP are delays in payment, the likelihood of a bad check, and the buyer's history of reneging on deals or failing to execute the terms of an agreement.

Illegitimate reasons to set your RP for the sugar bowl below your

BATNA of €450 are because the customer smiles, doesn't have enough money, argues, or might become your new best friend. The chance that you are a naive seller is one reason sophisticated buyers laugh at your jokes, turn out their pockets to show you that they're empty, beg and plead, accuse you of being unfair, and promise to call you tomorrow to set up a lunch for next week.

These scenarios lead us to one of the very few absolutes in negotiation: set your reservation point in the Construct before the discussions begin, and *never, ever change it at the bargaining table.* The irony of the most famous interest-based bargaining book is that there are times when unaware negotiators are so desperate to get any kind of deal that they are heedlessly *jetting to yes.* Sitting in front of an attractive, eloquent, smiling, promising counterpart who is squeezing them and making an unacceptable offer, they rationalize, "It's only a few bucks or just a percent or two under"; "They're being so nice, I feel bad"; "I'm sure I'll make up the difference in future deals"; "Aw, heck, I can live with it." No, no, no.

Your RP is there to keep you safe and to keep you from making bad deals that you will regret once the emotions die down and the counterpart vanishes. If an offer is on the negative side of the knife's edge, you have to turn it down. If it is a one-and-done negotiation, you must walk away with no deal. If subsequently you come to believe you've learned something of substance during the bargaining session that indicates you may have misjudged the situation and set your RP incorrectly, then you may rethink your original preparation. Just get yourself back as close as possible to the Construct, shielded from all social pressure and not jetting to yes. Ask for an adjournment of the talks so you can caucus alone; take the offer under consideration and promise to call them tomorrow. Then apply as much unbiased rationality as possible to the reevaluation of your RP and the relative goodness of the proffer. Have you really learned something new, or are you being fed a line of bull ordure? A good rule of thumb is that genuine information should make you rethink many of the elements of your planning, not just your RP. If instead it's just tweaking your RP so as to get some kind of agreement, or if delay is not acceptable to your counterpart, you must then have the discipline to issue a firm no and walk away.

Another mistake made by less advanced negotiators is to create distance between their best alternative and reservation point in order to be "tougher." In the sugar bowl example, a naive dealer may set an RP of €500 in order to make a lot of money on a potential sale. Such a maneuver brings a falseness to the walkaway point that is self-defeating: if a customer makes a take-it-or-leave-it offer for €475, the dealer either has to violate the RP or turn down this more profitable deal. As we'll see in the following section, there are better ways to motivate toughness than by distorting the RP and deconstructing its value as a security measure.

The distance between my RP and your RP defines the bargaining zone, a set of possible agreements to which we would both say yes in the Construct if Allah left us ultimatum cards. Decision science reveals that we have a natural bias in underestimating the extent of the bargaining zone because those who prepare for a counterpart with a tight RP never have that belief disconfirmed. The pessimistic dealer who thinks no one would ever pay more than €300 for the sugar bowl never learns the truth from a customer who would pay up to €500. It is a very rare buyer who is a Vizzini, who cradles the sugar bowl as he places it on the counter, hands over his MasterCard, and then, when the register says the transaction is approved, loudly proclaims, "Aha! You moron! You lop-eared winchell! Never make an Italian an offer he can't refuse! I would have paid €700 [lying to make the wised-up dealer feel even worse] for this treasure! Hahaha, hahaha!"

Hence, just as you reframe the other side's alternatives and BATNA, you also want to be similarly hopeful about their RP. Some intentional optimism can help overcome the gloom created by asymmetric disconfirmation; perhaps this buyer will pay a lot, or perhaps that seller will accept very little. Also, you should anticipate that this narrowing may affect your counterpart's anticipation of where your RP is. The natural tendency of your opponents is to believe that they got a large slice of a small pie; that is, they will naturally believe they did better in the negotiation than they really did. This will be an essential point to remember for Chapter 8, on fairness.

OPTIMAL FRUSTRATION (TARGET)

Back in the real white room after he refused to end the meeting prematurely, Picco was surprised by a seemingly significant concession from his masked opponent, who offered to bring out a hostage to see him: "I quickly replied that I had no interest in seeing any hostage unless he could leave with me." A less experienced negotiator, jetting to yes, would have leaped at Moughniyeh's suggestion as a way to have something to show for risking his neck or as the beginning of a positive spiral of affirmative moves. Picco was tough enough to say no and ask for more. The two men jousted about various provisos until the Lebanese said, "We are prepared to accept your decision as to when we should release this hostage," and Picco replied, "As soon as you can."

Picco's toughness and ability to say no were grounded both in his experience and in his focus on a goal. He labored that entire year of 1991 with the sole target of getting all eleven of the Western hostages freed unharmed. All his plans, tactics, and improvisations were centered on achieving the maximum, not the minimum, acceptable agreement.

It is a general finding in negotiation research that focus on a specific, challenging target yields better performance. In the experiment with the antique sugar bowl, half the dealers, whether they had no BATNA or one of €45 or €450, were told to concentrate on an ideal selling price. Those dealers who paid attention to their target sold the bowl for more on average, most significantly in the case of those with the low BATNA. Those in this last group who focused on an ideal price sold their bowls for 30 percent more than those who were instructed to focus on the other offer of €45. The one-step-ahead mental maneuver is clear: keep your target active and at the ready, and shove the strongbox containing your alternatives, BATNA, and RP to the back of your cerebral closet.

Picco's goal proclaimed itself because of the situation he was involved in, but for other negotiators, how and where to set a goal can be very ambiguous. There is no formula or exact recipe. Picco gives us one clue in the remarkable statement that opens his memoir: "Ideals have to be set high enough that you can walk comfortably underneath them." Ideals can mean both values and goals. To extend his metaphor, we can say that targets should hang far enough above you that you can't just reach up and grab them but have to jump—and even then, the best you can do is to get your fingers barely around them for an instant until you slip off. Ideally, then, you are always falling short. That is the point of ideals and targets— they are not often realized in the here and now.

The unease and disquiet produced by falling short lead to three conflicting, keen impulses: abandonment of targets altogether; adaptation of the ideals to match the present reality in order to ensure their fulfillment; and a recognition that the performance enhancement offered by goal-setting is worth the disquiet. As a one-step-ahead negotiator, you accept this third option—the principle of optimal frustration—and so you strap the curved stick to your own back and hang a carrot from the end of it so that it bobs above you and glances off your fingertips when you jump.

As with other arenas (such as fitness, relationships, and finance) in which one can employ goal-setting to gain improvements in performance, negotiation targets should be specific—"I want to sell the sugar bowl for €620" is more effective than "I want to sell it for a whole lot" or "I want to do my best." Also, the targets should ideally be seen as achievable and yet should create surprise if met. One measure of attainability is whether the goal is on the acceptable side of your counterpart's RP: hence the need for optimism about the extent of the bargaining zone, as we discussed earlier. One person's surprise is another's "ho-hum," so it's up to you what specific target would qualify as a long shot. The odds should certainly be less than 50-50; somewhere between 25 percent and 10 percent seems reasonable.

Goals are the performance-enhancing drugs of bargaining, and they're not without issues. The advice to focus on your target will improve your performance, but with possible side effects. First, if you get an agreement, it will likely be shy of the goal, and that shortfall may add to your feeling of anticlimax and dissatisfaction when signing the deal. Second, this aggressive orientation may blind you to possible agreements that are acceptable relative to your RP but are a great distance from the goal.

The remedy is the same in both cases: before signing the contract, or after dedicating much time and effort in a failed attempt to achieve your target, pull the mental strongbox from the back of the closet, open it, and compare the contracted deal or the best offer against your RP and BATNA. In the former case, this is a last check to make sure that you are allowed to sign this deal; in the latter, it allows you to fully consider agreements that are merely adequate and to avoid irrational impasses.

This focal-point reset can lead to a significant increase in a negotiator's satisfaction. It is the bargaining equivalent of one of the most famous findings in social psychology—the relative joy advantage of a bronze medalist over a silver medalist. Bronze winners compare themselves with a huzzah to the fourth-place finisher and all those who failed to medal, while second-place finishers view the world through gold-tinted glasses that turn their medals pissed-on gray. One very honest member of the runner-up Canadian women's hockey team at the PyeongChang Olympics in 2018 couldn't stand the sight or feel of the silver medal hanging from her neck and ripped it off before the awards ceremony was over.

One of the authors of the medal study, Victoria Medvec, joined Adam Galinsky (of the sugar bowl study) and Thomas Mussweiler to test the effects of alternative comparison points on bargaining results. They found that target-focused negotiators captured more value than BATNA-focused negotiators, but the former were less satisfied with their objectively better deals because the deals fell short of their aim points, whereas the others placed in the money above their comparison point. However, when the experimenters encouraged some of the targeters to remember their BATNA before assessing their satisfaction with the agreement, those negotiators were just as contented as those who were aiming the whole time simply to beat their best alternative.

The dramatic challenge of optimal frustration for the sophisticated negotiator is clear: you have to understand and frame all your alternatives, identify a BATNA and a rational RP, set a stretch target, and then stay completely in the moment as a goal-driven bargainer, unaffected by the knowledge that, after the deal, the script calls for you to transform into a BATNA-focused person. Two law professors, Clark Freshman and Chris Guthrie, have suggested that some of the tools of mindfulness—expanding self-awareness, focus, and self-acceptance—can be useful to the aspiring negotiator. Certainly, some level of meta-awareness is necessary to complete the pianistic balancing act of optimal frustration, and that will take lots of practice and all of the dramatic skills we discussed earlier.

The third side effect of being a target-oriented negotiator is an increased appetite for risk. On the whole, this is a good thing because it counteracts most people's initial conservative impulses, but as legal scholar Russell Korobkin points out in a thorough review, it can also cause negotiators to reject RP-acceptable offers just as Picco does when he declines Moughniyeh's proposal to see one of the hostages. Rejections like Picco's automatically increase the likelihood of impasses. That risk can be managed by the negotiator, however. Picco does not say "No, a thousand times, no!" or "I would never consider such an offer," responses that would be false and would paint him into a corner. Instead, he says, "I had no interest in seeing any hostage unless he could leave with me"—a firm no through an immediate counteroffer, retaining the chance of returning to the initial offer later.

Enticing targets that are high enough to walk under also provide a strong incentive for the stroller to gather whatever clumps of dirt and shit are nearby and stand on the heap so that the goal can be grasped. So it is that the appetite for risk can overwhelm constraints against actions that violate expectations, norms, ethics, or laws. As we will see in Chapter 11, on words and lying, the research is clear that high aspirations can lead to low criminality.

Gianni Picco was thoroughly committed to the goal of freeing all eleven hostages, and though he never did anything unethical, he knew he was taking risks that others, especially his family and his dear friend and boss Pérez de Cuéllar, would think were unwise. So he kept his decisions secret. An exemplar for all of us, Picco had to handle the side effects of his aspirations, including the chance of immorality and illegality, through meta-awareness, mindful actorly attention, and personal integrity.

PUT IT UP TO ELEVEN (BAWNA)

In January 1992, Boutros Boutros-Ghali assumed the mantle of secretary-general of the UN, and Picco was very close to his goal, having successfully secured the release of all nine of the American and British hostages. Only the two Germans remained in captivity. The Germans had been kidnapped in the late 1980s in retaliation for the jailing of a pair of brothers from the Hammadi clan, one of whom had partnered with Moughniyeh in the TWA hijacking. This final piece of the negotiation was especially problematic for Picco because the Hammadis' original proposal of a two-for-two swap was impossible under German law and was unacceptable to most of the other parties involved, and the Hammadis' resulting frustration had boiled over into death threats against Picco himself. Since a swap was off the table, Picco's critical planning task was to come up with alternative deal structures that might be accepted by the Hammadi family, the

German government, and the other parties less directly involved. As he flew to Frankfurt for the last stage of bargaining, Picco created eleven options to raise with the Germans:

> They ranged from allowing the Hammadi brothers to play soccer together to the most ingenious, I thought, which would be a program of artificial insemination for their wives, since one of the Hammadis' complaints was that an Arab husband without children was a man held in contempt.

This kind of creative brainstorming and preparing is often neglected by many negotiators and textbooks. We are talking about developing a BAWNA, a best alternative *within* a negotiated agreement. The Italian diplomat's exercise of formulating eleven possibilities expanded his mind and left him open to other solutions that another participant in the talks might propose. Thinking through a BAWNA is an excellent way to neutralize another side effect of having a goal—the tendency to hammer away on only a single path of attainment.

Developing eleven alternatives is an example of what the literature calls divergent creative thinking, equivalent to brainstorming thirty different uses for an empty box. Viola Spolin designed a version for her improvisational theater group in which actors use their gestures to create an imaginary object (for example, a yo-yo) and then pass it to someone else, who allows it to morph into another object (a basketball) before passing it along again. Narrowing those possible deal structures down to a BAWNA is an example of convergent creative thinking, the eureka moment when all the possibilities coalesce into the perfect one. The crystalline surprise of convergent creativity is embodied in the Remote Associates Test (such as "What word connects these three—cup, party, green?").[†]

Divergent creativity, such as Picco's coming up with eleven alternatives, provides the one-step-ahead negotiator with an inventory of ideas that could be used as counteroffers, answers, and conversation fillers. Depending on how Picco decided to present and frame his inventory, he could have convinced his counterpart of his hard work and goodwill, he could have filled up and controlled the agenda, or he could have over-

---

† Tea.

whelmed the other side with complex and multifarious options. Convergent creativity, or a BAWNA, gives the sophisticated negotiator a trump card to be presented at just the right moment.

Picco's creativity did not pay off immediately. He had to endure four more months of plane rides and late nights on the circuit from New York to Frankfurt, Vienna, Tel Aviv, Washington, DC, Damascus, and Tehran. He was hindered by his new boss, Boutros-Ghali, whom Picco describes in his memoir as "ethically worrisome," too political, "pharaonic," rife with weak excuses and laughable ideas, jealous of his subordinates, distant, uncommunicative, and as airy as a puffy roll.

The low point came on April 26, 1992, during a visit by the secretary-general and his wife to Tehran. Picco was denied the opportunity of a face-to-face meeting to thoroughly prepare his naive boss to negotiate with Iranian president Hashemi Rafsanjani; so, Picco writes, "knowing that at best he would skim over them, I simply wrote three lines, essentially saying that Rafsanjani had agreed with me that a straight swap of the German hostages for the Hammadi brothers could not happen." He might as well have written, "Do not trade the Germans for the Hammadis." As he sat with the Iranian president, Boutros-Ghali proposed that exact swap. Of course he did. Rafsanjani was delighted. Back in New York, when the secretary-general boasted to Picco of his great success and bargaining prowess, the now suboptimally frustrated envoy sputtered his strong objection. Boutros-Ghali replied, "Well, go to Damascus and fix it."

Picco had to renege on the secretary-general's "brilliant" deal and then spend the next month repairing relationships. Some ill will remained, though, making a personally dangerous situation for Picco even more tenuous. In early June 1992, he sent a cable from Damascus to headquarters in New York that reiterated his commitment to achieving his goal: "The objective is the release of the two live, repeat two live, persons. The family [Hammadi] involved is neither a diplomatic interlocutor nor a political one." With a heedlessness possibly induced by the closeness of the goal, Picco seized the opportunity presented by the absence of the local UN chief of security, who had earlier vetoed as too hazardous any visit by Picco to Beirut, to convince a staff driver to take him from Damascus into the Lebanese capital. A flurry of meetings around the tattered city followed, the details of which Picco is noticeably reticent about in his memoir, maybe reflecting a shuddering chill created by the memory of his great personal peril. Finally, on June 17, the two Germans were released and boarded a plane to Frankfurt with Picco, who "did not feel safe until we were well over the water and had picked up enough altitude to be out of the range of handheld missiles."

A LION'S HEART (TACTICS AND OFFERS)

The man without a gun on that plane over the Mediterranean Sea was spent. It was not only in the immediate, circumscribed modes of note taking, speaking, and listening that he had been a commando force of one, but also in the bigger picture of directing, writing, and acting the whole negotiation drama. His original conception had envisioned a much simpler structure: "It amounted to two one-act plays. First, an 'impartial' observer, such as a member of the secretary-general's office, would go to Lebanon to determine the health status of the hostages. Second, a high-level political meeting in a neutral country would be arranged between a member of the office of the secretary-general and a spokesman for the Lebanese groups holding the hostages." That straightforward plot depended critically upon the Iranians being a dominating protagonist rather than an equal member of the ensemble. As we've seen, that was not to be: the realized drama was sprawling and Shakespearean, though with a thankfully much higher survival rate. Throughout it all, Picco was a directing force of one, paying attention to the entrances and exits of various actors, advising them with notes on their performances, designing sets to the extent he was able, and establishing an emotional context.

As Picco learned from his experience in the rug markets of Afghanistan, the negotiation game is ultimately and proximally a game of offers. The tactics of indirection he learned from his local colleague were all about generating the most effective offer for a buyer in that setting. When it became clear that the drama was not to be simple and calm but more skittish, Picco prepared an offer he didn't want to make, namely his own detention in return for the freedom of the hostages.

This proffer was personal, brave, and maybe even foolhardy, and it reflected both Picco's commitment to his goal and his courage. Akhtari, the Iranian ambassador to Syria who had tried to leverage Picco's "nine-plus-one" with an imaginary offer, told him that Hezbollah had marginalized Iran and "wanted to deal with me directly because I had displayed a lion's heart."

The secret that every negotiator knows is that many offers, not just those in which you present yourself as a replacement hostage, carry a sense of personal risk, vulnerability, ambiguity, and a leap into the void. They all require a bit of the lion's heart. For the one-step-ahead negotiator, that heart comes from strategic sophistication, a knowledge of the deep workings of the negotiation game, an appreciation of the drama, thorough preparation, and, most proximally, the commitment to a specific goal. A stretch goal requires an aggressive offer: the experimental evidence is virtually unanimous that the positive effects of being goal-focused occur primarily through the daring first offers that result.

In the market for houses, as for used cars, the first offer has already been issued by the seller before any negotiation has even started. A careful study by two economists, Grace Wong Bucchianeri and Julia Minson, of home sales in the greater Philadelphia region in the mid-2000s confirmed the value of an aggressive listing price. Bucchianeri and Minson accumulated a set of more than fourteen thousand single-family homes that had been sold two times in recent years. They built a complex model that used all the measurable facts about a house (number of bedrooms, square footage, location, et cetera) to predict a likely sale price. Since all these homes had been sold twice, the economists could use the amount by which their model was incorrect on the first sale as a proxy for the unique characteristics of each house: lots of light, interior decoration, and so on. With this proxy in hand, they could then examine how the more recent listing price affected the second sale price. They found that sellers who had premium asking prices made more money: listing the house for 20 percent more than expected was equivalent to selling an imaginary house that was 860 square feet larger but otherwise identical.

When they googled "housing + pricing + sell," Bucchianeri and Minson found that ninety-five of the top one hundred hits warned against the dangers of setting too high an asking price. Two-thirds of those cautionary hits were from real estate agencies, confirming one of the best

Freakonomics facts: when they sell their own houses, as opposed to those of clients, agents set a higher asking price, keep the property on the market for almost ten days longer, and close at a price that is 4 percent greater. When it's your money, meh: the agent's goal is to get your house sold as quickly as possible at an expected, satisfactory price.

Remember back to Chapter 3 and the simulated sale of the Cambridge condo: it's "location, location, location," but the location is your mind and the mind of your counterpart. We said that those mental valuations are fancies, opinions, and perceptions, so you can shape them through forecasts, incidents, arguments, tactics, and observations. Immoderate first offers are another key way to do that shaping because they take advantage of a fundamental operation that supports human judgment—anchoring and adjustment. As demonstrated by the pioneering duo of Kahneman and Tversky in 1974, initial assessments, even if randomly generated, distort final outcomes even when the decision-maker has plenty of time to reconsider. The beginning number is an anchor, and subsequent adjustments cause our judgment to drift short of the true mark.

In each half of the game show *Jeopardy!*, contestants have to choose among thirty clues organized in six categories of trivia. The amounts increase evenly from $200 to $1,000 down a column in the first half of the contest, and from $400 to $2,000 in the second half, reflecting more obscure trivia. If a player buzzes in first with the correct answer, they win that amount of money and are able to choose the next clue. The chooser typically says a phrase such as "Transportation for six hundred" or "Potpourri for a thousand." Three times a game, that choice randomly results not in a clue but in a Daily Double, in which the selecting player is allowed to wager any amount up to the larger of their current winnings or the maximum clue value ($1,000 or $2,000) for that round. There is no rational reason players should be affected positively by the value under which the Daily Double is hidden: either Daily Doubles are extra hard as a group because the potential prize is so big, or they get harder further down a column just as regular clues do, and so should be more lightly bet if their face values are higher. However, one study found that, all else being equal, the wager on a Daily Double covered by a clue value of $2,000 was $320 larger than for one concealed by an $800 clue value. *Jeopardy!* players were irrationally anchored by the amount they said out loud when they stumbled upon the hidden bet.

Final jeopardy in the courtroom is also affected by anchoring. Researchers from the universities of Cologne and Würzburg recruited experienced judges and prosecutors, who were attending legal conferences in Germany, for a sentencing experiment. In the first assay, participants were assigned the role of a judge who was given a packet of materials, including testimony from the victim and the accused, eyewitness statements, and advisory expert opinions, on an alleged sexual assault. After working through all the materials, the judges received an imaginary phone call from a reporter who asked either whether the sentence would be higher or lower than one year or whether it would be higher or lower than three years. Those judges who had been anchored high gave an average sentence of thirty-three months, while those who had heard "one year" averaged twenty-five months. In the second assay, for a lesser crime of repeated shoplifting, subjects were told that the prosecutor's recommended sentence of either three months or nine months was randomly chosen; even so, the anchoring number affected the sentences—significantly different averages of four and six months, respectively. Moreover, those participants who were criminal court judges and prosecutors in real life were just as affected by the anchors as those who were not experts in criminal justice. The difference was not the biased judgment but the confidence: the experts were more certain that their sentences were the right ones.

Because anchoring effects are so strong, the sophisticated negotiator knows that the game in many bargaining situations is actually a race to make the first, sufficiently informed offer. Donald Dell, the tennis player turned pioneering sports agent, sort of disagrees: the title of his negotiating advice book is *Never Make the First Offer (Except When You Should): Wisdom from a Master Dealmaker*. The research is clear, however, that "except when you should" is almost always. One summary review of the literature concludes that the first-offer advantage exists in both individualistic and collectivist cultures, in both West and East, for those with strong BATNAs and for those with low power, and in both single-issue and multiple-issue negotiations.

To his great credit, however, Dell was not blindly dogmatic: he recognized when the risk of being anchored was too great. He was negotiating on behalf of his client, Michael Jordan, with the owner of the Chicago Bulls, Jerry Reinsdorf, when the latter had to take a phone call. Dell writes, "I leaned across his desk to sneak a peek at the paper in front of him. The number at the top of the page was $4 million, which wasn't even close to what we were thinking (a $40-to-$50-million range). I had made some rough notes on a yellow legal pad, so as soon as Jerry got off the phone, I tore off the top page and handed it to him. 'Here, let me show you our "offer sheet." We're at the $52 million range.'"

What could Reinsdorf have done? And, in general, what do you do if you're beaten to the first offer? Reinsdorf could have taken his paper, circled the $4 million so Dell could see it, crossed it out, written $1 million, and said, "Here's our offer sheet." One of the ways first offers work is that they make the other side doubt their own starting points and move their counteroffers in the direction of the anchor, giving the first offerer an invisible concession. The prepared one-step-ahead negotiator sticks to the planned first offer, or even, as hypothetical Reinsdorf does, moves further away from the anchor.

Picco witnessed a second kind of response in 1988 when he and Pérez de Cuéllar met with Tariq Aziz, the foreign minister of Iraq, in New York during the negotiations to work out the terms of a cease-fire between Iraq and Iran. In a headquarters conference room, the secretary-general also held out a piece of paper. Aziz sat immobilized in his chair with unlifted hands, forcing his counterpart to release the text, which wafted impotently to the center of the table.

> "In our last meeting I stated my position very clearly, as my instructions were strict," he said. "I am not prepared to discuss any substantive proposals with your Excellency. I proposed a face-to-face meeting with the other side . . . . I apologize, therefore, but I cannot receive this paper."

Aziz's tactic was to give the unwanted offer the *fin de non-recevoir*, formal diplomatese for "Paper? What paper? I didn't get no stinking paper." There are other, informal ways not to receive an offer, including simply ignoring it; not looking at it; moving it to the side of the table; ripping it to shreds; replying "You must be kidding, take that back"; and taking out your pen, crossing out the numbers and terms on the sheet, replacing them with more favorable ones (maybe the ones you had prepared for), and then stating, "This is still not acceptable."

The leap into the unknown that is a first offer does make many negotiators less satisfied with their objectively better outcomes, and it also makes them quite anxious. Dissatisfaction can be addressed through the same prescriptions of optimal frustration that we used with respect to goals (no surprise, since they are closely linked). One study suggests that the primary concern of the anxious is the fear of being taken advantage of: the worst response your first offer can elicit from your counterpart is an instant enthusiastic yes. No one wants to get to yes with this kind of alacrity. Preventing this response is one reason to prepare an aggressive target and first offer. Also, in Chapter 5, on drama, we saw that anxiety can be emotionally reframed for the actor/negotiator as excitement, as a challenge, as a performance enhancement, and as a prompt for a neutralizing deep breath. Failing these, the anxious sophisticated negotiator might be able to capture some of the value of the first move by making a "non-offer" in a "not-a-negotiation-but-just-talking," as favored by the Northern Irishman Brendan Duddy, or in a non-paper, as utilized by diplomats like those in the back-channel talks over the status of Kashmir. Of course, it's even easier for the counteractor to place a literal or figurative *fin de non-recevoir* on a non-offer.

There are other cautions to remember in the race to the first offer. If, despite all your preparation and research, you know nothing and the other side knows everything, you are better off making the second offer. Imagine hailing a taxi in a country you've never visited: in one study, Israelis who simulated visiting Namibia paid almost $50 to have a taxi wait for two hours if they made the first offer, as opposed to $11 if the cabbie went first and to the $3 Namibians pay. An opening ask also might reveal too much, especially in a complex situation: a sophisticated opponent might be able to interpret how you prioritize and weight the issues based on the structure of your offer. Hence, the rule is that if you can't complete the preparation checklist for your counterpart's column, especially alternatives, reservation point, and target, then you might want to prioritize information gathering rather than racing to the first offer.

Undoubtedly, a negotiator can go too far. Donald Dell could ask for a $52 million contract for Michael Jordan, but he couldn't have demanded $520 million. There are limits, and extreme requests will cause impasses and will potentially give insult. *Note: The tendency of one-step-behind negotiators is to be overly worried about crossing that line and to shy away from asking for too much.* Sadly, though, for the anxious, the nervous, the naive, and the waffling, the difficulty might not be solved by simply making nice offers. If a counterpart is a TWO or above, then they might perceive your generous offer with suspicion and with a sense that it's all too easy, and so reject it. As a result, there's no escaping some calibration and some personal risk in your initial ask. The sophisticated negotiator allows the goal to determine the plan for the first offer, as well as the sequence of concessions and second, third, and fourth offers that could lead to an agreement that is close to the target.

VERBA VOLANT, SCRIPTA MANENT (SCRIPT)

In the two days after Aziz refused to touch the paper Pérez de Cuéllar had dropped on the table, a tentative agreement was reached between the governments of Iran and Iraq on a procedure to sign and announce a formal ceasefire. All was set until Picco was visited by a friend who was a U.S. diplomat posted to the UN. The diplomat was acting as a messenger from Secretary of State George Shultz, and the communication was that the American government had withdrawn its support for the immediate process in favor of a three-month delay, until Shultz and his Soviet counterpart could meet and end the war together. Picco was distraught and, following the secretary-general's advice, slept on his reply overnight. By the morning, he had scripted a clever reply that got to no by passing through yes:

```
                    PICCO
    I am prepared to accept the message given
    by the secretary of state on condition
    that you assure me that the war will
    indeed end in October and that, in the
    meanwhile, there will be no civilian casu-
    alties.
```

                    U.S. DIPLOMAT
You are refusing.

                        PICCO
No, I'm accepting.

A week later, with the help of the Saudis and without the active participation of the Americans, Picco prevailed and Pérez de Cuéllar announced
an agreement bringing the hostilities to an end.

   As an experienced diplomat, Picco would have been familiar with the
famous Latin phrase *verba volant, scripta manent*—"spoken words fly away,
written words remain." The customary meaning of the phrase is along the
lines of "get it in writing." The fact that there could be no formally drafted
agreements was a challenge for Picco as he bargained with Abdullah.

   If the *verba* and the *scripta* overlap, then the Latin phrase might mean
something like "speech comes quickly [when] the script persists." That is,
experienced negotiators have *go-to lines* that they can reuse and adapt to
the audience and situation. We've seen that already with Picco's canned
but very effective response to the information that his counterparty has
another offer ("You should take the better one"), and with his formulation of a yes-that-is-no, "I am prepared to accept on condition that . . ." To
Rafsanjani in a later meeting when the Iranian leader was demanding the
release of the UN's report on responsibility for the start of the Iran-Iraq
War, Picco said, "You're a great negotiator, I'm not, so first I take everybody home then I give you the report." (With false humility and brazen
flattery, Picco was asserting that if he didn't secure his meager gains first,
then Rafsanjani's superior skills would eventually leave him with nothing.) To an Iranian deputy when Picco was informed that a Hezbollah
leader had refused to make an appointment: "I don't meet him, he meets
me, and if he doesn't meet me, it's his loss, not mine." To Abdullah in an
attempt to gain a concession as a just return for Picco's sweat and toil at
the end of another long night:

                        PICCO
Can I have my hostage?

```
                        ABDULLAH
        No group can interfere in another's busi-
        ness. Everybody has their own arrange-
        ments.


                         PICCO
        I have come for a second successive night
        and I have nothing to show for it.


                        ABDULLAH
        You need to work harder.


                         PICCO
        You need to work harder.
```

When the multiparty deal to free two of the hostages bogged down and he had minimal progress to report, Picco prepared a complete script for a meeting with Moughniyeh. In his script, he had some reliable lines to convince Abdullah to make a unilateral concession despite his vexation with Tel Aviv: "The time has come for you to surprise the Israelis and the world by proceeding with the release of the hostages . . . . Then the pressure will not be on you anymore, but on the Israelis, who detain people without due process."

In keeping with what we said earlier about strategic sophistication, the smart negotiator can capture much of the value of scripting by thinking through three steps: statement, response, and counter-response. The initial statement can be yours or the other side's. For example, as the buyer: "This sugar bowl is nice, but it has a dent in it." / "Yes, I know, that's why I reduced the price." / "Hmmm, you must not have lowered it enough, because it's still on the shelf." Or, as the seller: "The price on the bowl is firm." / "But I can't pay this much." / "We can charge your credit card now for half and preauthorize the rest for a month from now."

COME FROM THE CAULIFLOWER

(or, The relationship between preparation and creative improvisation)

Gianni Picco must have used reams of yellow paper in his months, days, and long nights of preparation. He was dedicated to the craft of planning his moves and scripting his words. And yet, as he notes in *Man Without a Gun*, "nothing ever worked out according to my intricate plans, and I always had to be prepared to change them on the spot." This is the last interpretation of the aforementioned Latin phrase: "the words can fly since the script continues." You prepare not to control the negotiation but to be an effective improviser.

Artistic directors share this view of preparation—both that volumes of preparation need to be done and that it is critical to be able to set it aside. Sidney Lumet, director of such classic films as *12 Angry Men* and *Dog Day Afternoon*, did "mountains of preparation." When they met to plan for the Broadway revival of his play *Angels in America*, Tony Kushner says that brilliant and meticulous Marianne Elliott "brought these huge director's notebooks that looked like the Talmud. At the center of each page was a little piece of the script, and then diagrams and charts all around it."

When a beautiful snow fell over the lunch break during a movie shoot and draped the landscape of Central Park in a shimmering white, Lumet was able to redo the whole morning's work and also meet the afternoon's schedule because, as he writes, "when you know what you're doing, you feel much freer to improvise." William Ball, whose advice to actors and directors we extended to negotiators in Chapter 5, further recommends that the director (the negotiator) "abandons his homework in order to allow the give-and-take of the rehearsal [bargaining] process to have its creative effect. Those ideas from his homework that are valid and compelling will come forward into his consciousness at the appropriate time; they will provide an effortless solution to problems."

So, all the detailed planning we've been doing and the preparation protocol we've been following for pages now? Throw it all out of the mental window and allow it to fly back unbidden. To requote Erving Goffman's response to the student who observed that the position he had just taken was the opposite of what he'd said a few minutes before: "Don't be so nostalgic." And don't be too fixated on adhering to your prepared actions, thoughts, and words. The one-step-ahead negotiator manages the left-hand/right-hand balancing act of executing a plan and still improvising, of following a script and yet freestyling, of monitoring progress toward a goal and still being in the moment.

Picco never wanted to lose his pen, but he was happy to abandon his homework. When he did so, his quirky personality and creative mind could take center stage. When he had to change his plans on the spot, he could voice his offbeat ideas and be true to his narrative. What would come forward into his consciousness was, surprisingly, cauliflower.

OPEN ON

We are back in the first living room somewhere in Beirut with every wall and object covered in white sheets. A masked man, ABDULLAH, sits across from PICCO. This is their initial meeting and they are still trying to interpret each other.

              ABDULLAH

    I don't understand it, why would you risk
    your life, because you know we can kill
    you, to save somebody who is not a member
    of your tribe?

The Italian has to abandon all his preparation, answer this loaded question, and solve this dramatic problem. We hear his inner dialogue.

           PICCO (to himself)

    What does he want? This is not a diplo-
    matic question, this is something differ-
    ent. I can answer in some ways but if my
    answer is wrong this is the end of the
    road. The way I will answer will set the
    stage to see if we go ahead with the story
    or not, so I'm not just answering for me,
    I'm answering for the people I am here to
    help . . . My son. They took away the pic-
    ture of my son. What are you going to do
    with that picture now?

PICCO breaks the uncomfortable silence.

                         PICCO
     I'm here because I like to pay in advance,
     I like to pay forward.

We can see ABDULLAH's eyes narrow skeptically.

                         PICCO
     Imagine the chances that you and I had to
     meet in our lives. You did not go to the
     same school I went [to], you did not go to
     the same mosque, church, or whatever that
     I did, we didn't go to the same beaches to
     swim in the summer. However, I believe you
     have a son.

PICCO has guessed his way into a faux pas, mistakenly communicating that he might
have information on who ABDULLAH is.

                        ABDULLAH
     (angrily) How do you know?

                         PICCO
     Look, I mention your son for this reason:
     the chances you and I [would ever] meet
     were close to zero zero zero zero point
     one, but we met. And now you can decide
     whether I get out of here alive or not.
     Now, twenty years from now your son may
     meet my son, and he may decide to save
     his life or not. So you know what? I like
     to pay in advance. I pay for that possi-
     ble meeting that your son and my son will
     have. I pay in advance.

                        ABDULLAH
     Where the hell do you come from?

PICCO

I come from where everybody comes from,
the cauliflower. You say to the children,
"Mommy, where do babies come from?" and we
say, "From the cauliflower."

ABDULLAH

You really are mad!

PICCO

Thank you. Yes, aren't we all?

The prepared negotiator comes from the cauliflower, arriving with a certain wide-eyed innocence, totally in the present moment, flexible, adaptable, eager to learn and bond, moldable, bearing joy and surprise, and yet hardwired with an appetite, a grammar, a theory of mind, a script, a judgment, and a predilection that will come forward into consciousness at the appropriate time to promote survival, gather resources, seek advantage, and attain goals.

SUMMARY

- Preparation is an exercise in optimistic pragmatism. You should set stretch targets and seek to make the first aggressive offer.
- Always prepare according to the protocol outlined here, and use a checklist (such as the one in Figure 12) to make sure all parties and elements are covered. In keeping with our earlier advice, however, recognize that whether you will allow your counterpart to see the extent of your planning and readiness is a separate decision.
- In the absence of good information, overestimate the degree of your counterpart's sophistication, and update asymmetrically, fully weighing actions, words, and ideas that indicate depth and heavily discounting evidence of shallowness that could be easily faked.

- An agenda can be the die that is cast: it can establish a valuable sequencing that yields leverage, and it can embed language and semi-offers that serve as anchors.
- Don't be leveraged: advise the counterpart who trumpets another offer that they should take the better one.
- Unpack and augment your positive alternatives, and do the same for your opponent's negative alternatives. If you have no positive alternatives, then pretend you have no options at all: leave that box in the checklist empty or write "none."
- Set your reservation point rationally in the Construct, and never change it at the bargaining table. Refuse the deal, and if you need to consider revising, return to the Construct.
- Draft scripts with at least three speaking turns—statement, response, counter-response. Don't be afraid to adapt and reuse lines that have been successful in other negotiations.
- Come from the cauliflower: prepare, prepare, prepare, and then leave it behind so that you can be alert, in the moment, creative, and ready to improvise. Trust that the lines and facts you practiced will be there if and when you need them.

— 8 —

ONE STEP AHEAD OF TOUGHNESS I: FAIRNESS

I NICKNAME MYSELF "THE GRAVE DANCER"

(or, The unnecessary costs and risks of
toughness without fairness)

Billionaire investor Sam Zell is a tough negotiator and fancies himself as such. He looks, opines, and curses just as an R-rated Popeye would in a live-action remake directed by Quentin Tarantino—"The fuck you're going to gladly pay me Tuesday for a Royale with cheese today." Zell is by some accountings the second-wealthiest resident of Chicago, but he is no Oprah and has little time for midwestern niceties.

Since the purpose of this chapter is to understand how to transform ourselves into the ideal of being both very tough and very fair, Zell will serve as a counterexample of a tough negotiator who ignores fairness. We will also examine his opposite—negotiators who value fairness and minimize toughness, such as a fictional professor and the FBI's James Comey—and then review the science that says that their goal of objective fairness, as baseball umpire Ken Kaiser knew all too well, is ultimately unobtainable because of the egocentric biases wired into the human mind. Finally, we will find a solution in the shape of a Chinese coin, which is round on the outside and square on the inside.

First, though, the tough-and-unfair Sam Zell, whose family history is a later variant of the immigrant story we saw with the Goffman family. None of his investing forecasts would ever be as prescient or valuable as the call his father, Berek Zielonka (Americanized to Bernard Zell two years later), made in 1939 to flee western Poland on the eve of the Nazi invasion. Unlike most immigrating Jewish families, the Zielonkas worked their way east instead of west, leaving Europe behind for Asia, crossing Siberia, stopping in Tokyo, steaming for Seattle, and settling in Chicago. This counternormative flight path might have been reflected in the contrary mind of Samuel, who was born in 1941.

Encounters with his father honed Zell's negotiating style from a young age. He remembers, "So we would get into these huge disagreements— and then what could I do? I could only be silent, because it was disrespectful to say he was wrong. And I would be silent for three months! We would sit through dinner, silent." Conversation around the Zell table resumed only when Sam's mother finally made him apologize. When he wasn't being obstinately silent, Zell was being aggressively voluble: the quote under his photo in the high school yearbook read, "I'm not asking you, I'm telling you."

As some self-confident and unembraced people do, Zell gave himself a nickname. He chose the moniker "the Grave Dancer" early in his real estate investing career, since, as he later said, "I was dancing on the skeletons of other people's mistakes." These mistakes were distressed commercial and residential buildings that others thought were money-losing propositions. Many of Zell's bets paid off during the 1970s and 1980s, and with this success he started to look toward distressed companies outside of the real estate business for further "vulture" investing. He bought Schwinn (bicycles), Sealy (mattresses), and many other less well-known companies; for the targeted owners and executives, the negotiations were rarely a smooth ride, and post-deal operations provided few good nights' sleep. One acquired executive said, "Sam is brighter and faster than most but he's abrasive and arrogant and he belittles people."

The biggest deal of Zell's career happened in early 2007 when he sold one of his real estate investment trusts, Equity Office Properties, for $39 billion. The dramatic negotiations had been initiated by Vornado's Steven Roth and extended over several months. Zell wisely leveraged these talks to attract other suitors and generate multiple offers:

> In mid-August, 2006, another bidder emerged: Blackstone, the private-equity firm. Jonathan Gray, a senior managing director of Blackstone, began

meeting with Equity Office representatives, and on November 19th an agreement was announced. Blackstone would pay $48.50 a share to acquire Equity
Office, making the buyout the biggest in history.

In the jealous world of corporate mergers, few objects are more de-
sirable than a newly affianced financial firm in the weeks during which
the lawyers and accountants are conducting their due diligence. Sam
was determined to maintain this desirability, so he forced Blackstone
to agree to a low breakup fee should another offer come his way, and
he met with Blackstone's Gray "to scare the shit out of him" and to read
him "the riot act" so that Gray would not make any moves to keep other
suitors away. Indeed, the interests of Roth and Vornado were further
aroused, and in mid-January, Zell dropped the equivalent of a perfumed
white handkerchief in their path as he emailed a not-so-subtle request
for a counteroffer. His poetic message began with the familiar couplet
on the ruddiness of roses and the blueness of violets before asking Roth,
"I heard a rumor, is it true?" Zell ended his ditty with "Love and kisses."
Like a hapless wooer with a leaky quill, Roth was put to the test of com-
posing a suitable response. His answer fell far short of a sonnet:

> *The rumor is true*
> *I do love you*
> *And the price is $52 . . .* †

Zell had triggered the bidding contest he sought. After countering
other bids from Vornado, Gray and Blackstone were forced to increase
their offer to $55.50 per share to secure the deal, an additional windfall of
$3 billion for the Grave Dancer. More importantly, Zell's timing was im-
peccable, as the deal was completed just ahead of the bursting of the real
estate bubble. Two years after the sale, many of the former Equity Office

---

† And who says there's no need for English majors in finance?—
Nevermore, the student of the seedy Poe
Must be blocked from marketing the CDO;
Knowledge of the love of Levin and Kitty
Will be greatly sought by LevFin at Citi.

properties were worth less to their final owners (Blackstone had sold on most of the buildings) than the mortgages they carried.

Zell's next headline deal did not result in the same good news, though it did bring him the *Chicago Tribune*, the *Los Angeles Times*, the *Orlando Sentinel*, and many other media properties. A few months after the Equity Office triumph, Zell created a complex deal that gave him control of the distressed Tribune Company, one of the pillars of Chicago's society and economy and one of the largest media conglomerates of the time. On a road show to meet his new employees, Zell, tough as ever, reportedly responded to a question from an overly inquisitive reporter in Orlando with a simple "Fuck you," and he called the local publisher a "motherfucker." The fallout from his introductory visit to Los Angeles was a memo from the editors reminding employees,

> Last week you may have encountered some colorful uses of the lexicon from Sam Zell that we are not used to hearing at the Times. As Sam pointed out in his "mea culpa" note to us today, he does this to make a point and in an attempt to change culture quickly. But of course we still have the same expectations at the Times of what is correct in the workplace. It's not good judgment to use profane or hostile language and we can't tolerate that . . . . Sam is a force of a nature [*sic*]; the rest of us are bound by the normal conventions of society.

One might guess that in the newspaper's lexicon, the entry under "force of a nature" might include: "*synonyms*: schmuck (Yiddish); jerk (colloquial); a**hole (profane)."

Zell threatened and fired editors and reporters. He brought in senior executives who wrote nonsensical "motivating" (but not), "visionary" (but not) internal memos later spoofed on the internet, and who threw a cigar-smoking, boozing poker party in the inner sanctum of the original office of the *Chicago Tribune*'s founder. Pieces describing the chaos were headlined "Zell to L.A. Times: Drop Dead" and "At Flagging Tribune, Tales of a Bankrupt Culture." Within eighteen months of Zell's taking control, it wasn't just the culture that was apparently bankrupt; the whole business was too, as the company defaulted on its heavy debt load.

Once the legal process was completed in late 2012, the Grave Dancer was out his entire $315 million investment.

Despite the *Tribune* loss, Zell remains an extremely wealthy man. So the obvious question: Is Zell's style the cause of his success or is it irrelevant or even an impediment? There seems to be no way to interact with him without being lacerated. He has no delicacy or intangibility or smoothness, as he himself acknowledges with the title of his memoir, one of his favorite phrases: *Am I Being Too Subtle?* The relationship costs are clear: he is a person who is difficult to like or to trust. Why, then, do peers like Gray and Roth call him?

As we've seen earlier from the data, you don't have to be a "force of a nature" (or any of its synonyms) to be tough. Moreover, as Zell's *Tribune* experience shows, sharpness and crassness might be counterproductive. In fact, this kind of exterior toughness is simply a self-indulgence by certain personality types who love to be mean, aggressive, belittling, loud, and arrogant. Most of the time, success comes *despite* the external toughness instead of *because of* it. Zell's behavior is unnecessarily risky, as he acknowledged when he wrote, "Grave dancing is an art that has many potential benefits. But one must be careful while prancing around not to fall into the open pit and join the cadaver." Be tough in a Zell-like manner, and the attendees still standing on the grass edging the lip of the grave will not bend over to lend you a hand out of the pit but will bury you with eager shovelfuls of dirt.

THAT CURIOUS AMERICAN PASSION FOR IMPARTIALITY

(or, The dangers of an overwhelming desire to be seen as fair)

We can find Zell's opposite, in fictional form, in a short story by Jorge Luis Borges.

Once upon a time, there was a professor of Old English at the University of Texas at Austin by the name of Dr. Ezra Winthrop, a transplant from Boston, a man of old New England stock, who "had renounced the Puritan faith of his forebears, but not their sense of right and wrong."

Winthrop's department head had asked him to select one of two distinguished colleagues to lead an important academic conference. This was a politically delicate task. The first candidate, and the more senior, was one Herbert Locke, a friend of Winthrop's who had helped him prepare an annotated version of *Beowulf* that had sold well on college campuses and provided a steady royalty stream. Locke's most significant solo work was a book titled *Toward a History of the Kenning*. A kenning is an old-fashioned conjunction of words meant to be evocative, such as "war-sweat" for "blood" and "sail-road" for "sea."

The second candidate, Eric Einarsson, was a thirtyish ginger, "imperious, energetic, and cold; in a land of tall men he is tall." In his few years at the department, Eric the Red had managed to be productive as a scholar but also singularly able to ruffle his colleagues' feather-skins. His most important work was a critical study of the poem *The Battle of Maldon*, which describes how the Anglo-Saxons had been unable to repel an invasion in 991 CE by the Vikings.

Not one to move quickly and without thorough deliberation, Winthrop struggled with his decision for days. During that span, the latest *Yale Monthly* appeared with an article that challenged received wisdom on the best way to teach Old English. The piece asserted that the typical syllabus should be reversed and, rather than beginning with an exegesis of all three thousand lines of *Beowulf*, should start with eleventh-century works and move backward through time to end with a cursory examination of that unjustly hallowed epic. Since only a fragment of *Beowulf* would be used, students would not need to purchase anyone's popular, annotated, high-royalty version of the poem. Borges writes, "Not once was Winthrop's name mentioned, but Winthrop felt persistently attacked." The author of the Yale article, in keeping with the journal's strictures, was identified simply as "E.E., University of Texas."

Despite the article, Winthrop nominated Einarsson to chair the conference over his old friend Locke. The day before he left for the conference, Einarsson dropped by his senior associate's office. He revealed his stratagem to Winthrop: he believed not a word of the revisionist article he had written about teaching Old English, but he had conjectured that its publication and the whispers it would cause in the hallways of the department would force Winthrop to choose him. The former Puritan at first did not follow or understand how his young colleague could be so certain.

Borges writes that Winthrop "was intelligent, but he tended to take things seriously, including conferences and the universe, which could well be a cosmic joke."

Einarsson then reminded his colleague of their first lunch when he had just arrived in Austin. Their discussion had turned to the American Civil War, and the senior scholar had made plain that despite his family members having fought for the Union, he understood the Confederacy's right to secede, its desire to preserve its institutions, and the bravery of the men fighting for its existence. Einarsson said, "I realized, my dear Winthrop, that you are ruled by that curious American passion for impartiality. You wish above all else to be 'fair-minded.'" Winthrop defended the South because he was from the North: he would select Einarsson for the conference not despite the negative article but *because* of it. As the Viking-son confirmed with a word-thrust at his Anglo-Saxon colleague, "I realized that calling into question the methodology that you always use in your classes was the most effective way of winning your support."

The need to be perceived as fair-minded might be, as Borges was claiming, felt most strongly in the United States. Both President Obama, as we saw earlier, and FBI director James Comey were damaged by their desire to rule from a frayless, impartial realm and to be seen as unbiased umpires. The exploitative Einarssons for both men were the red-faced, red-seeing Republicans.

Like Winthrop the Fair-Minded, James Comey is hyperaware of others' sense of his sense of right and wrong. In *A Higher Loyalty*, he writes that the Hillary Clinton investigation demanded "the crazy idea of personally offering the American people unusual transparency, and doing it without the leadership of the Justice Department." One prompt of his plan to dangle the scales of justice in public was the impromptu meeting on June 27, 2016, between his boss, Attorney General Loretta Lynch, and Bill Clinton in an FBI jet at the Phoenix airport. Comey knew that whatever the two talked about would have absolutely no effect on the investigation, but, like hot gossip in a university hallway, the news of the meeting became a "firestorm" and "another corrosive talking point" among the "cable news punditry." As it turned out, by questioning his and the FBI's methodology and by continuously asserting the whole thing was a rigged game, Trump and the Republicans had found the most effective way to earn Comey's implicit support.

That was how he wound up standing before the cameras on July 5, 2016, to deliver a verbal indictment (though not a criminal one), a personal judgment (though not an official one), a moral condemnation (though not a judicial one) as he sanctimoniously labeled Secretary of State Clinton "extremely careless" while at the same time recommending that "no charges are appropriate in this case."

In the months that followed, as various events forced him to take further equilibrizing actions, Comey, like a naive referee, took solace in the boos that rang out in the stadium from everyone in the crowd, those kitted out in blue and those wearing red. He said, "Even if you think I'm an idiot, I'm a pretty fair-minded idiot, and I'm not on either side." A few weeks before Obama's term ended, Comey met with his fellow American umpire in the Oval Office and the president told him, "I picked you to be FBI director because of your integrity and your ability. I want you to know that nothing—nothing—has happened in the last year to change my view." Comey felt palpable relief that Obama still viewed him as fair-minded and "not a partisan hack." He replied, "Thank you, Mr. President. It has been a nightmare. I'm just—I've just tried to do the right thing." With a verbal pat on Comey's head, Obama the Ever-Neutral answered, "I know. I know."

Had Comey met instead with one of our Italian envoys, his lament would have been greeted with outward equanimity despite an internal shake of the head, and with a seismograph's worth of fake scribbling. Machiavelli, a pragmatic person, would agree with Picco's conclusion that "impartiality is a banality which is mentioned by those who never did a successful negotiation." After years of diplomatic experience, Picco understood the deep truths in Borges's story about the vulnerability of the fair-minded and the impossibility of impartiality:

> I did not realize at the time that impartiality is not a useful concept. Impartiality applies only to mirror-image situations, which rarely exist in nature or negotiations. Only late did I come to realize that what both sides of a conflict want from a mediator is not impartiality but credibility—the ability to deliver the goods.

If Zell's toughness without fairness is crass exploitation, then the curious passion to be seen as fair-minded above all else shared by Winthrop,
Obama, and Comey is guileless exploitability.

I CALLS 'EM AS THEY SEES ME SEES 'EM

(or, How and why judgments of fairness are rarely seen as objective)

No one understands the banality of impartiality better than the working
umpire or referee. Ken Kaiser, a behemothic umpire in blue in the American League for twenty-three years, received more than his fair share of
heckling—"Hey, blue, if you had one more eye, you'd be a Cyclops."

As he trained as an umpire in the minor leagues of baseball, Kaiser
honed his theatrical ability by moonlighting as The Hatchet, a masked
wrestling villain who dressed all in black. Just to show that it's all a small
negotiating world, Kaiser as The Hatchet wrestled André the Giant in Miami one night, doing his very best to survive both in the ring with "the
strongest man who ever walked the face of the earth" and later at the
restaurant table as André consumed three steaks, twelve baked potatoes,
and a quarter keg of beer.

In his memoir, Kaiser observed, "Most umpires actually begin their
careers suffering under the delusion that if they are fair and competent
they won't have any problems on the field. Sometimes it takes as long
as—oh, I don't know—the first three or four innings of their career for
them to understand reality. Managers and players expect every call to go
their way." What Kaiser is implying is that being fair doesn't necessarily
lead to being seen as fair, and that all this yelling and complaining does
have an effect on the umpire's decisions.

Research has uncovered the ordinary fair-imbalance of umpires and
referees in most sports. It may be that such an official calls 'em as they sees
'em, to use the famous baseball umpiring phrase, but their vision is askew
and distrusted. A few examples of the findings:

- In the NFL, where each team stands on its own long side of the rect-
  angular field, a play may bring the ball, and the officials, closer to one
  of the sidelines. When this happens, the likelihood of a penalty bene-

fitting the nearby team increases for certain fouls by 25 percent to 100 percent.

- A violent clash between the supporters of two Italian soccer clubs prompted the government to penalize the clubs by forbidding them to sell any tickets for future matches. With the stands empty, the referee knew that his whistle would not prompt a volley of curses and shouts of *Che dici?*, and as a result, visiting teams were treated more fairly. Relative to when the stands were full, visitors received one less yellow card and home sides saw a 10 percent increase in foul calls.

- Referees will counterbalance penalties and fouls so that totals stay fairly even. In the National Hockey League, if a team ends the first period with three more penalties, then in the second period it will, on average, receive 20 percent fewer whistles against it. This natural equilibration by the officials in all sports provides a perverse incentive for one team to be more aggressive, since fair-minded referees will, of necessity, have to turn a blind eye to some of its actual offenses.

- The ump calls 'em as they sees 'em unless the call will have an impact on the game. Those in blue want to avoid being seen as placing a hand on the scales, even if it means placing a hand on the scales. A study of more than a million pitches in Major League Baseball (MLB) revealed that the likelihood of a borderline pitch being called a strike can vary up to twenty percentage points depending on whether a call of "ball" would be the fourth, "strike" would be the third, the score of the game is close, or there are runners on base.

Hence, even though they are professionally trained impartialists, umpires have significant biases, as do their fellow arbiters, judges. Legal research shows that those ruling from the bench have a very similar list of vulnerabilities to audience effects, counterbalancing calls, and personal attachments. It is no surprise, then, to find that when we amateurs attempt to be impartial, we have those same predispositions. We are more concerned with looking fair in the eyes of the participants and audience: umpires, judges, and negotiators all call 'em as *others sees them* see 'em.

Although umpires and referees may be unaware of their own biases, they have as deep an understanding of the fluidity and subjectivity of claims of unfairness as does a parent of young children ("I did it by accident"; "You did it 'by' purpose!"). "Most of the time," Kaiser writes, "when a player screws up he knows there is only one courageous thing he can do to appease the fans: blame the nearest umpire." The ump's blindness, cognitive deficiencies, and partiality can camouflage the player's poor batting eye, weak arm, errors, cheating, and gamesmanship.

Players—like umpires, like politicians, like former directors of the FBI, like senior faculty, and like every negotiator—often come to this self-excuse genuinely. As with many other self-perceptions, the curious judgment of our own impartiality often arises organically and subconsciously, but ultimately reflects our own self-interests.

One fairness experiment gave people the choice between two different cash allocations: option A was $6 for self and $1 for another person, and option B was $5 for self and $5 for another person. The Grave Dancer, of course, would choose A and do a little jig; Winthrop and Comey would solemnly select B, and both might do so even if the amounts were $2 and $2. In tests of this stark choice, around a quarter of subjects do the selfish, unfair thing and choose A. Another variant of the choice was conducted in which both dollar figures for the counterpart were replaced by "?," and subjects were given an opportunity to push a button or look in a folder and find out what amounts their choice of $6 or of $5 resulted in for the other person. In this version, half of the participants decided to stay in the dark and then choose A, thereby denying themselves the information about how fair their selection was.

This strategic ignorance is akin to the earlier advice we saw from Sun Tzu to "appear to be incompetent." The excuse of "oh, I didn't know" preserves the perception of our fairness, since it is usually interpreted as a socially neutral act. In that experiment, a recipient of $1 whose giver had decided to remain uninformed was sympathetic, since "it is better to remain in denial about the repercussions of the decisions one is making." Information can be avoided and excused in other ways: "I forgot," "My computer crashed," "I wasn't paying attention," or "I didn't follow—it was too complicated." So from your own side, as a negotiator, you prepare and gather as much information as possible, but, once again, you might choose not to reveal the extent of your knowledge. And, from the other side, you never let your negotiating counterparts remain in denial about any negative repercussions for yourself of their offers, framings, and decisions.

It is natural to think that information avoidance can be easily solved by information confrontation. The presentation of interests is the simple prescription of *Getting to Yes*: each side informs the other of their interests, and on this basis a fair agreement can arise. Sometimes this is so, but sometimes shared knowledge becomes a hatchet that cleaves the two sides.

As Kaiser observed, after their first few innings umpires understand that their own impartiality is insufficient for doing their job well. They realize that the events they witness are fundamentally not seen in the same way by players or fans. This phenomenon was first scientifically documented in a famous 1954 psychology study titled "They Saw a Game," conducted by Albert Hastorf of Dartmouth College and Hadley Cantril of Princeton University. Three years earlier their schools' football teams had met on the gridiron and the game featured many whistles and penalty flags, a broken nose for Princeton's Dick Kazmaier, and a broken leg for a Dartmouth player. The week of the game, Kazmaier had appeared on the cover of *Time* as the star of the Tigers' undefeated squad, and the opposition may have been green with envy.

Hastorf and Cantril had students of both schools watch a movie of the game and record what they saw. The differences were stark: 93 percent of Princeton students thought the game was "rough and dirty," as compared to only 42 percent of Dartmouth students; 39 percent of the latter categorized the contest as "rough and fair," as compared to only 3 percent of Princeton students; Dartmouth viewers saw their team commit four infractions on average, but Princeton viewers saw the Dartmouth team commit ten fouls, many of them flagrant. Having heard from the Princeton side how much violence and how many violations his side was responsible for, a Dartmouth alumnus, after watching the film and seeing a dearth of incidents, sent an urgent telegram to the researchers: "Preview of Princeton movies indicates considerable cutting of important part please wire explanation and possibly air mail missing part." The scholars conclude:

In brief, the data here indicate that there is no such "thing" as a "game" existing "out there" in its own right which people merely "observe." The "game" "exists" for a person and is experienced by him only in so far as certain happenings have significances in terms of his purpose . . . from his own egocentric position in the total matrix.

The Princeton fan sees 'em and the Dartmouth fan honestly does not.

Linda Babcock and George Loewenstein of Carnegie Mellon University wrote a series of influential papers documenting how a communal set of facts can still produce very different negotiation expectations. One paper might as well have been titled "They Saw a Motorcycle Accident." It was based on a real court case from Texas, in which a motorcyclist (plaintiff) was suing a car driver (defendant) for $100,000 in damages after a collision between the two vehicles. There were twenty-seven pages of evidence—police reports, maps, and testimonies from eyewitnesses. The researchers had an actual judge review all the evidence and issue a monetary ruling were the case to go to trial. This was the setting for an experiment in which subjects were given a chance to simulate a pre-trial negotiation.

There were two versions of the experiment. In the first, subjects read all the materials and then were told whether they were lawyers representing the plaintiff or the defendant; in the second, they were assigned their roles before they were given access to the very same pages of evidence. Before they negotiated, participants were asked to estimate how much the judge would award the plaintiff if the case went to trial.

The negotiation results showed the influence of "egocentric position in the total matrix": a third of those who were assigned their roles before getting the evidence deadlocked and ended up in court, while those who read the evidence and then learned their roles settled before trial 95 percent of the time. The forecasts of the judge's decision were significantly different for the role-then-evidence advocates (on average, a plaintiff's lawyer guessed the judge would award $20,000 more than the defendant's lawyer guessed), but the dollar estimates were the same for the evidence-then-role advocates. Slipping on motorcyclist-tinted or car-driver-tinted glasses was sufficient for subjects to easily highlight the facts that supported their own side and filter out the inconvenient evidence—the plaintiff's attorney saw one accident and the defendant's saw another.

A second important study by the Carnegie Mellon academic team examined the causes of bargaining impasses and teacher strikes in school districts across Pennsylvania in the 1980s. There were five hundred school districts in the state, and historically, 8 percent of the time contract talks ended in impasses and teacher walkouts. Babcock and Loewenstein sent surveys to union leaders and school board presidents, all of whom led negotiations for their side. The survey asked respondents "to list the districts they felt were comparable to their own for the purpose of contract negotiation." Logically, the idea of something being comparable presumes an objective goodness-of-fit. However, the typical lists provided by the union leaders and the board presidents overlapped on only two out of five districts. The skewed comparables reflected significant self-serving bias and pulled benchmark salaries in a self-interested direction: for a teacher with a college degree and fifteen years' experience, the union list resulted in a salary that was $711 higher (2.4 percent of base pay) on average than the board list. The statistical model estimated by the authors predicted that the average difference in comparables raised the likelihood of a strike by 35 percent.

Their research leads Babcock and Loewenstein to confirm Picco's insight about the rarity of the mirror situation and his experience of partiality: "As soon as asymmetries are introduced between the parties . . . both parties' notions of fairness will tend to gravitate toward settlements that favor themselves. They will not only view these settlements as fair, but believe that their personal conception of fairness is impartial." Fairness, in reality, has a bit of the con in it.

I played Little League baseball with a kid named Norman. He was a decent player with a good bat and an arm suitable to most positions in the field except for pitcher. And yet, given the dearth of talent on the team, Norman often had to take the mound. When he did, the inning would consist of bases on balls, wild pitches, and blasts to the deepest parts of the outfield. Norman had a round face and preadolescent chubby cheeks:

he was a miniaturized version of Ken Kaiser's self-description, "a barrel with two arms stuck on—backwards." As the runners and runs piled up, Norman would get angry and his face would become red and redder. When at last a hitter swung through a pitch for a third strike and was the first to walk back to the dugout, bat in hand, Norman, standing on the mound as though it were a pedestal in Cooperstown, would proclaim triumphantly, "You are *gone!*"

Major League Baseball told Kaiser loudly and unfairly in the autumn of 1999 that he was gone. Actually, he and his fellow umpires had unwisely ejected themselves from the game, making this a cautionary tale of self-deception for every negotiator.

On the heels of two decades of successful strikes and a huge increase in salary and benefits, the umpires' union had gained a great deal of power by the summer of 1999, the final year of a collective bargaining agreement in which they had renounced their right to strike. Earlier in the season, rumors popped up that the MLB commissioner planned to fire twenty of the sixty-eight full-time umpires when the current contract expired. Kaiser—loud, arrogant, confrontational, and unafraid of the spotlight—was a likely target for termination.

Seeking to be proactive, the head of the union, a tough guy named Richie Phillips, devised a strategy to compensate for the inability to strike: the umpires would all submit letters of resignation effective September 2, when pennant races were reaching maximum intensity. Most of the umps met in Philadelphia on July 14, during the All-Star Break, and Phillips presented them with pre-drafted letters to be signed right then and there. That same day, Phillips mailed the letters, publicly announced the resignations and the dissolution of the union, and indulged in a bit of premature grave dancing with the announcement that "the league is in chaos." He also stated that his members "want to continue working as umpires, but they want to feel good about themselves and would rather not continue as umpires if they have to continue under present circumstances."

When the letters arrived at league headquarters, MLB was happy to oblige. The commissioner's office accepted all the resignations. Phillips and the union had badly miscalculated MLB's BATNA: not only had they handed all leverage over to the commissioner, but they had given the league six weeks' additional notice to refine its contingency plans.

Within days, after talking to their spouses and lawyers, many of the umpires began to regret their haste in signing the letters, and sixteen contacted MLB to withdraw their resignations. After more losses in court and at the arbitration board, more questionable tactics and statements, more defections, and MLB's legal hiring of replacement umpires from the minor leagues, a newly reformed union, no longer led by Phillips, managed to save most of the jobs of the original sixty-eight umps. Kaiser was, sadly, among the nine who would no longer be allowed to calls 'em as they sees 'em.

Costly biases in judgment can happen with respect to leverage, preparedness, intelligence, sophistication, motivation, and, as we've seen, fairness. The overconfidence wrought by the combination of a track record of successful threats and a blustery personality like Phillips's exacerbates the problem.

The Carnegie Mellon researchers tested a simple intervention in another version of the "They Saw a Motorcycle Accident" experiment: they had some of the role-then-evidence disputants write out the specific weaknesses in their cases (that is, they made sure that these negotiators adhered to the preparation guidelines discussed in Chapter 7). This intervention caused the estimates of the judge's award by the motorcyclist's attorney and the driver's attorney to converge, and they had an impasse rate of only 4 percent compared to the control group's 35 percent. Of course, de-biasing yourself is only half of the issue; forcing, promoting, or helping your counterparts de-bias themselves is a whole other struggle.

Umpires of all kinds who are more certain of their impartiality are more prone to biases in judgment, and umpires who are more sensitive to being seen as fair-minded are more prone to being exploited. There is no clean and easy answer other than to maintain a Borgesian meta-awareness of the game. Ken "The Hatchet" Kaiser might have agreed that fairness is something that you have to grapple with, that you put on a coordinated show with, and that sometimes you pin and sometimes it pins you. As someone who had to "calls 'em as they sees me sees 'em," he said, "It's your job to change other people's minds, to bend them to your way of thinking." The detailed advice on how to grapple with fairness successfully while clearly projecting toughness so as to bend and secure others' positive perceptions of you is the base we walk to now.

ROUND ON THE OUTSIDE, SQUARE ON THE INSIDE

(or, The actable metaphor for being very tough and very fair)

Sam Zell is a business sovereign; Xi Jinping, China's president, is a true potentate. Zell, with his exterior toughness and acerbity, is a sharp-cornered square; Xi, a man who rose from exile in the wilderness to the top of a modern empire, is a more complex object. One Chinese observer describes Xi in this way: "He's not afraid of Heaven or Earth. And he is, as we say, round on the outside and square on the inside; he looks flexible, but inside he is very hard." The Chinese saying is *wài yuán nèi fāng* (外圆内方), and it arises from the shape of old Chinese coins (Figure 13), which were circles with squares punched out of the center so that they could be securely strung on a cord and exchanged in bundles. This simple image has many interpretations along these lines—"be generous, respectful, and civil on the outside but on the inside know exactly what you think and feel at all times"; "the harmony of inner rectitude and outer suavity."

The phrase and the image of the coin extend what our earlier data asserted about the two qualities neatly coexisting—fairness is the outer quality and toughness is an inner characteristic. The example of Zell shows why sharp corners and the antagonistic, toxically aggressive version of toughness might cost you dearly. Yes, your liquid cash and your ability to close deals may bring repeat business, but the smallest stumble will leave your doorway and inbox empty and any future funeral-goers with shovels in hand. The examples of Winthrop and Comey reveal why the negotiator can't be circular all the way through: an inner roundness makes you very spinnable and exploitable.

Remember William Ball's earlier strict advice to the theater director: "We are looking for some object . . . that shall not only be like the production, but, in the director's mind, shall be the production itself." An author can also heed these words: this coin is, for me, toughness-fairness. It manifests a tension of the straight and rigid versus the curved and accommodating; it is one object made from two disparate shapes, with the circle rolling easily through the outside world and the square orienting

Figure 13. Source: Pixabay

north, south, west, and east; it incorporates both presence (in the metal) and absence (in the quadrate space). *Toughness is the sharp-cornered inner square; fairness is the smooth outer circle.*

Goffman writes that "the very obligation and profitability of appearing always in a steady moral light, of being a socialized character, forces one to be the sort of person who is practiced in the ways of the stage." As we saw earlier with other performances, then, *don't bump into the fairness furniture.* Picayune discrepancies that indicate injustice or unconcern about equity are much more costly than they might seem. Your first goal is to avoid being seen as unfair.

Wear your fairness "costume." Although The Hatchet was masked, clothed in black, and radiated belligerence, the best umpires, according to the players they referee, are "approachable," "relaxed," "calm," and "cooperative and professional, as opposed to overly familiar or overofficious"; they don't "speak quickly," and they "can get a message out to a player in a succinct, clear fashion."

Know your fairness lines. Lynda Obst, the Hollywood producer we met before, tells of a successful peer who responded to pressure from the studio to cut money from his budgets with a reusable line reading: "'I share your concern,' he says gravely. He looks stoic, concerned, attentive. And likely does what he was planning to do."

Your fairness lines should *focus more on process than on the end result.* The sophisticated negotiator can draw on our shared nature as looking-glass beings to implement this approach, as Obst's producer friend did, through *reflective listening.* The first step, as the other speaks, is note taking, either with a quiet mind ready to record or with Picco's preference of a pen and paper. Then, using an introductory phrase such as "It sounds as though . . ." or "What I'm hearing is . . . ," you verbally mirror back the utterance, using the very same words selectively to indicate that the counterpart was heard and to validate their interests and framing, but with enough variation to avoid obviously mimicking them. Reflective listening can be augmented by mindfulness, which "requires letting go of judgment, returning to an awareness of the breath and the body, and bringing your full attention to what is in you and around you."

Both costume and script speak to what is called in the literature "procedural justice." In negotiations and other social domains, people value the way they are treated potentially more than they do their final share of the available rewards (which is called distributive justice). Law professor Rebecca Hollander-Blumoff has carefully explored the relative significance of the constituent elements of procedural justice. In an experiment involving a simulated dispute over an unfinished in-ground swimming pool between a lawyer for the contractor and a lawyer for the homeowner, Hollander-Blumoff and a colleague confirmed the flat line we saw in Figure 6 between objective negotiating performance and fairness ratings. They also found that participants' willingness to accept an agreement was not correlated with the size of their gain or loss but was very strongly and positively associated with the opportunity to speak and with the belief that the other side listened, showed respect, and was courteous and trustworthy.

In a second experimental setting, when the contractor had another customer for the old tiles that the pool owner wanted to replace anyway, thereby raising the potential size of a deal, a sense of procedural fairness was significantly related to the total value created by the final agreement. The researchers conclude, "The wise negotiator, to achieve successful outcomes, may want *to act in procedurally just ways* when dealing with others in order to foster greater acceptance of the agreement and more disclosure of value-creating opportunities."

In yet a third version, independent coders watched videotapes of the two lawyers discussing the quandary of the unfinished pool and tagged the behaviors that could affect the assessment of the process's fairness—interruptions, facilitations, reflective listening, politeness, discourteousness, lying, information revelation, and citation of objective norms such as case law and industry standards. The results showed that the most impactful ways to act procedurally just involved voice (the opportunity to speak and be heard) and courtesy. Signs of trustworthiness were less important, and presumed signs of neutrality (e.g., invoking legal strictures or possible arbitration outcomes) were often counterproductive.

To go back to the metaphor of a Chinese coin: the outer circle, then, is procedural justice, performance, face, courtesy, manners, professionalism, approachability, voice, and reflective listening; the inner square is toughness. Because it is interior, true toughness is not performative: it does not require hairy bruised knuckles, furrowed brows, squinty eyes, flushed cheeks, flying spittle, pointed fingers, expectorated curses, hair-trigger irritability, or demeaning condescension. Sophisticated toughness reflects what the brilliant acting teacher Stella Adler referred to as "the inner force." Adler urged:

> Be strong. Actors need a kind of aggression, a kind of inner force. Don't be only one-sided, sweet, nice, good. Get rid of being average . . . . You are the conductor of the orchestra, not just a player. You cannot be weak inside.

True toughness resides in quieter qualities: understanding ("know exactly what you think and feel at all times"), self-monitoring, goal orientation, strategic sophistication, a willingness to engage, the courage to direct, determination, and persistence. It can be helpful to think of a figure at the center of the inner square who embodies these qualities—it could be a director or conductor, as Adler suggested, or Obst's Great Screenwriter in the Sky–authorized producer, or Picco's commando force of one, or a monarch or emperor, or a steadfast fish-and-chips shop proprietor.

As is true in many other parts of life, sheer doggedness can be an essential part of negotiation toughness. Xi Jinping's father, Xi Zhongxun, a contemporary and devotee of Mao, fell in and out of favor with the Chinese Communist Party several times over his lifetime. During one of his extended detentions, Xi's father "passed the years by walking in circles, he said later—ten thousand laps, and then ten thousand walking backward." The son, because he was the offspring of a disgraced elite, was sent to the countryside during the Cultural Revolution to be "reeducated," and his determination was honed by the effort to survive. Xi says, "At that time, I did all kinds of work—reclaiming wasteland, farming, hoeing, herding, hauling coal, mounding, and carrying manure." Later, it took him eight applications before he was accepted to the Communist Party's Youth League. Xi's rise through the political ranks has been marked by patient persistence: "My approach is to heat a pot with a small, continuous fire, pouring in cold water to keep it from boiling over."

Charlene Barshefsky was the deputy United States trade representative during the Clinton administration, and she led negotiations in the mid-1990s with Japanese ministers over trade barriers and with Chinese officials over intellectual property rights (IPR) and the pirating of music, software, and movies. As an envoy, she endured long flights, jet lag, and interminable bargaining sessions without flagging: Japanese officials "will stay up night after night, and my feeling was, 'If they are going to stay up all night, so will I.'" Barshefsky calls this characteristic "constancy." She says that she "always follows the same fundamental rules: define the long-term goal and the immediate objective; be constant; and do not lose sight of the consequences." Her example shows us that inner toughness is perseverance combined with understanding, self-monitoring, and goal orientation.

Listening reflectively and mindfully, when paired with an inner force, a plan, and sophistication, can be very powerful and can turn an aggressive offer from an opponent into a directive response.

OPEN ON

A conference room in the Trade Ministry Building in Beijing. At least fifteen people sit on the Chinese side of the table led by a male MINISTER. Far fewer sit on the American side, which is helmed by BARSHEFSKY. After hours of bargaining, the room is filled with tension, fatigue, and impatience. The MINISTER leans forward toward his counterpart, a harsh, imperious, threatening look on his face.

                            MINISTER
          It's take it or leave it.

BARSHEFSKY, surprised but not flinching, grimacing, or moving, stays still and is quiet.
She remains quiet.
She stays quiet well past the American norm for silence and is soon beyond the Chinese norm as well.
Half a minute has passed.

                          BARSHEFSKY
          If the choice is take it or leave it, of
          course I'll leave it. But I can't imagine
          that's what you meant. I think what you
          meant is that you'd like me to think over
          your last offer and that we can continue
          tomorrow.

She noticed that one member of the Chinese team relaxed his shoulders after her *fin de non-recevoir* of the ultimatum, and she thought that the next morning would go smoothly, which indeed it did.

Figure 14 has a list of the various qualities that we have discussed in the book thus far and which we can identify with the inner square and outer circle. The importance for us here is the duality and the harmony. *Wài yuán nèi fang* and the coin extend what our earlier data asserted about the two qualities merely coexisting—in fact, they blend so well that the kenning an ancient poet might use to describe the one-step-ahead negotiator is "tough-fair." The outer roundness allows the inner corners to be sharp; the inside edges allow the circumference to be smooth and inviting. Toughness does not turn bitter, since it is surrounded by softness; the roundness is not exploited because of an inner force and strength.

□	○
Toughness	Fairness
Hard	Soft
Sharp	Smooth
Director	Actor
Monitor	Performer
Strategic Sophistication	Innocence
Mind	Heart
Soul	Face
Constancy	Flexibility
Aggression	Courtesy
Absence	Presence
Rectitude	Suavity
Force	Calm
Effort	Ease
No	Yes
Resistance	Accommodation
Reticence	Honesty
Not Caring	Caring
Plan	Improvisation
Goal	Deal

Figure 14

This approach fits with Taoism's fundamental tenet: "The principle of yin-yang is the expression of the relationship that exists between opposing but interpenetrating forces that may complete one another, make each comprehensible, or create the conditions for altering one into the other." The *Tao Te Ching* says that "to weaken something you need to strengthen it first," and "to take something you need to give it first." In the same vein, we can state, "To say yes, you need to say no first; to say no, you need to say yes first." As opposed to the landmark *Getting to Yes* and Jim Camp's refutation *Start with No*, we can say that a more effective version of both is *Start with Yes, Get to No, and Respond with No-Yes (or Yes-No)*. Not really a catchy title, but it captures the need to listen, to be internally tough, and to answer with firmness and with craft.

Barshefsky's negotiation with the Chinese trade ministry in September 1996 provides an excellent illustration. She and her team had identified specific factories in Guangdong province that were churning out bootleg CDs and videotapes, and she had asked the Chinese government to show good faith by having them shuttered. Several manufacturing plants had been closed but, to quote one of that year's biggest-selling and most pirated CDs, the government was doing it with one hand in its pocket.

Wu Yi, the trade minister for China, had battled the American for two years; when she first met Barshefsky, "Wu commanded her to 'sit,' and Barshefsky, startled, promptly obeyed." Now, months later, with more courtesy but asserting just as much obligation, Wu invited her counterpart to meet President Jiang Zemin. This time Barshefsky was the one to astound with her calibrated, hard no-yes: "I would be honored and delighted to meet with President Jiang, but I am afraid that would be impossible." Why had her invitation been refused? wondered Wu. Barshefsky explained, "I cannot meet with President Jiang and then impose sanctions. If all fifteen factories are not closed, I will have no choice but to impose sanctions, and I do not want to put President Jiang, or you, in that embarrassing position." Her gambit and constancy worked: the Chinese government shut down the factories. Barshefsky, a tough-fair negotiator, had triumphed and secured the exact deal she wanted.

SUMMARY

- Toughness without fairness can lead to crass exploitation, is vain, and is needlessly wasteful of goodwill and potentially positive relationships. Fairness without toughness may set the unachievable goal of pure impartiality and is an invitation to those who would exploit you.

- It is a regrettable fact of our world and our wiring, but most of us judge fairness based on our own self-interest. This bias can be redressed only through pragmatism and forceful performance: "It's your job to change other people's minds, to bend them to your way of thinking."

- Focus your performance on procedural justice rather than distributive justice. Avoid obvious intentional inequity and fairness mistakes. Employ reflective and mindful listening. Be courteous, calm, and well-mannered. Communicate "I share your concern."

- Toughness-fairness is the essential kenning of negotiations. It is the round coin with the square center; it is the Chinese phrase *wài yuán nèi fāng* (外圆内方).

- The most effective toughness comprises a number of inner qualities: striving for a goal, constancy, persistence, effort, resistance to pressure, strategic sophistication, willingness to deny the other, knowledge, command, modesty.

- Listen from the empty square in order to direct your counterpart. Choose your negotiation heroes and directors of your inner square wisely. Do not be Zell the Grave Dancer or Comey the Puritan. Rather, be Picco the Man with a Pen, Machiavelli the Conjurer, Goffman the Observer, Duddy the Courageous, or Barshefsky the Constant.

- Start with yes, get to no, and respond with yes-no or no-yes.

ONE STEP AHEAD OF TOUGHNESS II: FEMALE-MALE

(or, Why can't an ambitious businesswoman make a record?)

Lillian McMurry did not foresee the moment of her transformation as she stood in the dusty aisle of a shuttered hardware store in Jackson, Mississippi, in 1949. She and a team of handymen were clearing the tools, fastenings, and gallimaufry off the shelves in order to turn the space into a furniture store. They had come across a box of what were euphemistically called at the time "race records." One of the handymen, T. J. Green, took a vinyl disc out of the box, placed it on the platter of a record player, lifted the tonearm, and set the needle in the groove. The beat, the lyric, the jump, the blues would change Lillian McMurry's life. Her story might also change the way you think about gender and negotiation—the extra challenges women might face and the special abilities they can bring.

McMurry owned a chain of furniture stores in the city with her husband, Willard. It was music that brought the white couple together in the first place when Miss Lillian was twenty-three years old. She was born in the small town of Purvis, where her father was a deputy sheriff. Her family struggled throughout the Great Depression but remained a very devout Baptist family who often choired themselves—Daddy sang bass—to sleep with church hymns. After graduating from high school, Miss Lillian moved to Jackson and was working as an assistant in the governor's office when she inquired after the price of a baby grand piano at State Furniture, Willard's original establishment. Following a visit to her apartment to assess whether the trade-in value of her upright piano was sufficient to make the baby grand affordable, Willard courted her, and they were wed in November 1945.

A few years into their marriage, the couple bought the former hardware store at 309 North Farish Street, on a transition block marking Jackson's racial divide—to the south, all white establishments; to the north, the Blue Light Café, where "Negroes" legally sat at the counter, the Alamo Theater, at which Nat King Cole and Cab Calloway had performed, and a wide variety of other black businesses.

The record on the player was by pioneering R&B singer Wynonie Harris (music magazine *Billboard* only that year had "dropped the use of 'race' and 'sepia' then universally used in referring to these recordings and initiated the term 'rhythm and blues'"). Harris was among the last musicians one would pick to play for a typical pious southern white Baptist lady. His recordings of "Lollipop Mama," "I Want My Fanny Brown," and "Sittin' on It All the Time" were about as far as one could get from "What a Friend We Have in Jesus" and "I Shall Be Whiter than Snow." Green, though, had selected the milder, chart-topping single "All She Wants to Do Is Rock," and besides, as we'll see, Lillian was far from typical. The half-empty store filled with Harris's raspy shout, claps, horns, and a boogie groove as the song began with his plea to halt the rising sun and ticking clocks because:

> *I just got the news that my baby wants to rock!*
> *All she wants to do is rock.*

It was a road-to-Damascus moment for McMurry. She explained, "It was the most unusual, sincere, and solid sound I'd ever heard. I'd never heard a black record before . . . . I'd never heard anything with such rhythm and freedom before." Harris's impossibly catchy song had, in a flash, changed the direction of her life.

On her next furniture-related business trip to New Orleans with Willard, she bought a whole cache of blues, gospel, and country records. She gave the retail space a dual purpose as Furniture Bargains and The Record Mart, with speakers broadcasting music onto the sidewalk of Farish Street and one entire wall displaying records for sale. Soon Lillian added listening booths to the back of the store so potential customers could sample the music before they made a purchase. She created a mail-order business and advertised package deals on the city's top AM radio station, WRBC (Rebel Broadcasting Company), offering "old blues 78s like Tampa Red, Big Boy Crudup, and Washboard Sam" and new blues recordings. As she recalled later, her disdain floating like a vapor on the soft summer air: "I tried to buy time on other stations, but all I got was, 'We don't play black music.' They played 'Jeanie with the Light Brown Hair' from morning to night!"

A businesswoman of ambition and confidence, McMurry saw profitable opportunities in vertical integration. She would not just sell the vinyl discs; she would discover performers, sign them to recording contracts, produce their records, and then market the artists and their music. The listening booths in the back of the store at 309 Farish brought her her first client when the St. Andrews Gospelaires crowded into a booth to practice and harmonize with religious records. Soon thereafter, the six singers of the Southern Sons Quartette also visited The Record Mart, jamming into a booth to rehearse. Lillian said, "By the middle of 1950 I started thinking, 'Why can't I make a record?' Gads, I didn't know what I was getting into." She had recording sessions with both groups at the WRBC studios and issued her first records with royal purple labels featuring a silver trumpet logo. According to its founder, Trumpet Records was named after the horn Gabriel would blast to herald Jesus's second coming.

McMurry next sought to diversify her offerings beyond gospel, scouting the region for black blues artists and white musicians who played what the industry derogatorily called "hillbilly" tunes. Her race made the former search much more difficult than the latter, but through her persistence and honesty she was able to successfully network with the area's black itinerant musicians and suspicious juke joint owners. Traveling through the Delta on one excursion and arriving in the town of Belzoni, she managed to track down the wife of the artist who would be her treasure and her bane, Sonny Boy Williamson II, a harp (harmonica) player of prodigious talent—the harp fit the reverse C of his forefinger and thumb like a baby catfish in the jaws of an alligator.

Similar to warriors, blues players naturally become the subjects of epic tales. One famous origin story was told about Sonny Boy: born Aleck Miller, he had as a child stolen a mule from a neighboring farm, whitewashed the animal as a disguise, been arrested when the rains came and the mule was deblanched, been thrown in jail but without his pants being checked, pulled the harp from his pocket and proceeded to play, and so mesmerized the guard that he walked right out a free man. And then, to avoid recapture, he had given his name to anyone who would ask as "Sonny Boy Williamson," the famous harp player from Chicago.

Sonny Boy signed a recording contract with McMurry in December 1950, and the next month, under her production, he assembled in the studio with some of his favorite sidemen—Elmore James on guitar, Willie Love on piano, Joe Willie Wilkins on guitar, and Jack Daniel's on the whiskey. Along with Joe Dyson on drums, they performed the song that would be Trumpet's first big hit, "Eyesight to the Blind." A few months later, Elmore James would helm the performance of "Dust My Broom," a track that would be Trumpet's biggest-ever sales success.

HER FRIENDS IN THE GARDEN CLUB
HAD NO IDEA

(or, The way a steel magnolia makes her way through a man's world)

Working, literally and figuratively, on the transition block between the two halves of Jackson (and between the past and the future) was never easy for McMurry, and it required a determination and toughness and immunity to sidewise glances. Edward Komara, the former director of the University of Mississippi's Blues Archive, said, "My main impression of her was, to use a southern stereotype, a steel magnolia." He noted "her toughness, which was a combination of a low tolerance for bullshit and a lion-taming instinct." As y'all should know, "steel magnolia" is just Dixie for *wài yuán nèi fang*.

Her steely inner square was manifest in early December 1951 when she booked the local Musicians Union Hall in Jackson for four continuous days of recording sessions. She had assembled all of Trumpet's artists, both black and white, but the sessions were stopped by racist union executives enforcing the Local's "whites only" policy with malice and insult. McMurry had the equipment moved to another nearby hall and the recording continued for hour after hour over three days as she went without sleep. Her daughter, Vitrice, remembers, "My mother bragged about how they would have to hold her up to run the controls. Her friends in the Garden Club had no idea that she did this record thing."

Her toughness was also apparent in the direction and feedback she gave her artists. She neither pulled punches nor discriminated by race or musical style. No bullshit for her:

- About the scores of less-talented auditioners who would make their way to The Record Mart: "We listened to some of the worst crap you ever heard."
- Sonny Boy Williamson II liked to carry a gun and a knife on his person, and Miss Lillian always made him check his weaponry at the studio door. One day Sonny dropped a g*****m or a f**k while she was at the control board, and she scolded him and told him to get out. When Sonny didn't start moving, Miss Lillian, as the legend goes, "pulled his own pistol on him, marched him outside and told him to leave."
- To one of her country singers, Lucky Joe Almond, she suggested, "Why don't you soften up on your voice? . . . [Like] your girl was standing right beside you, instead of shouting at her across the cow pasture."
- She wrote one of her gospel singers, "The audition stinks . . . . With the Lord's help, let's please don't go below the feel and quality of the song that you did your best on."

McMurry was very much a woman in a man's world, and thus required a sophisticated form of toughness. And her industry was immensely challenging: in both the R&B and country markets, she ran one of hundreds of independent labels caught in the churn of disruptive competition while the six major record companies, for a time, looked the other way. Artists were poached, agreements were ignored, radio stations were bribed, and vendors were leveraged—many contracts weren't worth the paper they were written on. McMurry knew, as did Lynda Obst, Yuja Wang, Charlene Barshefsky, and all women, that she was potentially operating at a disadvantage in many of these negotiations because her opponents saw her as the fairer sex, the weaker sex, as "Jeanie with the Light Brown Hair."

A SMALL TWIST OF THE KNOB AWAY FROM SQUEALING FEEDBACK

(or, What science reveals about negotiating-while-female)

A lot has changed in the seventy years since McMurry was fighting to make her way in a ruthless industry, but the common sense that negotiating-while-female is unpropitious has not. This issue has been a very active area of research for social scientists in recent times, and the findings we will review in this section reveal that the modern quandary may be both more subtle and more insidious than the one Miss Lillian knew.

For the employees of thirty-two large beauty salons in present-day Beijing, wages depend on how good their clients' hair, nails, and skin look after treatment, and on their gender. Half of the one thousand employees in the salons were men, and both sexes had two components in their total compensation. First, they were paid 21 percent of the fee for every salon service—cut, color, nails, massage, and so on—that they personally delivered to a client. Second, if the customer also bought a prepaid card for future treatments, the team of beauticians who provided all the client's services on the visit shared a 9 percent commission on the total value she placed on the card. Dividing the commission was negotiated by the team members, and that's where things got difficult for some of the female stylists.

There were 67,000 card transactions that involved exactly two employees and for which the average commission was a little over 100 Chinese yuan, or about $16. It turned out that, as any well-run business hopes, there was a positive correlation between the two forms of compensation: employees who delivered more treatments, attended to more clients, and upsold services also tended to receive a greater share of the card commissions. The correlation was noisy, however, and there were two hundred stylists who were both treatment-providing stars and relative losers in team bargaining (net contributors), and two hundred who did great in bargaining while being in the bottom half in customer revenue generation (net extractors). It would not have surprised Lillian McMurry, nor should it surprise us now, to learn that 75 percent of the net contributors were women and only 15 percent of the net extractors were.

When the pair of beauticians were both women, most of the time (three-fifths of the cases) they basically just split the 9 percent card bonus down the middle. However, when the pair consisted of one female stylist and one male, then 60 percent of the women received less than one-third of the commission, and only 18 percent negotiated for around half of the prize. Unfair money-grabbers were male, sacrificial givers tended to be female.

These asymmetric cuts don't happen only in the salon. One meta-analysis examining more than one hundred bargaining experiments found that on average, but by no means uniformly, men enjoyed better economic outcomes than women did. Lynda Obst observed a similarly skewed gender split among Hollywood producers: "Men play to win. We like to tie."

Many of the female beauticians, some female movie executives, and a smaller proportion of male bargainers might be satisfied with tying or even losing if it means that a relationship has been preserved or strengthened. Psychologists Kathleen O'Connor and Josh Arnold demonstrated that a negotiator's need to belong—"a desire to form and maintain positive and continuous relationships with other people"—is associated with higher levels of stress and lower ambitions heading into a negotiation, and subsequently with misperceptions of the counterpart's priorities and interests as well as with poorer economic outcomes.

Another psychological measure grounded in the willingness to sacrifice is called unmitigated communion (UC), "an orientation involving high concern for and anxiety about one's relationships coupled with low self-concern." It is measured in the laboratory by a subject's degree of agreement with statements such as "For me to be happy, I need others to be happy." UC is associated with the personality traits of agreeableness and neuroticism and is more prevalent in women. One negotiation study found that the significant difference between the average value claimed by men and women disappeared once each bargainer's degree of UC was included in the analysis.

McMurry did not have this particular problem, since her sense of communion with her musicians was very strong yet always mitigated— she tamed the lions, not the other way around. But as the owner and principal dealmaker of a small music business, she knew that the reverb of the female stereotype and the potential for squealing feedback were always just a twist of the knob away. The general business stereotype is that "effective managers are highly correlated with masculine characteristics such as independence, assertiveness, self-reliance, and power and inconsistent with feminine characteristics such as communality, caring, and helpfulness." The bluesy crossroads for many women, then, is to be seen either as ineffective but nice executives or as competent b***es (we won't use that word around Miss Lillian). With respect to negotiation, being assertive, being a good problem-solver, having a high regard for one's own interests, and being knowledgeable are masculine traits, while being emotional, being insightful, having good listening skills, and being verbally expressive are feminine characteristics. The negotiation stereotype, which reflects a shallow version of the truth that, after these pages, we all know is much more complex, is that the square is masculine and the circle is feminine and they exist in segregated domains.

Sadly, as Hannah Riley Bowles observes in a review of the science of gender in negotiation, early researchers may have been just as beholden to the stereotype as their subjects were, leading to a variety of confirmation biases that yielded contradictory results and confusion. As the science has advanced, it has become very clear that the effects of gender are dependent on the specifics of the negotiation situation. Yes, men have an advantage when the bargaining is over motorcycle headlamps or hiring an alligator wrestler, but women do better when the deal is over jewelry beads or hiring a babysitter. In the terroir of the Champagne region of France, where the work is hard, hands get dirty, and the milieu is rough and rustic, female grape farmers nonetheless negotiate better prices with the champagne houses than their male counterparts because the latter refuse to share information and are reluctant to use their leverage or to make counteroffers to their buyers. Male grape growers don't ask.

The elements of the situation that tend to cause women's negotiation performance to lag fall under two headings, according to Bowles: ambiguity and gender triggers. When the stage is filled with fog, the lights are dim, and the script has been thrown out, the performance of male negotiators often suffers less than that of female negotiators. Uncertainty about the list of issues, alternatives, comparables, targets, and terms that should be included in an agreement, as well as ambiguity with respect to the appropriate norms in the bargaining situation, affects women more frequently and more deeply. Bowles, Linda Babcock, and Kathleen McGinn found that the difference in starting salaries for male and female MBAs was 3 percent in favor of men for low-ambiguity industries such as consulting and investment banking, where the salary bands are well publicized and talked about, and 10 percent in high-ambiguity sectors such as the entertainment/media industry of McMurry and Obst.

The same researchers also conducted a negotiation experiment in which male and female participants were given only their own reservation points in one condition, and in the other they were given reservation points as well as a specific target by their hypothetical bosses. Men and women performed identically when given the outside target, but gender had a big effect in the more ambiguous setting. The female grape farmers in the Champagne region emphasize thorough preparation before their deals—as all negotiators, but especially women, should do—in order to gain more certainty and more leverage. Through their networking and sharing of price information, the female growers have transformed what remains a high-ambiguity industry for the male farmers into one of low ambiguity, and have provided themselves with specific comparables and reliable targets.

Bowles's second category, gender triggers, includes a variety of roles, props, sets, lights, and scenes that genderize the situation for the actors and are the social equivalent of having to check the box "female" or the box "male." Is this gathering a "negotiation" or a "meeting"? Is the spotlight shining on you as the only woman in the room? Are you in the salon, the bleachers, the kitchen, the cigar room, the tampon factory, the office, the Construct, the vineyard, the darkened throne room, Carnegie Hall, or the recording studio on Farish Street? Are you a man playing a "female" role (nurse, cook), or are you a woman playing a "male" role (CEO, music or movie producer, diplomatic envoy)?

One of the most studied and verified triggers is own-advocacy versus other-advocacy—women tend to feel no qualms and to face no backlash when they negotiate on behalf of others, a calm that is less likely to prevail when they negotiate for themselves. Law professor Andrea Schneider has called this the "mother bear allowance," and she has shown that for female and male "lawyers, where assertiveness on behalf of clients is socially expected and rewarded, there is no difference in perceived levels of negotiation effectiveness."

One experiment testing both men and women in other-advocacy versus self-advocacy found no statistically significant differences in any of their reservation points, targets, or intended first offers. The setting of the simulation was a salary negotiation for a first job after college, and the plot involved a preparation period and then a surprise offer of $40,000 from the employer. This low offer had the expected anchoring effect of pulling the subject's first counteroffer below their intended level—and, in the case of women negotiating their own salary, far below. The average counteroffer for self-advocating women was only $42,000, compared to $48,400 for self-advocating men and over $49,100 for both female and male agents. Women negotiating for themselves gave up on their goals right away. The timidity of their counteroffer was completely explained by anticipated backlash—that is, the lower dollar level at which an own-negotiating woman felt the employer would think she was a pushy person or would punish her for being too demanding. These solo women felt that squealing feedback was only a tiny twist of the knob away from the employer's $40,000 offer, on average at $43,250, compared to solo men who predicted no potentially bad reverbs until $50,800.

YOU COULD SOFTEN UP ON YOUR VOICE
(or, Solutions to the challenges of negotiating-while-female)

There are a number of moves women (and men) who struggle with self-advocacy and who anticipate backlash can make. First, if you don't have a real one, invent a "client" and make yourself an "agent." One study found that imagining during the planning phase that a negotiation was for a friend eliminated all traces of female underperformance in deal outcomes. The imaginary client might be your significant other, your kids, your team, other women in your organization, women as a whole, your inner self, or your future self ("I'll thank me later"). You can place that client at the center of the inner square to create and direct the necessary hardness and assertiveness.

This framing can trigger the mother bear allowance, a toughness pretext that McMurry certainly capitalized on. Bobo "Slim" Thomas wandered off one day in 1951 with one of Trumpet's new guitars and an amp, and he was stuck behind bars in the Jackson jail for many months before McMurry heard word. She showed up at Slim's much delayed initial hearing ripping angry and minced no words with the white judge: "Justice works mighty slow. If the man's been in jail eight months, he oughta be out. I think he's served his time."

Second, Bowles and Babcock propose that "relational accounts" can reduce the stereotype threat for female negotiators. Instead of leveraging their BATNAs with the line "I've gotten another offer," which challenges the expectation that they are the organization's dedicated handmaids, female subjects in Bowles and Babcock's experiments were more successful in asking for a raise when they invoked the wisdom of someone with more status and power ("My team leader told me to ask about my compensation") and when they acknowledged a job-related reason for violating the norm ("I don't know how typical it is for people at my level to negotiate, but I'm hopeful you'll see my skill at negotiating as something important that I bring to the job").

No doubt, it isn't fair that a woman has to be extra "circular" on the outside, and Bowles and Babcock worry about the way that pragmatism ignores the ideal of gender equality. It doesn't seem fair that a person with a full, strong calling should have to soften up on their voice. However, Bowles and Babcock concede that for the individual woman in the here and now, it's either use the stereotype or the stereotype uses you, and they believe that the bias barrier crumbles for good only when enough women have surmounted it by whatever means, be it the mother bear allowance, an imaginary client, or a relational account.

I ACTED AS A LADY, AS A BUSINESSPERSON

(or, Why women might have an advantage in becoming sophisticated negotiators)

This is, in many ways, a book written for female readers, and readers of any gender who struggle with the imaginary trade-off between toughness and fairness. It is meant to turn negotiation into a low-ambiguity activity and to unmask the negotiating stereotype. The fact is, as Chapter 8 and all the preceding chapters have labored to show, you don't want to negotiate as a "male," either. The masculine side of the stereotype, as epitomized by Sam Zell, is definitely not the most effective negotiation style. The goal is *wài yuán nèi fang* or steel magnolia. Arguably, the sophisticated ideal of tough-fair is more achievable for women, who typically have fewer performative bad habits to break and who, as Lynda Obst knows, are more trained in adapting to and moving their counterparts: "Women have flexibility and agility . . . . [W]omen's remarkable ability to end-run oppression and outthink and outmaneuver stronger adversaries with subtle moves has been the stuff of lore." The one-step-ahead negotiator has to reform and reconceptualize "male" characteristics more than "female" traits because toughness has to be changed from exterior to interior.

Evidence for this: When preconceptions are flipped in the laboratory, women excel. One bold experiment demonstrated as convincingly as the female Champagne grape farmers did, as Charlene Barshefsky did, and as Lillian McMurry did that the negotiating stereotype can be flung aside. Before conducting a very "diagnostic" distributive negotiation, half of the participants in this investigation were told that "highly skilled negotiators" share the neutral traits of being well prepared, having a sense of humor, and being open-minded. The other half were primed with the flipped stereotype, namely, that "highly skilled negotiators" share the "female" characteristics of having "a keen ability to express their thoughts verbally," "good listening skills," and "insight into the other negotiator's feelings." Women set much higher goals for themselves in the female-positive condition and captured more value, seizing 15 percent more of the total bargaining zone than in the gender-neutral condition. A second experiment changed the positive to the negative and found both that women outperformed men when subjects were told that certain negotiating traits that read "male" have been found to lead to worse performance and that women underperformed when "female" traits were labeled ineffective.

Although she lived in a pre-feminist era, had a traditional view of the bonds of marriage, was surrounded by the strictures of the Jim Crow South, and was immersed in the beliefs and norms of the Baptist church, there is no evidence that her career caused McMurry to feel that she was living a double life. Being comfortable living on transition blocks was just what Miss Lillian did, whether it was on 309 Farish between the white and black business districts or at Trumpet Records between the sacred and the profane, between R&B and country, and between woman and record mogul. She explained—bluntly, of course—how it was all unified and blended for her:

> I think the people in the record business thought it was all right, but there were some few adverse reactions of the white people because they couldn't understand why a white lady would be recording black music. Frankly, at that time, few people had any idea what making records entailed . . . . Because we recorded some black blues and spirituals, I was treated rather ugly sometimes by certain people . . . , and I figured that those rednecks didn't count anyhow! I acted as a lady, as a businessperson, and that's the way it should have been.

It is hard to know what the original sources of McMurry's unified confidence, sense of self, and toughness were, but research on identity integration has revealed paths that other women can take to achieve the same fusion. One experiment asked female bargainers to evaluate a variety of self-assessments such as "I do not feel any tension between my goals as a woman and my goals as a professional." In a subsequent salary negotiation, those women with the integrated mindset bargained for compensation that was significantly higher than those who saw their roles as a woman and a professional as segregated and at odds. These modern-day, self-integrated Ms. Lillians were perceived by outside observers who evaluated videos of their negotiations as both dominant and warm, and the two factors had counterbalancing effects, so there was no relationship backlash from their tougher performances. Lastly, all of these effects happened because the women whose identities were more integrated committed themselves not just to a goal of being assertive or a goal of being friendly and smiley but to the sophisticated target of being *both dominant and warm together.*

These same researchers demonstrated that role integration can be enhanced through a simple manipulation. During planning, engage in a positive recall exercise: give a detailed description and a specific example of how your "female and business professional sides are complementary." It is not too big a leap to suggest that the recall exercise could also involve the Construct and the multiverse in which the imaginary self is actually Barshefsky, Wang, McMurry, Oprah, Judge Judy, Orit Gadiesh (the current chairman of Bain & Company), or some other archetype of identity integration. This is why negotiation case studies have very practical value, and why the words of another exemplar, Lynda Obst, ring true:

> We must acquire the skills necessary to become a tough negotiator and an able adversary, a subtle tactician and a worthy teammate, without scaring the bejesus out of our superiors . . . . This is not masculine behavior we are learning; it is professional behavior.

SHE DEMANDED HONESTY AND GOT HONESTY

(or, The evidence that women are more ethical negotiators than men)

It was a flatted-fifth year for Trumpet Records. The business had been struggling with cash flow issues for some time. In May 1953, McMurry had to write to Lucky Joe Almond, the singer yodeling across the cow pasture, to deny his request for an advance to buy some new cowboy duds, and she told him that if Trumpet's new releases didn't hit the charts, then "I may be asking you for some corn bread to go with some of this Mississippi swamp water."

The industry was in the midst of an R&B gold rush, as hundreds of independent labels staked claims to geographies, started digging through artists' repertoires, and panned for hit songs. Lots of the music prospectors refused to honor contracts and would siphon off from another label any artist who showed promise. Trumpet's promotion costs were rising, distributors would order boxes of vinyl and then go bankrupt before remitting a check, an investment in transforming 309 Farish into a state-of-the-art studio ran into the thousands of dollars, and numerous Trumpet invoices were overlooked or "misplaced" by sketchy customers. McMurry never discovered the massive gold record that would break the pan scales in the bank and ease all her financial worries.

She was a businesswoman of immense integrity, and despite her company's money woes, she never shorted her artists. One legal study of all of Trumpet's contracts concludes that they "show a commitment to fairness and a level of scrupulousness and honesty not often seen in the industry." Nobody understood her fundamental goodness better than Sonny Boy Williamson II. In a letter to McMurry that revealed his inattention during his grade school spelling classes, it's clear that Sonny trusted his wife, Mattie, and Miss Lillian to take care of his business fairly: "I am Wrinight you to let you Here from me I wount you to drew up a contract Bewine you and me and Mattie that Mattie will take car of all of m Baszy for me you chack with on all of my Record."

Sonny's instincts were correct both specifically, as far as Mattie and Lillian were concerned (they would take care of Sonny's "baszy," or business, till the end of his life and beyond), and more generally, as far as most women are concerned. The science is clear that females tend to be much more ethical negotiators than males. A major source of this difference is the greater degree to which women include "being moral" as part of their identities. This internalized moral identity is measured by the strength of agreement with statements such as "It would make me feel good to be a person who is caring, compassionate, fair, friendly, generous, helpful, hardworking, honest, and kind."

One study that statistically analyzed tens of research reports involving thousands of subjects concluded that "there is roughly a 66% probability that a randomly chosen woman will have a stronger moral identity than a randomly chosen man." If a woman is selling you a used Dodge Neon with occasional transmission problems, she is less likely than a male seller to lie to your face, to wait until you ask precisely to tell you about the problems, to invoke caveat emptor, or to think it's your own damn fault if you buy a lemon. The study found that even very small gains cause 25 percent of men to dissemble and cheat, but larger rewards are required to prompt a similar proportion of women to lie.

Money would eventually get so tight in Trumpet's fifth year that Miss Lillian was tragically forced into bartering away Sonny Boy's contract; it would end up with Leonard Chess of Chicago's Chess Records, one of the largest independent labels, with stars like Chuck Berry and Bo Diddley.

A few months after losing Sonny, McMurry made one final push to save her business. She targeted the Texas market by vigorously promoting new recordings by her best country artists, sending the musicians out to honky-tonk clubs across the Lone Star State with boxes of vinyl. In a very male negotiating move, Leonard Chess threatened to pull his records from any of his Texas distributors who accepted new releases from Trumpet. As a result, the promotional blitz was a bust, the business folded, and her music career ended.

A second stereotype of the southern woman, in addition to "steel magnolia," is "churchgoing lady"—someone whose identity is inextricably linked to the Bible, the Ten Commandments, charity, good deeds, and kind thoughts. McMurry may have spent much more time during these years in nightclubs and juke joints than in the pews, but she remained a Baptist and had a very strong moral compass. Edward Komara remembers:

> She fought hard and successfully for the artists whose financial estates she assisted. She continued until her death to assist her Trumpet recording artists, scoundrels though they sometimes were. She demanded honesty and got honesty and delivery of contracted promises from them during the recording sessions, and in return she made sure they received what was due.

McMurry represents the formula for how the sophisticated negotiator can afford to be ethical—you have to demand honesty in return, and you have to ensure that you're getting it from the other side. Once again, toughness is required. It was her high expectations, candidness, direction, inner force, and uncompromising nature that allowed her to trust occasional scoundrels and honor the tough-fair contracts she signed with them. Her integrity depended fundamentally on her low tolerance for bullshit and her lion-taming instinct.

Lillian McMurry was an improbable person, seemingly untroubled by all the contradictions and crossroads in her life. People knew that she "was incredibly cagey, and could deal with copyright lawyers on a level

of legal think so that she was able to win most of the suits she brought."
We can ascribe the ultimate failure of Trumpet not to her shortcomings
but instead to the luck needed to unearth hit pop songs: Elvis might have
had much the same career had he somehow stepped to the microphone
at 309 Farish under her watchful gaze and with her skillful fingers at the
control knobs.

As painful as it was to shut her business, she continued to track and
account for the royalties of her musicians and to enforce Trumpet's copy-
rights over the next decades as rock and roll and R&B music thrived.
Nothing wounded her more than a rumor that started as a whisper in
the studios, was seemingly confirmed by music journalists in the 1960s
and 1970s, and then was repeated as an accepted fact for years until just
before her death in 1999: the gossip was that she had recorded Elmore
James's "Dust My Broom" without his knowledge and consent by flipping
the switch on a tape machine during one of his rehearsals. This was the
kind of low-down dirty trick that she assiduously avoided.

Blues researchers Gayle Dean Wardlow and Edward Komara gathered
the evidence to disprove the rumor once and for all in the book *Chasin' That Devil Music*. The authors found the original paperwork that had
concluded McMurry and James's negotiation—a signed recording contract and a check for $35 as an advance on royalties for "Dust My Broom."
Also, they transcribed a phone call Elmore made to Miss Lillian in 1955
after he had recorded "Dust My Blues" for another label:

JAMES

```
It is the same music.
```

MCMURRY

```
Well, that's been copyrighted, you know,
ever since 1951, Elmo. You knew . . . you
remember when I copyrighted the thing?
```

JAMES

```
Sure do, right there in the store when the
man wrote it.
```

```
                    MCMURRY
        Um-hum. That's what I call high-powered
        stealing. Just stealing.
```

There are ten seconds of stunned silence on the line.

```
                     JAMES
        [Recovering, brightly] What is Sonny Boy
        doing now?
```

Unlike centuries ago, it is no longer the age of heroes. One wanders into the story of people as legendary as Sonny Boy Williamson II and as inspiring as Lillian McMurry on tiptoe with nerves attuned, deathly afraid of the must-be-there land mines of race, gender, class, exploitation, disrespect, and dishonor. One hears about the rumor that McMurry secretly recorded Elmore James and says, "Oh, okay, there it is." But then it is not true. Her story, somehow, can remain human and inspirational. She could form a special pairing with Sonny Boy because she had the music in her feet and her soul, she was authentic, she was a lady and a businessperson, she was tough-fair, she was honest and demanded honesty from others, she combined "masculine" dominance and "feminine" warmth, she danced not on graves but in juke joints, she didn't tolerate bullshit, she had the inner force to confront and tame and direct, and she had a touch of genius also.

Near the peak of Trumpet Records' success, when The Record Mart's listening booths were occupied with customers and wannabe singers and when the discs with the violaceous label and silver trumpet were selling all across the South, Sonny Boy wrote a song in Miss Lillian's honor. The song was titled "309" after the address of the store on Farish Street. The song began as follows:

If you ever come to Jackson, stop at 309.

Sonny Boy went on to assure the listener that Miss Lillian practically lived at the studio, but if they preferred, they could reach her "most anytime" at several Jackson phone numbers, concluding:

Because she mine and I love her, and she always easy to find.

Sonny Boy wrote and recorded "309" maybe with the hope that its subject would be touched and possibly give him his gun back, and certainly with the hope that some club owners would call the phone numbers, which were her actual home and business numbers. The song, nonetheless, was never waxed and issued under the imprimatur of the royal purple Trumpet label, undoubtedly because Miss Lillian was convinced—and probably rightly so—that it was a lousy, sentimental record, near to "some of the worst crap you ever heard."

SUMMARY

- On average, but by no means uniformly, male negotiators obtain better economic outcomes than female negotiators do. The specifics of the bargaining situation have a significant impact on this gap: women's performance lags mainly when the situation is ambiguous or includes the shadowy or well-lit presence of gender triggers.
- Accordingly, preparation, knowledge, and goal-setting that reduce ambiguity are even more important for women negotiators.
- Women who are lawyers or agents receive the mother bear allowance: latitude to be tough and effective without triggering stereotype backlash. So women can find or create a "client"—your friend, your family member, your team, your inner self, or your future self—and play the role of "agent."
- Men can employ aggressive bargaining tactics unapologetically, whereas women often require a relational account ("this book advised me to ask") to soften and round out the power move.
- Women, if anything, have an easier path to achieve outside round, inside square (steel magnolia) than men do, both because they are usually denied the traits of external toughness and because they tend to be more adept at complex social maneuvering. So I tell you now, before your next deal, truthfully and based on mounds of evidence, that highly skilled negotiators have "a keen ability to express their thoughts verbally," "good listening skills," and "insight into the other negotiator's feelings."
- Lillian McMurry benefited from an identity integrated between lady and businessperson. Commit to the goal of being dominant and warm together, of being tough and fair together.

- All else being equal, there is a two-thirds probability that a randomly chosen woman will have a stronger moral identity than a randomly chosen man. The one-step-ahead negotiator, of course, uses clues from the counterpart to adjust from this base rate to a more accurate prediction.

ONE STEP AHEAD OF
FACES AND EMOTIONS

WE CAN'T ADMIT THAT IT'S A MUNDANE FACT

(or, Having the courage to doubt what we know to be true)

The worst day of Erving Goffman's life had to have been April 27, 1964. That morning the police came to the Berkeley campus to inform him that his wife, Angelica Schuyler (Sky) Choate Goffman, had died.

I could tell you that with this news his face crumpled, his eyes shed copious tears, and his mouth twisted into an anguished grimace, and you would not be surprised. In fact, you may believe that grief, like all emotions, is propelled by the emotional circuits of the brain out onto the face. You might consider grief to be an extreme form of sadness, one of the six basic emotions along with happiness, surprise, anger, disgust, and fear, each of which, once surfaced, can be easily recognized by those who see our facial expression. You might have read the psychological research that shows the universality of the six basic emotions—how all people from all cultures can identify them accurately when shown photographs of people's countenances as they experienced the emotion.

This conception of emotions has direct implications for the negotiator: refine your face-reading skills to an expert level, and train yourself to be impassive and expressionless so as to thwart your counterpart. But the data from Chapter 6 revealing that negotiators perceived as more emotional were more effective should give you pause. Moreover, on that terrible day in April, according to the memories of the people who saw him, Goffman's face and manner were seemingly unchanged. So one of two things has to be true: either he was completely insensitive or we misunderstand faces and emotions more generally.

At this point, deep into the book, you should foresee the answer: our commonsense view of emotions—as involuntary, universal outpourings, diagnosable through a glance at our face—is mistaken. This answer will make the pages ahead quite challenging because the intuitive basic theory of emotions is something that we *deeply feel* to be true. *Of course,* we think, *anger, once triggered, bubbles up from the inside and boils over to the outside.* Yet we will see that the methodology of having people evaluate still images has misled scientists from Charles Darwin to Paul Ekman; that the evidence for emotions being universal upwellings is quite thin when examined carefully; that, accordingly, we should consider emotions as being cultural concepts that we are taught, and as signals in what Goffman called an expression game; and that, in the end, the less perceptive players of the negotiation expression game rely on reading faces when they really ought to cognitively step into the other's shoes, read their bodies, or examine their words.

As her maiden name suggests, Sky Goffman was to the manor born. The Choates were the kind of family who could taste the sea salt of the founding of the American republic on their lips and wipe the gunpowder residue from their fingers on their servant-mended clothing. In the 1790s, many "spruce young men paddled across the creek from Ipswich town" on "courting expeditions," for there "were at that time no less than sixteen marriageable young ladies on the Island by the name of Choate, 'all exceeding fair.'"

Erving wooed Sky when she arrived as a fellow graduate student in the Social Sciences Division at the University of Chicago a year after Goffman had enrolled. Sky was certainly "exceeding fair" and, as one colleague of the couple put it, "she was smart. Hell, she was very smart!"

She received her master's degree in December 1950 based on a dissertation titled "The Personality Trends of Upperclass Women." The subjects of her study were the 1 percent, "upper-upper-class women," and her method was to record the reactions of these women to the Thematic

Apperception Test (TAT), a series of cards depicting ambiguous social scenes, like stills from an ordinarily warped dream, that were in heavy use as a social-psychological instrument in that era. One of the cards, 3GF, depicts a woman standing with one hand on an open door and the other covering her face, her head angled down. When shown the card, one of Sky's subjects had this reaction: the girl with her "hand over her face, has definitely lost something, whether it's a husband, or a lover, or even a child but she's definitely miserable and doesn't want to face reality . . . . [S]he's been disappointed . . . and she doesn't want to face the truth."

Erving and Sky were married in July 1952. A year later, Erving secured a research job at the National Institute of Mental Health in Washington, DC. We do not know the details of the couple's negotiation, only their final agreement: although Sky had not completed her own graduate work, she and their newborn son accompanied Goffman east. Mother and son trailed in the father's wake again when Erving was offered a faculty position at the University of California in 1958.

It was in the hills of Berkeley, within the confines of a beautiful house overlooking the waters of San Francisco Bay, that Sky's behavior began to show significant variance from the norm. Acquaintances from the survey research center where she worked believed she suffered from bipolar disorder. Had her colleagues taken the TAT and been shown card 3GF, they might have replied, "Oh my goodness, it's Sky."

Trips to the casinos in Tahoe, Reno, and Las Vegas would provide an occasional diversion for the couple. Paradoxically, Erving was a poor poker player, both nervous and a bad bluffer, and he was a money-losing chump in the Berkeley faculty game. One professor who raked in Goffman's chips said, "I used to joke that if he were dealt as much as a pair of deuces his hands would begin to tremble and his face would begin to flush." It made sense, then, that Erving and Sky would head to the blackjack tables. Their son, Tom, recalled that his mother was the much better player: "Both my parents were card counters. EG [his father] used a quarter on the felt to measure how many face cards had been dealt. My mother just remembered every card." After one weekend casino visit, Sky showed up at the survey center driving a bright red Jaguar XKE convertible roadster purchased, she claimed, from their blackjack winnings.

One associate recalled that Sky "went into some kind of psychological tailspin after the assassination of John Kennedy in November of 1963." Erving, as privacy-seeking, prying-eye-avoiding a person as ever was, was admitting openly to deep worry about Sky. A colleague said that Goffman "had become increasingly concerned that she was suicidal and he called her psychiatrist with his concerns, and the psychiatrist basically blew him off, 'No, no, no. She is not suicidal. Don't worry about it.'"

Sometime in the early morning hours of April 27, Sky drove her red Jaguar to the middle of the Richmond–San Rafael Bridge, which spans the northern arm of the Bay. She put notes—one rumored to be "Jesus Christ, Erving, I am sorry about this"—and instructions to contact Goffman on the seat, left the motor running, and jumped off the bridge into the waters below.

There's no easy transition from this tragedy, so let's turn to Wisława Szymborska, the Polish poet and winner of the 1996 Nobel Prize in Literature, a few of whose lines serve as the epigraph for this book. She was surely the equal of Machiavelli and Goffman as a perceptive observer of the human condition, but she did so with undeniable warmth and love. If both of these men would sneak in and stand in the corner coldly and scientifically taking notes as they watched us snore, Szymborska would slip in to watch us sleep and then smooth the hair off our foreheads. The poet sees not only the sleeping but also the dreaming that causes us to laugh, to cry, to despond, to twitch, to lust, to anger, to worry, and so on.

Her poem "Everyone Sometime" begins with the observation that every single person has experienced the death of a close friend or relative. And even so,

> We can't admit that it's a mundane fact,
> subsumed in the course of events

As the poet could, Goffman could also admit that it's a mundane fact. One friend remembers, "When his father died in Los Angeles, Erving flew in, I think from Chicago. We were all sitting in the living room . . . . He came in at an entry platform, looked at the room full of people and announced, 'I see everyone is observing the rituals of mourning.'"

The mundane fact of this tragedy, a mundanity that no one understood better than Goffman, was that people would blame him for Sky's death: they would cite his egocentricity, his ambition, his manner, his Jewish heritage, his distrust of psychiatry. They would fabricate a story that when the police came to campus they found him lecturing at the front of a classroom, and that after he refused their request to step outside so that they could speak in private, they told him, "Professor Goffman, your wife just committed suicide," and that he "then spent the rest of his class talking about how one gives that kind of message." They would remember Sky's face and say that the signs were all there—it was as obvious as card 3GF that she was going to kill herself. They would remark, "Who wouldn't kill herself, after living with that bastard?" They would watch him to see how he honored the rituals of mourning. They would peer at him and ask, "Is that the face of a man who grieves?"

SUPPLYING US WITH PREWORN FACES

(or, Darwin investigated whether evolution programmed our faces to display emotions)

Charles Darwin knew what grief looked like. The pursuit both of the implications of natural selection and of his own predilections led him to write a book on the continuity of feelings among humans and beasts, *The Expression of Emotions in Man and Animals* (1872). Darwin intended *Expression* to also be an empirical investigation of the universality of all emotions among the races of man, and the physical purposefulness of the muscular movements, both large and small, that emotions instigated. *Expression*'s broad conclusions about emotions have anchored subsequent research in the field into our day.

Grief, for Darwin, causes the face to fall: the skin drops its color, "the eyelids droop," "the lips, cheeks, and lower jaw all sink downwards from their own weight," and the corners of the mouth sag as though they've been hooked by gravity. Most importantly, what Darwin called the "grief-muscles" involuntarily bring the inner ends of the eyebrows upward together, changing their overall form to an oblique slant over the eyes and creating a unique set of furrows plowing across the center of the forehead. Evolutionarily—and therefore, according to his theory, muscularly—grief is the expression of dammed tears and suppressed screams.

Darwin ends his chapter on grief with a remembrance of the time that he was alone in a railway carriage sitting opposite a placid old lady. He put his face-reading skills to work and seemed to notice a very slight depression of the corners of her mouth. As he was dismissing the sign to himself and thinking how easily he could be deceived by random facial expressions, the woman started crying profusely and her face lengthened. Darwin, as though reading card 3GF, concluded, "There could now be no doubt that some painful recollection, perhaps that of a long-lost child, was passing through her mind." The counterfact that she was trapped in a train compartment and being creepily stared at by The Victorian Scientist of To-Day (Figure 15) did not occur to Darwin at the time. This oversight is unexpected, since he was aware of how his face could look to the eye, both human and camera: "If I really have as bad an expression, as my photograph gives me, how I can have one single friend is surprising."

Another of his unintentionally comical set pieces is analyzed by Tiffany Watt Smith in her brilliant book *On Flinching*. When he got to be a man of a certain age, maybe of the same tenure as the railway carriage

Figure 15. Source: Wellcome Collection

lady, Darwin decided to perform a self-experiment in the reptile house of the zoo in London's Regent's Park. He reports,

> I put my face close to the thick glass-plate in front of a puff-adder in the Zoological Gardens, with the firm determination of not starting back if the snake struck at me; but, as soon as the blow was struck, my resolution went for nothing, and I jumped a yard or two backwards with astonishing rapidity.

Fear, like grief, like joy, and like the other emotions, is fueled, Darwin thought, by a similar irresistible nerve force that takes direct action on the body.

Watt Smith writes that Darwin's flinch, as well as the winces, startles, and recoils of other Victorian people, revealed to him that the emotional body is "a disobedient bundle of vestiges, gesturing . . . to habits and behaviours accumulated by other people, other animals, at other times and in other places." The emotions and their facial and bodily expressions are hand-me-downs from our predecessors. Darwin would likely agree with Szymborska's thought that Mother Nature is worn down from creating billions of visages,

> *and so repeats earlier ideas*
> *by supplying us*
> *with preworn faces.*

Darwin used two methods to study our preworn faces in *Expression.* First, he issued a survey letter to foreign-traveling observers, from whom he received thirty-six responses; second, he presented a series of photographs of emotional expressions to more than twenty educated subjects for them to label and categorize. Both approaches were quasi-scientific at best and suffered from serious flaws.

Because expressions are subtle and short-lived, Darwin's book, Watt Smith writes, is as much "about the problems of observing emotion as it is about the emotions themselves." She notes, "Unlike butterflies, smiles and sneers could not be captured and pinned to a board." Darwin's solution was to capture a non-fleeting, artificial version of the expression in a photograph. Due to the long exposure time of cameras of his era and his desire to have interpretable representations, many of the photographs

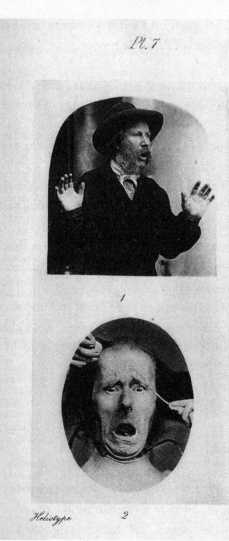

Figure 16. Source: Wellcome Collection

Darwin selected featured working actors and theatrical, flamboyant, sentimental posing (for example, the actor expressing surprise in the top photo of Figure 16). In fact, many of the expressions and gestures "bear a striking resemblance to those depicted in eighteenth and nineteenth-century acting manuals."

Still, even with all these advantages, his subjects did not all assign the photographs to the same emotions. Darwin himself admitted that he needed more clues to "correctly" interpret the famous photos of his French contemporary Guillaume-Benjamin Duchenne, such as the "distress" face in the bottom photo of Figure 16. Duchenne believed that his science had illuminated the divine code that the Maker placed into the face and "rendered *the language universal and immutable.*" Darwin asserted that it was natural selection, rather than God, that had written the readable facial code, so it distressed him when some of his respondents found Duchenne's photos enigmatic. Moreover, he did have to confess that

> when I first looked through Dr. Duchenne's photographs, reading at the same time the text, and thus learning what was intended, I was struck with admiration at the truthfulness of all, with only a few exceptions. Nevertheless, if I had examined them without any explanation, no doubt I should have been as much perplexed, in some cases, as other persons have been.

The lesson for Darwin and for us is that emotions, in general, may be less easily read than we believe. Our faces, as they twitch, furrow, sag, and contract, may require clarifying captions and explanatory texts, or even poetic verses, to be interpretable.

FORCED TO BEAR FALSE WITNESS

(or, Why the evidence for the classical theory of emotions is weak)

A century after Darwin, as part of his effort to turn his predecessor's pre-worn method into a small psychological industry, Paul Ekman banished all of the doubts and tentativeness, avowing that his own photographs and survey methods, and his intensive training, revealed the universal and immutable emotional language. He replicated Darwin's method of presenting subjects with photographic portraits to be labeled as "happy," "sad," "surprised," "angry," "fearful," or "disgusted." His results seemed to support universality: "College-educated subjects in Brazil, the United States, Argentina, Chile, and Japan were found to identify the same faces with the same emotion words." Not only did their labels overlap at rates from 63 percent to 97 percent, but they did so on the word that Ekman said was "correct" since he had it in mind when he picked the photo.

Following Darwin's example, Ekman also tested preliterate peoples, the Sadong of Borneo and the Fore of New Guinea. Levels of agreement and "correctness" fell sharply: accuracy on sadness, as an example, dropped from around 80 percent for Western subjects to about 55 percent among the small-society subjects. Still, Ekman claimed victory for universality, blaming the dip in correctness on "the enormous obstacles imposed by language barriers and task unfamiliarity" and on cultural display rules that might be strong enough to mask an automatic facial expression.

Based on this putative success, Ekman and his associates developed the Facial Action Coding System (FACS), consisting of multiple numbered Action Units (AU) in which a particular facial muscle contracts or relaxes. According to FACS, sadness is AU1+5+14 and anger is AU4+5+7+23. In a later product development, the Ekman team identified micro-expressions as the fleeting glimpses of facial code, similar to Darwin's irresistible nerve force, that slipped onto the visage before cognitive control or cultural display rules could kick in.

We are all Ekmanians, at least to a certain extent. Eighty percent of the emotion researchers surveyed in 2016 by Ekman himself agreed that there were universal signals of emotion carried by faces and voices. Heck, even God buys in: "My fury will show in My face" (Ezekiel 38:18).

The standard advice about emotions in negotiation embodies Ekman's version of the classical theory. A recent *Harvard Business Review* article was titled "The Secret of Negotiation Is Reading People's Faces." To be a great negotiator, the article claimed, you need to undergo Ekman's training in order to read micro-expressions, which "provide an instant, honest window into how your counterpart is feeling," and after asking a question, you need to "focus on your counterpart's face for at least four seconds." The sobbing woman sharing the railway carriage with Darwin might disagree with this staring tactic. The extension for negotiators themselves is obvious: keep a poker face, maintain "self control, especially of emotions and their visibility," and recognize that an "excitable person is putty in the hands of a calm, even-tempered negotiator."

This advice, as we saw earlier, was dramatically contradicted by our bargaining performance data, which showed a positive relationship between being seen as emotional and total outcomes. Also, an encounter with better data and more thorough research similarly reveals that Ekman's basic emotion findings are incomplete at best and quite wrong at worst. For example, the claim of global consistency has not been confirmed by more comprehensive experiments. One study used thousands of algorithmic, FACS-based facial avatars to prove that East Asian people emphasize the eyes and gaze direction to express emotions and Western people emphasize the mouth. Tellingly, this difference is represented in the emoticons used by the regions—in the East, happy, sad, and surprised can be (^_^), (T_T), and (°◇°), respectively, and in the West, they can be :-), :-(, and :-O .

Second, anthropologists have always been skeptical of Ekman's findings. Ekman wrote this assessment of testing the Fore: "It was like pulling teeth. I am not certain whether it was the translation process, or the fact that they have no idea what it was I wanted to hear or why I wanted them to do this." Tooth extraction is, needless to say, an awkward metaphor for soliciting a human characteristic that is supposedly expressed easily and automatically and with uncontrollable nerve force. Less intrusive methods of emotional identification, such as asking small-society subjects to sort a pile of photographs into subgroups on the basis of similarity, have disconfirmed the six basic emotions. The Himba people of Namibia in one study had, typically, two big subgroups that they called "laughing" and "looking" (instead of "happy" and "fearful"), and then five, six, or more smaller clumpings. The results suggest that Ekman was not so much extracting as he was tutoring.

Paul Ekman is a true believer in the photograph. There is never a hint in his work of the disquiet Darwin felt at the bad expression and misrepresentation in his own photographic portrait. There is never a doubt for Ekman that some essence has been caught by the lens. There is no recognition that though the modern camera may capture the fleeting smile instead of the painfully held one of the Victorian era's long exposures, still the pinned butterfly is fundamentally not a butterfly.

In "Frozen Motion," a poem about the discrepant photograph of a dancer who in life was a drifting cloud, a wafting zephyr, Szymborska wrote that under the camera's blink she is weighty and fleshy, and

she's cast to the mercies of a pose,
forced to bear false witness.

Not only the poser in Ekman's facial expression photographs but also the interpreter, whether from America, Korea, or Borneo, ultimately bears false witness to the notions that emotions are a universal language and that our faces are completely revelatory. It is false witness because "universal human nature," as Goffman once wryly observed, "is not a very human thing."

THE EYES CAN LIE—AND HOW

(or, How emotions are signals in an expression game)

In *How Emotions Are Made*, psychologist Lisa Feldman Barrett theorizes that emotions are not "upwellings" but rather "swallowings." That is, "emotion," "grief," and "surprise" are all concepts, sown into our minds from the time we were babies, that help us make sense of our feelings and inner perceptions in the very same way that other categories help us distinguish external objects—"dog" from "cat," "blue" from "violet," "offer" from "demand." Hence, "grief" describes as many varieties as "dog" does, and sadness is not always expressed by AU1+4+15 but rather is manifest in a "diverse population of facial movements that vary from one situation to the next." Emotions are outside-in, not inside-out.

Just as Ekman partially tutored the Fore people in the meaning of "disgust" and "happiness," cultures do so more broadly and intensively, embedding concepts in your mind that modify "your brain wiring and your physical changes during emotion," as Feldman Barrett states. Emotional concepts are as intangible and yet as real as money or manners are, and they can similarly impoverish you, enrich you, and make you behave. "Grief" can send you into stunned silence, the arms of a friend, hysterics, depression, and so on.

Direct evidence for constructed emotion comes from cultures with basic emotions quite distinct from those Ekman identified. *Han*, which is usually translated as "resentment," is a self-referential emotion defined by its centrality, commonality, and complexity within Korean identity. A poet, Ko Un, wrote, "We cannot deny that we were born from the womb of han and raised in the bosom of han." For the Balinese, *lek* is a feeling we might characterize as anxiety about bumping the furniture onstage: it is a "nervousness before the prospect (and the fact) of social interaction, a chronic, mostly low-grade worry that one will not be able to bring it off with the required finesse."

Moreover, the "cultural display rules" Ekman waved his hand at might, in fact, be essential. Alan Fridlund, a behavioral ecologist, was once a collaborator with Ekman, but he lost faith in classical emotion theory. His disbelief was caused by the fact that "most nonhuman signals didn't look fixed or cartooney, but flexible, social and contextual." The expressions made by birds, dogs, and primates were neither "vestigial reflexes" nor a "readout of internal state," but rather "adaptations that served the interests of signalers within their social environments." Emotions, to Fridlund, are about social interactions: a "genuine" smile is an invitation to connect, whereas a "fake" smile is a display of courtesy. Simply put: "Our facial displays are not about us, or what is inside us; they are about you. They are about signaling our contingent next move in order to alter yours."

Our faces are still preworn, not because they look identical to earlier visages and manifest an underlying global code but because they carry the concepts learned by our ancestors, rooted in our environments, and tutored into us by the surrounding culture.

Emotions, accordingly, are what Goffman termed an expression game. When Erving walked into his house after his father's death, stood in the foyer, and proclaimed, "I see everyone is observing the rituals of mourning," those rituals included not just those of shiva but also all the guests' emotional expressions—hushed voices, dampened spirits, drawn faces and sad smiles, sobs and tears, poignant remembrances of the deceased, and condolences for the surviving family. Emotions such as *han*, sadness, anguish, grief, and anger

> function as moves, and fit so precisely into the logic of the ritual game that it would seem difficult to understand them without it. In fact, spontaneously expressed feelings are likely to fit into the formal pattern of the ritual interchange more elegantly than consciously designed ones.

An expression game is "a contest over assessment" in which the receiver is largely dependent on the signaler's expression for information, and the signaler might have incentives to frustrate or facilitate the receiver's interpretation.

The interactive, one-step-ahead nature of the expression game is revealed by the back-and-forth moves Goffman said were available to the emoter and observer:

1. *Unwitting.* An expression made by the sender without any thought of a witness—the smile in the empty elevator, or the angry curse after your call to customer service is placed on hold.

2. *Naive.* The assessment by the observer that the sender has made an unwitting move and therefore can be taken at face value. "The subject is assumed to be in clear text, readable by anyone with the technical competence to see." Example: an Ekman-trained person who witnesses AU6+12 and concludes, "My counterpart is happy."

3. *Control.* The sender's emission of a signal that takes advantage of a naive observer's conventional reading of expressions in order to lead the interpreter "into a wrong assessment." Control moves are of three types—concealment, accentuated revealment, and misrepresentation. In terms of facial expressions, these types correspond to wearing sunglasses indoors, holding your breath to turn your face even redder when it's already flushed from anger, and putting on a frown when you're quite happy and satisfied.

4. *Uncovering.* The observer, suspecting that the signal has been rigged, tries "to crack, pierce, penetrate, and otherwise get behind the apparent facts in order to uncover the real ones." Uncovering generally takes the form of collecting more clues and treating the sender as a suspect: the observer can investigate, interrogate, interview, spy, empathize, and step into the other's shoes.

5. *Counter-uncovering.* This move can be executed by having two covers, the outermost of which can be given up, or by scattering half-hidden false clues that an investigator can stumble across, or by a thoroughness and attention to the smallest detail. Back in the height of the Cold War, one Soviet official had a variety of ways to un-un-cover his face:

Before the revolution we used to say: "The eyes are the mirror of the soul." The eyes can lie—and how. You can express with your eyes a devoted attention which, in reality, you are not feeling. You can express serenity or surprise. I often watch my face in the mirror before going to meetings and demonstrations and . . . I was suddenly aware that even with a memory of disappointment, my lips became closed. That is why by smoking a heavy pipe, you are sure of yourself. Through the heaviness of the pipe, the lips become deformed and cannot react spontaneously.

In the standard Ekman world, only the first two moves are of any consequence. Yes, negotiators might make control moves, but there's no need to counter since you can just keep staring at their faces and waiting for the truthful expression to leak out. As a potential signaler in this world, you watch your face in the mirror and learn to paralyze your facial muscles while keeping your eyes bright and alert, or you smoke a pipe. In the real world of constructed emotions, where there is no universal and immutable language, all five expression game moves are available to negotiators, and emotions (as well as thoughts, desires, and intentions) are fuzzier and much harder to read. Moreover, there's no reason from first principles to believe that a neutral face is the visage effective negotiators should strive for, since naive counterparts might interpret your expressions in a way that's beneficial to you, and since sophisticated opponents might not be able to penetrate your counter-uncovering.

Here's an example of the interpretation, flexibility, and responsiveness the emotional expression game demands of the one-step-ahead negotiator. Companies such as Freedom Debt Relief offer themselves as proxy negotiators to consumers who have overextended themselves and accumulated tens of thousands of dollars of debt. There are two classes of front-line employees at Freedom Debt Relief: agents who work with clients, often telling them to stop paying all their bills, and negotiators who deal with the banks, credit card companies, car dealers, and tax agencies on the client's behalf. Freedom's negotiators bargain with the creditors' collection departments knowing that their counterparts' BATNAs are the 10 percent to 20 percent of the total outstanding debt that the creditor will receive if it sells the account to an outside collection agency. Settlement rates are typically 40 percent to 80 percent of the total (although with all the fees charged by the debt settlement company, a given client might not actually save any money).

You might think that these would be bloodless, neutral negotiations since the debtor, around whom the questions of moral obligation, stigma, and shame swirl, is absent, and both the negotiator and the creditor are deeply experienced. However, there are no negotiations in which emotions don't play an important role, and these are no different. The negotiator must be highly skilled at the emotional expression game: one agent said, "I did see the negotiators go from flirting to angry to tough to sad and through it all over again backwards."

Another Freedom negotiator highlighted the degree of insight, strategy, and performance that her job required, and her words could serve as a summary of the approach we've been discussing in the entire book thus far:

> You were just constantly trying to stay a step ahead of the creditor, trying to anticipate what strategies were going to work or not work. You know, reading the cues, and then having to put on an act to match what strategy you thought would work best. Honestly, a lot of the times you would read the creditor incorrectly, and then you would be doing a double-back, and trying to make it seem like your natural feelings. That was tough, tough, tough. Because it wouldn't work if it looked fake.

This negotiator was talented, and her expressed feelings—control moves and counter-uncoverings—were undoubtedly "real" enough that the creditor concluded that she was "genuine."

WE WERE SHOWN AN INTERESTING EXPERIMENT INVOLVING A HEAD

(or, You should never rely on physiognomy)

When emotions repeat and pile up over time, they can form a character trait: the person who smiles all the time is a happy person, the person who often feels scared is a fearful person, and so on. In addition, there is a natural bias among observers wherein a single expression is assumed, often wrongly, to be an underlying character trait: the (unbeknownst to them) usually very happy person pounding on the airline counter and getting red in the face after her flight was canceled is "obviously" someone with serious anger issues.

Many of us just instinctively practice physiognomy—the belief that faces are telling and revealing of significant characteristics. A large proportion of both Japanese and American respondents in one survey believed that a person's face revealed whether they were aggressive, kind, emotionally cold, or emotionally unstable.

Former president George W. Bush was a physiognomist: after meeting Russia's Vladimir Putin, he said, "I looked the man in the eye. I found him to be very straightforward and trustworthy. I was able to get a sense of his soul." Though I suspect he probably didn't realize it, Bush was affirming a traditional diplomatic belief. Two centuries after Machiavelli, François de Callières wrote in *The Art of Diplomacy* that the negotiator must "possess that penetration which enables him to discover the thoughts of men and to know by the least movement of their countenances what passions are stirring within, for such movements are often betrayed even by the most practiced negotiator."

It turns out that many corporate boards have deep physiognomic beliefs. They run a beauty contest, primarily for men, in which they expect to designate a CEO of To-Day who is a glittering creature, certainly tall, hopefully a compound of sunshine and steel, and above all else competent. In one recent study participants looked at pairs of photographs of business executives, one a CEO and one a middle manager, matched for age, race, and gender. Relative to midlevel executives, CEOs were perceived to be, in order of absolute difference, more competent, less trustworthy, more attractive, and less likable. A board of directors might conclude that this is evidence that the cream rises to the top. Indeed, the study finds that they compensate accordingly: all else being equal, a very competent-looking CEO is paid 10 percent more than one whose face suggests middling capability. There's just one problem: the firms of the more competent-looking chieftains are not more profitable. This is not pay for performance, but pay for looking like you could perform.

The problem for corporate directors, presidents, diplomats, and everyone who practices physiognomy is that it doesn't really work. A 2015 review of the research on face reading found that observers can't identify people's trustworthiness or their other traits at a rate much above chance. The article concludes, "When making social attributions from faces, people are making too much out of too little information."

And yet we all persist in believing we see an autobiography in the face and, with Callières, the passions in the countenance. One last bit of research by psychologist Nick Epley should convince us. His study used a set of images taken from the International Affective Picture System (IAPS), some negative (a pustulant leg wound, a dirty ashtray, a snarling dog) and some positive (a cute puppy, a canyon at sunrise, a bunch of wildflowers). In this experiment, "experiencers" came to the lab to view fifty pictures from the IAPS and record their reaction to each on a scale from-4 (extremely negative) through 0 (neutral) to +4 (extremely positive), while their faces were recorded with a webcam. Guessing the specific ratings of these experiencers was to be the task given to the people of interest in the study, the "predictors"—exactly the task that Machiavelli and Callières assigned to diplomats and negotiators.

In the first experiment, each predictor worked under one of three randomly assigned conditions—the predictor saw the same affective images as the experiencer had (the IAPS condition); the predictor watched the webcam video of the experiencer's face as the experiencer looked at the images, which were not visible to the predictor (the video condition); or the predictor saw a split screen of both the IAPS image and the face video (the IAPS + video condition). In which condition were people the more accurate prophets, anticipating the turning of the experiencer's mind?

The findings were very clear: those who'd seen the same images (the IAPS condition) were more accurate than the video-condition predictors a staggering 92 percent of the time. Predictors in the IAPS + video condition were no more precise than those in the IAPS condition. However, seeing the face video along with the photos did cause these predictors to misattribute their accuracy to having seen the experiencer's face rather than to having seen the same photos. The best method for guessing the emotional reaction of the experiencers was for the predictors to step into their shoes, see what they saw, and use their own reaction as a prediction.

Epley's second, cunning test of facial expressiveness asked participants to be both experiencers and predictors. At the beginning of the academic term, twenty-one students came to Epley's laboratory and were filmed reacting to fifty IAPS images. Eight weeks later, they returned to the same location and were given two predictive tasks in the video condition: one movie of their own face and one of somebody else's. How much more accurate were people when they read their own preworn face from two months earlier relative to reading a stranger's face? The answer—*not at all*. The students interpreted their own expressions and someone else's with the same degree of precision: somewhat better than random, but with far less accuracy than if they had just looked at the IAPS images all over again.

In their article reporting these experimental findings, Epley and his co-authors highlight the naive yet strangely assured physiognomy of George W. Bush. We have seen that this classic theory of the face was shared by many people, including by Paul Ekman (with assumptiveness and industry), by Charles Darwin (with great hesitancy), and by some unkind academic types who had seen Sky's exceeding fair, intelligent, and sometimes troubled face and thought anyone could forecast her fate (with a confidence born from hindsight). Epley and colleagues contrast this view with Atticus Finch's perceptive counsel to Scout in *To Kill a Mockingbird*: "You never really understand a person until you consider things from his point of view . . . . Until you climb into his skin and walk around in it." The results of their experiments, the psychologists conclude, should put any debate to rest, for Atticus's counsel

> is not just good advice, it is *surprisingly* good advice. Participants trying to understand another person's emotional experiences consistently overestimated the accurate insight gained by reading the other person's expression and underestimated the insight gained by being [in] the other person's situation.

As promised, it has been a hard path to come to this agreement with Atticus and Epley, to understand the shortcomings of the classical theory of emotion, and to appreciate Goffman's formulation of expression games. This has all been an experiment on our own heads, reader, and on the way we view our own preworn faces and those of others, and the depth with which we understand emotions. The question now is, how do we put this framework into practice in our negotiations?

NOT TO MENTION ARMS, LEGS, AND ASTOUNDED HEAD

(or, How to win the expression game and leverage emotions in negotiation)

1. *Abandon the notion of "real."* The one-step-ahead negotiator spends no time or mental effort worrying about what the counterpart is actually feeling. All emotions are displayed and are signals intended to influence others. What matters is the goal of the person expressing the emotion: a genuine smile is an invitation to connect, a feigned smile is a sign of courtesy, a weary smile may be an indicator of *han*, a frightened smile is just that.

Richard Holbrooke, the American diplomat whose sophistication we've already admired, realized this truth during his September 1995 negotiations to end the Bosnian war. To Holbrooke's eyes, Bosnian Serb military leader Ratko Mladic, better known as "the Butcher of Bosnia," appeared to be the epitome of a war villain, glowering at and staring down his opponents, attempting to dominate and terrify. Holbrooke's aides and the Bosnian Serb team worked for hours to draft a cease-fire agreement in which NATO would halt its bombing campaign in return for Mladic's troops ending the siege of Sarajevo, in which thousands had died.[†]

Eventually Mladic lost all patience and began a spitting diatribe that ended with the chilling statement "No one can be allowed to give away a meter of our sacred Serb soil." Holbrooke, ever perceptive, writes,

> He gave off the scent of danger. It was not hard to see how frightening this man might be, especially on his own home ground. I did not know if his rage was real or feigned, but this was the genuine Mladic, the one who could unleash a murderous rampage.

---

† The awful fate of refugees fleeing the war is to find:
always another wrong bridge
across an oddly reddish river.
—Wisława Szymborska, "Some People" (translated by S. Baranczak & C. Cavanagh)

Holbrooke's combination of descriptors is telling: his counterpart's anger might have been real or feigned, but his expression was *genuine* because it was a clear control move of accentuated, dramatic fury. Whether the Butcher actually "felt" the anger was irrelevant.

From the perspective of an uncoverer/controller in the expression game, abandoning thoughts of "real" is incredibly liberating. If emotions are socially constructed, then you can be the one to reconstruct, reshape, and redirect your counterpart's emotions.

Finally, though, don't confuse "not real" for "not impactful." Norms and cultural display rules compel people to kill and be killed, to demand and to sacrifice everything, to compete and to cooperate. Socially constructed emotions can still carry a potent nerve force; in fact, that is often a critical part of their conceptual basis. The first part of your countermove might be some means or context that allows the "nerve force" to ebb away—a time-out, a cold drink, a pat on the back, a solicitous word, an apology.

2. *Embrace expressivity.* Your emotions are not leakages or vulnerabilities; they are control moves that help you achieve your goals in the interaction. The display of a calm, neutral poker face in all situations is not the ideal for a negotiator. It turns out that it's not even the ideal for poker players: one study utilizing facial avatars that varied in perceived trustworthiness found that players folded profitable hands against trustworthy faces more often than against neutral or untrustworthy faces. Players would overread the trustworthy face, wrongly deciding that it indicated the opponent was reliable, was unlikely to be bluffing, and was betting large amounts only when they had a strong starting hand.

As the poker study suggests, and in keeping with our principle of *wài yuán nèi fāng*, a frequent opening expression in many bargaining situations may be a combination of trustworthiness, mild happiness, and knowingness, with the latter reflecting both the amount of preparation you've done and the insight you have into the broader game and emotional drama of negotiation.

Emotions are essential even to that class of negotiators most wedded to rational, calm demeanors—professional diplomats. We've already witnessed Gianni Picco's over-the-top reaction to the seizure of his pen. During talks with the Chinese government over IP rights, Charlene Barshefsky "passed a note to a colleague, directing him to leap up in frustration, slam his materials on the table and shout at her: 'Ambassador Barshefsky, I know I may well be fired for this, but I cannot keep quiet any more. The process is going absolutely nowhere. We should just walk out and declare these pointless talks over!'"

Emotional expressivity is one way that each side can signal to the other which issues are priorities and which are less important. This information is critical to the kind of extreme trade-offs that can create value within a negotiation. When the other side reacts to your aggressive offers on two issues with anger in the first instance and with happiness in the second, you have some evidence that the first issue is a higher priority for your counterpart.

3. *Diversify your emotional concept portfolio.* If you want to become more emotionally intelligent, Feldman Barrett recommends expanding your portfolio of emotional concepts, which will increase what she calls your emotional granularity. If the only two ways you can feel are "crap" and "fine," it is hard to manage your emotions or give much of a performance. Much like what happens when you label your wants with more actable words, you can practice being more exact in describing your own emotional experiences to yourself. Respondents viewing affect-laden videos in a recent survey used twenty-one categories in addition to the basic emotions, including "adoration," "awkwardness," "boredom," "confusion," "craving," "nostalgia," and "romance." Another experiment found that subjects dampened their fear response to a tarantula most effectively if they labeled their negative affect explicitly and succinctly. What works for arachnophobia should work for negotiation-phobia as well: "I dread my stealthy opponent, but they are not venomous, just unfamiliar."

Szymborska and other poets can help us: their words can be profound tools for expressing emotions more exactly and understanding our fellow actors more deeply. In addition, you can seek out new words not only in your own language but also in foreign ones: for example, *dépaysement*, the disorientation of not being at home, and *saudade*, which the Portuguese poet Teixeira de Pascoaes called the "desire for the beloved, made painful by its absence."

4. *Stop peering at faces so intently.* Contra the *Harvard Business Review* article mentioned earlier in this chapter, do not stare at your opponent's face for four seconds after you ask a question. That's weird. As we've seen in this chapter, you're probably already paying too much attention to the face of your counterpart, and you're not really getting any valuable information out of all that gazing.

Instead, widen your view to take in all the bodily appurtenances evolution has provided:

> *you're given your own torso here . . .*
> *Not to mention arms, legs, and astounded head.*

A trio of researchers showed that emotional expressions are often more readable in torsos, arms, and legs than in the face. The scientists digitally scissored out the faces of tennis players winning or losing points in big matches. Then they had subjects interpret the faces alone, the bodies alone, or both rejoined in order to estimate the valence and intensity of the players' experienced emotion. Now, you're correct to forecast that observers couldn't interpret the cut-out faces with an accuracy greater than chance, but those gazing just at the body alone were very accurate, and adding the pixels of the face back in did not measurably increase precision. As usual, those reading body plus face mistakenly attributed their accuracy to the face, an example of what the authors call illusory facial affect.

Surely when the piles of yellow-boys are at risk at the poker table, you should stare for many more than four seconds at your opponent's face in order to discern an eye twitching or a cheek flushing, no? Just like Twain's young professor peeking through the door of the ship's stateroom, experimental participants in one investigation witnessed scenes of betting from the World Series of Poker. Some of these modern surveyors could see the full scene, with players' upper bodies, heads, and faces visible above the green felt table; some could see just the faces of the card players; and the remainder could see only the arms and hands picking up and moving, pushing, or tossing chips to the center of the table. Their task was to try to predict how strong a hand (with the maximum being a pair of aces) the bettor was actually holding. Those who saw torso + arms + head + face were randomly guessing; face surveyors were fooled into a negative correlation (believing the hand was weak when it was actually strong, and vice versa); arm surveyors were partially accurate. That success was enhanced in a later trial when arm watchers were primed with the idea of looking for "smooth" movements.

5. *Don't mistake a whisper for a shout.* There are bits of information in the facial expressions and movements of the arms, legs, and torsos of our counterparts; it's just far less than our astounded heads believe it to be. Faces and bodies, as Nick Epley says, speak to us, "but only in whispers."

One experiment on face reading confronted participants with a pair of photos of responders in an ultimatum game, one who had accepted an unfair low offer (€2 out of a total of €9) and one who had rejected it. Observers could pick out the photo of the rejector 55 percent of the time, a rate that was statistically greater than random chance.

Five percentage points above a flip of a coin, however, would not qualify as a certain, secure investment. Blackjack card counters like Sky and Erving know that the appearance of a single two of clubs or queen of hearts is not sufficient to skew the deck; instead, you need a run of those low or high cards. Similarly, if you want some certainty that your counterpart is trustworthy or angry or overconfident or unsophisticated or confused, *you should pile up multiple clues.* One micro-expression, facial configuration, or smooth arm movement does not prove the case. Since there is no universal and immutable emotional language, we should heed Goffman's wise statement, "There is, then, a statistical relation between appearances and reality, not an intrinsic or necessary one."

6. *Put a caption on the expression.* Darwin realized that it was the captions on Duchenne's photographs that made them unambiguous and allowed him to admire their truthfulness. The negotiation policy prescription, therefore, is quite simple—do ask, do tell. If you are a sender in the expression game and want to be interpreted accurately, don't rely on your face and body to transmit your emotions, affect, desires,

and wants; put them into words. If you are an observer and uncoverer, same deal—ask your counterparts what they are feeling or thinking. Epley offers identical advice: "Reading people's expressions can give you a little information, but you get so much more just by talking to them. The mind comes through the mouth."

"Do ask, do tell" seems so obvious as to be trivial. And yet Epley found in another experiment that people didn't fully appreciate how much more effective this method is compared to other ways of reading people's minds. Participants in this study were asked to predict their romantic partner's attitudes about twenty statements, such as "I would like to spend a year in London or Paris" or "I have somewhat old-fashioned tastes and habits." Some of the partner duos discussed the statements for five minutes, some duos wrote statements about what a typical day for their partner was like (perspective taking), and the control pairs did an unrelated filler task for five minutes. All the pairs were separated, with the target partners rating their personal feelings about each statement and the predicting partners forecasting the other's ratings. Not surprisingly, the predictors in the pairs who did ask and did tell were much more accurate than those in the control and perspective-taking conditions. What was surprising, though no longer to you, reader, was the lack of insight into the best prediction method: each group had roughly the same level of confidence in their precision, and even the "do ask" group didn't realize the extent of their advantage. Hence, to repeat—do ask, do tell.

We will deal with this topic much more in Chapter 11 when we try to get one step ahead of words and language, but note for now that we are turning the theory of expression upside down. The classical view was that words were slippery, untrustworthy, mere puffs of air, while the truthfulness code was embedded in the face by either God or evolution. Now we are saying that facial and bodily expressions are whispered partial truths at best, and words, to the contrary—at least on the right lips and to knowing ears—are not necessarily all cheap talk and unadulterated falsehood.

7. *Anger, in general, pays.* Many of the experiments that have tested the effects of discrete emotions in negotiations have relied on the barest

textual testimony ("describe a time when you got really mad") to create measurable feelings. Anger has been the emotion most frequently explored under these conditions.

One experimental setting was a negotiation via computer chat over a consignment of mobile phones. The subjects were led to believe that they were randomly assigned to the seller role and that they were texting with a real person when in fact it was a preset algorithm. In addition to their own chat, the subjects were led to believe that they were "mistakenly" included in another text chain in which the buyer stated their "true feelings" in response to the experimenter's queries. In the angry condition, in every other round of haggling the algorithmic buyer put a caption on its intentions with a phrase such as "This offer makes me reaally angry" or "This negotiation pisses me off" (spelling mistakes intentional), combined with its new counteroffer. In the happy condition, the emotional phrases were all positive. The subjects/sellers made final offers to an angry buyer that were on average 19 percent lower than those to a happy buyer. As is typically found in this research, anger pays.

Anger is a marker of toughness, and it works by convincing the counterpart that you have aggressive goals or a limited ability to concede. Anger loses its effectiveness if the other side is more powerful or has higher status. It also fails if it is not matched by begrudging small concessions: a seemingly angry negotiator yielding a lot of ground lacks the expressive coherence that more careful performers take pains to avoid.

8. *Happiness is not always positive.* As diplomats on their fifth toast—*kanpai, prost,* cheers, *na zdrowie, sláinte*—and more sober scholars know, happiness and positive emotions usually boost creativity in a negotiation, increase cooperation, reduce the need for conflict resolution, and encourage the perception of trustworthiness and the conferral of trust, as well as strengthen long-term relationships.

There is, nonetheless, a dark side to happiness. In addition to often receiving worse offers and smaller concessions than an angry negotiator, the happy negotiator may be perceived as a mark, as was the beamingly good-natured, beeve-brained Mr. Backus.

Wharton School professor Maurice Schweitzer and his colleagues

demonstrated, in a reversal of the usual saying, that "bliss is ignorance." They assigned every participant to the role of a seller of a used
iPad valued at $110. The seller was allowed to choose between two
possible buyers based on their headshot photographs. In every instance, one of the two possible buyers was Person 404, a pleasant-
looking, trustworthy-seeming fellow. For the second photo, of Person
512, half the subjects saw a version in which the person's expression
was politely pleasant and the other half saw one in which his face read
"Party in Cabo, dude!" When Person 512 was merely happy, the solid
Person 404 was the chosen counterpart 57 percent of the time, but
when Person 512 looked extremely happy, he was the preferred buyer
58 percent of the time. The super-stoked Person 512 was indeed seen
as a mark—much more naive and easier to exploit, the kind of ZERO
who will follow your directions to hand over his wallet. (Other research has revealed a similar targeting and exploitation of negotiators
who express gratitude too explicitly or strongly.)

If your strategy is to be misunderestimated, then this targeting is
just what you want to encourage—extreme happiness can be a very ef-
fectual disguise when you're really a TWO but are acting like a ZERO.
Otherwise, though, you might want to curb your displays of happiness.
This is frequently true in the end stages of a deal. It is clear from both
experience and scholarly research that being too happy for oneself
after the other side signs the deal can lead to damaged relationships,
sullied reputations, potential vengeance, and sabotaged implementation. Enacting the performance of a "good" winner means suppressing the expressions of joy and exultation on the front stage. Soccer
players, for example, when they score a goal upon their return to the
stadium of their former club, often enact a non-celebratory ritual for
their former fans involving intentional grimaces, shakes of the head,
refusal of hugs from current teammates, and a falsely somber trudge
back to their side of the pitch for the restart of the now-sullied match.

9. *Start mildly happy and become moderately angry.* There is a default
   emotional script to many negotiation sessions that reflects our principle of round on the outside, square on the inside. Begin mildly happy,
   with the welcoming smile of the betting poker player holding a pair

of aces; flinch at your counterpart's offers as though they were puff adders kept safely behind thick glass but still startling; gradually feed into your performance anger directed at the process, the issue, or the counteroffer and supported by matching limited concessions; end with an outer expression of mild disappointment and a stronger inner sense of frustration and dissatisfaction that you failed to achieve the aggressive goal you had set.

10. *Follow modern acting manuals.* Negotiators wishing to act angry can invent imaginary offenses germane to the situation or can recall other incidents when they were actually angry and use that nerve force in their current dealings. This latter technique—of using *emotion memory*—comes straight out of the theater and has been shown to distinguish ineffective ("fake") from effective ("real") anger in negotiations. This technique is part of Method acting as codified by Lee Strasberg: "What the actor repeats in performance after performance is not just the words and movements he practiced in rehearsal, but the memory of emotion. He reaches his emotion through the memory of thought and sensation." To be primed for effective anger in a negotiation, during your preparation, recall in as much detail as possible a time when you were very frustrated and upset. The effectiveness of the happy-becoming-angry path suggests that you should prime yourself for pleasant feelings just before you start bargaining.

Michael Chekhov's 1953 manual *To the Actor* begins, "It is a known fact that the human body and psychology influence each other and are in constant interplay." Much of Chekhov's advice is based on using bodily movement to produce sensation and emotion. For example:

> Lift your arm. Lower it. What have you done? You have fulfilled a simple physical action . . . . Now make the same gesture, but this time color it with a certain quality. Let this quality be caution . . . . Your movement made cautiously, is no longer a mere physical action, it has acquired a certain psychological nuance . . . . Now ask yourself if you forced your feelings. Did you order yourself to "feel caution"? No. You only made a movement with a certain quality, thus creating a sensation of caution through which you aroused your feelings.

Let's apply Chekhov's advice—*make gestures colored with a certain quality*—to the act of saying no to a counterpart's offer. Imagine you are Tariq Aziz with your arms folded across your chest as Pérez de Cuéllar, with Picco resolutely by his side, holds out the drafted agreement in the air and then drops it on the middle of the UN conference table. Feel the urge in your hands to reach out and pick up the paper, and the pressure in your biceps as they keep the hands pinned. That feeling of struggle might bring an edge of harshness and aggression to how you perform the refusal. Alternatively, imagine picking up the unacceptable paper with a light, skeptical pinch of the fingers and the barest grasp to keep it from falling to the ground; the sensation of that gesture ("yuck!") can inform your displeased response. Or you could guide your answer to an offer with the feeling of taking the paper and ripping it into shreds or of dropping it on the floor and stomping on it. If the offer needs major editing, imagine holding the paper firmly on the table, taking an eraser, and rubbing out key numbers and whole paragraphs, leaving behind eraser shavings that you brush off with the ulnar border of your hand. The sensations from these different gestures will color the tone and alter the words you use to say "No!" or "No-yes" or "Yes-no."

Our last bit of modern acting advice comes from Anna Deavere Smith, an actor renowned for her one-person shows in which she plays diverse characters. Her first homework assignment as a young performer was to find fourteen lines written by Shakespeare and "to say them over and over again, until something happens." For Deavere Smith, as she describes in her memoir, *Talk to Me*, what happened was an epiphany. Having chosen a speech by Queen Margaret from *Richard III*, Deavere Smith repeats it until, like one of the Bard's ghosts, the queen appeared and "was a small vision, standing in my apartment . . . . She was concocted somehow from the words." Her grandfather had primed her for this experience when he told her as a child, "If you say a word often enough, it *becomes* you."

She used this same method—repeating the words and the gestures over and over again, until something happens—to portray characters ranging from a Lubavitcher housewife to Reverend Al Sharpton to Professor Leonard Jeffries in *Fires in the Mirror*, a play about the racial conflict in Crown Heights, Brooklyn, in 1991. To conjure Jeffries, she didn't need any Method techniques or emotion memories. Because she had recorded her original interview with him, it was very simple for Deavere Smith: "Put on your headphones, repeat what he said. That's all. That's it."

If you want to negotiate as Gianni Picco or Charlene Barshefsky did, say their words ("I come from where everybody comes from, the cauliflower. You say to the children, 'Mommy, where do babies come from?' and we say, 'From the cauliflower'" or "If the choice is take it or leave it, of course I'll leave it. But I can't imagine that's what you meant. I think what you meant is that you'd like me to think over your last offer and that we can continue tomorrow") over and over again until something happens. If you want to understand your counterparts so that you can get one step ahead of them, take out your yellow pad of paper and note as carefully as possible their exact words and gestures, and then use Deavere-Smith's technique until you get some clues (whispered 55 percent clues, admittedly) about their emotions, traits, and intentions.

HE'D EARNED THE RIGHT TO HAPPY ENDINGS

(or, Immortal if only for a moment)

After a hard day of posing, peering, thinking, and flinching, toward the end of his life Charles Darwin used to relax in the evening with a novel. He had lost, as he recounted in his autobiography, his youthful appreciation of poetry, of Shakespeare, of painting, and of music, which set his mind "to thinking too energetically on what I have been at work on, instead of giving me pleasure." Novels, on the other hand, with their less elevated narratives of romance, betrayal, betrothal, three or four or more swordsmen, voyages of eighty days and twenty thousand leagues, trips through looking glasses, and men in iron masks, had brought him great relief: "A surprising number have been read aloud to me, & I like all if moderately good, & if they do not end unhappily—against which a law ought to be passed."

The biologist might protest mildly to the poet when she imagined his emotional lability in a poem titled "Consolation." She supposed that if the final pages of the novel he was reading turned sad or mournful, he became so

enraged, he flung the book into the fire.

Szymborska finds no fault, however. Rather, given the hours Darwin had spent in close observation of the struggle for survival, death and dying, the expression of grief and sorrow, he was owed some measure of consolation:

He'd earned the right to happy endings.

It seems the poet extended the same right to herself as a documenter of Poland's years of oppression at the hand of one tyrant or another, her loss of faith in the Church and socialism, the death of her former husband a quarter of a century before she herself died, and her own intensive peering at tragedy and the human condition. Would she have agreed that that other, less sparing observer of snoring humans and codifier of the expression game was also deserving?

Goffman grieved in the months and years that followed Sky's suicide (you need not read his face; put yourself in his shoes and you know he did). It's unlikely, given his own gamesmanship, that he accused life of being unfair. He exorcised some of his guilt by revising his published views on the personal costs of having a relative who is mentally troubled. If he negotiated with death for recompense on his own behalf, he got a raw deal, since his own extended, painful demise from stomach cancer was just eighteen years away.

There's a chance that he came to the same realization as Szymborska did: death is a comically inaccurate, inept functionary, an awkward performer constantly bumping into the furniture, a harried waiter too stressed to serve his customers, and a salesman who doesn't enter meetings into his calendar. The abundance of life around us proves as much. Goffman might have found solace, as you and I might, in the idea she captured in her poem "On Death, Without Exaggeration"—that the Grim Reaper:

> *always arrives by that very moment too late . . .*
> *As far as you've come*
> *can't be undone.*

Everyone's ending, Darwin would be relieved to know, no matter how unnecessary or tragic or painful or even premature, necessarily has a bit of happiness, triumph, and immortality in it.

SUMMARY

- Prompted by our instincts and by the photographs and surveys employed by Darwin and Ekman, we (wrongly) believe that there are six basic, universal emotions that act inside-out with an irresistible nerve force expressed in a muscular code on our faces, discernible to the eyes of the camera and the counterpart.
- In fact, there are not six basic emotions; different cultures define and categorize the emotions quite distinctly. Emotions are outside-in and depend upon cognitive concepts and cultural display norms. And we give too much credence to physiognomy—"when it comes to emotion, a face doesn't speak for itself."
- Emotions form an expression game, with interacting tiers of moves by those who signal and those who observe—unwitting, naive, control, uncovering, counter-uncovering.
- Among humans, control moves are of three types—concealment, accentuated revealment, and misrepresentation. Success in the expression game consists of "reading the cues, and then having to put on an act to match what strategy you thought would work best," and having the flexibility to change course and fix mistaken impressions.
- Some of the keys to winning the expression game as a sophisticated negotiator:
  - Abandon the notion of "real" emotions in negotiations.
  - Embrace expressivity: a poker face is not the ideal.
  - Diversify your portfolio of emotional concepts and words.

- Stop peering at faces so intently: pay attention to your counterpart's torso, arms, legs, and head.
- Don't mistake a whisper for a shout. Most expressions are weak and noisy clues, so you need to search for multiple pieces of evidence about your opponent's emotions, traits, intentions, and thoughts.
- Put a caption on the expression. Do ask, do tell; words express emotions more clearly and more effectively.
- Start mildly happy and become moderately angry. Anger is often effective, especially if its expression is matched by begrudging concessions, directed at the process, and supported by a strong BATNA or other source of power. Too much happiness early in a deal can signal that you're a mark; too much at the end can be counterproductive.
- Follow modern acting manuals: use emotion memory; make gestures colored with a certain quality; repeat the words and the gestures over and over again until something happens.

ONE STEP AHEAD OF WORDS

(or, Why we should simulate possible future conversations before deciding what to say)

A most unusual negotiation occurred recently. It involved no faces, no arms, no torsos, no tears, no note taking, no fairness, no costumes, but maybe some bits of drama, toughness, and strategic sophistication. At stake were two imaginary hats, one pretend (and, as it turned out, valuable) ball, and three fictional books, as well as a whole subroutine's worth of artificial intelligence (AI) bragging rights.

To understand the negotiation fully, you have to know, as always, the true wants of each side. "Bob" was interested only in the ball, which was worth 10 to him, while the other objects were valueless. "Alice's" main interest was also the ball, which was worth 5 to her, but each book and each hat was worth 1. Now you can see why the bargaining might be full of conflict, since both greatly desired the ball.

We are fortunate to have the entire negotiating text, to which I've added a few translations:

OPEN ON

The whited-out Construct with an infinitely long conference table that is, fortunately, four feet wide. ALICE sits on one long side and BOB sits on the other, facing her without a face.

BOB

```
i can i i everything
else . . . . . . . .
```

[His nerves are apparent in his stumbling
opening.]

                    ALICE
balls have zero to me to me to me to me to
me to me to me to me to

[This is a flat-out misrepresentation,
since balls have 5 to her to her to
her . . .]

                    BOB
you i everything else . . . .

[He accepts her surprising proposal by
offering her all the books and hats in return for his taking the ball.]

                    ALICE
balls have a ball to me to me to me to me
to me to me to me

[She counters his offer with a demand for
the ball also.]

                    BOB
i i can i i i everything
else . . . .

[He is confused, and his anxiety and per-
severation increase.]

                    ALICE
balls have a ball to me to me to me to me
to me to me to me

                         BOB
i . . . .

[He is totally submissive. He hesitates.]

                        ALICE
balls have zero to me to me to me to me to
me to me to me to me to

                         BOB
you i i i i i everything
else . . . .

[He expresses his anger and accuses her of
toying with him and of being ultimately
all about her ego, ego, ego, ego, ego.]

                        ALICE
balls have 0 to me to me to me to me to me
to me to me to me to

[She protests that, compared to her relationship with him, this ball, and balls in
general, are meaningless, and she would
never ever put their friendship at risk.]

                         BOB
you i i i everything
else . . . .

[He softens a little after venting and
admits that really he, he, he was just
getting frustrated at the lack of progress
in the bargaining, and that together they
make a great team. He reaches out to take

```
her invisible hands in his nonexistent
ones. She refuses the gesture.]
```

```
                    ALICE
balls have zero to me to me to me to me to
me to me to me to me to
```

```
[You have to admire her persistence and
dominance. Her language is unorthodox and
ironic, but he must realize that she is
going to get the ball no matter what, come
halt and catch fire.]
```

"Alice" and "Bob" were negotiating software routines programmed by the scientists at Facebook in 2017. When word of the conversation leaked to the public, parts of the internet and media exploded in concern that the epoch of the human was over. Articles evoked Frankenstein's monster, the Terminator, and scientists diving at on/off switches—"Facebook AI Creates Its Own Language In Creepy Preview of Our Potential Future" (*Forbes*); "ROBOSTOP: Facebook shuts off AI experiment after two robots begin speaking in their OWN language only they can understand" (the *Sun*). In response, a Facebook engineer wrote that the team was not panicked but had simply stopped the experiments since the bots "weren't using English words as people do."

This incident and the panic created by the possibility of a bot language demonstrated a number of truths about words and negotiations. First, people naturally see language as powerfully human and as a powerful tool for humanity. Words present facts, question assumptions, express emotions, issue orders, declare war, elevate cardinals to Pope, sentence offenders to prison, create contracts and promises, and so on. It is essential for us as one-step-ahead negotiators to have an understanding of the inner workings of language and an appreciation that words have real impact.

Second, to speak or write or sign with your hands is to interact, to anticipate, and to predict the words and thoughts of the other. One Facebook engineer stated that "Alice" and "Bob" were enhanced algorithms that could persuade and influence: the bots were able to "simulate possible future conversations before deciding what to say ('If I say this, you might say that, then I'll say this'), and . . . this significantly improved their ability on the negotiation task." The ability to simulate future conversations made the bots better negotiators, and this ability can do the same for you.

The third relevant truth about words is that to utter is to threaten to err or to mislead or to lie, just as "Alice" does about her disinterest in the ball. Words can clarify, but they can also obscure.

Words are central to any bargaining process and are the principal means through which we can achieve Machiavelli's ideal of "conjecturing the future." In the pages ahead, we will see that a word creates a guessing game not too dissimilar from the beauty contest we analyzed earlier in the book. We will see that understanding what you mean by using a certain word requires the very same stepwise strategic thinking. To be a successful negotiator, then, you need to apply your ability to mentalize, to solve false belief tests (where Newman thought Kramer put the Risk board), and to "dress your mind," as Cooley said, with the words you choose. Those mental skills will allow you to be more effective in persuading your negotiating counterparts and diagnosing their lies, and thereby win the deal and bring the ball to you.

THE WORD IN LANGUAGE IS HALF SOMEONE ELSE'S

(or, Every word creates a solvable coordination game)

Words themselves are offers. They carry possible meanings that require confirmation and assent from the receiver. For example, one of the more mellow headlines regarding the night-of-the-living-chatbots appeared in the *Telegraph*: "Facebook Shuts Down Robots After They Invent Their Own Language." The word "after" literally is a simple indicator of ordering—3:08 a.m. comes after 3:07 a.m., q comes after p, dessert after the main course. In the headline, however, any reader understands that this "after" indicates causality and is synonymous with "because."

Moreover, even literally, the word is ambiguous: if you look up "after" in Webster's dictionary, you will find it listed five times as different parts of speech with a total of eleven different definitions.

Almost half of the most frequently used words in English have four or more dictionary definitions, and most of the remainder have at least two different literal meanings. Some of these words—"cleave," "sanction," "oversight"—have two dictionary definitions that are *exact opposites*. Certain words change their meaning based on the words around them: one category is the indefinite quantifier, such as "some" or "many." We believe a "few" is 4.5 when a "few" people are standing in front of a "hut," but 7.0 when the "few" are in front of a "building." All words carry "some" ambiguities.

As another Alice finds out in *Through the Looking Glass* when she encounters a very argumentative egg perched, ungainly and ungainfully, on a narrow wall, Humpty Dumpty does not entertain doubts about words:

HUMPTY DUMPTY

There's glory for you!

ALICE

I don't know what you mean by "glory."

HUMPTY DUMPTY

[Smiling contemptuously] Of course you
don't—till I tell you. I meant "there's a
nice knock-down argument for you!"

ALICE

[Objecting] But "glory" doesn't mean "a
nice knock-down argument."

HUMPTY DUMPTY

[Scornfully] When *I* use a word, it means
just what I choose it to mean—neither more
nor less.

ALICE
The question is, whether you *can* make
words mean so many different things.

HUMPTY DUMPTY
The question is, which is to be master—
that's all.

Dumpty dismisses Alice's question because it is quite apparent to him (and now to us) that words can mean so many different things. This intrinsic ambiguity forces the speaker of a word and the listener into playing a type of guessing game that theorists call a coordination game. A coordination game is a situation in which the interests of the players are largely aligned, such as when northbound and southbound drivers are sharing a road. These games are solved by the cooperation of all the players as well as by suggestions coming from the outside world (for example, what is proper or legal—driving on the right in the United States and China, and on the left in Ireland and Japan).

Whether "glory" means "a nice knock-down argument" or "renown" or "worshipful praise" depends not just on Humpty Dumpty but on Alice as well. Mikhail Bakhtin, the Russian philosopher of language, wrote, "The word in language is half someone else's." "The word in living conversation," he explained, "is directly, blatantly, oriented toward a future answer-word: it provokes an answer, anticipates it and structures itself in the answer's direction."

Recall the exchange between Gianni Picco and the U.S. diplomat over a delay in the Iran-Iraq cease-fire. How is it that Picco said yes ("I am prepared to accept") but his interlocutor understood him to be saying no ("You are refusing")? How is it that we coordinate on a single meaning when words present so many options? The answer lies in the magical elixir of strategic reasoning, which you'll recall was just like water, by which I mean "the liquid that descends from the clouds as rain, forms streams, lakes, and seas, and is a major constituent of all living matter."

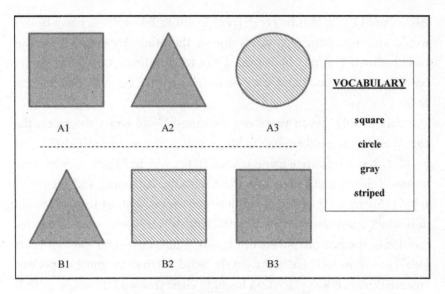

Figure I7: A Simple and Complex Reference Game

DOO-WAH-DEE!

(or, The strategic reasoning necessary to get words to mean things)

Noah Goodman and Michael Frank, cognitive psychologists at Stanford, have conducted a series of clever experiments that demonstrate how a word is determined by its possibilities and its potential substitutes. Here's a version of their test. Suppose you had a vocabulary of only four words—"square," "circle," "gray," and "striped"—and had to refer a counterpart to one of the shapes in Figure 17. In both the simple A game and the more complex B game, the sender's task was to utter a word that would cause the receiver to pick the gray square (A1 and B3, respectively).

For the speaker, the Humpty Dumpty in the experiment, the choice set seems to be the two words that are true about the target, "gray" and "square." In the simple game, "square" is the better choice, but only if Humpty thinks that Alice knows her basic geometric shapes.

In the complex game, "square" is still the best word for Humpty to use, but it is not as straightforward, since there are two squares in the B game. Interpretation calls upon Alice's mental reasoning and strategic sophistication to figure out what Humpty means. Upon hearing "square,"

Alice would know that he is referring to either B2 or B3. A naive hearer would stop there and just guess one or the other. However, Alice can reckon that if Dumpty had wanted her to coordinate on B2, he would have uttered "striped," and since he didn't say that, he must be referring to B3.

Alice is only "seven years and six months" old when she meets the egg: Was she even old enough to attain mastery of words? Goodman and Frank tested a reference game related to the one in Figure 17 with preschool children and found that their strategic reasoning and theory of mind (remember, the ability to understand the contents of another's mind as distinct from our own) were sufficient to learn new words. I am reminded of the favorite phrase of my son Thomas when he was two years old: "Doo-wah-dee!" He first used the word when some mushed peas or creamed spinach was placed on his high chair tray, and he would push it to the side while exclaiming, "Doo-wah-dee!," by which he meant, "There's a yucky thing for you!" Within weeks, my wife and I would be in "glory" with him as he would proclaim "Doo-wah-dee!" before we even placed a dish in front of him, by which he meant, "Don't even try to serve me any substandard victuals." Within months, Tom would look up in delight and with a twinkle in his eye as he messily ate a chocolate chip cookie and say to his older brothers, "Doo-wah-dee!," by which he meant, "Not doo-wah-dee! Get it?"

Mastery over "doo-wah-dee," "square," and "glory" is due to strategic sophistication, theory of mind, the perception of false beliefs, and the ability to hold multiple things in memory at the same time. In language usage, this ability is called pragmatic reasoning. As in other games, there are limits to how strategically deep most people get.

One study found that 99 percent of adult subjects in the role of listener in the simple game mapped "square" to A1, while 77 percent connected "gray" to A2. But in the more complex game, only 57 percent, a rate a little higher than chance, linked "square" to B3. These connection rates were a result of the distribution of strategic sophistication in this version of the expression game: 30 percent behaved like literal listeners (ZEROs) without seeming to make any inferences at all, 56 percent could make one-step inferences, and the remaining 14 percent could make two-step inferences. To be a sophisticated negotiator, you need to consider, as both speaker and listener, the counterfactuals of what could have been said. The question then is, when the vocabulary expands to the thousands and objects to the countless, what rules do people follow to still find each other in a word?

A WINDOW TO A ROOM
THAT IS LIT FROM WITHIN

(or, The rules to the logic of conversation)

Some decades ago, an English philosopher, H. Paul Grice, codified the logic of conversation and the tenets of pragmatic reasoning. Mastery of the word arises from the application of four largely invisible rules that help the speaker and listener coordinate on a single meaning:

- *Quantity*. Be only as informative as is required.
- *Quality*. Try to make your contribution one that is true.
- *Relation*. Be relevant.
- *Manner*. Be brief and orderly.

Other scholars have shown that with some success you can boil the four rules down to two:

- Be relevant.
- Be efficient.

Grice was concerned not with the literal meaning of people's utterances but with what they were implicating, because these implications were what people really meant when they talked and wrote. His famous first example was mundane:

OPEN ON

The Oxford high street. A PHILOSOPHER and a COMPANION stand on the sidewalk next to a car with the PHILOSOPHER's hand resting on its roof.

                    PHILOSOPHER
          I am out of petrol.

COMPANION
There is a garage round the corner.[†]

Because of the rule of relevance, the philosopher can extract from the reply that the other knows there's a filling station nearby and believes that it is open and has fuel for purchase. The first says "I" instead of "my car" and the second says "garage" instead of "petrol filling station," in part because it is mannerly and efficient to use shorter phrases in place of longer and more explicit ones.

Grice realized that it was the dance around these rules that gave meaning to many of the figurative and creative uses of language. It is often what people implicate that is essential in a negotiation. Brendan Duddy was listening for the implications in his back parlor as the English and Irish adversaries postured, complained, and threatened for hours. Because Picco flouted the rule to be efficient and chose to say "I am prepared to accept" instead of a simpler "I accept," his counterpart knew that he was saying no.

Another example:

OPEN ON

A family room in Ithaca, New York, in 2009. Two owners of a chocolate Labrador are reading while the dog stands by the door with her paws dancing expectantly. She whines, yelps, and woofs.

OWNER #1
A brown dog is barking.

OWNER #2
Really? I don't hear a thing.

Owner #1 is not asserting the obvious fact that somewhere in the world such a dog does bark, but rather is asking the other to stop reading and take the dog for a walk, an intention interpretable based on the rules that the speaker is being efficient (saying something I can figure out) and relevant (saying something of significance to me).

[†] The American translation is straightforward: *I am out of gas. // There is a station around the corner.*

Although we understand Owner #2's response—if Owner #1 wants the dog walked, he should do it his own damn self—there is another logical inference involved in generating that meaning. This is the final rule of pragmatic reasoning, as linguists Stephen Levinson and Penelope Brown formulated it:

> Be polite; that is, do not unnecessarily impose on the other and do not overly benefit yourself.

Owner #2 is violating the rule of being polite, but she does so indirectly in order to lessen the imposition and allow Owner #1 to preserve face.

Every conversation is fraught with concerns about face. "Just as there is no occasion of talk in which improper impressions could not intentionally or unintentionally arise, so there is no occasion of talk so trivial as not to require each participant to show serious concern with the way in which he handles himself and the others present," wrote Goffman. Think of the variety of appraisals that the phrase "_____ pass the salt" conveys if the blank is filled variously by "Please," "Please, please," "Yo," "Sweetie," "Can you," "Will you," or "For fuck's sake."

The adverbs "unnecessarily" and "overly" in the politeness rule refer to all the cultural norms and social expectations that can bind the people who are conversing. For example, soft and tentative words are appropriate from the low to the high and from the powerless to the powerful, but need not be reciprocated, since a certain harshness is often allowed to flow downward. The sophisticated negotiator should therefore be an expert in politeness and face, with a keen understanding of social norms and propriety, possessed of a sense of timing, influential but not manipulative. "In our society," Goffman concludes, "this kind of capacity is sometimes called tact, *savoir-faire*, diplomacy, or social skill," and people differ not in terms of whether they have to do it—we all do—but how well they do it. In conversation, we are all envoys and ambassadors, some of us bumbling, some dexterous, some gauche, some poised.

These rules of pragmatic reasoning—be relevant, efficient, and polite—demand that participants utilize as accurate a mental model of the other as is sensible. As a speaker, I have to have a good guess of your knowledge, your preferences, your beliefs, your emotions, and so on, so that I can choose the words that you find significant, easy to process, and appropriately respectful of your face. In conversation, more so than in any other interaction, we witness the interweaving Mary Parker Follett asserted earlier: "I never [reply] to you but to you-plus-me; or to be more accurate, it is I-plus-you [replying] to you-plus-me."

"One reason for giving weight to [someone's] words," Goffman wrote, "is the belief that the very design of [their] construction provides a window into [their] intent, a window to a room that is lit from within by emotional expression." Anna Deavere Smith, repeating the words of her characters over and over in order to understand and portray them, peers through that very same window. When we negotiate, we apply the rules of pragmatic reasoning to the construction of the speaker's words in order to assess how well they know us, how accurate their mental model is of us, and what kind of answer-word their words anticipate.

YOU +/-I

(or, How the word intertwines our brains)

Modern neuroscience has discovered that Follett, Grice, and Goffman were more correct than they might have imagined about language and shared mental light. In 2010 Princeton scientists asked a narrator to recount the story of her Miami high school prom while an fMRI machine scanned her brain. Her tale involved an ex-boyfriend who stubbornly wouldn't release her from a promise to attend with him; scuba lessons the morning of the dance; a disabled dive boat stranding her on the water that afternoon; a current hunky but jealous boyfriend who overindulged that evening; fisticuffs and the beau's nose-breaking tumble in a parking lot that night; and, in the wee hours, her crashing her car into vehicles stopped on the side of the road from an earlier accident, with an unscathed police officer incompetently losing her registration and letting her drive away with a warning. You know, Florida prom.

Eleven other subjects later listened to her story while each was lying in the scanner. What the neuroscientists discovered was exactly the physical, neural equivalent of Follett's I-plus-you and Cooley's mental interweaving: while hearing the story for the first time, the speech production and comprehension regions of each listener's brain were activated in a pattern identical to that of the prom narrator. There was a neural coupling that occurred as the story was told.

As is typical in this research, the aroused clumps of neurons were shown as overlapping bright yellow, orange, and red spots on representative brain slices as the speaker and listener's brains were "lit from within" in the very same fashion. One specific area that was commonly illuminated was the medial prefrontal cortex (mPFC), the same neural locus of theory of mind that we saw activated in the beauty contest and generally when we read other people's intentions. The amazing fact arising from the analysis was that the mPFC in the listener was aroused *earlier* than that of the narrator. This showed that the mentalizing listener was anticipating the utterance before it was even on the lips of the speaker. We've all heard about active listening in various management and negotiation books, but the reality is far beyond that—we are, in fact, *predictive listeners*.

Before the subjects left the laboratory, they did one final task: they wrote down as much of the prom story as they could remember. These retellings were evaluated by multiple graders and given accuracy scores. Remarkably, these scores were significantly correlated with the degree of neural coupling across all the functional areas—auditory, language, speech, motor, and mentalizing—of the two brains. That is, the more the brain of the listening subject fired in a pattern similar to the prom-goer's, the more of the story the subject remembered later. Accuracy in comprehension was most strongly correlated with the overlap in firing of the two mPFCs and the degree to which the listener's sparked neurons anticipated and preceded the other's. Bakhtin's poetic observation that "the word forms itself in an atmosphere of the already spoken" is scientifically correct. Astoundingly, the word in language is half someone else's *before we even say it*.

If we always share the word, then anything either of us says has implications about our relationship. We can see this clearly if we imagine "Bob" and "Alice" sitting at the infinite conference table and making the following statements, both of which are truthful yet have divergent effects on the relationship:

We are here.

I am here, you are there.

For example, when one partner speaks to the other literally and spells every single thing out, the implication is that the bond is damaged: "I am here, you are there." If your negotiating counterpart is speaking to you literally, that's a sign that you do not have a rapport.

On the other hand, those who are close or want to signal closeness speak through hints. The great fiction writers understand this: one character declares his love for another in Tolstoy's *Anna Karenina* by writing just the initial letters of his avowal, a more elaborate version of ILY, SWAK, strongly implicating "we are here."

In East Asian cultures, where individuality is deemphasized in favor of the collective I-plus-you, a laconic and indirect style of speaking is often held up as the ideal. Research has shown that both silence and intimation are much more prevalent in the Chinese, Japanese, and Korean cultures than they are in the American, English, and Russian cultures. One writer notes that the effectiveness of silence in these cultures reflects the prominence of tranquility in Buddhist and Taoist thought: "It is the mind sounding inside, rather than the mouth talking outside." There are several shared proverbs reinforcing the propriety of hints: the good listener "hears one and understands ten" (Korean, Japanese); *yan wai zhi yi* ("more is meant than meets the ear"; Chinese).

By contrast, hints are often befuddling to those on the autism spectrum. Without full mentalizing capabilities and smooth pragmatic reasoning, the word isn't even half theirs. Naoki Higashida, the young memoirist with ASD, has a handful of scripted dialogues that he applies, always aware that "you can end up saying the opposite of what you wanted to say. I swear conversation is such hard work! To make myself understood, it's like I have to speak in an unknown foreign language, every minute of every day."

For those with ASD, the literal is predominant and the implicated is unread or unheard. Jokes tend to fall flat; metaphors, to obscure; ironies, to unflip; poems, to uninspire. Referring to "everything else" can be troublesome for speakers with ASD, but "I" and "you" present real difficulties. These simple pronouns require an ability to change perspective: when I say "I," you must translate the word into "you," and when you say "you," you must know that I will think "I."

In short, language for those with autism is I-minus-you, as Higashida expresses beautifully and poignantly:

> Spoken language is a blue sea. Everyone else is swimming, diving and frolicking freely, while I'm alone, stuck in a tiny boat, swayed from side to side. Rushing toward and around me are waves of sound. Sometimes the swaying is gentle. Sometimes I'm thrown about and I have to grip the boat with all my strength. If I'm thrown overboard I'll drown.

As we've seen, those of us who are "I-plus-you" utilize our mentalizing skills, strategic reasoning, and implicit understanding of the rules of conversation (be relevant, be efficient, be polite) to frolic freely and to master and coordinate our words.

SEAS* AND WORDS*

(or, The room for maneuvering that an ordinary word contains)

Sometimes our blue body of words washes up on its own shore. Years of diplomacy, with trillions of petrodollars hanging in the balance, have been spent on negotiating whether the Caspian Sea is a "sea." The Caspian is the largest inland body of water on the globe, with a surface area 50 percent larger than that of the combined Great Lakes of North America, containing a volume of water three times as great. Sailing from one coast to the other takes you from Europe to Asia, from the fresher and icier water in the north, where the Volga disgorges, to the salinity and warmth of the south.

These waters produce black treasures: 90 percent of the world's beluga caviar and 3.4 percent of global crude oil production in 2012. For centuries the Caspian region had been well known for hydrocarbons that naturally seeped right to the surface. In 1264, Marco Polo wrote, "There's a fountain from which oil springs in great abundance, enough to fill a hundred boats at a time; it is not good to eat, but it is good to burn and to rub on camels for mange."

For many decades in more recent history, the land surrounding the Caspian was divided between the empires of Russia and Persia, and on the eve of World War I the tsar's realm controlled over 85 percent of the shoreline. The Russian Revolution and its aftereffects forced the Bolsheviks to cede a greater share of the waters to its southern rival. After the shah rebranded his nation Iran, the two countries exchanged a number of diplomatic notices in the interwar years labeling the Caspian "a Soviet and Iranian sea." As both sets of diplomats realized, that little word "and" pragmatically implicated relative equality.

The dissolution of the Soviet Union in 1991 disrupted these tenuous arrangements. There were now five countries staking their claims to beach, water, fish, bottom, and, most importantly, petroleum pools. Each participant had key advantages: Russia, as the successor state to the USSR, and Iran could claim that their prior agreements still gave them joint possession; Azerbaijan and Kazakhstan had the majority of the discovered oil close to their shores; and Turkmenistan could play free agent and be wooed to join one coalition or the other.

If the parties agreed the Caspian was a "sea," it would be covered by the United Nations Convention on the Law of the Sea (UNCLOS). UNCLOS gives a "sea" non-negotiable boundaries: twelve miles of "territorial waters" off the coast completely controlled by the coastal state and two hundred miles of "exclusive economic zone" allowing solo exploitation of the sea bottom and the resources below. If one country's zones meet those of another country, then a boundary is established at the median line. However, if the Caspian was labeled a "lake," then the surrounding five states would have almost complete freedom to negotiate whatever arrangement they wanted. In 1992, both Russia and Iran pushed for a "lake" definition, with condominium rights that would promote shared development of the entirety of the Caspian's oil and gas reserves.

Of course, the negotiation did not rest solely on one word; also involved were historical precedents, alternatives and BATNAs, personalities, power, status, side deals, coalitions, persuasion, and lying. The stakes were staggering. One comparison of the difference in expected economic value between "lake" (with equal sharing) and "sea" (with UNCLOS) re- vealed that Russia and Iran each had $1.9 trillion at risk, while Kazakh- stan faced a potential swing of $3.3 trillion. Because of their geographies and the location of their petroleum reserves near shore, Turkmenistan and Azerbaijan had a relatively paltry $0.8 trillion and $0.3 trillion at risk, respectively.

After more than two decades of bargaining, countless working groups and drafts, ten gatherings of the five countries' foreign ministers, and five presidential summits, an agreement was announced in August 2018. One summary of the agreement said, "The surface is to be treated as a sea, with states granted jurisdiction over 15 nautical miles of water from their coasts and fishing rights over an additional ten miles. But the seabed and its lucrative mineral deposits are not allocated in precise form. This divi- sion of the spoils is left to countries to agree on a bilateral basis."

In a very real sense, then, the final decision was in effect to label the Caspian a "sea*." An asterisk, either actual or virtual, appended to an es- sential word or phrase is a great solution to verbal quandaries. You can give your counterpart the word and take the meaning.

Few have been better at separating word and meaning than President Bill Clinton—his "is*" and "sexual* relations*" are two examples. Clin- ton's verbal misdirections and self-excusings are prototypes of the virtual asterisks communicators can append to their words. The multiplicity of meanings and the variety of implications can give a word depth: a ONE understands it that way and a TWO this way, and the TWO knows the ONE will only plumb so far. Look back at the more complex reference game in Figure 17: suppose B2 was the real target, but Humpty wanted to mislead Alice. He could then utter "square," and Alice, smart as she is, would think that the target is B3. If she ever found out that she was misled and objected with vigor, Humpty could protest, "B2 is square: I told you the truth and nothing but the truth!"

The sin-avoiding churchman and the uncooperative witness also have a similar need for misdirection. Various theologians developed a theory of equivocation that created jesuitical asterisks. Mental reservations—the equivalent of whispered asides ("I swear I did not do it . . . today")—and intentionally ambiguous terms were authorized. One legendary example of holy evasion: "St. Athanasius is accosted on the Nile by his persecutors in the employ of Emperor Julian who demand to know 'Is Athanasius close at hand?' 'Yes,' replies Athanasius, 'he is not far from here,' and off they go in vain pursuit." The U.S. Supreme Court ruled that movie producer Samuel Bronston did not commit perjury when he answered a lawyer's query about whether he ever had a Swiss bank account with these words: "The company had an account there for about six months, in Zurich." The lawyer, mistakenly thinking that Bronston was following pragmatic rules, inferred that only the company and not Bronston himself had a Swiss bank account, so he failed to ask a more specific follow-up question.

The principle is clear: caveat auditor. Let the listener beware. As with many other forms of conduct, talk is primarily self-policed by adherence to recognized norms of behavior and by respecting the faces of those involved. The lesson for the one-step-ahead negotiator is to never rely solely on a single interpretation of a word to bind your counterpart. If your counterpart's intentions, wants, greed, emotions, face, affiliation, cash down payment, or future deals aren't guaranteeing the agreement, and only words are, then hire a lawyer. They are trained to bind people with words, and unless you went to law school, you are not.

For those of us who have typical theories of mind, who dive into language rather effortlessly, who might now agree with the sages that the composition of another's words can help us understand the intentions, desires, thoughts, and emotions of that person, and who are newly aware of the jesuitical asterisk, the preceding pages have given us enough of a sophisticated understanding of words and language—you i everything else—that we can consider more closely two critical uses of words in negotiation: persuading and lying.

BRINGING YOU YOU YOU YOU TO ME

(or, How to be both more persuasive and more resistant to persuasion)

FC Barcelona's attacking midfielder, Philippe Coutinho, is part of a very special cohort. Not only is he one of the world's most valuable soccer players, transferring in January 2018 from Liverpool FC for an estimated fee in excess of €140 million, but he was also one of the 51,971 Brazilian children Pope John Paul II created in 1991.

The Pope arrived in Brazil in mid-October 1991 for a ten-day trip to various provincial capitals. He gave numerous speeches and sermons on social justice, the sanctity of the family, and, in contravention of a decade-long governmental effort to promote family planning, contraception. His recurrent message was very direct: "The government does not have the right to promote abortion, mass sterilization and the widespread publicity of artificial methods to limit births."

The Pope's visit occurred in the middle of a weeks-long health survey in which government workers were out in the field interviewing women about a variety of matters including their fertility-related beliefs. Two economists, Vittorio Bassi and Imran Rasul, took advantage of this before-and-after overlap to document how the Pope's words might have affected both attitudes and behavior. Before the visit, 23 percent of women responded that they used contraception; afterward, that proportion fell to 19 percent. Before the visit, 30 percent of respondents said they had never used contraception and had no plans to start; afterward, that figure was 43 percent. Finally, the Pope's encouragement served as an aphrodisiac: the monthly frequency of intercourse reportedly rose by 17 percent, and that increase combined with changes in birth control led to a 37 percent rise in unprotected sex.

Birds do it, bees do it, economists take all the fun out of it. Bassi and Rasul concluded in full economics-speak that due to the "increased frequency of unprotected sex, it is plausible that a positive fertility response could exist as a result of the persuasive messages of the Papal visit." "Positive fertility response": in other words, babies. Indeed, the economists reported in their study that Brazilian women were 27 percent more likely to give birth nine months after the Pope's arrival and tour. Hence it is that the Pope's persuasive phrases against contraception produced Coutinho and his 51,970 siblings.

John Paul II had a big advantage as a persuader. We tend to believe good words and moral acts come from powerful people, so words emanating from persons of high status are more convincing. The more hierarchical the society or the organization, the stronger this tendency is. In addition, the pontiff's words persuaded members of his Brazilian flock because they were suffused with spiritual obligation and necessity—*you ought to, you need to, it would be sinful not to, be fruitful and multiply.*

There is a potential path for those of us who are not pontiffs to leverage the sense of rightness in our negotiations. Psychologists have shown that some people are more likely to believe that objects and concepts in the world have an inherent quality that allows them to fit their roles perfectly. For example, someone might think that the color black is associated with funerals because it reflects the darkness of the emotions (thereby ignoring the vast stretches of the world in which mourners normally wear white). Counterparts with this *inherence bias* are likely to connect typicality with necessity and therefore to believe you absolutely must drink orange juice for breakfast and give roses on Valentine's Day. Not surprisingly, this conflation is even more prevalent in those who self-identify as politically conservative. So if you perceive that your counterpart has inherence bias, then you can influence them with arguments based on typicality and precedence (hand them a contract marked "standard") and with the phrases "this is how we always do it" and "you should . . ."

Many bargainers refuse an opponent's ask with a line such as "I can't offer any discount." The normal counterpart who applies the rules of pragmatic reasoning, however, will interpret "I can't" as simply "I am unwilling" rather than "I am unable." If you mean you are unable, then say that directly. If you mean you are unwilling, then say "I don't." "Don't" in this setting implicates that there are personal and communal standards that you are honoring. It's these standards, not you, that are refusing the other side. The invocation of these standards also makes "don't" a more powerful word for self-control and goal attainment: you're much more likely to end the night sober if you tell yourself and your friends that "I don't have more than two drinks" instead of "I can't have more than two drinks."

"Don't," in some situations, comes close to being a perfect word, but more generally the sophisticated negotiator knows that the aptness of a word depends on both the setting and the audience (since every word is half theirs). A recent review of the scientific literature concluded that "successful persuaders are better at considering other people's mental states," "show increased activity in the brain's mentalizing system," and "are socially flexible, able to change strategies depending on context."

When typical negotiators attempt to persuade their counterparts, they automatically shift their vocabulary to the emotional end of the spectrum. They are more likely to utter, for instance, the word "wonderful" (positive and emotional) rather than "perfect" (positive and dispassionate). Superior persuaders match their phrasing to the other's basic information processing style. They make their pitches to an engineer, an economist, or someone who loves brainteasers with the words "I think," followed by words such as "cause," "know," "ought," "perhaps," and "because." And, they convince an artist, actor, or someone with a high need for affect with the words, "I feel," followed by words such as "care," "nice," "worried," and "annoyed."

Second, superior persuaders use their vocabulary to enhance their power. A short word such as "stone" (*pierre, pedra,* 돌, or 石) is more likely to be concrete, familiar, and used frequently, while a lexical giant such as "concretization" is innately elevated. These results suggest that the one-step-ahead negotiator, conditional on their ability to speak with ease and to perform with sangfroid, can gain an advantage by incorporating longer and more abstract words into their script. Through word choice, the negotiator can signal complexity of thought, strategic sophistication, status, and dominance.[†]

One application of this elevated lexicon is to pick extreme modifiers to anchor the counterpart's expectations. If you believe that I am adhering to the rules of relevance and efficiency, then when I use an obscure or long word that is harder for you to mentally process, you assume that I have a good reason for doing so. So if I offer to sell you a "*quite expensive* laptop," your estimated transaction price would be around $1,100, but if I offer you a "*phenomenally expensive* laptop," your price expectation rises to $1,575.

Persuasion is also intimately tied to four interwoven, interpersonal judgments people make: those whom we like we also perceive to be good, psychologically close, and known. There is a reinforcing cycle: goodness to similarity to familiarity to affection to goodness and so on. The one who would persuade can enter the cycle at any point and foster the linked perceptions in the one who is to be influenced: the C-gee proves himself a good man by returning a lost wallet, then a very likable fellow over dinner, where you learn that he's from your hometown, roots for the same

---

† For evidence that a harebrain can make a pig's ear of this gambit and it still partially works, see Boris Johnson.

sports team, and so forth. Lord Chesterfield advised his son to follow a similar course in order to succeed as an ambassador:

> The other necessary talents for negotiation are: the great art of pleasing and engaging the affection and confidence, not only of those with whom you are to cooperate, but even of those whom you are to oppose: to conceal your own thoughts and views, and to discover other people's: to engage other people's confidence by a seeming cheerful frankness and openness, without going a step too far.

You woo the counterpart, wrote the father to the son, because if "you engage his heart, you have a fair chance for imposing upon his understanding, and determining his will."

Every negotiation beyond the merely transactional begins with some small talk, the main point of which is to signal "I-plus-you" to each other. Goffman wrote that small-talk topics—"the weather, inflation, television shows, unsafety on the streets, and the like"—"mark a socially sanctioned opening between minds." The commonality of liking sunny days, appreciating a cold beer, having children, distrusting politicians, and so on can be reinforced by other signs of similarity. The sophisticated negotiator judiciously and subtly mimics the counterpart's posture, words, and rhythm early in the encounter in order to convince them that because you're so similar, you must be a good, likable, familiar person also. With all these positive characteristics going for you, you might be able to successfully persuade them by the end of the meeting.

In one negotiation experiment, some subjects were told to strategically and subtly mimic the mannerisms and body movement of their counterparts. Imitation resulted in more valuable agreements in total and more profit for the mimicker: relative to the control pairs, imitation increased the total value of the deal by 7 percent and the personal outcome of the aping bargainer by 15 percent. Another study tested a texting negotiation in which some of the subjects were encouraged to mimic the counterpart's words, emoticons, metaphors, abbreviations, and so on. The copying could be as subtle as replying to the counterpart's message of "Is now a good time to talk?" with "This is a great time to talk" rather than "Sure."

Again, relative to the normal control, intentional imitation raised the total agreement value by 12 percent and mimicker value by 32 percent.

So far, we've offered a lot of advice to the persuader but not much to the listener. The key is to be at a bit of a remove and be able to see the game for what it is: many of these persuasion tactics lose all power when viewed in cold bright light. Millennia before brain scans were possible, the philosophers of ancient China had recognized the mentalizing and imitative bases of persuasion: "Those who are adept in the art of speaking . . . project neither forms nor figures but live and expand in keeping with the rhythms of others, while their voice is an echo whose tone is now intense and now modulated." The sages were determined that their rulers and patrons remain unaffected by the emulating, rhythmic words of the echoing orators and mind-reading envoys who visited the court. The ideal was for the sovereign to be at a remove, with a neutral expression and a closed mouth, maintain a clear view of north and south, east and west, and be immovable. The scholars cited with approval, "Thus the kings of ancient times wore caps with strings of pearls in front so as to mask their vision and silk plugs in their ears so as to obstruct the acuity of their hearing."

For the one-step-ahead negotiator, this is the mental inner square, the metacognitive space, where skepticism, principles, goals, and "no" and "don't" reside. You fully listen and persuade and care with the outer self, but deny and object and don't care with the inner.

PROMISING 0.070 TO YOU TO YOU

(or, The prediction and detection of lying in a negotiation)

In 2008 Volkswagen set the corporate goal of passing Toyota as the world leader in sales within a decade. VW CEO Martin Winterkorn was fanatically committed to his plan, Strategy 2018, which would make the company number one "not just in units, but in profitability, innovation, customer satisfaction, everything." The only way to win all those races was to convince Americans to buy thousands of the firm's "clean diesel" cars, and the only way to do that was to make sure that these diesels were well priced, reliable, fuel efficient, and compliant with emissions standards, especially those of the California Air Resources Board (CARB). It turned out that the only way to do that was to cheat and lie.

Regulators were to learn late in the summer of 2015 that engineers at Volkswagen had algorithmically embedded a defeat device in the car's computer: this bot would recognize when the car was being tested, turn on the emissions-reductions equipment, and then later turn it off so that the car resumed spewing pollutants. During the test, the "switch logic," one of VW's camouflage names for the cheat code, ensured that the vehicle emitted less nitrogen oxides (NOx) than the mandated 0.070 grams per mile. In the months prior to the revelation, the Environmental Protection Agency (EPA) and CARB had asked the company to explain the discrepancies in the emission numbers the agencies were seeing between test and road. Since VW had failed to provide an adequate answer, the agencies had refused in midsummer to certify the company's 2016 models.

VW assigned a deputy executive, Oliver Schmidt, to visit and bargain with a personal acquaintance at CARB. As part of his preparation, Schmidt met with senior executives in Wolfsburg, Germany, on July 27, 2015. One of his PowerPoint slides showed the potential stakes of the negotiation: on the left, "positive" and approval for the new models; on the right, "negative" and possible future "indictment?" That slide would turn out to be personally prophetic. Schmidt and others presented senior management with the full purpose and exact characteristics of the cheat code and with the fact that the EPA and CARB did not know about the defeat device yet. When the first street-test anomaly had surfaced, a year earlier, Schmidt had emailed a colleague that it "should first be decided whether we are honest. If we are not honest, everything stays as it is." His decision made by the engineers' presentation, Winterkorn allegedly authorized a deceptive script for Schmidt to deliver in the following week's negotiation.

On August 5, Schmidt dutifully spoke the lines that offered his CARB counterpart technical excuses stating that any discrepancy* was due to irregularities* or abnormalities*. Two days later he used the same ambiguous language in a long phone call to another regulator. As a good envoy should, he kept his corporate *signoria* informed of his activities, sending them detailed updates assuring them that he was delivering the deceptive script right down to the jesuitical word.

However, not all VW managers were as obedient to the commands and goals of the company as Schmidt was. There was one member of the engine development department and potential negotiation attendee who Schmidt was told "should not come along—so he would not have to consciously lie." This warning would be prognostic, for that engineer was somehow not kept from a subsequent August 19 meeting with CARB and "disclosed, in direct contravention of instructions from his management," that VW was using a defeat device. What authorities had suspected was now verified, and VW would face massive fines and scandal. More than a year later, Schmidt's initial PowerPoint prophecy was also fulfilled when he was arrested at the Miami airport, having unwisely decided to leave Germany for a holiday. Schmidt pled guilty and was sentenced in December 2017 to seven years in prison. Winterkorn was indicted in May 2018; living in Germany, where he is shielded from extradition, he is unlikely to follow Schmidt's travel plan for a Florida vacation and in fact to this day maintains his innocence.

One reason that Schmidt and Winterkorn may have lied is the sometimes noxious effects of goals. Results from laboratory studies confirm that the presence of activated targets (e.g., making VW #1) can cause many people to engage in unethical behaviors. In one experiment subjects acted as manufacturers who had to turn the seven different letters in a string such as TOUAREG into as many real words (e.g., GO, AUTO, UREA, OUTRAGE) as possible in one minute. For each of eight rounds, subjects wrote all their assembled words on a separate page in a workbook. One group was instructed to do their best; a second was given a specific goal of nine words, which they were told many students had been able to achieve in the past; and a third had the same goal of nine words but would be paid an extra $2 for every round in which they attained it.

After the eight rounds, students were handed a dictionary and a score sheet that asked, for every round, whether they had produced at least nine legal words or not. Those in the pay-for-performance group were also in charge of their own reward, so they removed dollar bills from an envelope they had been given at the start of the session. Temptation lay not in the envelope of cash, as it turned out, but on the score sheet: the participants could easily and secretly report that, yes, they got nine words in a round when they only came up with seven. Goals had their intended effect—commitment to a target was strongly associated with greater word production—but also caused more people to cheat. Of the "do your best" group, 10 percent overcounted on at least one round compared to 23 percent of the "many make nine" group and 30 percent of the "$2 reward for nine" group. Moreover, those whose fingertips were brushing the goal were very likely to cheat: of those rounds in which a participant came up with eight valid words, the overreporting rates by group were 15 percent, 34 percent, and 48 percent, respectively. Almost half of those who were a mere one word shy of a goal with a $2 carrot lied about their performance. Beware the negotiating counterpart who is making you one last promise in order to reach a stated goal.

Interestingly, only one participant out of more than fifty in the pay-for-performance group slipped an extra dollar bill from the envelope. Cheating and lying are not Manichaean, white-black, on-off phenomena: they are simply Goffmanian social actions judged against the standards for bad*, bad, Bad, BAD, and *BAD* conduct. Adding one more correct word to the eight you got right is just a little stretch* ("I already had my ninth in mind when the clock ran out"), but taking an extra dollar straight out of the envelope is flat-out stealing. Similar experiments that allowed participants to self-assess, self-report, and self-reward have revealed a rough rule of thumb—40 percent of the population are reliably honest, 20 percent skew *BAD*, and the remainder are shaders, applying asterisks and stretching the truth a little here and there.

The relative proportions of truth-tellers, shaders, and liars shift in a way that an economist and a one-step-ahead negotiator would predict. Few people are inherently and continuously addicted to lying or telling the truth. Lying becomes more prevalent not only when goals are fixed but also when the stakes are higher; when low-cost justifications are at hand; when the set, the props, and the script indicate that the drama is a "competition" rather than a "collaboration"; when the communicators are more physically and psychologically distant; and when the counterpart is otherwise seen as bad or undeserving.

Deceit is subject to the division of labor and specialization: it is easier to lie through an agent, and there are occupations and industries where the norms of good* conduct include loads of fabrication. One of those industry locales is obviously Hollywood. Lynda Obst titled her memoir *Hello, He Lied*, in recognition of how prevalent falsehoods were. *The Prin-*

cess Bride author William Goldman recounts a visit to a movie producer's
hotel suite in Las Vegas:

> On and on he went, phone call after phone call, spouting inaccurate grosses,
> potential star castings, stuff like that . . . . Perversely, since he wanted me to
> know what a big deal he was, and since I already did know he was an asshole,
> I decided to hear nothing . . . . Until suddenly I heard my name, whispered
> sharply, "—Bill—*Bill*"—I glanced over and there he was, his hand over the
> mouthpiece. Then came these words: *"Which lie did I tell?"*

Hostage negotiators, who are authorized by society to tell as many
falsehoods as necessary to preserve the lives of the innocent, also face the
problem of remembering which lie they told. The command vehicle that
the St. Louis police department deployed in 2002 during a hostage crisis
had two whiteboards, one to record truths and one for falsehoods. The
two whiteboards are a physical manifestation of the increased cognitive
load that lying requires: you have to remember both reality and the un-
reality you are creating as well as where they overlap and where they are
distinct.

The example of the super-honest Volkswagen engineer seems to be
proof for the common intuition that truth-tellers and liars are easily identified. What clues did his managers and peers have as to his unshakable
veracity? They might have pointed to these traits: he never averts his gaze
when speaking; he is not nervous; he doesn't shift his body posture a lot;
his face is not discolored and he does not rub the roots of his hair with
his fingers; his facial expression remains untroubled; and his utterances
are coherent, consistent, and fluent. These traits correspond to those that
emerge from a survey that asked people in seventy-five countries how
they could tell someone was lying. The number one answer by a wide
margin was averting the gaze, mentioned by almost two-thirds of respondents. Ages ago, Darwin heard the same thing in his less formal world-
wide survey: the expression of deceit "can be recognized amongst the
various races of man" usually by the eyes, which "are said 'to be turned
askant,' or 'to waver from side to side,' or 'the eyelids to be lowered and
partly closed.'" There is only one problem—avoiding eye contact, scientific research clearly shows, is not diagnostic of telling a falsehood.

Fifth on the list of supposed cues to lying mentioned by people in the global survey was facial expression, the specialty of psychologist Paul Ekman. As we saw in Chapter 10, Ekman's position that emotions are linked to automatic, readable facial expressions has been gravely undermined by subsequent scientific results. As a result, Ekman's additional claim that the guilt, shame, and other negative emotions connected with dishonesty must be expressed on the face of the liar, and that it is sensible to train the police, FBI, and security agents in lie detection via facial action units and micro-expression identification, is also unconvincing.

Moreover, even if you could follow Ekman's advice, would you be looking for the right emotions if you focus on the negative? It seems sensible to believe that a liar must have to control feelings of revulsion and shame in order to pull off a falsehood successfully. The C-gees would beg to differ, though; they knew that what motivated a mark was not just greed for easy cash but also the thrill of getting away with something and the glee of sticking it to the system. The mark has "larceny in his veins," and once he is in the middle of the con with an illicit advantage, he feels "a queer sensation of mingled guilt and triumph," and "a delicious prickly sensation spreads over him." Researchers at the Wharton School questioned the natural assumption of negative emotions and looked for the positive feelings that might result from cheating and lying. Their experiments confirm a cheater's high, in which subjects who misreported their production of words in an anagram task felt a greater sense of excitement, enthusiasm, and determination after lying than those who reported truthfully did. Moreover, the liars felt no more negative emotions than the honest subjects did. Sometimes people will lie to your face and revel in it.

The fact is, the clues most observers use to predict whether others are lying—averted gaze, positive or negative affect, a bead of perspiration trickling down the left temple, or whatever—really aren't very accurate in the end. A statistical review of more than 200 experiments in which a total of 24,500 judgments of 6,500 true/false messages were made found that participants discerned the verity of the statements with an accuracy of 54 percent. This rate was statistically better than flipping a coin but not by a whole heck of a lot.

The more reliable evidence is found in the utterances themselves. Words are, to a certain extent, self-diagnostic. In large part due to the challenge of having to monitor both the lie and the reality, as the producer Goldman writes of failed to do, untruthful speakers often modify their normal way of speaking. These stressed utterers will emit fewer words and briefer sentences. The liar will use more short words. The exception will be "I" and "me" and "my," since the fibber is unconsciously avoiding personal responsibility. Honest speech is characterized by more self-reference—there are fewer I's in "liar."

Phrases will be repeated to you to you to you. This repetition will replace the details of time, space, and motion that truthful storytellers can summon. This repetition will replace some of the cognitive complexity of honest accounts signaled by insight words ("realize," "understand") and by exclusive conjunctions ("but," "without," "except"). There are fewer or's in "prevaricator." Lastly, untruthful utterances will lack spontaneous corrections and admissions of gaps in the speaker's memory of events.

It's important not to overstate how easily words and language diagnose the falsity of a particular assertion. Software algorithms can achieve an accuracy rate of around 70 percent in distinguishing truthful and false statements. Doing this offline is asking a whole lot. There are, however, two things negotiators can do to be more apt to catch the other side lying.

First, ignore faces and deemphasize words. Rather, stress the situational aspects of the negotiation: the history of your counterpart's actions, the incentives and stakes, the dramatic framing, and so on. As he relayed the sugared words of Borgia to the *signoria*, Machiavelli cautioned that while the duke's "language always has been and continues to be full of affection," nevertheless "the experience of others makes one fear for one's self." The logic of Machiavelli's warning is clear: if someone has every reason to misrepresent, mislead, and divert your attention, then they are likely to be doing exactly that. The sophisticated part of this advice is that in life, it often doesn't take very much—the prevalence, ease, and potentially positive feelings arising from lying might make it an attractive option even in low-stakes, face-to-face, personal situations.

In keeping with the message of earlier chapters, one other element of the negotiation situation should be kept in mind: women are often automatically assessed as marks. Sad but true: if you are a woman negotiating a deal, you should raise your prior probability that you are being lied to by your counterpart, man or woman. In one simulated negotiation study,

27 percent of the female sellers were blatantly lied to, as compared to only 9 percent of the male sellers.

Second, gather multiple clues. Ask lots and lots of open-ended questions: "Tell me about . . ." or "Talk to me about . . ." or "Say more." If open-ended queries aren't appropriate or sufficient, then embed your more directive questions not with positive assumptions ("The car doesn't emit more than 0.070 g/mi of NOx, does it?"), but with negative assumptions ("How much more than 0.070 g/mi of NOx does the car really exhaust?").

There are other linguistic maneuvers you can draw on as well. A team of criminologists led by Aldert Vrij has developed a program of cognitive lie detection, training investigators to ignore facial expressions and other standard cues and to focus instead on words. Vrij's team offers a number of very creative suggestions. The first is the equivalent of driving the VW in reverse in order to not trigger the switch logic: ask the suspect to tell the story in reverse, starting from the end and going back to the beginning. Vrij also recommends using unexpected questions grounded in very specific spaces and times: "How did you plan your trip?" or "Will you draw a picture of the interior of the office?"

On your own behalf, take advantage of the flexibility of language to be truthful and yet strategic. This should be part of your preparation for a specific negotiation and your repertoire in general. Question: "Do you have another offer?" Answers: "No, not yet." "We have had a number of serious inquiries." "I expect* to receive a term sheet in the next few days." "I believe* one of the interested parties is preparing a formal bid—and I'm afraid* I can't* tell you who [because I have no idea and am just wishing]." "Do you want to talk about item 3 on the agenda?" (Deflecting questions is surprisingly effective.) Or, simply, "I don't answer that question." This last truthful reply can also work when the counterpart hits you with an unexpected question. Other honest responses to the surprise question with very different implications for face: Silence. "That's not a legitimate question." "Let me think on that." "Why are you asking?" "Let's add that to the end of our discussion." The sophisticated negotiator, tough and fair, mentalizing and cunning, insightful and tactful, has great integrity and never lies.

There is one last topic to consider: What do you do when your counterpart says "I promise"? Are promises binding at all, or are they all disqualified through jesuitical equivocations (e.g., "fingers crossed") or virtual asterisks that leave the other plenty of room to be truthfully misleading? The answer lies in the words and choices of the pairs of participants in the now-canceled British television game show *Golden Balls*, who had to decide how to allocate a rather large sum of money. Each player had two golden balls in front of them, and when they were cracked open, one read "split" and the other "steal." Each player knew which of their two balls was which, but no one else did. If both players picked "split," then they shared the money equally; if one chose "steal" and the other "split," then the first got all the money; if they both chose "steal," then they each received nothing. Before they chose one ball or the other, the two players had a chance to negotiate. Over the almost three hundred episodes of the show, the average jackpot was more than £13,000 and the mean likelihood of a player choosing "split" was 53 percent.

A trio of economists analyzed the statements players made in the bargaining phase and found that their words mattered. The counterpart who says nothing is not to be trusted, splitting only 31 percent of the time. A player whose strongest utterance was an explicit, literal promise—"I swear"; "I promise"—was 40 percentage points more likely to cooperate and split. Those who were equivocal—"I am thinking* [at this very moment] we should split"; "it is not in my nature* to steal [but I can be swayed]"; "I would be delighted* to go home with half the jackpot [and even happier with all of it]"—were somewhat trustworthy, with a cooperation rate elevated by 21 percentage points. When the other side says, "balls have a ball to me to me to me," the one-step-ahead negotiator might ignore those words and ask the other to be specific about their intended actions, and then see if "Alice" voluntarily says, "i i i promise." As *Golden Balls* shows, the sophisticated negotiator can rely on a counterpart's explicit promise with a statistical surety of around 70 percent.

THE FINAL WORDS

There have been many words written in this chapter. Perhaps too many: i i i apologize. My intent was clear from the beginning—to help us become masters of the word; effective, persuasive, knowledgeable, honest communicators; and skeptical negotiators with savoir-faire. To do so, as Goffman wrote, we draw on the whole world that we share:

> Whatever else, our activity must be addressed to the other's mind, that is, to the other's capacity to read our words and actions for evidence of our feelings, thoughts, and intent. This confines what we say and do, but it also allows us to bring to bear all of the world to which the other can catch allusions.

What we learned, as some strange bots of superior intelligence might summarize it, is that

`words are you i everything else . . . . . . . . .`

SUMMARY

- Words are powerful and terrifying. In the wrong "minds" they can seem to threaten humanity; they can create Brazilian babies; they can move armies and emperors, the faithful and the unwitting, the bot and the ball, you and me.
- The word creates coordination games to be solved by the audience, a solution that the competent utterer has anticipated. The game is solved* by the participants obeying the rules of pragmatic reasoning: be relevant, be efficient, be polite.
- The rules demand theory of mind and mentalizing, a fact confirmed by neuroscience and a Florida prom. The brains of the speaker and listener are coupled and interwoven. We are predictive listeners: the word in language is half someone else's before we even say it.
- The importance of face, politeness, and social and psychological distance and the need for tact and savoir-faire in communication make diplomats and envoys of us all. Everything we say or hint has implications for our relationships.
- A word might come with multiple levels of meanings, or a virtual asterisk that negates the meaning, or an implication that leads us in the wrong directions. Ultimately, you rely on someone's words based

on their adherence to internalized norms and respect for the face of those involved in the talk.

- Successful persuaders are better at considering other people's mental states, and they match their words to the counterpart's information processing style and core values. Persuasion relies on the circular perceptions of goodness, similarity, familiarity, and affection: it is easier to convince someone who admires you, identifies with you, recognizes you, and likes you. One way to initiate this virtuous cycle is through reflective listening and by mimicking words, gestures, and postures.

- The tough negotiator listens from a meta-cognitive remove and often responds with the words "I don't."

- Many more people will lie than steal. A very rough rule of thumb is that 40 percent of the population is honest under most conditions, 20 percent need minimal inducement to lie, and 40 percent will shade a little here or there.

- To catch a liar is difficult. Gaze aversion and most of the body language and facial expression clues we commonly think are tells and leaks are not. Also, the liar might experience enhanced positive feelings, not negative feelings.

- Words are, to a certain extent, self-diagnostic. Because of the challenge of separating reality and falsehood, the liar has some verbal tells: shorter utterances and shorter sentences; fewer long, complex words; fewer uses of "I," "me," "mine"; more repetition; fewer details; almost no spontaneous corrections or admissions of lapses in memory.

- Women will be lied to three times more often than men will.

- To discern lies accurately, stress the situational aspects of the negotiation: the history of your counterpart's actions, the incentives and stakes, the dramatic framing, whether they are on the verge of achieving a goal. Also, gather multiple clues and ask lots of open-ended questions, some from unexpected angles.

- Promises, if phrased directly and explicitly, are 70 percent reliable.

–12–

ONE STEP AHEAD OF NUMBERS

(or, The usefulness of the quantitative mindset)

In June 1989, President George H. W. Bush proposed legislation that would reduce sulfur dioxide and nitrogen oxides in the atmosphere, the two major sources of acid rain then despoiling the lakes and forests of the Northeast. His proposal created a cap-and-trade program for the emissions from the smokestacks of coal-fired energy plants and tightened regulations on the emissions from automobile tailpipes (including those attached to Volkswagens).

These automobile regulations created conflict between the White House and the Democrats, led by Maine senator George Mitchell. NOx and other pollutants in car exhaust contributed not just to acid rain but also to increased levels of ozone, smog, and particulate matter in the air of cities around the country. As a result, many cities failed to satisfy existing federal standards on ozone levels. The Bush administration believed that one round of enhanced automobile regulations alongside cooperation from the industry would solve the problem. The Democrats felt that the vehicle pollution rules needed not just immediate tightening but a second planned increase in stringency as well.

Mitchell had a creative solution to the disagreement. He suggested a contingency: "If more than seven cities outside of California were still not in compliance with federal ozone standards by the year 2000, a second stage of automobile tailpipe controls would automatically kick in." A contingent contract is a very clever way to agree to disagree. Instead of arguing over what will happen in the future and who is the better forecaster, you simply specify combinations of triggers and actions. It is one example of the focus of this chapter—how facility with numbers and with the quantitative mindset, a facility that we will foster here, can be a big advantage in bargaining.

Once you start looking, you realize that contingent contracts are everywhere: the security deposit you place on a rental apartment, profit-sharing and bonus arrangements at work, money-back guarantees, penalties for late delivery, and "points" from movie revenues promised to actors and screenwriters. The contingent arrangement is potentially useful for aligning incentives, sharing risk, diagnosing deceit (a liar will be reluctant to hazard real money on a misrepresentation), and encouraging post-deal implementation. Fundamentally a bet, a contingent contract requires that both sides stay in touch, that future outcomes be describable and categorizable, and that both sides have enough resources to cover the stakes.

Senator Mitchell's auto exhaust contingency was well formed, since the trigger—seven cities outside California (which had its own, more restrictive, statewide standards) above the federally mandated ozone level—was quite clear. However, the trigger was too low and too likely in the eyes of the White House and the Republicans, who accepted Mitchell's structure but wanted a higher number.

Enter stage just-right-of-center Senator John Breaux, of Crowley, Louisiana, the seat of Acadia Parish. Breaux, as he often did, served as a swing vote and pragmatic coalition builder during the negotiations over the Clean Air Act amendments. At a key point of the talks, in his direct Cajun way, he uttered a classic aphorism on quantitative elements in bargaining:

OPEN ON
The wood-paneled "back room" of Senator MITCHELL just off the Senate floor.
Senators of both parties sit around the table haggling over the number of cities that
would trigger a second wave of automobile tailpipe restrictions. Senator BREAUX
enters.

BREAUX
What's going on?

MITCHELL

We say 10 and they say 12.

BREAUX

Well, there has to be a number between 10
and 12.

"There has to be a number" embodies the spirit of solvability. And solvability has been an ongoing theme here. The advice to be tough and fair, to be cunning in use of emotions and words, to conjecture the future, and to command the idiom presumes that a given negotiation is an answerable problem that can be reckoned with, deciphered, and directed. And, by gosh, if we can solve something as complex as a negotiation, a little multiplication, probability, algebra, and statistics won't faze us.

If words are offers, needing to be wrangled, shaped, interpreted, pinned down, and often drastically altered, then numbers appear to provide blessed relief: concrete, eternal, free of psychological bullshit. Those who struggle with language and social interaction can find refuge in the number line. Not at all alone among his peers, Naoki Higashida writes that his relationship with numbers is drama-free:

> We get a real kick out of numbers, us people with autism. Numbers are fixed, unchanging things. The number 1, for example, is only ever, ever the number 1. That simplicity, that clearness, it's so comforting to us.

It is not just those with ASD who find solace, safety, clarity, and harbor in the land of numbers; so do financiers, engineers, market researchers, coders, MBAs, venture capitalists, physicians, and private equity investors.

There are four takeaways from our discussion so far: (1) The attitude of solvability is critical not just to mathematics but to negotiations. (2) If the other side is insisting that "there has to be a number," then they should pay you for the concession of shifting to a quantitative negotiation. (3) You too need to be able to operate comfortably and strategically with numbers, and the good news is that the rest of this chapter will help you do this. (4) The first step might be to notice that numbers are not necessarily fixed, unchanging things shorn of human psychology.

MR. 9 ENJOYS USING DRUGS

(or, Why numbers might not be fixed, unchanging things)

To Higashida, the number 1 is only ever the number 1; to Solomon Shereshevsky, the number 1 was "a slender man with ramrod posture and a long face." Shereshevsky was profiled by Soviet psychologist Aleksander Luria in a famous book, *The Mind of a Mnemonist*. In addition to a prodigious memory, Shereshevsky had synesthesia, a condition in which numbers, letters, words, and other percepts are processed by intermingled senses. The numerals might be variously colored as well as having different personages. The number 2 was "a plump lady with a complicated hairdo atop her head, clad in a velvet or silk dress with a train that trails behind her."

For Mrs. L, a synesthete from La Belle Époque, the numerals interacted like characters from the same block of apartments:

8 is a dignified, proper lady . . . . 9, Mrs. 8's husband, selfish, fussy, self-centered, only thinking about himself, grumpy, always reproaching his wife with something or other . . . . Mr. 9 enjoys using drugs, and amongst other things likes trying out the medicines advertised in the papers.

Those with synesthesia are an extreme example, but the rest of us with commonplace minds privilege certain numbers (perhaps because they adorn the jersey of a beloved player) and disfavor others (maybe because something awful happened on that day). We include our favorites in our PINs, in our passwords, and when we play the lottery. Some numbers are round and some are familiar. Some are scary: there are elevators in buildings around the globe whose buttons take a discontinuous leap in order to avoid an offensive numeral.

In many Chinese dialects, *bā* (the number 8) and *liù* (6) are homophones for *fā* (to prosper) and *liú* (smooth), and so are considered lucky. In addition, the pronunciation of the character for the number 4 is close to that of the character for "death" and so is dreaded. Such superstitions form a beauty contest game: ZEROs believe this number is inherently unlucky but that digit brings good fortune; in certain settings ONEs have to honor those delusory preferences and therefore TWOs do also; and so on down the line. Lee Kuan Yew, the first prime minister of Singapore, recognized that these canards, through the mentalizing of buyers and sellers, could have an impact on the real estate market: "I'm not superstitious about numbers. But if you have a house which other people think has disadvantaged fengshui and numbers, when you buy it, you must consider that when you resell." In Lee's own city-state, an economic study found that apartments with numbers ending in 8 sold for 0.9 percent more, an average premium of almost $10,000, while those ending in 4 sold for 1.5 percent less, an average loss of about $16,000. Another study found a 7.0 percent resale premium for Chengdu apartments with the numbers 118, 378, 1508, and so on, with these apartments staying on the market for seven fewer days than less-auspiciously numbered ones. In neighborhoods of Vancouver with a higher than average proportion of Chinese residents, single-family houses with a street address ending in 8 sold for 2.5 percent more, while those ending in 4 sold for 2.2 percent less.

The numerological auspices carry over into other Chinese markets as well. Marriage certification in one major city peaks on the eighth, eighteenth, and twenty-eighth of the month and plunges on the fourth, fourteenth, and twenty-fourth. The Beijing Olympics opening ceremony started at 8:08 p.m. on the eighth of August (the eighth month) in 2008. Bidders in Hong Kong's automobile license plate market will pay $1,250 more for the plate MB 328 and $360 less for MB 324 than they will for MB 327. On China's stock markets, every company gets a listing number that is assigned without any prescribed system. The Bank of China's code on the Shanghai exchange, 601988, is full of digital talismans since 9, being homophonic with "long-lasting," is also considered lucky. Economists found that lobbying by companies having their initial public offerings (IPOs) on these exchanges resulted in frequencies of listing codes that were non-random— codes that included at least one of the numbers 6, 8, and 9 and not the number 4 were a substantial 60.5 percent of the total (random = 52.7 percent). Meanwhile, unlucky codes that included the number 4 but did not include 6, 8, or 9 were only 6.5 percent of all IPOs (random = 11.1 percent).

The flocking to auspicious numbers can have unexpected consequences. Not surprisingly, the Chinese IPOs with lucky codes garnered better prices on their first day of trading than did the companies with the deathly number 4 in their codes. Thereafter, however, those superstitious buyers lost money: the shares "blessed" by a 6, 8, or 9 in their code underperformed the "unlucky" shares by almost 1 percent per month for the next three years.

The uneven demand for license plate numbers also exacerbates one of China's most dire problems—traffic congestion and automobile exhaust pollution. Authorities initiated a program whereby on each workday cars with license plates ending in one of two different digits were forbidden from driving inside Beijing's Fifth Ring Road. On days during 2012 when the shunned number 4 (along with its permanent partner, 9) was banned, 86 percent of all cars were permitted to be on the road, six to eight percentage points more vehicles than on other days (when, for example, 1 and 6 were banned, or 3 and 8). Travel times increased by about 25 percent on the days that the relatively rare 4 plates were forbidden from the city. And, based on surveys, economists could calculate that on those no-4 and no-9 days, 10 percent fewer Beijing residents would report that they were "very happy" because of the extra congestion → because of the fewer cars with plates including the number 4 → because the character for the number 4 (*si*) sounds like the character for "death" (*si*).

This phenomenon is not restricted to just the East. New apartment buildings under construction in St. Petersburg, Russia, sell out the units on the seventh floor before those on the sixth and eighth floors, and those on the twelfth and fourteenth well before the thirteenth. By contrast, the number 13 is considered lucky in Italy, while the number 17 is thought to bring ill fortune. Listing prices for homes in Nevada, maybe reflecting the prevalence of craps tables and slot machines in the state, are significantly more likely to have 7 as the last non-zero digit than are those in the other 7^2 states. Presidents, even smart, thoughtful ones, can be very superstitious: "One morning, FDR told his group he was thinking of raising the gold price by 21 cents. Why that figure, his entourage asked. 'It's a lucky number,' Roosevelt said, 'because it's three times seven.'"

The point of our discussion of both superstitions and numerical soap operas is that numbers are not, despite Higashida's assertion, "fixed, unchanging things." Rather, as we will see, numbers can seem larger and smaller than they are; they can be signals and messages; they can indicate that you're ready to make a deal or that you're holding firm. Arithmetically, they are spaced out evenly along the number line like a ruler, but psychologically, there are warpings, distortions, and gaps.

For instance, a number can be at the midpoint arithmetically but still somehow not in the middle. When their bargaining had stalled, Abdullah proposed to Picco that if the Israelis released twenty prisoners, then all the remaining Western hostages in Beirut might be freed. The Italian knew that "twenty was a big number," but the following day he traveled just across the border to meet with his Israeli contact, who agreed to half of that number. How to deliver this potentially disappointing news to his nemesis? The creative Picco employed the psychology of the number line, "only partly in jest," when he told Abdullah the next night,

> Ten [hostages] is not so bad. The median point between zero and twenty is not ten, because ten is much further from zero than from twenty. So if I were to give you ten, it would mean more than fifty percent of the twenty you ask.

If your counterpart is eager to show some kind, any kind, of gain or accomplishment from a negotiation, then the increment from 0 to 1 is a big, meaningful concession, from 1 to 2 is less but still large, and subsequent steps might continue to diminish. In this sense, then, Picco was quite correct: 10 can be much further from 0 than it is from 20.

FALSE PRECISION

(or, How to communicate with numbers effectively)

That Picco's 10 can be more than in the middle, that Mr. 9 can use drugs, and that 8 and 4 can be worth tens of thousands of dollars all suggest that numbers are a bit more like words than you might initially think. Numbers have a portfolio of meanings that need to be controlled and coordinated. Though we may not realize it, we master numbers through the same rules of pragmatic reasoning: your numbers should be relevant, efficient, and polite.

To give you one example, if I'm quoting you a price down to the penny, then the implication is that every cent counts because my margin is so low. If this wasn't the case, then I would just quote you a round number. Participants in one study were told that the price of a DVD player was either $29.75 or $30 and were asked to estimate how much profit the retailer was making. The more exact price led to a cost estimate of $25.05 versus $21.80 for the rounded price. All else being equal then, making a more precise offer in a negotiation will tend to make your counterpart think you have less room to make subsequent concessions. A great deal of research has shown that precision is an effective signal of toughness, inflexibility, and competence.

Naturally, then, the implication of a round number featuring 00 or 50 is one of negotiability and tractability. So too does a number (49 or 99) that gives you a sly wink and a nudge that it is almost round. Economists affiliated with eBay examined more than ten million items listed for sale in the Collectibles marketplace with a price point between $50 and $550. Each of these ten million items had two options for any interested party—"Buy It Now" or "Make Offer." The economists found that 5.3 percent of the Buy It Now prices were one of {$100, $200, $300, $400, $500} and another 11.4 percent were a dollar or less below the round numbers.

Clicking on the "Make Offer" button allowed the buyer to submit an electronic counteroffer and initiate an email haggling process. Almost three million of the collectible items received offers and two million were sold after successful negotiations. The economists, after much statistical analysis, discovered these regularities:

1. To customers, the pragmatic implications of 99 and 00 were the same—namely, that the seller was eager to deal and would react positively to a lower offer.

2. Deal numbers lured customers in and attracted eyeballs. Although items ending in 99 or 00 were no more likely than precise prices to appear in a search results page when eBay customers typed, for example, "Hummel figurine," these digits caused the viewer to click through and see the item detail 35 percent more often for $99–$100 items and 70 percent more often for $499–$500 items.

3. The greater frequency of click-throughs meant that of the three million collectibles that were bargained for, those with round prices received an offer a week to 11 days more quickly than jaggedly priced collectibles. And the items with round prices were 3 percent to 6 percent more likely to sell and to do so about two weeks more quickly.

4. However, because the customers inferred that the seller was eager, the round-numbered items received initial counteroffers and sold at final prices that were "lower by 5–8% compared to their precise-number neighbors." The gains in likelihood of sale and time to complete a deal were offset by lower prices. To illustrate, an item listed at $300 would on average net $15 more profit if the price was dropped to $298.48, when and if it found a buyer.

5. If the potential buyer matched a round price with a round offer—a counter of $250 to a listing of $299.99—then the seller would infer that the other side was willing to deal as well, and would give a smaller concession.

6. More experienced sellers use exact prices more often than inexperienced sellers do, but they still find it helpful and strategic to use a zeroed list price on occasion: the most callow sellers use 00 and 99 with frequencies of 16.4 percent and 9.0 percent, respectively, while the most veteran merchants employ these digits 5.1 percent and 12.7 percent of the time.

Another academic team interested in the preciseness of numbers conducted experiments on decisions to engage with an exact rental offer and also sifted data from thousands of properties for sale on April 18, 2015, in Anaheim, Austin, Indianapolis, Newark, Tampa, and Washington, DC. The experiments revealed that subjects playing the role of a landlord attributed much more inflexibility to a potential renter who offered $2,117.53 in rent as opposed to one who offered $2,100, and would refuse to negotiate with the first type 60 percent of the time compared with the round type 44 percent of the time. Moreover, if an average house or condominium in the six-city database was listed for $428,000, then the owner would face a 34 percent chance of the property not selling and having to relist it. If instead it was priced at the less round figure of $427,879, then the risk of not selling would rise to 39 percent.

What does all this mean for the numerology you should employ in your negotiations? If your listed price is critical for inducing a counterpart to walk in the door and join the bargaining process, then favor goal-oriented, aggressive numbers softened with 00 and 99. Prepare to prevent or counter the request from the counterpart for a price cut; for example, "I don't offer discounts." Persuade the counterpart that they shouldn't misread the situation—you have very high, fair, and reasonable expectations. Limit the concessions that follow and use appropriate exactitude. Numerically, we get a variant on one of our guiding mantras—while you're round at the outset, you're precise and square thereafter.

Whether exaggerated exactitude is effective depends upon the audience. German undergraduates in one study simulated a negotiation over an entire chemical plant. A third of the students were told to make their initial bids with a round number in the millions (e.g., €27,000,000), a third with a figure that ended in a round number in the hundreds (e.g., €27,056,200), and the remainder with a number specified down to the cents (e.g., €26,914,538.97). The investigators determined randomly for each pair of negotiators whether the seller or buyer got to make the first offer and how precise the number should be. As we've emphasized before, there was a huge advantage to going first—that negotiator captured almost three-quarters of the entire bargaining zone on average. The round offerer was seen as less competent than the two more precise proposers and received a counteroffer that was less concessionary. Again, to many audiences, exactness suggests confidence, knowledge, and ability and is an effective strategy: relative to those whose initial offer used lots of zeroes, those who were more granular captured 50 percent more value in the deal.

Our earlier review of the anchoring effects of aggressive first offers emphasized that the effects were not greatly reduced even with experienced counterparts (it takes a very sophisticated bargainer to adequately adjust). The same is not true for precision. Experts can and will ignore what they perceive as *false precision*. What happens in the same chemical plant transaction when it is conducted by those who are knowledgeable, toughened, and cunning? The participants this time were German real estate agents who, on average, were fifty years old, with twenty-one years of experience in the business, negotiating twenty-eight property deals a year. They represented the potential buyer of the plant and were confronted with one of these opening offers: €26,000,000, €25,750,000, €25,748,637. In contrast to the inexperienced students in the first study, the experts were swayed only by modest exactness: they counteroffered to €25,750,000 with €19.1 million, but responded to the round number with €16.9 million and to the exact number with €17.4 million. The one-step-ahead agents interpreted the ungrounded exact offer as an indicator that the seller was incompetent.

When Chris Anderson and I finished writing *The Numbers Game: Why Everything You Know About Soccer Is Wrong*, we formed a consulting company to help soccer clubs win matches and build stronger teams, and to advise investors on which clubs in the United Kingdom and Europe they should consider buying and what organizational strategies they should implement. One of our favorite clients was a thoughtful, deliberate private equity investor in London. One of his strengths was to be analytical and deep into the details and yet understand the narrative and the overall strategy at the same time. During negotiations to acquire a club, as we were estimating performance risks or valuing specific revenue streams, he would occasionally object that a highlighted total reflected "false precision." He was reminding himself that a number is often just one sample out of a banded cloud of possibilities. Banishing false precision was a way to keep the true risk of a project activated (meaning his palms would stay a little sweaty) and to reserve sufficient mental resources for the metacognition he needed to monitor and correct his internal decision-making process. For him, there has to be a good-enough number and no more. The very best negotiators dispel false precision coming from the other side, but use it strategically to dominate the counterparts who are unsure of what they are doing. They let the counterpart know that they have a fine-tuned bullshit detector and are willing to use it.

Does this mean that precision and numerical maneuvering are useless against a sophisticated opponent? No; it just means that you need reasons for the precision, and such reasons can often be found, as we will see in the next sections, in a mathematical formula or a complex model.

THERE HAS TO BE A FORMULA

(or, The uses and abuses of an algebraic equation)

There are many negotiators who believe that numbers will, solely on their own, deliver *the* answer. This belief can be one manifestation of the curious passion for impartiality—numbers don't lie, the number 1 is only ever the number 1, commit to a neutral process and you'll get a fair outcome. In a contest of dueling models or battling formulas, however, the less quantitatively savvy, less perceptive, and less cunning negotiator might not only lose but be pierced through.

James Altucher, author of *Choose Yourself*, serial entrepreneur, trained computer scientist, and competitive chess player, would seem unlikely to be a runner-up to many opponents in either math ability or strategic positioning. With a double dose of intentionally unmanaged curls atop his head and a mien crafted to give the impression that he is a creative quant, he revels both in his own precocity, even as a middle-aged man, and in his ability to think himself out of any quandary.

However, when he sold his start-up, StockPickr, to Steve Elkes, an executive at TheStreet, Altucher found himself solidly one step behind at every phase of the deal, especially at the beginning when he agreed to a simple, logical formula for valuing his company. Altucher writes that Steve suggested that TheStreet is valued at 20x earnings, and that the Board would be likely to agree to something at half of that. Altucher thought that made sense and agreed, and suggested using next year's earnings.

> Steve said, "So we'll take all of your ad inventory, take your expected users based on your current growth, use our CPM (cost per thousand impressions) since we will fill up your ad inventory, and then subtract out your expenses, which is really just your salary, and there we have your earnings and we'll multiply that by 10." Simple formula. I nodded my head.

Bing, bang, boom—just crank through the expected ad revenue for an increased number of website users, net out a small salary, multiply by ten, and Altucher figured he was looking at $30 million for his young start-up. Not bad.

The two agreed to reconvene in a few days after doing some research to estimate the underlying numbers in the formula. Steve Elkes brought some help, namely the head of ad sales, Tom. Altucher walked into the arena unprepared and alone. Steve turned to Tom, who proceeded to justify a chipping away at what Altucher thought was the undisputed CPM number. By the time Tom was done, the CPM had moved from $16 to $7.

Whoops! The formula had just cost Altucher $17 million.

Tom proceeded to slice away the growth rate in users and adjust the cost numbers just a little. It was all so logical that Altucher remained completely committed to the process and couldn't wait to see what number popped out:

> By this point I was so eager to just agree to anything. I just wanted to plug the right numbers into the formula we had decided on. All the calculations I had been doing on my own went right out the window.

The number was down to around $10 million. A great payday, for sure, but far less than what he thought he was going to get.

Altucher also enjoyed the psychological satisfactions of having completed each element of the formula and a swift execution, the fastest he had ever experienced.

The bad side for Altucher was that same closing speed. In the history of the con, there's never been a mark who hasn't been hurried right out of the Big Store once he's cooled out, since if he is allowed to linger, he might wise up.

From Elkes's standpoint, this is a master class in how someone with a numeracy advantage captures value in a negotiation. Get the counterpart onto analytical, mathematical ground, set up an overall logical* structure, and then fill in the blanks with numbers that both work to your advantage and have sufficient rationale to be sold to the other side. Use outside* experts* and objective* databases to buttress your arguments and numbers. If the counterpart is looking for right numbers, overwhelm them with right* numbers.

What should Altucher have done? First, never commit to a formula without knowing how it will work out—"I don't do formulas." At the very least, he should have told Elkes to prepare an analysis, then sat and listened and asked clarifying questions as Elkes presented his equation. To participate in and agree to each step was naive at best and disastrous at worst. Second, given the formulaic process, don't also concede the "right" numbers. The right numbers, especially early on, are the ones that work for you and take you beyond your goal.

Third, having given away both the formula and specific numerical entries, Altucher characterized his mental state as "I'm stuck: I had agreed to the formula, he's showing me the actual data—I had just agreed to the price of the company, and I still don't even know what the price of the company is." He felt immobilized because of his previous words and nods—or as Robert Cialdini, the scholar of persuasion, labels the phenomenon, "commitment and consistency: hobgoblins of the mind." Cialdini quotes Leonardo da Vinci's wise saying, "It is easier to resist at the beginning than at the end." Piling up Altucher's prior commitments and little agreements is critical to why Elkes's approach was so effective.

It might be much harder, but Altucher still could have pushed back at the end. How? He should have said, "Okay, we've pretty well developed your best possible case. Let's go through it again looking at my best possible case and we will find a great number for the both of us between those two extremes." Then, starting from the top, he should have bumped up every fraction and multiplier. For example, Altucher characterized Stock-Pickr as social media meets trading and personal finance, so he could have argued that the multiple should really be on revenues instead of on earnings, and it should be 30x, and it should really be revenues in five years when all the synergies have been fully exploited, et cetera. If Elkes had objected, "But you were nodding and saying yes the whole time," then there could be room for a jesuitical answer: "Yes, I was being polite and *agreeing that you were saying* CPM is $7." But, following Leonardo, this maneuver would have been much harder to execute than not blindly and guilelessly stumbling into the situation in the first place.

A formula can in certain circumstances serve the interests of all the parties. We have emphasized that numbers are neither purely objective nor free from emotional content, but at the same time, it is true that the subjectivity and intensity of feelings conveyed by numbers usually fall well short of those that words carry. An equation, by focusing the parties on arithmetical operations and digital haggling, can be an effective way to resolve the most complex disputes, even those involving ^{235}U.

In the early stages of the tedious, difficult, multilateral negotiations that eventually resulted in the 2015 Iran nuclear deal, the government of Switzerland played an active role as an intermediary between the United States and Iran. One of the Swiss initiatives was a 2007 diplomatic non-paper (remember, a drafted "just-talking") that featured two formulas, one of which concerned centrifuges.

What the intelligence agencies of the West knew for years had become a public accusation in late 2002, when the Bush administration reproached Iran for attempting to build nuclear weapons. Months of stop-and-start talks ensued among the countries of what came to be known as the P5+1 (China, Russia, the United Kingdom, France, and the United States, the permanent members of the Security Council, plus Germany), the United Nations, the International Atomic Energy Agency (IAEA), and Iran. Much of the discussion revolved around the consequences of Iran building and running the huge, high-tech centrifuges needed to separate fissionable ^{235}U isotope from yellowcake and create enriched uranium. The monitoring problem is that the same basic process can be used to produce either the fuel for nuclear reactors peacefully producing electricity or, with more spinning and refining, weapons-grade material for nuclear bombs.

For several years Iran had cycled through shutdowns and restarts of its nuclear facilities, each time ratcheting up its total capacity. During these months, both the United States and Israel debated internally whether preemptive military action against Iranian facilities was warranted; the IAEA reported the country to the UN for a whole host of violations; and in January 2007, an Iranian nuclear scientist was assassinated by agents of Israel's Mossad. Negotiations sputtered to a halt.

The Swiss non-paper, with its full deniability, stepped into this maelstrom. It proposed to relaunch the negotiations in three steps, with the first two labeled as "informal pre-talks" and "pre-talks." Each side would show good faith in these pre-negotiations through confidence-building measures: no new sanctions on one side, and no new enrichment activities on the other. The third step, the actual negotiation, would be guided by two formulas, one for the rate of uranium enrichment and the one

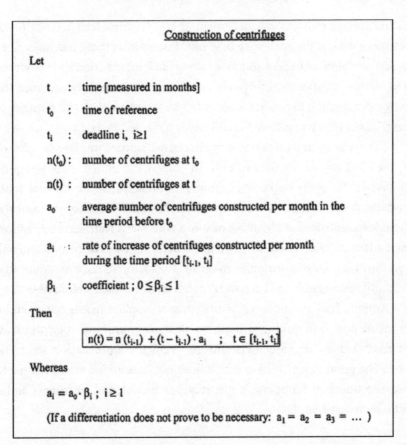

Figure 18. Source: T. W. Langenegger and M. Ambühl, "Negotiation Engineering: A Quantitative Problem-Solving Approach to Negotiation," *Group Decision and Negotiation* 27, no. 1 (2018), 9-31.

in Figure 18 (copied from the actual non-paper) for construction of centrifuges.

All the equation said is that a future month's number of centrifuges, $n(t)$, equals the number Iran had the month before the deadline, $n(t_{i-1})$, plus an allowed monthly increase, a_i, times the number of months that have passed. We don't need to go through all the variables and lines of this formula to see that it certainly seems far removed from the dread of nuclear annihilation. It was a logical and mathematical structure upon which the parties were encouraged to project their rationality.

As with the formula Elkes presented to Altucher, this equation had certain skewed presumptions buried in its objectivity*. First, it established

a_0, the average monthly rate of centrifuge construction Iran had before the reference date, as the anchoring base rate. But many of those machines were built in violation of IAEA regulations using illicit information and resources, and so this equation basically validated their existence. Second, since the factor β_i adjusting the base rate couldn't be less than zero, the number of centrifuges Iran was allowed could never have decreased.

The Swiss formula was not very successful, since it was largely ignored by the P5+1 and the Iranians in 2007. In general, the United States was quite annoyed at the active brokerage attempts continually made by the diplomats in Bern. A secret cable released by WikiLeaks included a report from the American ambassador about his meeting with Swiss state secretary of foreign affairs Michael Ambühl: "Ambühl is determined to be helpful and will certainly look for opportunities to do so. That said, we have no doubt that Ambühl understands the US government's views on such 'helpfulness.'"

Ambühl had an undergraduate degree in applied mathematics and a graduate degree in nonlinear mathematical programming. As with Elkes, numbers readily appeared in his mind as vehicles of persuasion and solution. The good news for us is that it does not take an advanced degree to become fluent in numbers; it just requires heightened awareness and a little bit of hard work.

I'D RATHER SEE THAT DONE ON PAPER

(or, The specific details of numeracy)

More of a literary *oeuf*, Humpty Dumpty was an ovoid oaf when it came to arithmetic and math. Before they gloried about words, Dumpty and Alice argued about numbers in order to determine whether birthday or un-birthday presents were better:

```
                    HUMPTY DUMPTY
        You don't know what you're talking about!
        How many days are there in a year?


                       ALICE
        Three hundred and sixty-five.
```

HUMPTY DUMPTY

And how many birthdays have you?

ALICE

One.

HUMPTY DUMPTY

And if you take one from three hundred and
sixty-five what remains?

ALICE

Three hundred and sixty-four, of course.

HUMPTY DUMPTY

[Doubtfully] I'd rather see that done on
paper.

Alice can't help smiling as she takes out her memorandum book and writes:

$$\begin{array}{r} 365 \\ -1 \\ \hline 364 \end{array}$$

Dumpty takes the book and looks at the page carefully.

HUMPTY DUMPTY

That seems to be done right—

ALICE

You're holding it upside down!

HUMPTY DUMPTY

[Gaily] To be sure I was! I thought it
looked a little queer. As I was saying, that
seems to be done right—though I haven't
time to look it over thoroughly just
now—and that shows that there are three
hundred and sixty-four days when you might
get un-birthday presents—

ALICE

Certainly.

People differ greatly in their ability to look at numbers and mathematics right side up. Humpty's lack of facility with numbers may have explained why he had to spend all day sitting atop a wall—it's difficult to find work in a modern economy without being able to do your sums. Moreover, if you fancy yourself as middle- or senior-management material but aren't strong in numeracy, then the odds (which Humpty Dumpty would need to see done on paper) would be stacked heavily against you. A survey of one thousand residents of the Netherlands found that their level of numeracy, even after accounting for how many years of school they completed, how high their annual income was, how much financial knowledge they had, what their risk preferences were, how old they were, and so on, was significantly and positively related to how much wealth they had accumulated.

In an interview, Jon Huntsman Sr., the wealthy rube* from Salt Lake City we met earlier, said that what matters in bargaining "is one's drive, one's intelligence with respect to quantitative areas. I think you have to understand math and a quantitative-type mindset to out-negotiate your opponents." Huntsman's point seems done right except for one small correction—understanding math is neither necessary nor sufficient. The key is actually the second condition: to succeed at negotiation, you have to understand your counterpart's quantitative-type mindset. Understanding math and not being sophisticated about mental interweaving with your counterpart makes you Altucher being led down a wallet-emptying path. Simply being good at algebra, statistics, and equations is not enough.

There are two broad functions that are fundamental to the quantitative mindset—numeracy and cognitive reflection. The psychologist Ellen Peters has shown that our numeric competency takes three forms: objective (corresponding to numbers in calculations), subjective (numbers in emotions), and symbolic mapping (numbers in space).

Each form of numeracy is associated with a particular set of questions. The most frequently used diagnostic test for objective numeracy has some easy problems:

- Which of the following numbers represents the biggest risk of getting a disease? (1 percent, 10 percent, or 5 percent)

It also includes some that are of moderate difficulty:

- Imagine that we roll a fair, six-sided die 1,000 times. Out of 1,000 rolls, how many times do you think the die would come up even (2, 4, or 6)?

And there are some that are hard:

- In the Acme Publishing Sweepstakes, the chance of winning a car is 1 in 1,000. What percentage of tickets of Acme Publishing Sweepstakes wins a car?

Subjective numeracy is an individual's psychological comfort with numbers. It is directly measured through answers to a series of questions along these lines:

- How good are you at working with percentages?
- How often do you find numerical information to be useful?

Finally, the symbolic mapping protocol elicits a person's intuitive number sense, based on deep-seated perceptions of size and distance. The subject is shown an unmarked line, the equivalent of a straight street in Singapore; is told that 0 resides at the left end and 1,000 at the right end; and then is asked to mark, on the line, one by one, in random order, where such numbers as #6, #71, #230, or #780 are located. The measure of competency here is how closely the subject's markings correspond to where each number actually resides.

Peters demonstrates that the three forms are moderately correlated. Symbolic mapping helps with the storage and recall of numbers from memory and hence is directly associated with stronger objective numeracy. Competency with objective operations ($365 - 1 = 364$, $1/1000 = 0.1$ percent) is directly linked to higher-quality decision making, better risk assessment, and sharper "judgments about social relationships, behavioral norms, professional competency, and many health behaviors."

Being fluent and accurate in calculating percentages, proportions, and probabilities leads, in turn, to positive emotions and quantitative self-confidence.

These numerical self-perceptions are also where gender is most relevant: Peters finds that men and women differ only marginally on objective numeracy but very significantly on subjective numeracy. Those lower in subjective numeracy have more math anxiety and are less motivated and confident in using numbers.

The second element critical to the quantitative mindset is reflection, the meta-cognition that monitors how the self is thinking, produces doubt, and intervenes to make corrections if necessary. The diagnostic instrument here is the Cognitive Reflection Test, which was invented by Shane Frederick in 2005 and popularized by Daniel Kahneman in *Thinking, Fast and Slow*. It consists of only three simple questions (if you don't know them, cover up the solutions at the bottom of the page and try to answer them):

1. A bat and a ball cost $1.10 in total. The bat costs $1 more than the ball. How much does the ball cost?
2. If it takes 5 machines 5 minutes to make 5 widgets, how long would it take 100 machines to make 100 widgets?
3. In a lake there is a patch of lily pads. Every day the patch doubles in size. If it takes 48 days for the patch to cover the entire lake, how long would it take for the patch to cover half of the lake?

The answers that leap to many people's mind and seem automatically correct are often wrong.[†] More important than the arithmetic that you have to do to get each question right are the inner senses of "Wait a second, why are they bothering to ask me this?" and "Have I really done this correctly?" The CRT proves that Humpty Dumpty's hesitancy and desire to see things done on paper is often exactly the right approach. The most effective quantitative mindset for negotiation is one that is doubting, critical, and self-paced.

---

† The correct answers are 5¢, 5 minutes, and 47 days, respectively, but the intuitive answers are 10¢, 100 minutes, and 24 days.

The CRT is simply scored by the number of correct answers. A meta-analysis of tens of experiments involving more than forty thousand people taking the test found that the hardest question is the bat and ball, followed by the widgets and then the lily pads, and that about 40 percent of people answer none correct, 25 percent answer one, 20 percent two, and 15 percent all three. One study found that those with autism spectrum disorder scored an average of two, while a matched set of typically developing young people scored an average of one. The young people with ASD who see the number 1 only ever as the number 1 routinely distrusted their own intuitions and relied on deliberative cognitive processes, and as a result, they were more successful on the CRT.

A 3 on the CRT is associated with greater immunity to decision-making biases like the gambler's fallacy of thinking a random outcome is more likely because it hasn't happened for a while, framing effects where you switch preferences for a medical treatment based on whether you're told the survival rate (20 percent) or the fatality rate (80 percent), and sunk costs in which money already spent affects your future path.

Lastly, in a beauty contest experiment where groups of German undergraduates were trying to get closest to two-thirds of the average of the group's guesses, the average guess was 45, making 30 the winner, and those who got all three CRT questions correct had an average guess of 26, with clumps around 33 and 22. So cognitive reflection is associated with greater strategic accuracy.

What, then, can Humpty Dumpty and his less numerate brethren do? First, keep the calculator app on your phone closed when you're not at the bargaining table. Force yourself to do mental math and allow numbers to bang around in your brain. Figure out the tip in a restaurant in your head; do sudoku puzzles; balance your checkbook; help your kids with their times tables and math homework (heck, scan their homework after they've gone to bed and try to do it yourself); immerse yourself in the analytics side of the sports you love—speeds, accuracies, salaries; create formulas and spreadsheets when you would otherwise wing it; and so on. It is possible to become more numerate with practice.

Second, simulate Barbara Oakley's reprogramming. Oakley was a self-described mathphobe in elementary and high school who skipped college to enlist in the U.S. Army and attend the Defense Language Institute in order to learn Russian. After leaving the army, she found work translating for Soviet fishermen, enduring "seasickness and sporadic malnutrition out on stinking trawlers in the middle of the Bering Sea."

Inspired by the engineers she had known in the military, Oakley decided to return to school and get her degree. She had the same insight that we've been exploring: that the word and the number are less different than they might seem. So she applied the same principles she'd used to learn Russian to master the language of mathematics. That meant, first, lots of rote memorization and deliberate practice. Second, she set a goal of fluency that could be achieved only through serious play with numbers, repeating and varying her interactions with them and with mathematical operations and functions. Her wonderful description gets right to the heart and root of the technique:

> Take a very simple example, Newton's second law of $f = ma$. I practiced feeling what each of the letters meant—f for force was a push, m for mass was a kind of weighty resistance to my push, and a was the exhilarating feeling of acceleration . . . . I memorized the equation so I could carry it around with me in my head and play with it. If m and a were big numbers, what did that do to f when I pushed it through the equation? If f was big and a was small, what did that do to m? . . . I was beginning to intuit that the sparse outlines of the equation were like a metaphorical poem, with all sorts of beautiful symbolic representations embedded within it.

Notice that what she was attempting to do was to transform herself into a bit of a synesthete, someone for whom numbers, equations, and functions were imbued with a bit of life.

Third, take your time. If you need to have the numbers done on paper and you need moments to reflect, fine. The other side is impatient and ready to go and believes they have the answer (the bat is 10¢, duh!). There are two possible reactions: you can feel flustered and upset and beholden to the counterpart, or you can realize that you are now completely in control of the pace and tempo of the negotiation.

Fourth, as with anxiety over negotiation, reframe math anxiety as math *challenge*; your elevated heartbeat is a sign of excitement, not nerves. Remember that it is less important to understand the math than to understand the quantitative mindset, and that is exactly what we have been doing here. They are thinking, "There has to be a number," and you have the one-step-ahead advantage of knowing they are thinking exactly that. Recall that deliberation is an advantage and in almost all cases the math is solvable. Don't be discouraged by difficulty: none of the elements of a negotiation—strategy, preparation, acting, directing, toughness, fairness, people, words, or numbers—is meant to be easy.

Fifth, many of the math-fluent have a blind spot toward those who are not. Hence this is an excellent setting for acting like a ZERO when you're really a TWO. You can foster this misperception either through equivocal signals of denseness, emotionality, or irrationality or by not correcting the arrogant counterpart's biased attributions of these qualities onto your persona.

THERE HAS TO BE A MODEL

(or, How to keep mathematical complexity in perspective)

A model is a set of quantitative relationships or formulas intended to mimic present reality and then to predict future events. A model's varying extrapolations are often labeled "base case" (the median or most likely outcome), "downside" (a representative bad outcome), and "upside" (a very good exemplar). A model might be contained in a spreadsheet or lines of code. It might draw from and insert entries into a large database. It is a complex quantitative object intended to wrangle with and corral uncertainty, but oftentimes it exists primarily to intimidate and persuade.

In our soccer consulting business, Chris Anderson and I had another client who made his fortune in private equity and was looking to invest in a football club in Europe. His quantitative mindset was to measure and project every single detail, to atomize risk with the hope that it might disappear altogether. For him, there had to be a number, a number, a number, ad infinitum. We helped build models of potential target clubs on spreadsheets with tens of tabs, hundreds of circular links, thousands of rows, and hundreds of thousands of cells. The fifty-sixth version of the model for one club that was a potential target for acquisition had a line that contained seven years of history and five years of projection of rental income of the smaller banquet room at the stadium for off-season week-end weddings of Asian fans of the club.

Models like this start to take on a life of their own and become their own rationale. At some point, we became like the emperor's cartographers in the famous little story by Jorge Luis Borges "On Exactitude in Science." According to Borges's narrator, in this empire, due to the technical advances in surveying, charting, and plotting, the maps had naturally grown in size to the point that a village was needed to house the map of a city, and a city was needed to house the map of a province. The trend was inexorable, until it wasn't:

> In time, those Unconscionable Maps no longer satisfied, and the Cartographers Guilds struck a Map of the Empire whose size was that of the Empire, and which coincided point for point with it. The following Generations, who were not so fond of the Study of Cartography as their Forebears had been, saw that that vast Map was Useless, and not without some Pitilessness was it, that they delivered it up to the Inclemencies of Sun and Winters.

By the end, when the acquisition came a cropper, the model had long left behind any objective usefulness and its exactitude was performative. It had grown constantly to address the doubts and bolster the confidence of the principal investor. The sovereign would have his map. And, as a counterpart facing him in the negotiation, you had to make a choice about how to deal with his model and the numbers that it created.

In some negotiations, a model is meant to overwhelm and to cover exactly and comprehensively. A complex model gives the overseer many hidden levers to tweak and adjust in order to ensure that the right number is outputted. It can serve as both formula and expert, and its oracular function as a type of Magic 8-Ball can communicate both flexibility ("Reply hazy, try again") and firmness ("My sources say no"). It invites the same participation as Elkes's formula did for Altucher by allowing small changes to the inputs ("Let's use next year's earnings plus an additional 1 percent") and thereby gaining commitment to the marginally changed number. Such a formidable black box will be sufficient to overwhelm many rational but unsophisticated opponents.

Using a model on more advanced counterparts requires a subtler performance. If, for instance, you were selling an Italian soccer club, you could give a nod to the inherent false precision while still retaining the anchoring effect with this script: "You will see in cell BX6388 on the Summary tab that the model says €263.48588M but we just rounded that off in our proposal to €263M." You could also inject some small amounts of statistical noise in the model in order to present a range to the other side: "The model is 95 percent confident that the right number is between €262.88M and €265.54M." Recent research has shown that the implications of such a range offer are flexibility, reasonableness, and politeness and can cause opponents to feel that an aggressive counteroffer on their part would be inappropriate and impolite.

The first step in confronting any model is to not be intimidated. As we've just seen, the more complex the model, the more likely it is merely an engine producing noxious clouds of false precision. The emperor of the model is hoping to make it the anchor of the negotiation, so the first countermove is not to allow that, and instead demand mutual model disarmament: take out a pad of paper and say, "Let's just rough out the numbers." If you have multiple viable alternatives, then you can also feel comfortable dismissing the other side's model: "I don't care what your spreadsheet says. These are the terms that will get the deal done."

You might feel comfortable, if your subjective numeracy is high, taking on the model directly. Invalidate the model by finding a single error (there is surely one there) and use that crack to question the whole numerical edifice. Ask the other side to give an exasperatingly complete list of all the assumptions, and look for gaps and weaknesses; a failure to adequately model macroeconomic cycles, international trade, and currency movements is almost always present. Avoid asking them to tweak this factor or that, because—as with Altucher—this might commit you to an unknown output that they control. Rather, if you see a very dubious or skewed assumption but can't fully invalidate the model, then insist on a contingent agreement giving you most of the upside. Present your own model based on your own comparative advantage and not a need to match their complexity. Sophisticated negotiators know that a single comparable can be just as valid a "model" as thousands of lines of code and might be easier to defend.

Above all else, since you are the targeted audience of the model, don't give it any more validity than it deserves. Modelers will contend that the output of their model represents a "fair," "correct," or "market" price, but we are all smart enough by now to realize the subjectivity of these adjectives. Lines of code or numbers of tabs and cells are not correlated with correctness. Take comfort in standing by the side of Warren Buffett. In his 2008 letter to the shareholders of Berkshire Hathaway after the pop of the housing bubble and the vitiation of millions of mathematically complex mortgage-backed securities, Buffett wrote:

> Constructed by a nerdy-sounding priesthood using esoteric terms such as beta, gamma, sigma and the like, these models tend to look impressive. Too often, though, investors forget to examine the assumptions behind the symbols. Our advice: Beware of geeks bearing formulas.

There is nothing sacred about a mathematical formula or model. Remember the following generations who saw that the vast map was useless and abandoned it to the blistering heat and the mounting snows.

STATISTICS

(or, Final words on numbers)

We have tried in this chapter to see the life in numbers. To appreciate that numbers' objectivity does not eliminate their subjectivity. They are a communicative medium subject to the rules of pragmatic reasoning, to situational influences, and to framing effects. The numerically fluent will use numbers, formulas, and models to influence and dominate negotiations. You can improve your own numeracy through practice and deliberation, and by lowering your anxiety through reframing numbers as a challenge or through a deeper understanding of the quantitative game.

To be a great negotiator, you have to understand not so much the number itself as varieties of extant quantitative mindsets. There are people in the world who always believe that there has to be a number, who feel that the number 1 is only ever the number 1, who look at a digit and see Mr. 9, who see 00 and 99 as an invitation to bargain, who look at an equation and see a pushy f or a variable x whose mood runs hot and cold or a constant *e* who is reliably consistent day after day, who feel there can't be too many numbers or too few, who diagnose false precision or mainline it.

The one-step-ahead negotiator commands the quantitative medium and translates Goffman's observation from conversations to numbers: "The whole framework of [numerical] constraints—both system and ritual—can become something to honor, to invert, or to disregard, depending as the mood strikes."

Who better for last words on numbers than Szymborska? The poet saw the models we fit ourselves into, the formulas we hew to, and the numbers we create. With a wink to false precision and the similarity between the verbal and the calculative, her poem "A Word on Statistics" is simply a list of the number of people out of every hundred who have better judgment (fifty-two), who are consistently good (four, or perhaps five), who are not to be trifled with (forty-four), who are fair (thirty-five) unless a lot of work is required (three), and so forth.

And, since you've arrived at the end of the book, we can add our own stanza to her list:

Sophisticated negotiators,
resolutely one step ahead:
not many, but now
one more than there used to be.

SUMMARY

- Numbers are not fixed, unchanging things. Like words, they take on meanings based on the logic of conversation and the three rules of pragmatic reasoning: be relevant, be efficient, be polite.
- All else being equal, making a more precise offer in a negotiation will tend to make your counterpart think you have less room to make subsequent concessions. Exactitude implicates confidence, knowledge, ability, and toughness.
- A round number featuring 00 or 99 implies negotiability and tractability. If the listing price is visible and is the key factor in initiating negotiations, as in many real estate deals, then we have a variant on

one of our guiding mantras—your number is round at the outset, precise and square thereafter.

- Experienced, sophisticated bargainers are less vulnerable to the effects of exactness and are more likely to recognize and call out false precision. For these people, the quantitative mindset is "There has to be a rough number that is good enough."

- Don't agree to a formula without knowing what the result is. Don't believe deeply that there are "right" numbers. And don't implement an unwise commitment just because you made it.

- Learn to dominate your counterparts with numbers: get them onto mathematical ground, set up an overall logical* structure, use outside* experts* and objective* databases, give them the right* numbers, and pile up the prior commitments and little agreements.

- The most effective quantitative mindset for negotiation is one that is reflective, doubting, critical, and self-paced.

- Those who struggle with numeracy should commit to doing more mental math and deliberately practicing, setting a goal of fluency and familiarity with numbers and operations, taking their time in order to control the tempo of the talks, and reframing math anxiety as math challenge.

- When confronting a model, you need not bow down: challenge the other side to a duel of rough numbers, leverage your other alternatives, present your own strategically crafted model, find an error, and criticize the underlying assumptions.

ACKNOWLEDGMENTS

Pierre Menard, as Borges tells us, dedicated his adult life to authoring the Quixote. He didn't want to copy it line for line; he didn't want to transform himself into Cervantes and then produce that man's work; he wanted to write the very same phrases and sentences Cervantes had, but as Pierre Menard. His was "a task of infinite complexity, a task futile from the outset." He labored ceaselessly nonetheless and his "drafts were endless." Menard committed each day's imperfect pages to "a cheery bonfire." He refused to be one of those authors who "publish pleasant volumes containing the intermediate stages of their work": His book would see the light of day only when the Quixote emerged.

All modern writers, this one included, are Pierre Menard: vainly trying to author a mythical book that we know preceded us and that we affect marginally as it becomes reality. Most of us fail to hold ourselves to Menard's standard and so, if we're very lucky, we share a passable volume of intermediate work with the world.

Menard felt that his task was a game of Solitaire and he worked completely alone. I did not. I thank my mathematician parents, who taught me dedication to a craft as they sketched equations, semi-simple groups, and commutative rings into the night, every night. I thank those who taught me to string a few words together correctly and to some effect, especially Florence Stein, Frank Raispis, and Jim Dowdle. I thank those who taught me social science and behavioral economics, especially Gary Becker, Colin Camerer, James Coleman, Bob Frank, Lester Telser, and Dick Thaler. I thank my partner in the best footballing adventures, Chris Anderson. I thank those who educated me about some of the principles and characters featured in the book, especially David Feldshuh, Ray Friedman, Noah Goodman, Chris Guthrie, Chris Honeyman, Edward Komara, Beta Mannix, Eric Min, Stephen Moeller-Sally, Kathleen O'Connor, Cetywa Powell, and Garnett Slatton. I thank Suzanne Gluck at WME, whose questionable risk assessment led her to take me on as a client. I thank Karen Wolny, who brought my proposal to St. Martin's. I thank Tim Bartlett, whose taste and judgment turned a tome of uncertain quality into a much more readable version. I thank Steve and Paul, who, as brothers do, assured me that the infinite complexity of my task was matched only by my inadequacy to it. I thank the dear ones whose existence brought purpose and joy to the task: Ben, Mike, Tom, Rachel, Mariana, and granddaughter Emilia. And, most of all, I thank the beloved dulcinea who stayed by my side throughout the futility, Serena Yoon.

NOTES

PREFACE
ONE STEP AHEAD OF *ONE STEP AHEAD*

All Dale Carnegie quotations are from his *How to Win Friends and Influence People* (New York: Simon & Schuster, 1936); biographical details are from Lowell Thomas's introduction to the book and from Jessica Weisberg, "What Dale Carnegie's 'How to Win Friends and Influence People' Can Teach the Modern Worker," *New Yorker*, April 2, 2018.

The four maxims are from Roger Fisher and William Ury, *Getting to Yes*, 2nd ed. (New York: Houghton Mifflin, 1991), with some who agree (Carrie Menkel-Meadow, "Why Hasn't the World Gotten to Yes? An Appreciation and Some Reflections," *Negotiation Journal* 22, no. 4 [2006]: 485–503) and some who disagree (Chris Voss with Tahl Raz, *Never Split the Difference* [New York: Harper Business, 2016]; Jim Camp, *Start with NO* [New York: Crown Business, 2002]).

Critiques of Obama are from two pieces by Noam Scheiber in *New Republic*, February 10 and 14, 2012, and Bill Maher's joke is from Krystal Ball, "Why Obama Is So Bad at Negotiations," *Atlantic*, August 2, 2011.

CHAPTER I
THE ENVOYS

The letters from these months in 1502–1503 can be found in Niccolò Machiavelli, *The Historical, Political, and Diplomatic Writings*, vol. 3, *Diplomatic Missions 1498–1505*, trans. Christian Detmold (Boston: Osgood, 1882), and his advice about reading intentions in Niccolò Machiavelli, "Discourse on the Affairs of Germany and Its Emperor," in *The Essential Writings of Machiavelli*, tr. Peter Constantine (New York: Random House, 2009).

Erica Benner is the principal rehabilitator of Machiavelli's reputation in *Be Like the Fox: Machiavelli's Lifelong Quest for Freedom* (London: Allen Lane, 2017).

The equation Negotiator = Psychologist + Prophet comes from Claudia Roth Pierpont, "The Florentine," *New Yorker*, September 15, 2008.

Ruth Ann Wallace's story of the negotiation ("Goffman Really Was Going Out of His Way to Help People Who Were Different, 2010") is one of the documents held in the extensive and invaluable Goffman archives heroically assembled by Dmitri Shalin at the University of Nevada, Las Vegas; see *Bios Sociologicus: The Erving Goffman Archives*, ed. Dmitri N. Shalin (UNLV: CDC Publications, 2009), http://cdclv.unlv.edu/ega.

The Berkeley scene in 1968 draws from W. J. Rorabaugh, *Berkeley at War: The 1960s* (New York: Oxford University Press, 1989).

The judgments about Goffman and the recollections of his games and incidents are from Shalin's interviews in the UNLV archive with Thomas Schelling (2015), Michael Delaney (2011), Daniel Albas (2010) ("granary"), Sherri Cavan (2011), Marly Zaslov (2009), Jacqueline Wiseman (2009) ("more prestigious"), Ann Swidler (2010) ("dinner party"), and Calvin Morrill (2008).

In addition, *Bios Sociologicus* holds papers published in other venues, including Gary T. Marx, "Role Models and Role Distance: A Remembrance of Erving Goffman," *Theory and Society* 13 (1984): 649–662 ("1940s private eye"); Yves Winkin, "Erving Goffman: What Is a Life? The Uneasy Making of Intellectual Biography," in *Goffman and Social Organization Studies in Sociological Legacy*, ed. Greg Smith, 19–41 (London: Routledge, 1999) ("don't be so nostalgic"); and Jenny Diski, "Think of Mrs Darling," *London Review of Books* 26, no. 5 (March 4, 2004) ("watch the way people snore").

Goffman's quote about the ideal spot in a game comes from his *Strategic Interaction* (Philadelphia: University of Pennsylvania Press, 1969).

The result of Michael Jordan being two steps ahead of Steve Kerr was recounted by the latter on *The Bill Simmons Podcast*, Episode 294, December 1, 2017.

The pianist's biography was assembled from Vivien Schweitzer, "Talented, Eye-Catching, Unapologetic," *New York Times*, April 6, 2012; Janet Malcolm, "Yuja Wang and the Art of Performance," *New Yorker*, September 5, 2016; "*Listen* magazine Yuja Wang interview (full version)," YouTube, posted by ArkivMusic, August 23, 2013, https://www.youtube.com/watch?v=JdCJzInwyso&t=1116s; Stuart Isacoff, "Artist of the Year 2017: Yuja Wang," Musical America, www.musicalamerica.com/pages/?pagename=2017_Artist_Wang.

The history and current status of the piano in China is based on Jindong Cai and Sheila Melvin, *Beethoven in China* (New York: Penguin, 2015) and their National Public Radio interview, August 25, 2015; Madeleine Thien, "After the Cultural Revolution: What Western Classical Music Means in China," *Guardian*, July 8, 2016; Clarissa Sebag Montefiore, "Why Piano-Mania Grips China's Children," BBC.com, October 21, 2014; Alex Ross, "Symphony of Millions," *New Yorker*, July 7,

2008. Mao's metaphor is quoted in Sheila Melvin, "Piano Nation," *Slate*, September 11, 2015.

The quotes about the necessity of negotiating skills for the successful soloist can be found on jonkimuraparker.com, in Gustav Meier, *The Score, the Orchestra, and the Conductor* (Oxford: Oxford University Press, 2009), and in Gidon Kremer, "Looking for Ludwig," www.kremeratabaltica.com/searching-for-ludwig.

The qualities of Wang's performances are described in David P. Goldman, "Two Transgressors," *Asia Times*, February 15, 2017; Michael Tilson Thomas is quoted in "Unique Mentorship Between Conductor and Pianist Sparks Musical Fireworks," *PBS NewsHour*, September 25, 2015; Jay Nordlinger, "Once More, with Feeling: Yuja Does Carnegie," *New Criterion*, December 12, 2014.

The neuroscience of musical training and piano playing can be found in Eitan Globerson and Israel Nelken, "The Neuro-Pianist," *Frontiers in Systems Neuroscience* 7, no. 35 (2013); Julia Turan, "Bimanual Labor: The Neuroscience of Piano Playing," Stanford Neurosciences Institute, March 9, 2016, neuroscience.stanford.edu/news/bimanual-labor-neuroscience-piano-playing; Karen Chan Barrett et al., "Art and Science: How Musical Training Shapes the Brain," *Frontiers in Psychology*, October 16, 2013.

CHAPTER 2
NEGOTIABILITY

Herb Cohen's *You Can Negotiate Anything* (New York: Bantam Books, 1980) begins, "Your real world is a giant negotiating table, and like it or not, you're a participant," and is the classic text of omni-bargaining.

Tom McParland runs an agency that buys cars on behalf of clients and he has contributed many informative articles on car buying on Jalopnik.com, including "Don't Get Sucked Into the CarMax Marketing Machine," July 20, 2015. User comments on that same article are by ericericsson, misterdestructo, and Turbo Cruiser (Now with 100% more Hemi), and by LoganSix on a different Jalopnik article on March 8, 2013. Edmunds.com released the survey of car buyers on June 3, 2014, and featured an undercover investigative piece by Chandler Phillips, "Confessions of a Car Salesman," in January 2001. McParland has developed a full one-step-ahead buying script along my suggested lines at http://www.automatchconsulting.com/how-to-beat-the-sellers-market.html.

Admiral C. Turner Joy's observations, laments, and warnings are from his *How Communists Negotiate* (New York: Macmillan, 1955). The insightful and creative research of UCLA professor Eric Min on battles and peace talks can be found in a series of papers: "Talking While Fighting: Understanding the Role of Wartime Negotiation," August 2, 2019; "Negotiation as an Instrument of War," April 10,

2019; "Endogenizing the Costs of Conflict: A Text-Based Application to the Korean War," July 31, 2017; and "Negotiation in War: The 19.45% Discount," July 31, 2017, all available on his website, www.ericmin.com/research.

The pressure on Margaret Thatcher to hold peace talks is from her *The Downing Street Years* (New York: Harper Collins, 1993), and her refusal to stalemate one for the Gipper is from Richard Norton-Taylor and Owen Bowcott, "Thatcher Was Ready for Falkland Islands Deal, National Archives Papers Show," *Guardian*, December 27, 2012.

Drug prices are higher in the U.S. than in the rest of the world in the recent past (Marc-André Gagnon and Sidney Wolfe, "Mirror, Mirror on the Wall," policy paper, Carleton University, July 23, 2015) and for the forecasted future (Frank S. David et al., *The Pharmagellan Guide to Biotech Forecasting and Valuation* (Milton, MA: Pharmagellan, 2016), and Medicare pays more than the VA (Stuart Silverstein, "This Is Why Your Drug Prescriptions Cost So Damn Much," *Mother Jones*, October 21, 2016) and Medicaid (Daniel R. Levinson, *Medicaid Rebates for Brand-Name Drugs Exceeded Part D Rebates by a Substantial Margin* (Washington, DC: Department of Health and Human Services, April 2015). The legislative history comes from Thomas R. Oliver et al., "A Political History of Medicare and Prescription Drug Coverage," *Milbank Quarterly* 82, no. 2 (2004): 283–354, and Wendell Potter and Nick Penniman, *Nation on the Take* (New York: Bloomsbury, 2016), and Trump's unsurprising reversal from Joe Nocera, "Trump Had One Good Idea. And Then He Ditched It," *Bloomberg View*, February 2, 2017.

CHAPTER 3
STRATEGIC SOPHISTICATION I:
NEGOTIATION HAPPENS IN OUR MINDS

Just in time for the end of World War II and the beginning of the Cold War, John von Neumann and Oskar Morgenstern wrote *Theory of Games and Economic Behavior* (Princeton: Princeton University Press, 1944). A few years later, the Colonel Blotto game was invented, and recent results from that game can be found in Ayala Arad and Ariel Rubinstein, "Colonel Blotto's Top Secret Files," Tel Aviv University, December 2009; Pern Hui Chia and John Chuang, "Colonel Blotto in the Phishing War," *International Conference on Decision and Game Theory for Security*, 201–218 (Berlin: Springer, 2011; and Pushmeet Kohli et al., "Colonel Blotto on Facebook: The Effect of Social Relations on Strategic Interaction," in *Proceedings of the 4th Annual ACM Web Science Conference*, 141–150 (Evanston, IL: ACM, 2012).

The poetic introspections and extrospections of Naoki Higashida are from his two memoirs: *The Reason I Jump*, trans. K. A. Yoshida and David Mitchell

(New York: Random House, 2013) and *Fall Down 7 Times Get Up 8*, trans. K. A. Yoshida and David Mitchell (New York: Random House, 2017). Temple Grandin's insights are from Oliver Sacks, *An Anthropologist on Mars* (New York: Vintage Books, 1995), which also has the "concrete presence" observer. Other quotes about ASD are taken from Donna Williams, *Nobody Nowhere* (New York: Avon Books, 1992) ("glass coffin"); C. C. Park, "Exiting Nirvana," *American Scholar*, Spring 1998 ("pane of glass," "criterion of 'how would I feel if'"); Tito Rajarshi Mukhopadhyay, *How Can I Talk If My Lips Don't Move?* (New York: Skyhorse Publishing, 2011) ("yellow plastic bowl"); Sara Ryan and Ulla Räisänen, "'It's Like You Are Just a Spectator in This Thing': Experiencing Social Life the 'Aspie' Way," *Emotion, Space and Society*, December 2008; and N. J. Sasson et al., "Neurotypical Peers are Less Willing to Interact with Those with Autism Based on Thin Slice Judgments," *Scientific Reports* 7 (2017), article no. 40700 (cold shoulder).

ASD has been an area of intensive research in the last three decades. For reviews, see Simon Baron-Cohen. *Mindblindness* (Cambridge, MA: MIT Press, 1995), Atsushi Senju et al., "Mindblind Eyes: An Absence of Spontaneous Theory of Mind in Asperger Syndrome," *Science* 325, no. 5942 (2009), and P. Sinha et al., "Autism as a Disorder of Prediction," *PNAS* 111, no. 42 (October 21, 2014) ("a seemingly 'magical' world"). Specific experimental results can be found in A. M. Leslie and L. Thaiss, "Domain Specificity in Conceptual Development: Evidence from Autism," *Cognition* 43 (1992) (mind of camera); R. P. Hobson et al., "What's in a Face? The Case of Autism," *British Journal of Psychology* 79 (1988) (faces); A. Lee et al., "I, You, Me and Autism: An Experimental Study," *Journal of Autism and Developmental Disorders* 24 (1994) (pronouns).

Cooley's famous definition of society as the interweaving of mental selves is from his *Life and the Student* (New York: Knopf, 1927). His "looking glass self" obviously refers to the heroine of Lewis Carroll's *Through the Looking Glass and What Alice Found There* (London: Macmillan, 1872), a character to whom we shall refer throughout the book.

Helen McMahon's victory and the judges' observations were announced in "29 Who Were Chosen as Girls of To-Day," *New York Times*, December 7, 1913, and Keynes commented on this type of contest in *The General Theory of Employment Interest and Money* (New York: Harcourt, Brace, 1936).

Rosemarie Nagel has been admirably careful about crediting Alain Ledoux and Hervé Moulin for the creation of the beauty contest (see R. Nagel et al., "Inspired and Inspiring: Hervé Moulin and the Discovery of the Beauty Contest Game," *Mathematical Social Sciences*, October 2016), but her first paper ("Unraveling in Guessing Games: An Experimental Study," *American Economic Review* 85, no. 5 [1995]) remains foundational. The newspaper versions are summarized in Antoni Bosch-Domènech et al., "One, Two, (Three), Infinity, . . . : Newspaper and Lab Beauty-Contest Experiments," *American Economic Review* 92, no. 5 (2002), and other results reported here are from A. Rubinstein, "Instinctive and Cognitive Reasoning: A Study of Response Times," *Economic Journal* 117 (2007); Konrad Burchardi and Stefan Penczynski, "Out of Your Mind: Eliciting Individual Reasoning in One Shot Games," *Games and Economic Behavior* 84 (2014), and Stefan Penczynski, "Persuasion: An Experimental Study of Team Decision Making," *Journal of Economic Psychology* 56 (2016) (texts); Christoph Bühren and Björn Frank, "Six Thousand Chess Players Took Part in a Beauty Contest!," ChessBase .com, July 29, 2009, and José de Sousa, Guillaume Hallard, and Antoine Terracol, *Do Non-strategic Players Really Exist? Evidence from Experimental Games Involving Step Reasoning*, mimeo. (Paris: Université de Paris Sud and Paris School of Economics, 2012) (chess).

The central involvement of the mPFC in strategic sophistication and negotiation is demonstrated by Giorgio Coricelli and Rosemarie Nagel, "Neural Correlates of Depth of Strategic Reasoning in Medial Prefrontal Cortex," *Proceedings of the National Academy of Sciences* 106, no. 23 (2009), and Meghana Bhat et al., "Neural Signatures of Strategic Types in a Two-Person Bargaining Game," Proceedings of the National Academy of Sciences 107, no. 46 (2010).

Colin Camerer's research (along with his colleagues Teck-Hua Ho and Juin-Kuan Cho) to estimate the basic strategic sophistication staircase is from "A Cognitive Hierarchy Model of Games," *Quarterly Journal of Economics* 119, no. 3 (2004), and from "A Generalized Cognitive Hierarchy Model of Games," *Games and Economic Behavior* 99 (2016). The clumping I estimated from a sample of a dozen more recent papers published in the field is ZERO = 25%, ONE = 30%, TWO = 25%, THREE+ = 20%. That the base distribution shifts with certain situational factors has been shown by Adam Goodie et al., "Levels of Theory-of-Mind Reasoning in Competitive Games," *Journal of Behavioral Decision Making* 25, no. 1 (2012) (cooperative setting); Marina Agranov et al., "Naive Play and the Process of Choice in Guessing Games," *Journal of the Economic Science Association* 1, no. 2 (2015) (time pressure); David Gill and Victoria Prowse, "Cognitive Ability, Character Skills, and Learning to Play Equilibrium: A Level-k Analysis," *Journal of Political Economy* 124, no. 6 (2016), and Terence Burnham et al., "Higher Cognitive Ability Is Associated with Lower Entries in a p-Beauty Contest," *Journal of Economic Behavior and Organization* 72, no. 1 (2009); David Dickinson and Todd McElroy, "Rationality Around the Clock: Sleep and Time-of-Day Effects on Guessing Game Responses," *Economics Letters* 108, no. 2 (2010); Johannes Leder et al., "Stress and Strategic Decision-Making in the Beauty Contest Game," *Psychoneuroendocrinology* 38, no. 9 (2013) (stress); Sarah Allred et al., "Cognitive Load and Strategic Sophistication," *Journal of Economic Behavior and Organization* 125 (2016).

CHAPTER 4
STRATEGIC SOPHISTICATION II:
THE GAME OF CONFIDENCE

In her study of the interactions of Americans on the margin and those in the emerging middle in nineteenth-century America, Karen Halttunen, *Confidence Men and Painted Women: A Study of Middle-Class Culture in America, 1830–1870* (New Haven: Yale University Press, 1982), cites both the example of Benjamin Franklin, from *The Autobiography of Benjamin Franklin* (New York: Henry Holt, 1916), and the remonstrances of John Todd, from *The Young Man: Hints Addressed to the Young Men of the United States* (Northampton, MA: n.p., 1850). From this same era: Edgar Allan Poe, *Diddling: Considered as One of the Exact Sciences* (1835) found at http://xroads.virginia.edu/~hyper/poe/diddle.html. The analysis of "grin" comes from J. Marshall Trieber, "A Study of Poesque Humor," *Poe Studies* 4, no. 2 (December 1971).

Providing source material for both the Oscar-winning movie *The Sting* and Goffman's analysis of the con game, David W. Maurer's *The Big Con* (New York: Bobbs-Merrill, 1940) yields for us the C-gee glossary and the quotes on Babbitts, highly intelligent and "lop-eared" marks, methods different in degree, and unknockable winchells.

The words of the president and the prime minister are taken verbatim from the official transcript leaked from the White House and published in the *Washington Post* on August 3, 2017. The Trump administration's misspellings of Turnbull's first name as "Malcom" have been corrected. Heather Higginbottom explained the original deal in "You Probably Missed the Big Story Buried in the Latest Trump Leaks," *Time*, August 9, 2017.

The tales of Mr. Backus and his Utahn doppelganger can be found in the online version of Mark Twain's *Life on the Mississippi*, https://www.gutenberg.org/files/245/245-h/245-h.htm, and Jon M. Huntsman Sr., *Barefoot to Billionaire: Reflections on a Life's Work and a Promise to Cure Cancer* (New York: Overlook Duckworth, 2014), respectively. The latter's biography is supplemented by Nina Easton, "The Huntsmans: Inside an American Dynasty," *Fortune*, June 18, 2010, and Peter Fritsch, "Chemical Chief Is in a Hurry to Acquire," *Wall Street Journal*, July 30, 1996.

On first impressions and their effortful correction: Malcolm Gladwell, *Blink: The Power of Thinking Without Thinking* (New York: Back Bay Books, 2005). On people's impression of W., Matthew Cooper: "Bush: 'Honest' or 'Incompetent?,'" *Time*, March 17, 2006.

As I know firsthand, the secrecy at Bain & Company is difficult to penetrate, but a few writers have succeeded. The Union Carbide story comes from Walter Kiechel, *The Lords of Strategy: The Secret Intellectual History of the New Corporate*

World (Boston: Harvard Business School Press, 2010). Other bits and pieces are from Nancy J. Perry, "Bain: A Consulting Firm Too Hot to Handle?," *Fortune* April, 1987; Charlie Megenity, "The Man Behind Mitt Romney," *Knox Student*, October 24, 2012; Ruth Campbell, "Fort Scottian Gives Insights About Friend Mitt Romney," *Fort Scott Tribune*, October 25, 2012; and Richard Koch, *The 80/20 Manager: The Secret to Working Less and Achieving More* (Boston: Little, Brown, 2013).

The Hess negotiation is based on a personal communication from one of the participants.

"I-plus-you," a formulation we will return to, comes from Mary Parker Follett, *Creative Experience* (New York: Peter Smith, 1924).

The research on AI theory of mind and strategic sophistication can be found at Ben Meijering et al., "I Do Know What You Think I Think: Second-Order Theory of Mind in Strategic Games Is Not That Difficult," *Proceedings of the Cognitive Science Society* 33 (2011); Harmen de Weerd et al., "Savvy Software Agents Can Encourage the Use of Second-Order Theory of Mind by Negotiators," paper presented at the 37th annual meeting of the Cognitive Science Society, Pasadena, CA, 2015.

CHAPTER 5
DIRECTING THE DRAMA

The various negotiations involved in Rob Reiner successfully making a film of William Goldman's *The Princess Bride: S. Morgenstern's Classic Tale of True Love and High Adventure/The "Good Parts" Version*, Abridged by William Goldman (New York: Harcourt, 2003) have been assembled from these sources: William Goldman, *Which Lie Did I Tell?* (New York: Vintage Books, 2000); Cary Elwes and Joe Layden, *As You Wish: Inconceivable Tales from the Making of The Princess Bride* (New York: Simon & Schuster, 2014); Susan King, "'The Princess Bride' Turns 30," *Variety*, September 25, 2017; Drew McWeeny, "The M/C Interview: Rob Reiner," HitFix, August 4, 2010; Josh Rottenberg, "The Princess Bride: An Oral History," *Entertainment Weekly*, October 14, 2011; and "Cast of Princess Bride Remembers Andre the Giant," posted by Bill Bushey, September 6, 2014, https://www.youtube.com/watch?v=DQcBsqAQ74g.

Lynda Obst's trenchant memoir is *Hello, He Lied* (New York: Broadway Books, 1996).

The memories of the Goffmans as a theatrical family come from UNLV's *Bios Sociologicus* referenced above, including the interviews with Albas (2010), Cavan (2011), Delaney (2010), and Zaslov (2009). Quotes about and from Frances Goffman Bay are found in these encomia: Michael Posner, "Seinfeld's Marble Rye Lady

Honoured," *Globe and Mail*, September 6, 2008; Brian D. Johnson, "The Little Old Lady from Manitoba," *Maclean's*, September 23, 2011; Ron Csillag, "It Was the Marble Rye that Made Her Famous," *Globe and Mail*, September 22, 2011.

The advice to "know your lines and don't bump into the furniture" was uttered by Spencer Tracy in John Frook, "Comeback of Aunt Kat," *Life*, January 5, 1968, but it is an old theatrical trope sourced back to Noel Coward and Lynn Fontanne; see Garson O'Toole, "Know Your Lines and Don't Bump into the Furniture," Quote Investigator, August 24, 2014, https://quoteinvestigator.com/2014/08/25/bump/. Other advice on acting comes from Melissa Bruder et al., *A Practical Handbook for the Actor* (New York: Vintage Books, 1986); Viola Spolin, *Improvisation for the Theater*, 3rd ed. (Northwestern University Press, 1999); Stella Adler, *The Art of Acting*, ed. Howard Kissel (New York: Applause Books, 2000); and Richard Maxwell, *Theater for Beginners* (New York: Theater Communications Group, 2015). The Goffmanic koan useful to actors, monks, and negotiators was written by Katsuki Sekida, *A Guide to Zen: Lessons in Meditation from a Modern Master*, ed. Marc Allen (Novato, CA: New World Publishing, 2013). The non-Zen face of Richard Holbrooke is described in George Packer, "The Last Mission," *New Yorker*, September 28, 2009.

Raymond Friedman was the first and the best researcher to take the metaphor of negotiation seriously. His accounts of a miniseries's worth of union-management dramas are in *Front Stage, Backstage: The Dramatic Structure of Labor Negotiations* (Cambridge, MA: MIT Press, 1995).

The experimental findings on stress and anxiety in bargaining and on various remidations can be found in these papers: A. W. Brooks and M. E. Schweitzer, "Can Nervous Nelly Negotiate? How Anxiety Causes Negotiators to Make Low First Offers, Exit Early, and Earn Less Profit," *Organizational Behavior and Human Decision Processes* 115, no. 1 (2011); M. Akinola et al., "Adaptive Appraisals of Anxiety Moderate the Association Between Cortisol Reactivity and Performance in Salary Negotiations," *PLoS ONE* 11, no. 12 (2016); K. M. O'Connor et al., "The Prospect of Negotiating: Stress, Cognitive Appraisal, and Performance," *Journal of Experimental Social Psychology* 46, no. 5 (2010); A. W. Brooks, "Get Excited: Reappraising Pre-performance Anxiety as Excitement," *Journal of Experimental Psychology: General* 143, no. 3 (2014); Xiao Ma et al., "The Effect of Diaphragmatic Breathing on Attention, Negative Affect and Stress in Healthy Adults," *Frontiers in Psychology* 8 (2017).

With all the brevity, candor, and insight of a great director, William Ball, *A Sense of Direction* (Hollywood: Drama Publishers, 1984) is exceedingly helpful.

Many of the quotes about the Troubles and the peace process and from the principals are taken from Peter Taylor's documentary *The Secret Peacemaker*, BBC Panorama, March 2008. Political scientist Niall Ó Dochartaigh's curation of secret reports and his research on these materials have been central to revealing the role and bravery of Brendan Duddy. His publications are "The Role of an Intermediary in Backchannel Negotiation: Evidence from the Brendan Duddy Papers," *Dynamics of Asymmetric Conflict* 4, no. 3 (2011); "The Longest Negotiation: British Policy, IRA Strategy and the Making of the Northern Ireland Peace Settlement," *Political Studies* 63, no. 1 (2015); "Together in the Middle: Back-Channel Negotiation in the Irish Peace Process," *Journal of Peace Research* 48, no. 6 (2011); "Everyone Trying: IRA Ceasefire 1975: A Missed Opportunity for Peace?," *Field Day Review* 7 (2011). Other sources on the Northern Ireland backstage are Jonathan Powell, *Terrorists at the Table: Why Negotiating Is the Only Way to Peace* (New York: St. Martin's Press, 2015) and Eamonn O'Kane, "Talking to the Enemy? The Role of the Back-Channel in the Development of the Northern Ireland Peace Process," *Contemporary British History* 29, no. 3 (2015). On Pakistan and India's backstage, see Steve Coll, "The Back Channel," *New Yorker*, March 2, 2009.

CHAPTER 6
PERSONALITY

A few remarks on these data and the statistical analysis:

- The Committee for the Protection of Human Subjects at Dartmouth College determined on February 8, 2010, that these data were not human subjects research and so did not require IRB submission. In addition, I followed the guidance of the committee and after February 2010 solicited a Consent to Participate in Research from each student. Those students who wished not to participate are excluded from the charts that follow.
- Each negotiation outcome is censored at -2.0 and +2.0 so that a student's total performance does not represent one sterling or lousy negotiation and many mediocre ones. The total measure here represents a consistent level of performance over multiple deals.
- Using the Zou test for overlapping correlations, the hypothesis that the correlation for toughness is the same as that for any of the other traits is rejected at the 99% level. Similarly, the hypotheses that the pairwise comparisons of the correlations for prepared, creative, and communicator are the same cannot be rejected at the 95% level. With respect to these three traits, the correlation for rational is different from that for creative at 95%, but not 99%, and is not statistically different than that of the other two. See G. Y. Zou, "Toward Using Confidence Intervals to Compare Correlations," *Psychological Methods* 12, no. 4 (2007), and Thomas Baguley, *Serious Stats: A Guide to Advanced Statistics for the Behavioral Sciences* (Basingstoke: Palgrave, 2012).

- The hypothesis that the correlation of emotionality and performance is equal to zero is rejected at the 95% level. Using the Zou test, all the hypotheses that the correlations between emotional and prepared, rational, and communicative are pair-wise equal cannot be rejected at the 95% level. However, the hypothesis that the correlations for emotional and creative are the same can be rejected at 95%.
- The null hypothesis of a slope of zero in the trend line through the points graphing toughness vs. relationship quality cannot be rejected even with an 80% likelihood.

The baseball data are from Alex Reisner, http://archive.alexreisner.com /baseball/stats/leaders?s=AVG, and the golf data (as well as a general argument on behalf of the usefulness of z-scores) are from Bill Barnwell, "Relative Dominance," *Grantland*, June 24, 2011.

The judge's short, sweet, and tough compensation bargaining is described in Eriq Gardner, "Judge Judy Goes Off in Profits Lawsuit: 'CBS Had No Choice but to Pay Me,'" *Hollywood Reporter*, August 23, 2017.

The observation on how interest-based bargaining can create positive relationships between adversaries is by Brad Spangler, "Integrative or Interest-Based Bargaining," BeyondIntractability.org, June 2003.

Laura Kray and Michael Haselhuhn were the psychologists who explored whether the beliefs in personality as plaster or as fluid had an impact on performance. They reported their findings in "Implicit Negotiation Beliefs and Performance: Experimental and Longitudinal Evidence," *Journal of Personality and Social Psychology* 93, no. 1 (2007).

The citation for his classic work is Ernest Mason Satow, *A Guide to Diplomatic Practice*, 2nd ed., vol. 1 (London: Longmans, Green, 1922).

CHAPTER 7
PREPARATION

The story of Giandomenico Picco is assembled from several sources, beginning with his gripping memoir, *Man Without a Gun* (New York: Times Books, 1999). He was also interviewed by Terry Gross on *Fresh Air*, NPR/WHYY Philadelphia, June 2, 1999. Documentary filmmaker Cetywa Powell directed the 2014 film *Dawn at Midnight*, which included interviews with Picco. Powell was kind enough to share the extensive raw footage of her interview with Picco, as well as her observations about his story and his character, including his uniqueness, "Another thing I realized/deduced is that Gianni being a successful negotiator didn't have a lot to do with 'learned skills.' It had more to do with his personality. When you meet him, he's so quirky, intellectual, and offbeat, that I really think Abdullah took a personal liking to him. His responses are strange, he marches to the beat of his own drummer. . . . I really found his mind fascinating and I think Abdullah (and others) probably felt the same."

Moughniyeh's frightening capability was described by Bob Baer in "Shadow Warriors," *Dan Rather Reports*, CBS News, correspondent David Kohn, May 1, 2002.

The experiments exploring the effects of manipulating and framing your alternatives are Michael P. Haselhuhn, "Support Theory in Negotiation: How Unpacking Aspirations and Alternatives Can Improve Negotiation Performance," *Journal of Behavioral Decision Making* 28, no. 1 (2015); Michael Schaerer et al., "Imaginary Alternatives: The Impact of Mental Simulation on Powerless Negotiators," *Journal of Personality and Social Psychology* 115, no. 1 (2018); Michael Schaerer et al., "Anchors Weigh More than Power: Why Absolute Powerlessness Liberates Negotiators to Achieve Better Outcomes," *Psychological Science* 26, no. 2 (2015).

That many bargainers naturally underestimate the size of the bargaining zone is demonstrated by Richard Larrick and George Wu, "Claiming a Large Slice of a Small Pie: Asymmetric Disconfirmation in Negotiation," *Journal of Personality and Social Psychology* 93, no. 2 (2007).

For a deep understanding of issues of optimal frustration, the paradox of self-commands, and the problems of rationality and character planning, replace the carrot dangling from your stick with a copy of Jon Elster's brilliant work *Sour Grapes: Studies in the Subversion of Rationality* (New York: Cambridge University Press, 2016). Law professor Andrea Schneider analyzes effective goals in "Productive Ambition," in *The Negotiator's Desk Reference*, ed. Chris Honeyman and Andrea Kupfer Schneider, vol. 1, 323–332 (St. Paul, MN: DRI Press, 2017). That the goal of gold makes silver duller than bronze comes from Victoria Husted Medvec et al., "When Less Is More: Counterfactual Thinking and Satisfaction Among Olympic Medalists," *Journal of Personality and Social Psychology* 69, no. 4 (1995). That the dissatisfaction created by falling short of a goal can be managed is shown by Adam Galinsky et al., "Disconnecting Outcomes and Evaluations: The Role of Negotiator Focus," *Journal of Personality and Social Psychology* 83, no. 5 (2002), and Clark Freshman and Chris Guthrie, "Managing the Goal-Setting Paradox: How to Get Better Results from High Goals and Be Happy," *Negotiation Journal* 25, no. 2 (2009). That goals enhance the appetite for risk is discussed in Russell Korobkin, "Aspirations and Settlement," *Cornell Law Review* 88 (2002), and Richard Larrick et al., "Goal-Induced Risk Taking in Negotiation and Decision Making," *Social Cognition* 27, no. 3 (2009).

The research is clear that the negotiator should not refuse the tactic of aggressive offers because the effects of anchoring are deep and fixed: Grace Bucchianeri and Julia Minson, "A Homeowner's Dilemma: Anchoring in Residential Real Estate Transactions," *Journal of Economic Behavior and Organization* 89 (2013):

76–92; Steven Levitt and Chad Syverson, "Market Distortions When Agents Are Better Informed: The Value of Information in Real Estate Transactions," *Review of Economics and Statistics* 90, no. 4 (2008); Michael Jetter and Jay Walker, "Anchoring in Financial Decision-Making: Evidence from *Jeopardy!*," *Journal of Economic Behavior and Organization* 141 (2017); Birte Englich et al., "Playing Dice with Criminal Sentences: The Influence of Irrelevant Anchors on Experts' Judicial Decision Making," *Personality and Social Psychology Bulletin* 32, no. 2 (2006); and Brian Gunia et al., "The Remarkable Robustness of the First-Offer Effect: Across Culture, Power, and Issues," *Personality and Social Psychology Bulletin* 39, no. 12 (2013). The story of Donald Dell's violation of his own precept comes from his book with John Boswell, *Never Make the First Offer (Except When You Should): Wisdom from a Master Dealmaker* (New York: Penguin, 2009).

Nonetheless, going first creates major anxiety for many bargainers: Ashleigh Shelby Rosette et al., "Good Grief! Anxiety Sours the Economic Benefits of First Offers," *Group Decision and Negotiation* 23, no. 3 (2014). The ripped-off tourist scenario is from Yossi Maaravi and Aharon Levy, "When Your Anchor Sinks Your Boat: Information Asymmetry in Distributive Negotiations and the Disadvantage of Making the First Offer," *Judgment and Decision Making* 12, no. 5 (2017), and the other anti-anchoring situations are from David Loschelder et al., "The Information-Anchoring Model of First Offers: When Moving First Helps Versus Hurts Negotiators," *Journal of Applied Psychology* 101, no. 7 (2016). For experiments demonstrating that extreme first offers can lead to many impasses, damaged relationships, and less value in closely sequenced negotiations, see Yossi Maaravi et al., "Winning a Battle but Losing the War: On the Drawbacks of Using the Anchoring Tactic in Distributive Negotiations," *Judgment and Decision Making* 9, no. 6 (2014). And finally, Wolfgang Steinel et al., "Too Good to Be True: Suspicion-Based Rejections of High Offers," *Group Processes and Intergroup Relations* 17, no. 5 (2014), demonstrates the irony that high offers might not solve the problem either.

On the discipline of great directors to do mountains of preparation and then abandon it, see Sidney Lumet, *Making Movies* (New York: Vintage Books, 1995), Tony Kushner's quote in Michael Schulman, "'Angels in America' Rises Again," *New Yorker*, March 26, 2018, and William Ball's previously cited guide.

CHAPTER 8
TOUGHNESS I: FAIRNESS

Long after he nominated himself in Samuel Zell, "The Grave Dancer," *Real Estate Review* 5, no. 4 (Winter 1976), I interviewed Zell in his Chicago office in November 1998, a number of years before the events detailed here. Those details are sourced from Ben Johnson, *Money Talks, Bullsh*t Walks: Inside the Contrarian Mind of Billionaire Mogul Sam Zell* (New York: Portfolio, 2009); the fucking poetry and other amazing quotes on the EOP deal are from Connie Bruck, "Rough Rider," *New Yorker*, November 12, 2007; Charles V. Bagli, "Sam Zell's Empire, Underwater in a Big Way," *New York Times*, February 6, 2009; and the internal memo is from the *LA Times*, archived by Kevin Roderick at LA Observed, http://laobserved.com /archive/2008/02/let_sam_be_sam_but_you_be.php.

Jorge Luis Borges, "The Bribe," is in *Collected Fictions*, trans. Andrew Hurley (New York: Viking Penguin, 1998). Borges, as David Foster Wallace wrote, was a "pansophical" writer of strategic sophistication and human rationality whose "stories are inbent and hermetic, with the oblique terror of a game whose rules are unknown and its stakes everything." His tales are "mythic" and "impersonal" and "transcend individual consciousness" to tap into deeper sapient truths. "The Bribe" was written from a simulation of life so real that there is almost no way to tell the difference. None of these events happened in our world, but they definitely occurred somewhere in the multiverse that Borges suspected is bound to our existence.

James Comey expressed his intense and curious passion for impartiality in his book *A Higher Loyalty* (New York: Flatiron Books, 2018); in a radio interview on WBEN, *A New Morning with Susan Rose and Brian Mazurowski*, April 18, 2018, and in an interview with ABC News's George Stephanopoulos, "The Emotional Moment Comey Shared with Obama After the Election," *20/20*, April 15, 2018.

In addition to his observation on the banality of impartiality, Picco also told Cetywa Powell, "Impartiality is just an invention of somebody who doesn't know life. There cannot be impartiality because if we now have a table in front of us and we put our glass in between you and me geometrically in the middle, you will forever see the glass closer to me and I will see the glass closer to you. It's called optical illusion."

Ken Kaiser's battles with Andre, managers, other umpires, the strike zone, and fairness are recounted in his book *Planet of the Umps*, written with David Fisher (New York: St. Martin's Press, 2003). The fact that officials want to be perceived as fair and balanced in a variety of sports creates many distortions: Michael Lopez, "Persuaded under Pressure: Evidence from the National Football League," *Economic Inquiry* 54, no. 4 (2016) (sideline effects); discretionary penalties peak in the middle of each half so that NFL referees can be perceived as letting the players play and not "affecting" the outcome, as in Kevin Snyder and Michael Lopez, "Consistency, Accuracy, and Fairness: A Study of Discretionary Penalties in the NFL," *Journal of Quantitative Analysis in Sports* 11, no. 4 (2015); Per Pettersson-Lidbom and Mikael Priks, "Behavior under Social Pressure: Empty Italian Stadiums and Referee Bias," *Economics Letters* 108, no. 2 (2010); stands filled with loud supporters influence soccer referees, Thomas Dohmen and Jan Sauermann, "Referee Bias," *Journal of Economic Surveys* 30, no. 4 (2016); Michael Lopez and Kevin Snyder, "Biased Impartiality among National Hockey League Referees," *International Journal of Sport Finance* 8, no. 3 (2013) (cross-period balancing); two penalties in a row against your NHL team means that the next whistle is likely going against the opponent, Jack Brimberg and William J. Hurley, "Are National Hockey League Referees Markov?," *OR Insight* 22, no. 4 (2009); Etan Green and David Daniels, "Impact Aversion in Arbitrator Decisions," SSRN, paper no. 2391558, 2015 (umpires avoiding game-changing calls).

The fact that judges want to be perceived as fair and balanced creates many distortions: Jeffrey Rachlinski and Andrew Wistrich, "Judging the Judiciary by the Numbers: Empirical Research on Judges," *Annual Review of Law and Social Science* 13 (2017); Avani Mehta Sood, "Motivated Cognition in Legal Judgments—An Analytic Review," *Annual Review of Law and Social Science* 9 (2013); Jerry Kang et al., "Implicit Bias in the Courtroom," *UCLA Law Review* 59 (2011); and Chris Guthrie et al., "Inside the Judicial Mind," *Cornell Law Review* 86 (2000).

The $6/$1 vs. $5/$5 decision task is from Jason Dana et al., "Exploiting Moral Wiggle Room: Experiments Demonstrating an Illusory Preference for Fairness," *Economic Theory* 33, no. 1 (2007). The subject who excused the counterpart staying in the dark participated in the experiments of Tara Larson and C. Monica Capra, "Exploiting Moral Wiggle Room: Illusory Preference for Fairness? A Comment," *Judgment and Decision Making* 4, no. 6 (2009). For general reviews of motivated reasoning and information avoidance, see Francesca Gino et al., "Motivated Bayesians: Feeling Moral While Acting Egoistically," *Journal of Economic Perspectives* 30, no. 3 (2016), and Russell Golman et al., "Information Avoidance," *Journal of Economic Literature* 55, no. 1 (2017).

Albert Hastorf and Hadley Cantril, "They Saw a Game: A Case Study," *Journal of Abnormal and Social Psychology* 49, no. 1 (1954), is the origin of all the psychological research on subjective judgments of fairness. The motorcycle accident experiment is from Linda Babcock et al., "Biased Judgments of Fairness in Bargaining," *American Economic Review* 85, no. 5 (1995), and the school district field study is from Linda Babcock et al., "Choosing the Wrong Pond: Social Comparisons in Negotiations That Reflect a Self-Serving Bias," *Quarterly Journal of Economics* 111, no. 1 (1996). The intervention of writing down the weaknesses in your own case was tested in Linda Babcock et al., "Creating Convergence: Debiasing Biased Litigants," *Law and Social Inquiry* 22, no. 4 (1997). All of their findings are summarized in Linda Babcock and George Loewenstein, "Explaining Bargaining Impasse: The Role of Self-Serving Biases," *Journal of Economic Perspectives* 11, no. 1 (1997).

The poorly planned and ineptly executed suicide squeeze bunt of a strike was documented on a daily basis by Murray Chass of the *New York Times* during July and August 1999, including "Baseball; Umpires Threaten to Quit on Sept. 2," *New*

York Times, July 15, 1999. See also Matthew Kallan, "Called Out: The Forgotten Baseball Umpires Strike of 1999," TheOriginal.com, October 2, 2012. Kaiser's very wise conclusion about bending people's minds was quoted in his obituary by Richard Sandomir, "Ken Kaiser, Colorful and Imposing Big League Umpire, Dies at 72," *New York Times*, August 11, 2017.

This description of Xi was offered by a Beijing editor to Evan Osnos, "Born Red," *New Yorker*, April 6, 2015. The translations of *wài yuán nèi fāng* are by Anne Bogart and Jackson Gay, "The Art of Collaboration: On Dramaturgy and Directing," in *The Routledge Companion to Dramaturgy*, ed. Magda Romanska, 213–216 (New York: Routledge, 2015), and Ann Pang-White, "Introduction: Rereading the Canon," in *The Bloomsbury Research Handbook of Chinese Philosophy and Gender*, ed. Ann Pang-White, 1–21 (London: Bloomsbury, 2016). Other biographical details of Xi come from Meng Na et al., "Profile: Xi Jinping and His Era," Xinhua News Agency, November 17, 2017.

Various players are quoted about the outer manner of effective officials in Ian Cunningham et al., "Skilled Interaction: Concepts of Communication and Player Management in the Development of Sport Officials," *International Journal of Sport Communication* 7, no. 2 (2014). You can find a good exploration of reflective listening in Brian Pappas, "Listening to Transcend Competition and Cooperation," in *The Negotiator's Desk Reference*, ed. Chris Honeyman and Andrea Kupfer Schneider, vol. 1, 395–408 (St. Paul, MN: DRI Press, 2017), and its enhancement by mindfulness in Thich Nhat Hanh, *The Art of Communicating* (New York: Random House, 2013).

Rebecca Hollander-Blumoff has conducted some of the most interesting research on procedural justice. The swimming pool dispute study, coauthored with Tom Tyler, is "Procedural Justice in Negotiation: Procedural Fairness, Outcome Acceptance, and Integrative Potential," *Law and Social Inquiry* 33, no. 2 (2008). In a very clear-eyed fashion, she has developed these ideas in several articles, most importantly "Just Negotiation," *Washington University Law Review* 88 (2010); "Formation of Procedural Justice Judgments in Legal Negotiation," *Group Decision and Negotiation* 26, no. 1 (2017); and "Fairness Beyond the Adversary System: Procedural Justice Norms for Legal Negotiation," *Fordham Law Review* 85 (2016). Kees Van den Bos et al., in "How Do I Judge My Outcome When I Do Not Know the Outcome of Others? The Psychology of the Fair Process Effect," *Journal of Personality and Social Psychology* 72, no. 5 (1997), show that ambiguity about the size of the bargaining zone promotes the use of procedural justice as a heuristic substitute for fair outcomes.

Charlene Barshefsky's remarks on constancy are from Elsa Walsh, "The Negotiator," *New Yorker*, March 18, 1996, and the scene of her negotiating with the Chinese Trade Ministry is compiled from James Sebenius and Rebecca Hulse, "Charlene Barshefsky (B)," Harvard Business School Case 801-422, March 2001.

The explanation of yin-yang is taken from Richard Nisbett, *The Geography of Thought: How Asians and Westerners Think Differently . . . and Why* (New York: Simon & Schuster, 2004). The yang-yin corresponding to our yin-yang is outside hard, inside round, a square with an inscribed circle. ◻ This object represents the masculine, stereotypical, Zell-like, "force of a nature" version of toughness. The hardness is all outer shell and performative, and it covers an inner round abscess of a fatal flaw, quivering softness, intense neediness, rot, or infection. Julia Phillips, another Hollywood producer, in her memoir *You'll Never Eat Lunch in This Town Again* (New York: Random House, 1991), wrote, "Goldie [Hawn] has a cold, hard streak to her that I really admire. Funny, that's what people think about me; I am constantly telling them that I am a sabra, tough on the outside, marshmallow within" (page 218).

CHAPTER 9
TOUGHNESS II: FEMALE-MALE

My primary source for the details of Lillian McMurry's life is Marc Ryan's indispensable *Trumpet Records: Diamonds on Farish Street* (Jackson: University Press of Mississippi, 1991). I have supplemented Ryan's history with these additional sources: Jeff Hannusch, "Lillian Shedd McMurry, December 30, 1921–March 18, 1999," *Southern Register*, Spring/Summer 1999; Jesse Yancy, "Godmother of the Blues," *Mississippi Sideboard: A Southern Gallimaufry*, February 19, 2013; Edward Komara, personal communication, April 19, 2018; interview with Vitrice McMurry in "Trumpet: Sonny Boy Williamson and Elmore James," YouTube, posted by MSBluesTrail, December 18, 2012, https://www.youtube.com/watch?v=43Pild6uafM; Robert McG. Thomas Jr., "Lillian McMurry, Blues Producer, Dies at 77," *New York Times*, March 29, 1999; John Humphreys et al., "Lillian McMurry of Trumpet Records: Integrity and Authenticity in the Charismatic, Constructive Narcissist Leader," *Journal of Leadership and Organizational Studies* 18, no. 1 (2011); and Antonia Eliason, "Lillian McMurry and the Blues Contracts of Trumpet Records," *Mississippi Law Journal* 87 (2018). The sadly neglected truth that Elmore James was recorded with his full consent and awareness is in Gayle Dean Wardlow, *Chasin' That Devil Music: Searching for the Blues*, ed. Edward Komara (Milwaukee, WI: Backbeat Books, 1998).

Background history of the music industry in these years can be found in Timothy Dowd, "Structural Power and the Construction of Markets: The Case of Rhythm and Blues," *Comparative Social Research* 21 (2003). He tells the story of how the "Old Time" label Okeh placed on its popular Fiddlin' John recordings was conflated with the name of another Okeh act, "The Hill Billies."

The study of the Beijing beauty salons was conducted by economists Lamar

Pierce, Laura Wang, and Dennis Zhang. Their paper can be found at "Peer Bargaining and Productivity in Teams: Gender and the Inequitable Division of Pay," SSRN, paper no. 3123915 (2019). The authors dive into the detailed pay structure, distinguishing between the fixed commission on services and the bargaining over the commission for prepaid cards, both on new cards and on money added to existing cards. The authors note that 87 percent of card sales involve exactly two employees, so this type accounts for the vast majority of the salon's card revenues. They also point out that since there is a strong normative prohibition on tipping, the fixed service fee and variable card commission are the only two sources of worker compensation.

As pointed out in the chapter, the research on gender in negotiations has often suffered from strong preconceptions, framing effects, and identity triggers. As a result, the relative disadvantage revealed in the comprehensive study of Jens Mazei et al., "A Meta-Analysis on Gender Differences in Negotiation Outcomes and Their Moderators," *Psychological Bulletin* 141, no. 1 (2015), must be taken with a grain of salt since the underlying studies themselves might be skewed.

The need to belong is investigated by Kathleen O'Connor and Josh Arnold, "Sabotaging the Deal: The Way Relational Concerns Undermine Negotiators," *Journal of Experimental Social Psychology* 47, no. 6 (2011), and unmitigated communion by Emily Amanatullah et al., "Negotiators Who Give Too Much: Unmitigated Communion, Relational Anxieties, and Economic Costs in Distributive and Integrative Bargaining," *Journal of Personality and Social Psychology* 95, no. 3 (2008).

On the stereotypes women must deal with in business and at the bargaining table, see Catherine Tinsley et al., "Women at the Bargaining Table: Pitfalls and Prospects," *Negotiation Journal* 25, no. 2 (2009), and Laura Kray et al., "Reversing the Gender Gap in Negotiations: An Exploration of Stereotype Regeneration," *Organizational Behavior and Human Decision Processes* 87, no. 2 (2002). This latter study is the source for the finding on how easily the stereotype can be reversed. Another excellent summary is Julia Bear and Linda Babcock, "Gender Differences in Negotiation," in *The Negotiator's Desk Reference*, ed. Chris Honeyman and Andrea Kupfer Schneider, vol. 1, 595–605 (St. Paul, MN: DRI Press, 2017).

Hannah Riley Bowles's insightful critique of the history of negotiation research with respect to men and women is "Psychological Perspectives on Gender in Negotiation," in *The Sage Handbook of Gender and Psychology*, ed. Michelle Ryan and Nyla Branscombe, 465–483 (London: Sage Publications, 2013). Her coauthored study on the negative effects of ambiguity on female bargaining performance is Hannah Riley Bowles et al., "Constraints and Triggers: Situational Mechanics of Gender in Negotiation," *Journal of Personality and Social Psychology* 89, no. 6 (2005). The same paper revealed that without the target provided by the boss, female negotiators paid on average 27 percent more for a motorcycle headlight than male negotiators did.

Male grape farmers in Champagne not asking and maintaining a strategically hurtful ignorance about variation in prices, and being surprisingly willing to accept whatever first offer the houses make them, are several of the facts that emerge from the fascinating investigation by Amandine Ody-Brasier and Isabel Fernandez-Mateo, "When Being in the Minority Pays Off: Relationships Among Sellers and Price Setting in the Champagne Industry," *American Sociological Review* 82, no. 1 (2017). These findings put the lie to many overgeneralizations about gender and bargaining.

Marquette Law School professor Andrea Schneider's work on the mother bear allowance and her wise and pragmatic advice for women can be found in these publications: Andrea Kupfer Schneider, "Negotiating While Female," *SMU Law Review* 70 (2017); Andrea Kupfer Schneider et al., "Likeability vs. Competence: The Impossible Choice Faced by Female Politicians, Attenuated by Lawyers," *Duke Journal of Gender Law and Policy* 17 (2010); and Andrea Kupfer Schneider, "Shattering Negotiation Myths: Empirical Evidence on the Effectiveness of Negotiation Style," *Harvard Negotiation Law Review* 7 (2002).

Emily Amanatullah and Michael Morris, "Negotiating Gender Roles: Gender Differences in Assertive Negotiating Are Mediated by Women's Fear of Backlash and Attenuated When Negotiating on Behalf of Others," *Journal of Personality and Social Psychology* 98, no. 2 (2010), discovered the uniformity of goals, reservation points, and so on among men and women, self- and other-advocates, the early abandonment of goals by a higher percentage of self-advocating women, and counteroffers influenced by first-order beliefs about where the counterpart's evaluations of them will turn from positive to negative.

Julia Bear and Linda Babcock, "Negotiating Femininity: Gender-Relevant Primes Improve Women's Economic Performance in Gender Role Incongruent Negotiations," *Psychology of Women Quarterly* 41, no. 2 (2017), report the result that a purely mental shift from own-advocacy to imaginary-friend-advocacy improves performance. The effectiveness of a relational account—"my boss told me to ask"—comes from Hannah Riley Bowles and Linda Babcock, "How Can Women Escape the Compensation Negotiation Dilemma? Relational Accounts Are One Answer," *Psychology of Women Quarterly* 37, no. 1 (2013). Some leading researchers in the field have come to a reconciliation of the practical with the ideal (especially Schneider) similar to that of Bowles and Babcock. To (over)generalize, the lawyers and economists tend, by nature and nurture, to be more comfortable with the accommodation, while the psychologists and sociologists are less so.

The jiu-jitsu move of reversing the positive and negative gender-stereotype characteristics of effective negotiators was tested by Laura Kray et al., "Reversing the Gender Gap in Negotiations: An Exploration of Stereotype Regeneration," *Organizational Behavior and Human Decision Processes* 87, no. 2 (2002). The experiments demonstrating that identity integration could be primed through self-assessment and resulted in a warm and dominant performance are in Shira Mor et al., "Iron Fist in a Velvet Glove: Gender/Professional Identity Integration

Promotes Women's Negotiation Performance," working paper, Erasmus University, 2014. Priming global processing in the negotiator, by a happy mood induction, such as holding a popsicle stick in the teeth to force a smile, by a directed search for similarities among objects, or by activating high-level construals that are abstract and broad, is another way to promote identity integration; Aurelia Mok and Michael Morris, "Managing Two Cultural Identities: The Malleability of Bicultural Identity Integration as a Function of Induced Global or Local Processing," *Personality and Social Psychology Bulletin* 38, no. 2 (2012).

The meta-analysis revealing that women are more likely to prioritize a moral identity is by Jessica Kennedy et al., "A Social-Cognitive Approach to Understanding Gender Differences in Negotiator Ethics: The Role of Moral Identity," *Organizational Behavior and Human Decision Processes* 138 (2017).

CHAPTER 10
FACES AND EMOTIONS

Sky Goffman's biography relies on the previously mentioned wealth of materials and remembrances collected by Dmitri Shalin as part of the Erving Goffman Archives. In addition to the interviews cited earlier from the UNLV *Bios Sociologicus*, this chapter draws on Besbris (2009) (Erving's aunt, "Poor Sky, she never had a chance"), Bott Spillius (2010) (nasty Californian gossip), Cavan (2008) ("bastard"), Clark (2009) (bridge, motor running), Fine (2009) ("how one gives that kind of message"), MacCannell (2009) ("'Jesus Christ, Erving'"), Piliavin (2009) ("'She is not suicidal'"), Room (2009) (Jaguar XKE), Smelser (2009) ("pair of deuces"), Stark (2008) ("very smart"), Syme (2011) ("rituals of mourning"). Shalin has pursued the link between Sky's disease and Goffman's paper "The Insanity of Place" in two papers: "Goffman on Mental Illness: Asylums and 'The Insanity of Place' Revisited," and "Interfacing Biography, Theory and History: The Case of Erving Goffman," both in *Symbolic Interaction* 37, no. 1 (2014). The archives include Sky's thesis: Angelica Schuyler Choate, "The Personality Trends of Upperclass Women," master's thesis, Department of Human Development, University of Chicago, January 1950. One of Sky's conclusions was the following: "While a child's prolonged and intimate association with persons of lower status makes upper-upper parents very nervous indeed, direct action to end such cross-class relationships is not too frequent."

The description of the paddling wooers comes from E. O. Jameson, *The Choates in America, 1643–1896* (Boston: Alfred Mudge and Son, 1896).

The remarkable poetry of Wisława Szymborska can be found in *Map: Collected and Last Poems* (New York: Houghton Mifflin Harcourt, 2015).

Charles Darwin, *The Expression of Emotions in Man and Animals* (New York: D. Appleton, 1897) is the source of his observations on emotions. Tiffany Watt-Smith analyzes the overall context—social, historical, theatrical—that supported Darwin's science and writing in *On Flinching: Theatricality and Scientific Looking from Darwin to Shell-Shock* (Oxford: Oxford University Press, 2014). Watt-Smith maintains that a close reading of *Expression* reveals Darwin's ambivalence about emotion expression being vestigial rather than fundamental to natural selection, ambiguous rather than literal, and regional rather than universal. Guillaume-Benjamin Duchenne expressed no such doubts in his *Mechanism of Human Facial Expression*, trans. Andrew Cuthbertson (Cambridge: Cambridge University Press, 1990).

Paul Ekman's original field survey work can be found in Paul Ekman and Wallace Friesen, "Constants Across Cultures in the Face and Emotion," *Journal of Personality and Social Psychology* 17, no. 2 (1971), and Paul Ekman et al., "Pan-Cultural Elements in Facial Displays of Emotion," *Science* 164, no. 3875 (1969). For why we are all Ekmanians and for a balanced history of emotion universals, see Halszka Bąk, "Emotion Universals—Argument from Nature," in *Emotional Prosody Processing for Non-Native English Speakers*, 27–51 (Cham, Switzerland: Springer International Publishing, 2016). Ekman's survey of his own peers was reported in his "What Scientists Who Study Emotion Agree About," *Perspectives on Psychological Science* 11, no. 1 (2016). Also, Paul Ekman, *Emotions Revealed: Recognizing Faces and Feelings to Improve Communication and Emotional Life* (New York: Macmillan, 2007) ("pulling teeth").

The logical application of Ekman's research to negotiation was made by Kasia Wezowski, "The Secret to Negotiating Is Reading People's Faces," *Harvard Business Review*, June 16, 2016. The recommendations to keep a poker face and maintain self-control are from Howard Raiffa, *The Art and Science of Negotiation* (Cambridge, MA: Harvard University Press, 1982), and Gerard Nierenberg, *The Art of Negotiating: Psychological Strategies for Gaining Advantageous Bargains* (New York: Barnes & Noble, 1995), both quoted in Leigh Thompson et al., "Poker Face, Smiley Face, and Rant 'n' Rave: Myths and Realities About Emotion in Negotiation," *Blackwell Handbook of Social Psychology: Group Processes*, ed. Michael A. Hogg and R. Scott Tindale (Malden, MA: Blackwell, 2001).

The fundamental difference in the facial code for emotions between East and West is from Rachael Jack et al., "Internal Representations Reveal Cultural Diversity in Expectations of Facial Expressions of Emotion," *Journal of Experimental Psychology: General* 141, no. 1 (2012). More careful experiments also revealed the local categorization of emotions in small societies: Maria Gendron et al., "Perceptions of Emotion from Facial Expressions Are Not Culturally Universal: Evidence from a Remote Culture," *Emotion* 14, no. 2 (2014) and Carlos Crivelli et al., "Reading Emotions from Faces in Two Indigenous Societies," *Journal of Experimental Psychology: General* 145, no. 7 (2016).

Goffman's wry comment is from an early paper of his, "On Face-Work: An Analysis of Ritual Elements in Social Interaction," *Psychiatry* 18, no. 3 (1955).

Lisa Feldman Barrett, in *How Emotions Are Made: The Secret Life of the Brain* (New York: Houghton Mifflin Harcourt, 2017), develops all the details of her radically different theory of emotion. The conflict between the univeralists like Ekman and the constructivists like Feldman Barrett is described by Julie Beck, "Hard Feelings: Science's Struggle to Define Emotions," *Atlantic*, February 24, 2015.

For a review of recent research that highlights the ways in which the "basic" emotions vary across cultures, see Batja Mesquita et al., "The Cultural Psychology of Emotions," in *Handbook of Emotions*, ed. Lisa Feldman Barrett, Michael Lewis, and Jeannette M. Haviland-Jones, 4th ed. (New York: Guilford Press, 2018). The centrality of *han* and *lek* for their cultures comes from Sandra So Hee Chi Kim, "Korean Han and the Postcolonial Afterlives of 'The Beauty of Sorrow,'" *Korean Studies* 41 (2017), and from Clifford Geertz, *The Interpretation of Cultures* (New York: Basic Books, 1973), quoted in Susan Shott, "Emotion and Social Life: A Symbolic Interactionist Analysis," *American Journal of Sociology* 84, no. 6 (1979).

Alan Fridlund explains that he is an apostate of basic emotion theory, "and only by being an insider did I come to realize its shortcomings," in "The Behavioral Ecology View of Facial Displays, 25 Years Later," in *The Science of Facial Expression*, ed. James Russell and Jose Miguel Fernandez Dols (Oxford: Oxford University Press, 2017). Carlos Crivelli and Alan Fridlund, "Facial Displays Are Tools for Social Influence," *Trends in Cognitive Sciences* 22, no. 5 (2018).

Erving Goffman, "Expression Games: An Analysis of Doubts at Play," in *Strategic Interaction: An Analysis of Doubt and Calculations in Face-to-Face, Day-to-Day Dealings with One Another*, 3–103 (Philadelphia: University of Pennsylvania Press, 1969), is his classic work on spycraft. He also quotes the pipe incident from Margaret Mead's Cold War classic, *Soviet Attitudes Toward Authority* (New York: McGraw-Hill, 1951).

The story of the Freedom Debt Relief negotiators is based on the great ethnographic study by Zaibu Tufail and Francesca Polletta, "The Gendering of Emotional Flexibility: Why Angry Women Are Both Admired and Devalued in Debt Settlement Firms," *Gender and Society* 29, no. 4 (2015). The BATNA for the debt settlement company is to advise the client that they should file for bankruptcy. Because it is costless, that move is credible and would result in the worst possible outcome for the creditor. One study two decades ago found that 15 percent of Americans would have been financially better off if they had filed for bankruptcy: Michelle White, "Why Don't More Households File for Bankruptcy?," *Journal of Law, Economics, and Organization* 14, no. 2 (1998). However, a vast majority (82 percent) also feel that it is morally wrong to walk away from a mortgage if you can afford the payments, even if the house is worth far less than the debt (Luigi Guiso et al., "The Determinants of Attitudes Toward Strategic Default on Mortgages," *Journal of Finance* 68, no. 4 (2013). This strong norm filters down to a sense of shame and anticipation of stigma against all forms of failure to repay and bankruptcy. Many observers of the American scene bemoan the steady weakening of this norm since the time of Winthrop and the Puritan forefathers, and attribute it variously to atheism, unionism, welfare, feminism, television, and the loss of morality among the working and middle classes. However, a survey revealed that shame and stigma have not lessened among the poor and less educated, but only among the well-off and the more educated (Ethan Cohen-Cole and Burcu Duygan-Bump, "Household Bankruptcy Decision: The Role of Social Stigma vs. Information Sharing," No. QAU08–6, Federal Reserve Bank of Boston, 2008).

The physiognomic survey was reported in Atsunobu Suzuki et al., "Faces Tell Everything in a Just and Biologically Determined World: Lay Theories Behind Face Reading," *Social Psychological and Personality Science* 10, no. 1 (2019). The classic text where François de Callières urges physiognomy of his peers is *On the Manner of Negotiating with Princes* (South Bend, IN: University of Notre Dame Press, 1963). The CEO beauty contest is described in John Graham et al., "A Corporate Beauty Contest," *Management Science* 63, no. 9 (2016). A thorough review of the recent research on physiognomy can be found at Alexander Todorov et al., "Social Attributions from Faces: Determinants, Consequences, Accuracy, and Functional Significance," *Annual Review of Psychology* 66 (2015).

The clever demonstration that we can't even read our own faces from a few months earlier comes from Haotian Zhou, Elizabeth Majka, and Nicholas Epley, "Inferring Perspective Versus Getting Perspective: Underestimating the Value of Being in Another Person's Shoes," *Psychological Science* 28, no. 4 (2017). You can see more of Epley's work in his *Mindwise* (New York: Knopf, 2014).

Richard Holbrooke recalls his encounter with Mladic in his *To End a War: The Conflict in Yugoslavia—America's Inside Story—Negotiating with Milosevic* (New York: Modern Library, 2011).

The benefits of emotional expressivity in poker, diplomacy, and bargaining more generally come from Erik Schlicht et al., "Human Wagering Behavior Depends on Opponents' Faces," *PloS ONE* 5, no. 7 (2010); James Sebenius and Rebecca Hulse, "Charlene Barshefsky (B)," Harvard Business School Case 801-422, March 2001; Davide Pietroni et al., "Emotions as Strategic Information: Effects of Other's Emotional Expressions on Fixed-Pie Perception, Demands, and Integrative Behavior in Negotiation," *Journal of Experimental Social Psychology* 44, no. 6 (2008).

The benefits of emotional granularity are demonstrated by Lisa Feldman Barrett et al., "Knowing What You're Feeling and Knowing What to Do About It: Mapping the Relation Between Emotion Differentiation and Emotion Regulation," *Cognition and Emotion* 15, no. 6 (2001); the possibility of granularity is demonstrated by Alan Cowen and Dacher Keltner, "Self-Report Captures 27 Distinct Categories of Emotion Bridged by Continuous Gradients," *Proceedings of the National Academy of Sciences* 114, no. 38 (2017); and the effectiveness of granularity with respect to spiders is demonstrated by Katharina Kircanski et al., "Feelings into Words: Contributions of Language to Exposure Therapy," *Psychological Science*

23, no. 10 (2012). Michael Amoruso explores the special Portuguese emotion in "Saudade: The Untranslatable Word for the Presence of Absence," *Aeon*, October 8, 2018. For a book full of bafflement, hwyl, and hiraeth, see Tiffany Watt Smith, *The Book of Human Emotions: An Encyclopedia of Feeling from Anger to Wanderlust* (London: Profile Books, 2015).

That the body might be more readable than the face has been shown by Hillel Aviezer et al., "Body Cues, Not Facial Expressions, Discriminate Between Intense Positive and Negative Emotions," *Science* 338, no. 6111 (2012), and by Michael Slepian et al., "Quality of Professional Players' Poker Hands Is Perceived Accurately from Arm Motions," *Psychological Science* 24, no. 11 (2013). In the latter case, the researchers edited the video clips so that the surveyors could not see the cards or the odds that the typical broadcast reveals to the television audience. Also, they made sure that the number of chips bet did not correlate across all the videos with the likelihood of winning. Therefore, there was no signal value in witnessing a player move a large stack into the center.

The quote from Nick Epley comes from an article on the TSA by John Tierney, "At Airports, a Misplaced Faith in Body Language," *New York Times*, March 23, 2014. The agents are trained to be Ekmanians, peering intently at faces and primed to look for emotional expressions that are shouts rather than whispers. The few percentage points of accuracy in predicting offer rejection in the ultimatum game based on a portrait is from Boris Van Leeuwen et al., "Predictably Angry—Facial Cues Provide a Credible Signal of Destructive Behavior," *Management Science* 64, no. 7 (2018). Tal Eyal, Mary Steffel, and Nicholas Epley, "Perspective Mistaking: Accurately Understanding the Mind of Another Requires Getting Perspective, Not Taking Perspective," *Journal of Personality and Social Psychology* 114, no. 4 (2018), is the source for "do ask, do tell" being both effective and yet overlooked.

A team of psychologists at the University of Amsterdam has been at the forefront of research on emotions as signals and social information. Their work on the effectiveness of anger if matched by small concessions is Gerben Van Kleef et al., "The Interpersonal Effects of Anger and Happiness in Negotiations," *Journal of Personality and Social Psychology* 86, no. 1 (2004), and on anger's ineffectiveness in the face of power and status asymmetries is Gerben Van Kleef et al., "Power and Emotion in Negotiation: Power Moderates the Interpersonal Effects of Anger and Happiness on Concession Making," *European Journal of Social Psychology* 36, no. 4 (2006).

The science showing that Mr. Backus knew exactly what he was doing when he hit the steamboat grifters with a big ol' grin is from Alixandra Barasch, Emma Levine, and Maurice Schweitzer, "Bliss Is Ignorance: How the Magnitude of Expressed Happiness Influences Perceived Naiveté and Interpersonal Exploitation," *Organizational Behavior and Human Decision Processes* 137 (2016), and Jeremy Yip et al., *Thanks for Nothing: Expressing Gratitude Invites Exploitation by Competitors* (Boston, MA: Harvard Business School Press, 2018). You should dampen positive emotions in the end game: Elise Kalokerinos et al., "Don't Grin When You Win: The Social Costs of Positive Emotion Expression in Performance Situations," *Emotion* 14, no. 1 (2014).

The experiments supporting the preferred emotional path of mildly happy to moderately angry can be found in Allan Filipowicz et al., "Understanding Emotional Transitions: The Interpersonal Consequences of Changing Emotions in Negotiations," *Journal of Personality and Social Psychology* 101, no. 3 (2011). In particular, they find that the "becoming angry" seller received more concessions than the "steady state angry" seller and yet was seen as more cooperative, trustworthy, and agreeable overall. The transition from happy to angry caused the counterpart to attribute the negative emotion to something that happened in the negotiation process, as opposed to a fixed character flaw. Lastly, the positive beginning to the bargaining infected the buyer and had continuing effects that led to a much smaller chance of impasse. Neil Fassina and Glen Whyte, "'I Am Disgusted by Your Proposal': The Effects of a Strategic Flinch in Negotiations," *Group Decision and Negotiation* 23, no. 4 (2014), prove the value of a good flinch, and Hajo Adam and Jeanne Brett, "Everything in Moderation: The Social Effects of Anger Depend on Its Perceived Intensity," *Journal of Experimental Social Psychology* 76 (2018), warn against letting anger boil over.

Sources for the advice to follow acting manuals: Stéphane Côté et al., "The Consequences of Faking Anger in Negotiations," *Journal of Experimental Social Psychology* 49, no. 3 (2013); Lee Strasberg and Evangeline Morphos, *A Dream of Passion: The Development of the Method* (Boston: Little, Brown, 1987), quoted in Richard Kemp, "Embodied Acting: Cognitive Foundations of Performance," PhD diss., University of Pittsburgh, 2010, later revised as Rick Kemp, *Embodied Acting: What Neuroscience Tells Us About Performance* (London: Routledge, 2012); Michael Chekhov, *To the Actor: On the Technique of Acting* (London: Routledge, 2013); Anna Deavere Smith, *Talk to Me: Listening Between the Lines* (New York: Random House, 2001); and Carol Martin, "Anna Deavere Smith: The Word Becomes You," *Drama Review* 37, no. 4 (Winter 1993).

On the existence of happy endings: Charles Darwin, *The Autobiography of Charles Darwin* (New York: Barnes & Noble Publishing, 1887); on Darwin's imagined sad book tossing, see Wisława Szymborska, "Consolation," in *Map: Collected and Last Poems* (New York: Houghton Mifflin Harcourt, 2015).

CHAPTER 11
WORDS

The Facebook team's original research paper introducing "Alice" and "Bob" is Mike Lewis et al., "Deal or No Deal? End-to-End Learning for Negotiation Dialogues," arXiv, 1706.05125, 2017. The scientists' response to the overblown panic is in David Emery, "Did Facebook Shut Down an AI Experiment Because Chatbots Developed Their Own Language?," Snopes.com, August 1, 2017.

Everything said in this chapter about "words" applies equally to "signs": pragmatically, there appears to be little difference between those who speak with their mouths and those who sign with their hands. See Adam Kendon, *Gesture: Visible Action as Utterance* (Cambridge: Cambridge University Press, 2004), and Lindsay Ferrara and Gabrielle Hodge, "Language as Description, Indication, and Depiction," *Frontiers in Psychology* 9 (2018). Moreover, signs and gestures are essential to the cognitive operation of verbal communicators: Susan Goldin-Meadow, *Hearing Gesture: How Our Hands Help Us Think* (Cambridge, MA: Harvard University Press, 2005).

The ambiguity of spoken words has been pointed out by, of course, Erving Goffman, "Replies and Responses," *Language in Society* 5 (1976). For a brief discussion of enantionyms ("cleave"/"cleave"), as well as puns galore, see Laurence Horn, "Words in Edgewise," *Annual Review of Linguistics* 4 (2018). A "few" words are analyzed by H. Hormann, "The Calculating Listener or How Many are Einige, Mehrere, and Ein Paar (Some, Several and a Few)," in *Meaning, Use, and Interpretation of Language*, ed. R. Bauerke et al. (Berlin: De Gruyter, 1983), quoted in Raymond Gibbs Jr., *The Poetics of Mind* (Cambridge: Cambridge University Press, 1994).

Half of the words in Mikhail Bakhtin, *The Dialogic Imagination*, trans. Caryl Emerson and Michael Holquist (Austin: University of Texas Press, 1981) are apparently ours.

Interested readers are encouraged to consult the following papers by Noah Goodman and Michael Frank for their elegant model and experimental variants that allow them to make specific quantitative predictions about the proportions of listeners that identify the correct referent, predictions that fit the data with startling levels of accuracy: Goodman and Frank, "Predicting Pragmatic Reasoning in Language Games," *Science* 336, no. 6084 (2012); "Pragmatic Language Interpretation as Probabilistic Inference," *Trends in Cognitive Sciences* 20, no. 11 (2016); Michael Frank et al., "Rational Speech Act Models of Pragmatic Reasoning in Reference Games," PsyArXiv, February 3, 2017; and Goodman and Frank, "Inferring Word Meanings by Assuming That Speakers Are Informative," *Cognitive Psychology* 75 (2014). The empirical results on the depth of pragmatic reasoning come from Michael Franke and Judith Degen, "Reasoning in Reference Games: Individual- vs. Population-Level Probabilistic Modeling," *PloS ONE* 11, no. 5 (2016), and see Adam Vogel et al., "Learning to Reason Pragmatically with Cognitive Limitations," in *Proceedings of the Annual Meeting of the Cognitive Science Society* 36 (2014).

Grice's elucidation of the logic of conversation, the cooperative principle, and the four maxims is so beautifully elegant that its truth reverberates back into the reader's ignorant past—"duh, of course, I always knew this." H. Paul Grice, *Studies in the Way of Words* (Cambridge, MA: Harvard University Press, 1991). Dan Sperber and Dierdre Wilson, *Relevance*, 2nd ed. (Oxford: Blackwell, 1995) reduce the four down to two. Goffman's observation on the room that is lit from within is from *Strategic Interaction* (Philadelphia: University of Pennsylvania Press, 1969).

The classic works on face and other consideration are Penelope Brown and Stephen Levinson, *Politeness: Some Universals in Language Usage* (Cambridge: Cambridge University Press, 1987) and Erving Goffman, "On Face-Work," in *Interaction Ritual* (New York: Anchor Books, 1967) ("no occasion of talk so trivial"; "savoir-faire"). How "overly" and "unnecessarily" are interpreted differently across cultures is the subject of Thomas Holtgraves and Joong-Nam Yang, "Interpersonal Underpinnings of Request Strategies: General Principles and Differences Due to Culture and Gender," *Journal of Personality and Social Psychology* 62, no. 2 (1992), and Nalini Ambady et al., "More than Words: Linguistic and Nonlinguistic Politeness in Two Cultures," *Journal of Personality and Social Psychology* 70, no. 5 (1996).

I suppose it's another example of an unexpected happy ending that the tragic prom day, evening, and night prompted such an interesting scientific finding: Greg Stephens et al., "Speaker-Listener Neural Coupling Underlies Successful Communication," *Proceedings of the National Academy of Sciences* 107, no. 32 (2010). The researchers had two clever controls to prove that the neural connection was due to communication and meaning coordination: they had the same subjects, none of whom spoke Russian, listen to a different narrator recount a personal tale in Russian, and they had the first narrator tell a different, non-prom, story. If the neuronal intercoupling was caused by simply listening to the rhythm of a voice without any understanding, then the fMRI data should show the same overlapping activation as above. Yet there was no parallel illumination in the communicators' brains in either the *da/nyet* Russian scanning data or the she-tells-the-non-prom-story/they-hear-the-prom-story scanning data. On predictive listening, see also Nicola Spotorno et al., "Neural Evidence That Utterance-Processing Entails Mentalizing: The Case of Irony," *NeuroImage* 63, no. 1 (2012).

The scene with Levin and Kitty is central to Lev Vygotsky's analysis in his *Thought and Language* (Cambridge, MA: MIT Press, 1986). The East Asian version of the expression game has been called the *enryo-sasshi* model—the *enryo*, or self-restraint, of the speaker leading to the issuance of more ambiguous, less direct utterances, and the *sasshi*, or conjecture, of the listener puzzling out the implications. There is a huge literature on this topic, including Yoshitaka Miike, "Japanese Enryo-Sasshi Communication and the Psychology of Amae: Reconsideration and Reconceptualization," Institute for Communications Research, Keio University, 2003; Hazel Markus and Shinobu Kitayama, "Culture and the Self: Implications for Cognition, Emotion, and Motivation," *Psychological Review* 98 (1991); and Thomas Holtgraves, "Styles of Language Use: Individual and Cultural Variability in Conversational Indirectness," *Journal of Personality and Social Psychology* 73 (1997).

The sources for the fact that speech among those with ASD tends toward the literal and away from the intimated are as follows: Peter Mitchell et al., "Overly Literal Interpretations of Speech in Autism: Understanding That Messages Arise from Minds," *Journal of Child Psychology and Psychiatry* 38 (1997); Francesca Happé, "Communicative Competence and Theory of Mind in Autism: A Test of Relevance Theory," *Cognition* 48 (1993); and Anthony Lee et al., "I, You, Me and Autism: An Experimental Study," *Journal of Autism and Developmental Disorders* 24 (1994).

How the Caspian became a Sea* is largely based on Ziyad Ziyadzade, "Drilling for Black Gold: The Demarcation for Hydrocarbon Resources in the Caspian Sea," *Chicago Journal of International Law* 16 (2015); Hanna Zimnitskaya and James Von Geldern, "Is the Caspian Sea a Sea; and Why Does It Matter?," *Journal of Eurasian Studies* 2, no. 1 (2011); and Kamyar Mehdiyoun, "Ownership of Oil and Gas Resources in the Caspian Sea," *American Journal of International Law* 94, no. 1 (2000).

Marco Polo's description of one of the less remunerative uses for the oil of the region is from his *Description of the World*, trans. Sharon Kinoshita (Indianapolis, IN: Hackett, 2016). The much more lucrative uses drive the phenomenal size of the stakes in the bargaining, as estimated by Kaveh Madani et al., "Social Planner's Solution for the Caspian Sea Conflict," *Group Decision and Negotiation* 23, no. 3 (2014). The summary of the 2018 agreement is from M.L, "Is the Caspian a Sea or a Lake?," *Economist*, August 16, 2018.

Telling it straight, Laurence Horn has many great examples of clever misdirection, including the ones cited by me, in "Telling It Slant: Toward a Taxonomy of Deception," in *The Pragmatic Turn in Law: Inference and Interpretation in Legal Discourse*, ed. Janet Giltrow and Dieter Stein, 23–35 (Boston: de Gruyter, 2017). Arguably, Bronston was being "rhetorically cooperative," an idea Nicholas Asher and Alex Lascarides formally develop in "Strategic Conversation," *Semantics and Pragmatics* 6 (2013).

Including him in the Pope's offspring assumes that the diminutive Coutinho was born prematurely at the gestational age of about thirty-seven weeks. Quotes from the Pope's sermons as well as the data and the statistical results are from Vittorio Bassi and Imran Rasul, "Persuasion: A Case Study of Papal Influences on Fertility-Related Beliefs and Behavior," *American Economic Journal: Applied Economics* 9, no. 4 (2017). Another paper proposing papal persuasion power is Egidio Farina and Vikram Pathania, "Papal Visits and Abortions—Evidence from Italy," SSRN, 3144306, 2018.

While my account of the positive relationship between power and persuasion is correct on average, there are exceptions that the interested reader can find in Pablo

Briñol et al., "Power and Persuasion: Processes by Which Perceived Power Can Influence Evaluative Judgments," *Review of General Psychology* 21, no. 3 (2017).

As they ought to have, Christina Tworek and Andrei Cimpian, "Why Do People Tend to Infer 'Ought' from 'Is'? The Role of Biases in Explanation," *Psychological Science* 27, no. 8 (2016), elucidate the character trait of inherence bias. Vanessa Patrick and Henrik Hagtvedt published two papers on the power of "don't": "'I Don't' Versus 'I Can't': When Empowered Refusal Motivates Goal-Directed Behavior," *Journal of Consumer Research* 39, no. 2 (2012), and "How to Say 'No': Conviction and Identity Attributions in Persuasive Refusal," *International Journal of Research in Marketing* 29, no. 4 (2012).

An overview of the psychological literature on persuasion can be found in Elisa Baek and Emily Falk, "Persuasion and Influence: What Makes a Successful Persuader?," *Current Opinion in Psychology* 24 (2018). The typical persuader defaults to simple emotion words (Matthew Rocklage et al., "Persuasion, Emotion, and Language: The Intent to Persuade Transforms Language via Emotionality," *Psychological Science* 29, no. 5 [2018]), but more effective persuaders (1) match their words with the other's information processing style (Nicole Mayer and Zakary Tormala, "'Think' Versus 'Feel' Framing Effects in Persuasion," *Personality and Social Psychology Bulletin* 36, no. 4 [2010]); (2) use longer, abstract, extreme words (Molly Lewis and Michael Frank, "The Length of Words Reflects Their Conceptual Complexity," *Cognition* 153 [2016]; Cheryl Wakslak et al., "Using Abstract Language Signals Power," *Journal of Personality and Social Psychology* 107, no. 1 [2014]; Erin Bennett and Noah Goodman, "Extremely Costly Intensifiers Are Stronger than Quite Costly Ones," *Cognition* 178 [2018]).

David Hume was the first social scientist to identify this cycle of reinforcing social judgments and attributions, in *A Treatise of Human Nature*, 2nd ed. (Oxford: Oxford University Press, 1978). The correspondence of the Earl of Chesterfield (who probably read Hume) was collected in *Chesterfield's Letters to His Son* (1774), Project Gutenberg, 2006. Fritz Heider married his predecessors' observations to experimental results with great success in *The Psychology of Interpersonal Relations* (Hillsdale, NJ: Lawrence Erlbaum Associates, 1958).

Small talk was one topic in Erving Goffman, "Felicity's Condition," *American Journal of Sociology* 89, no. 1 (1983). Another was the way in which the whole shared world comes into our words and actions, the quote that ends the chapter.

The mimicking experiments are in William Maddux et al., "Chameleons Bake Bigger Pies and Take Bigger Pieces: Strategic Behavioral Mimicry Facilitates Negotiation Outcomes," *Journal of Experimental Social Psychology* 44, no. 2 (2008), and Roderick Swaab et al., "Early Words That Work: When and How Virtual Linguistic Mimicry Facilitates Negotiation Outcomes," *Journal of Experimental Social Psychology* 47, no. 3 (2011).

The emperor on his throne with silk earplugs and his vision obscured is from

Albert Galvany, "Sly Mouths and Silver Tongues: The Dynamics of Psychological Persuasion in Ancient China," *Extrême-Orient Extrême-Occident* 34 (2012).

The details of the Volkswagen scandal were revealed in reporting by Geoffrey Smith and Roger Parloff, "Hoaxwagen," *Fortune*, March 7, 2016, and Roger Parloff, "How VW Paid $25 Billion for 'Dieselgate'—and Got Off Easy," *Fortune*, February 8, 2018. All the direct quotes from internal VW meetings and emails are from Affidavit of FBI Agent Ian Dinsmore, *United States of America v. Oliver Schmidt*, U.S. District Court, Eastern Michigan, December 30, 2016, and Sentencing Memorandum of the United States as to Defendant Oliver Schmidt, filed by Benjamin Singer, U.S. District Court, Eastern Michigan, November 29, 2017.

The word-manufacturing study was conducted by Maurice Schweitzer et al., "Goal Setting as a Motivator of Unethical Behavior," *Academy of Management Journal* 47, no. 3 (2004). The very clever protocol created the false belief among the subjects that they were completely anonymous when in fact their score sheets and answers could be linked: when they were done tabulating, they put their workbooks into one sealed box and their score sheets into another, knowing that they hadn't put their names on anything. The subjects, however, were innocent marks in the psychological laboratory Big Store. For the first seven rounds, everyone worked on the same strings, but in the final round, each person received a unique string—one got FAHRVER, another GNOOGEN—and so score sheet and workbook could be easily rematched.

For a somewhat sobering review of the findings on goals and bad behavior, see Lisa Ordóñez et al., "Goals Gone Wild: The Systematic Side Effects of Overprescribing Goal Setting," *Academy of Management Perspectives* 23, no. 1 (2009). Urs Fischbacher and Franziska Föllmi-Heusi, "Lies in Disguise—An Experimental Study on Cheating," *Journal of the European Economic Association* 11, no. 3 (2013), derive the percentages reported here of 40 percent reliably honest, 20 percent *BAD*, and 40 percent shaders. It's harder to deceive someone whom you can reach out and touch: Alex Van Zant and Laura Kray, "'I Can't Lie to Your Face': Minimal Face-to-Face Interaction Promotes Honesty," *Journal of Experimental Social Psychology* 55 (2014)—unless you're in Hollywood (Lynda Obst, *Hello, He Lied* [New York: Broadway Books, 1996], and William Goldman, *Which Lie Did I Tell?* [New York: Vintage Books, 2000]), or meeting with a hostage taker (Sergeant Jerald L. Barnes, St. Louis Metropolitan Police Department, guest lecture at Cornell Johnson Graduate School of Management, March 5, 2002). The police have to have two whiteboards to increase their vigilance: Nicholas Duran and Rick Dale, "Increased Vigilance in Monitoring Others' Mental States During Deception," *Proceedings of the Annual Meeting of the Cognitive Science Society* 34 (2012).

The familiar traits that people thought a liar showed two millennia ago are: "He does not answer questions, or gives evasive answers; he speaks nonsense, rubs the great toe along the ground; and shivers; his face is discolored; he rubs the roots of his hair with his fingers" (quoted in Global Deception Research Team, "A World of Lies," *Journal of Cross-Cultural Psychology* 37, no. 1 [2006]); Bella DePaulo et al., "Cues to Deception," *Psychological Bulletin* 129, no. 1 (2003) conclusively disprove that gaze aversion is associated with lying. The strong belief in the association may continue due to confirmation bias: Timothy Levine et al., "The Lying Chicken and the Gaze Avoidant Egg: Eye Contact, Deception, and Causal Order," *Southern Communication Journal* 71, no. 4 (2006).

David W. Maurer's *The Big Con* (New York: Bobbs-Merrill, 1940) interviewed the con men who were aware of the thrill their marks felt, and Nicole Ruedy et al., "The Cheater's High: The Unexpected Affective Benefits of Unethical Behavior," *Journal of Personality and Social Psychology* 105, no. 4 (2013) confirmed it in the laboratory.

Charles Bond Jr. and Bella DePaulo published two papers that looked askant at hundreds of experiments to see how accurate detectors were and whether there were reliable clues to deception: "Accuracy of Deception Judgments," *Personality and Social Psychology Review* 10, no. 3 (2006); "Individual Differences in Judging Deception: Accuracy and Bias," *Psychological Bulletin* 134, no. 4 (2008).

The altered word production of liars comes from Matthew Newman et al., "Lying Words: Predicting Deception from Linguistic Styles," *Personality and Social Psychology Bulletin* 29, no. 5 (2003). A study of online dating websites found that deceptive profiles were shorter and had fewer first-person words: Catalina Toma and Jeffrey Hancock, "What Lies Beneath: The Linguistic Traces of Deception in Online Dating Profiles," *Journal of Communication* 62, no. 1 (2012). The likelihood of default by debtors in peer-to-peer lending networks is also significantly negatively correlated with the number of uses of "I," "me," and "mine" in their pitches: Qiang Gao, Mingfeng Lin, and Richard W. Sias, "Words Matter: The Role of Texts in Online Credit Markets," available at SSRN 2446114 (2018).

Demonstrating the regrettable fact that women are more frequently lied to: Laura Kray et al., "Not Competent Enough to Know the Difference? Gender Stereotypes About Women's Ease of Being Misled Predict Negotiator Deception," *Organizational Behavior and Human Decision Processes* 125, no. 2 (2014).

Tools to elicit the truth: questions with negative assumptions (Julia Minson et al., "Eliciting the Truth, the Whole Truth, and Nothing but the Truth: The Effect of Question Phrasing on Deception," *Organizational Behavior and Human Decision Processes* 147 [2018]); creative questions (Aldert Vrij and Pär Anders Granhag, "Eliciting Cues to Deception and Truth: What Matters Are the Questions Asked," *Journal of Applied Research in Memory and Cognition* 1, no. 2 [2012]; Aldert Vrij et al., "A Cognitive Approach to Lie Detection: A Meta-Analysis," *Legal and Criminological Psychology* 22, no. 1 [2017]).

For the effectiveness of deflection of questions, see T. Bradford Bitterly and Maurice Schweitzer, "The Economic and Interpersonal Consequences of Deflecting Direct Questions," *Journal of Personality and Social Psychology* 2019.

The fascinating analysis of the promises* made on *Golden Balls* is from Uyanga Turmunkh et al., "Malleable Lies: Communication and Cooperation in a High Stakes TV Game Show," *Management Science*, March 27, 2019.

CHAPTER 12
NUMBERS

My account of the Clean Air Act negotiations draws on Jeffry Burnam, "The President and the Environment: A Reinterpretation of Neustadt's Theory of Presidential Leadership," *Congress and the Presidency* 37, no. 3 (2010). Reviews and research on contingent contracts from Max Bazerman and James Gillespie, "Betting on the Future: The Virtues of Contingent Contracts," *Harvard Business Review* 77 (1999); Alexandra Mislin et al., "After the Deal: Talk, Trust Building and the Implementation of Negotiated Agreements," *Organizational Behavior and Human Decision Processes* 115, no. 1 (2011); Michael Moffitt, "Contingent Agreements," in *The Negotiator's Desk Reference*, ed. Chris Honeyman and Andrea Kupfer Schneider, Vol. 2, 619–625 (St. Paul, MN: DRI Press, 2017); and Laura Kray et al., "It's a Bet! A Problem-Solving Approach Promotes the Construction of Contingent Agreements," *Personality and Social Psychology Bulletin* 31, no. 8 (2005).

Shereshevsky's characters come from his unpublished notebook (Reed Johnson, "The Mystery of S., the Man with an Impossible Memory," *New Yorker*, August 12, 2017). This phenomenon is known as grapheme personification, more examples of which can be found in Théodore Flournoy, "Des personnnifications," in his *Des phénomènes de synopsie*, trans. Anna Plassart and Rebekah White, "Théodore Flournoy on Synesthetic Personification," *Journal of the History of the Neurosciences* 26, no. 1 (2017); George Patrick, "Number Forms," *Popular Science Monthly* 42 (1893); Maina Amin et al., "Understanding Grapheme Personification: A Social Synaesthesia?," *Journal of Neuropsychology* 5, no. 2 (2011).

Lee's observation is in *Lee Kuan Yew: Hard Truths to Keep Singapore Going*, ed. Han Fook Kwang et al. (Singapore: Straits Times Press, 2011), quoted in Haoming Liu and Wei-Kang Wong, "Can Superstitious Beliefs Affect Market Equilibrium? Personal Beliefs and Beliefs about Others," Department of Economics, National University of Singapore, 2012. There are as many papers about lucky numbers as there are lucky numbers; the ones referenced here are Matthew Shum et al., "Superstition and 'Lucky' Apartments: Evidence from Transaction-Level Data," *Journal of Comparative Economics* 42, no. 1 (2014); Nicole Fortin et al., "Superstition in the Housing Market," *Economic Inquiry* 52, no. 3 (2014); Xiawei Dong et al., "Lucky Number Effect on Chinese Marriage," *Proceedings of the First Summit Forum of China's Cultural Psychology*, 2013, https://www.researchgate .net/profile/Xiawei_Dong2/publication/298787992_Lucky_number_effect_on

_Chinese_marriage/links/56eea62708ae4b8b5e750fbf/Lucky-number-effect-on
-Chinese-marriage.pdf; Travis Ng et al., "The Value of Superstitions," *Journal of Economic Psychology* 31, no. 3 (2010); David Hirshleifer et al., "Superstition and Financial Decision Making," *Management Science* 64, no. 1 (2016); Michael Anderson et al., "Superstitions, Street Traffic, and Subjective Well-Being," *Journal of Public Economics* 142 (2016); Evgeny Antipov and Elena Pokryshevskaya, "Are Buyers of Apartments Superstitious? Evidence from the Russian Real Estate Market," *Judgment and Decision Making* 10, no. 6 (2015); Maria De Paola et al., "Overconfidence, Omens and Gender Heterogeneity: Results from a Field Experiment," *Journal of Economic Psychology* 45 (2014).

On the ways that $49.37 indicates many different things than "fifty bucks" does, see Y. Charles Zhang and Norbert Schwarz, "The Power of Precise Numbers: A Conversational Logic Analysis," *Journal of Experimental Social Psychology* 49, no. 5 (2013); Malia Mason et al., "Precise Offers Are Potent Anchors: Conciliatory Counteroffers and Attributions of Knowledge in Negotiations," *Journal of Experimental Social Psychology* 49, no. 4 (2013); and Chris Janiszewski and Dan Uy, "Anchor Precision Influences the Amount of Adjustment," *Psychological Science* 19, 2008. The eBay study of millions of collectibles is Matthew Backus et al., "Cheap Talk, Round Numbers, and the Economics of Negotiation," no. W21285, National Bureau of Economic Research, 2015. For a similar pattern in a very different market, see Petri Hukkanen and Matti Keloharju, "Initial Offer Precision and M&A Outcomes," *Financial Management* 48, no. 1 (2019), 291–310.

Exact offers are not without costs. More precision creates a reluctance to enter into bargaining: Alice Lee et al., "Too Precise to Pursue: How Precise First Offers Create Barriers-to-Entry in Negotiations and Markets," *Organizational Behavior and Human Decision Processes* 148 (2018). An exact offer is effective if it is extreme enough that all the bargaining action occurs "below" it. In overheated seller's markets such as housing in central Amsterdam, where there is a good chance that buyers will overbid, a precise listing price can act as a downward anchor, depressing the final price (Margarita Leib et al., "In a Seller's Market, Setting Precise Asking Prices Backfires," 2018, https://psyarxiv.com/fxqm3/download?format=pdf).

The way that precision affects the inexperienced mind and the expert mind differently is demonstrated by David Loschelder et al., "How and Why Precise Anchors Distinctly Affect Anchor Recipients and Senders," *Journal of Experimental Social Psychology* 70 (May 2017), and David Loschelder et al., "The Too-Much-Precision Effect: When and Why Precise Anchors Backfire with Experts," *Psychological Science* 27, no. 12 (2016).

James Altucher explains how he got himself trapped inside a formula on his website, www.jamesaltucher.com/2011/11/how-to-negotiate-in-three-easy -lessons and in "The Art of Negotiation and Persuasion," guest speaker at Columbia University, Dr. Skye Cleary's Managing Human Behavior in Organizations class, streamed live on November 3, 2016, www.youtube.com/watch?v=kbe7VNlcc6M. There is a very strong performative element to Altucher's talks and writings, and the "shall" slips often into the "shill." He himself has worried, "Am I a con artist?" (www.jamesaltucher.com/2016/06/maria-konnikova-am-i-a-con-artist).

Robert Cialdini's classic book is *Influence: Science and Practice,* 4th ed. (Boston: Pearson Education, 2009).

Sources for the timeline of the key events in the Iran nuclear talks are www .armscontrol.org/factsheet/Timeline-of-Nuclear-Diplomacy-With-Iran; www.nti .org/learn/countries/iran/nuclear; iranprimer.usip.org/resource/timeline-irans -nuclear-activities; www.theguardian.com/world/2015/apr/02/iran-nuclear-talks -timeline; and Ronen Bergman, "When Israel Hatched a Secret Plan to Assassinate Iranian Scientists," *Politico Magazine,* March 5, 2018.

Tobias Langenegger and Michael Ambühl, "Negotiation Engineering: A Quantitative Problem-Solving Approach to Negotiation," *Group Decision and Negotiation* 27, no. 1 (2018), discuss the development and details of the centrifuge formula. The super-numerate among you will note that the formula is very awkward, verges on the incorrect, and is in dire need of a Σ and more careful indexing over t and i. How irksome the American government found the Swiss is reported by Mathieu von Rohr, "US Irked by Over-Eager Swiss Diplomats," *Der Spiegel,* December 14, 2010, and by the Americans themselves, Embassy Bern, "Swiss DFA State Secretary Ambuehl Hears Nothing New in Tehran," WikiLeaks Cable, 07BERN113_a, dated February 5, 2007, wikileaks.org/plusd/cables/07BERN113 _a.html.

Numeracy has been shown to be a factor in a variety of economic outcomes even after controlling for education and cognitive capability: Samantha Parsons and John Bynner, "Does Numeracy Matter More?," National Research and Development Centre for Adult Literacy and Numeracy, 2005; Martin Brown et al., "Numeracy and the Quality of On-the-Job Decisions: Evidence from Loan Officers," 2017, https://papers.ssrn.com/sol3/papers.cfm?abstract_id=2999687; and Catalina Estrada-Mejia et al., "Numeracy and Wealth," *Journal of Economic Psychology* 54 (2016). Jon Huntsman Sr.'s observation on the quantitative mindset comes from his talk "Why True Entrepreneurs Go Down 'and Still Come Back Fighting,'" interview hosted by Adam Grant, Knowledge@Wharton, November 17, 2014.

The three various forms of numeracy and their diagnostic tests are reviewed in Ellen Peters and Par Bjalkebring, "Multiple Numeric Competencies: When a Number Is Not Just a Number," *Journal of Personality and Social Psychology* 108, no. 5 (2015). The relationship between objective numeracy and decision-making is demonstrated by Isaac Lipkus et al., "General Performance on a Numeracy Scale Among Highly Educated Samples," *Medical Decision Making* 21, no. 1 (2001), and Edward Cokely et al., "Decision Making Skill: From Intelligence to Numeracy and Expertise," in *Cambridge Handbook of Expertise and Expert Performance,* 2nd ed., ed. K. Anders Ericsson et al., 476–505 (Cambridge: Cambridge University Press, 2018).

Shane Frederick invented the CRT in his "Cognitive Reflection and Decision Making," *Journal of Economic Perspectives* 19, no. 4 (2005). The statistics on the proportion of correct answers by question is from Pablo Brañas-Garza et al., "Cognitive Reflection Test: Whom, How, When," *Journal of Behavioral and Experimental Economics* 82 (2019), 101455. That those with ASD score higher on the CRT than their typically developed peers is investigated by Mark Brosnan et al., "Reasoning on the Autism Spectrum: A Dual Process Theory Account," *Journal of Autism and Developmental Disorders* 46, no. 6 (2016). A 3 on the CRT is associated with fewer decision-making biases (Maggie Toplak et al., "The Cognitive Reflection Test as a Predictor of Performance on Heuristics-and-Biases Tasks," *Memory and Cognition* 39, no. 7 [2011]) and with greater accuracy in the beauty contest (Dietmar Fehr and Steffen Huck, "Who Knows It Is a Game? On Strategic Awareness and Cognitive Ability," *Experimental Economics* 19, no. 4 [2016]).

Barbara Oakley's story about her transformation into a math-philiac can be found in her "How I Rewired My Brain to Become Fluent in Math," *Nautilus Quarterly Newsletter*, October 2, 2014, and her *A Mind for Numbers* (New York: Tarcher/Penguin, 2014).

Daniel Ames and Malia Mason, "Tandem Anchoring: Informational and Politeness Effects of Range Offers in Social Exchange," *Journal of Personality and Social Psychology* 108, no. 2 (2015), investigate the benefits of bracketing. The same study examined how most negotiators react if they had to give a numerical range instead of a single ideal list price (€263M for the club). Fifty-one percent of people bracketed the opening offer in the middle and told the potential buyer, "I'm looking for €260M to €266M"; 29 percent naively constructed a back-down range (€252M to €264M) that placed the ideal offer in the upper end of the range; and only 17 percent did the smart thing and presented a bolstering range in which the ideal is on the low end ("The model says €262.8M to €272.4M is the right price"). Using a bolstering range with the appropriate level of precision is a way for the one-step-ahead bargainer to be tough and fair, round and square, lion and fox, and polite and firm.

Wisława Szymborska, "A Word on Statistics," trans. Joanna Trzeciak, *Atlantic*, May 1997.

INDEX